Capitalizing on
Environmental Injustice

Nature's Meaning

Series Editor: Roger S. Gottlieb, Professor of Philosophy, Worcester Polytechnic Institute

Each title in Nature's Meaning is created to have the personal stamp of a passionate and articulate spokesperson for environmental sanity. Intended to be engagingly written by experienced thinkers in their field, these books express the comprehensive and personal vision of the topic by an author who has devoted years to studying, teaching, writing about, and often being actively involved with the environmental movement. The books will be intended primarily as college texts, and as beautifully produced volumes, they will also appeal to a wide audience of environmentally concerned readers.

Integrating Ecofeminism, Globalization, and World Religions,
    by Rosemary Radford Ruether
Environmental Ethics for a Postcolonial World,
    by Deane Curtin
The Ecological Life: Discovering Citizenship and a Sense of Humanity,
    by Jeremy Bendik-Keymer
Sacramental Commons: Christian Ecological Ethics,
    by John Hart
Capitalizing on Environmental Injustice: The Polluter-Industrial Complex in the Age of Globalization,
    by Daniel Faber

Capitalizing on Environmental Injustice

The Polluter-Industrial Complex in the Age of Globalization

Daniel Faber

ROWMAN & LITTLEFIELD PUBLISHERS, INC.
Lanham • Boulder • New York • Toronto • Plymouth, UK

ROWMAN & LITTLEFIELD PUBLISHERS, INC.

Published in the United States of America
by Rowman & Littlefield Publishers, Inc.
A wholly owned subsidiary of The Rowman & Littlefield Publishing Group, Inc.
4501 Forbes Boulevard, Suite 200, Lanham, Maryland 20706
www.rowmanlittlefield.com

Estover Road
Plymouth PL6 7PY
United Kingdom

British Library Cataloguing in Publication Information Available

Library of Congress Cataloging-in-Publication Data

Faber, Daniel, 1961–
  Capitalizing on environmental injustice : the polluter-industrial complex in the age of
globalization / Daniel Faber.
       p. cm.— (Nature's meaning)
  Includes bibliographical references and index.
  ISBN-13: 978-0-7425-3391-2 (cloth : alk. paper)
  ISBN-10: 0-7425-3391-3 (cloth : alk. paper)
  ISBN-13: 978-0-7425-3392-9 (pbk. : alk. paper)
  ISBN-10: 0-7425-3392-1 (pbk. : alk. paper)
  eISBN-13: 978-0-7425-6344-5
  eISBN-10: 0-7425-6344-8
  1. Environmental justice—United States. 2. Environmental policy—Economic
aspects—United States. 3. Environmental economics—United States. I. Title.
  GE230.F33 2008
  363.7—dc22   2008004124

Printed in the United States of America

This book is dedicated to my best friend
and partner in life, a wonderful mother,
community activist, family therapist, musician,
and so much more!

Laura Kurman

Contents

Acknowledgments

This book has been four years in the making, with some detours along the way. During this time, I received strong support from my family and friends. It is often difficult to give up precious time with your family in order to write, but mine never complained. So, I wish to extend a special thanks to Emma, Jonah, and Laura for being so wonderful and patient with me. You all have my eternal love.

Secondly, I would like to offer a special thanks to Roger Gottlieb, G. William Domhoff, Laura Kurman, as well as Amy Lubitow, Kat Rickenbacker, Mark Hengen, Matt Judge, Lora Karaoglu, Corey Dehner, Nahide Konak, Shobha Hamal Gurung, Ronald Sandler, and other members of the Northeastern Environmental Justice Research Collaborative for their excellent editorial comments, criticisms, and suggestions. A special word of appreciation also goes out to my co-investigators on related research projects over the past ten years: Eric (Luke) Krieg and Deborah McCarthy. I would also like to express my gratitude to James O'Connor, Barbara Laurence, Joel Kovel, Bristow Harding, Tom Estabrook, Frank Ackerman, Victor Wallis, Michael Goldman, Sandra Meucci, Alan Rudy, and my other friends with *Capitalism, Nature, Socialism*. Another word of thanks to Brian Romer, Sarah Stanton, and Melissa McNitt at Rowman & Littlefield for their excellent work in producing the book.

Finally, I would like to acknowledge those individuals who aided me in my research on the environmental justice movement and foundations over the past seven years The following persons granted me a significant portion of their valuable time and energy to be interviewed: James Abernathy, Environmental Support Center; Leticia Alcantar, Tides Foundation; Ann Bastian, New World Foundation; Bob Bingaman, Sierra Club; Harolynne Bobis, Bullitt Foundation; China Brotsky, Tides Foundation; Karie Brown, Tides Foundation; Millie Buchanan, Jessie Smith Noyes Foundation; Carol Cheek, Lannan Foundation; Jack Chin,

Director of the Funders' Forum on Environment & Education; Cynthia Choi, Environmental Justice Fund; Diana Cohn, Solidago Foundation; Fernando Cuevas, Jr., Farmworker Network of Economic and Environmental Justice (FWNEEJ); Vic De Luca, Jessie Smith Noyes Foundation; Veronica Eady, Massachusetts Executive Office of Environmental Affairs; Marjorie Fine, Unitarian Universalist Veatch Program at Shelter Rock; Lois Marie Gibbs, Executive Director of the Center for Health, Environment, and Justice (CHEJ); Warren Goldstein-Gelb, Alternatives for Community and Environment (ACE); Tom Goldtooth, Indigenous Environmental Network (IEN); Julie Herman, Beldon Fund; Deborah Holder, Unitarian Universalist Veatch Program at Shelter Rock; John Hunting, Beldon Fund; Joshua Karliner, Transnational Resource and Action Center (TRAC); Orin Lengelle, Action for Community and Ecology in the Rainforests of Central America (ACERCA); Penn Loh, Alternatives for Community & Environment (ACE); Jane McAlevey, Unitarian Universalist Veatch Foundation at Shelter Rock; Vernice Miller-Travis, Ford Foundation; Stephen Mills, Sierra Club; Richard Moore, Southwest Network for Environmental and Economic Justice (SNEEJ); Tirso Moreno, Farmworker Network for Economic and Environmental Justice (FWNEEJ); Dan Nicolai, Louisiana Labor-Neighbor Project; Ali Noorani, Greater Boston Urban Resources Partnership; Deepak Pateriya, Environmental and Economic Justice Project; Christopher Peters, Seventh Generation Fund; Janet Phoenix, Northeast Network for Environmental Justice (NEJN); Rachel Pohl, Hemenway & Barnes; Alejandro Queral-Regil, Sierra Club; Cynthia Renfro, Beldon Fund; William J. Roberts, Beldon Fund; Christina Roessler, French American Charitable Trust (FACT); Jane Rogers, San Francisco Foundation; Peggy Saika, Asian Pacific Environmental Network (APEN); Peggy Shepard, West Harlem Environmental Action (WE ACT); Khalida Smalls, Greater Boston Environmental Justice Network (GBJEN); E. Gail Suchman, New York Lawyers for the Public Interest; Diana Takvorian, Environmental Health Coalition; Elizabeth Tan, French American Charitable Trust (FACT); Midge Taylor, Public Welfare Foundation; Connie Tucker, Southern Organizing Committee for Economic and Social Justice; and Stephen Viederman, Jessie Smith Noyes Foundation.

Finally, I would like to express my deepest appreciation and respect to my incredible extended family members—especially Zane, Kyffin, Kendra, Zach, Mindy, Debbie, Paul, Jay, Susan, and my father Charles—for all of your love and support. Each one of you has done so much to make this work a better place. I am also very fortunate to have a wonderful group of in-laws: Avery, Noah, Eli, Hannah, Max, Jessica, Judy, David S., Marsha, Brad, Ursula, David A., Shirley, Clara, and Israel. Our time together is always special. And, as always, the remembrance of Shelley and my mother Pat fills my spirit and soul.

The Polluter-Industrial Complex: Capitalizing on Environmental Injustice

The Earth provides enough to satisfy everyone's need, but not everyone's greed.

—Mahatma Gandhi

THE EVOLUTION OF AMERICAN ENVIRONMENTALISM

Growth of the Conservation and Preservation Movements

In the United States, the contemporary environmental movement partly evolved out of the preservationist and conservationist battles of the late nineteenth and early twentieth centuries. Conservationists and preservationists initially sought to prevent environmental abuses stemming from the "irrational" overexploitation of natural resources by robber-baron capitalism as well as to prevent the commodification of wilderness and other unique natural wonders by rapacious corporations.[1] After World War II, these movements became more broadly based among the rapidly growing middle and working classes. Buoyed by the construction of the federal highway system, citizens were afforded the opportunity to visit and enjoy America's most splendid landscapes and natural wonders. As a result, traditional conservation/preservation groups expanded in size and worked successfully in Congress to achieve the 1964 Wilderness Act and other legislation. By the early 1980s, some 109 million acres were included in the national forest system and were regulated on a "multiple-use" (read "multiple-profit") basis. Over 77 million acres in the national park system were closed to mining, timbering, and grazing, while the national wilderness preservation system included over 79 million acres. Thus, the conservation/preservation movement won

1

important protections for America's most unique and treasured landscapes, especially in the West.[2]

Conservation organizations were also partially merged into a more broadly based environmentalism that challenged not only the destruction of distant wilderness but also the degradation of nature near major population centers. The nineteenth- and early twentieth-century preservationists fought to prevent mountains, marshes and wetlands, valleys, and other valued landscapes from becoming capitalist private property. The modern environmental movement broadened and democratized these struggles to include nature protection for the middle class in the form of residential zoning and local greenbelts and other public lands. The efforts of the urban and suburban middle classes expanded the number of local parks and protected areas. Struggles to "Save Our Land," "Save Our Valley," "Save Our Mountains," "Save Our Forests," "Save Our Farmland," and "Save Our Wildlife" abounded. In these efforts by communities to protect themselves from the worst excesses of sprawl and development, a "no-growth" politics emerged, along with demands for greater local democratic control and regulation of land and natural resources. Today, these struggles are evolving smart-growth initiatives all over the country.

Birth of the Environmental Health Movement

The years following World War II also witnessed an explosive growth in the use of chemicals by American business. Free of any significant government controls, industry freely released massive quantities of pollution and toxic waste into the nation's air, land, and waterways. By the middle of the 1960s, industrial poisoning of the environment had reached crisis proportions. In Cleveland, Ohio, for instance, pollution was so bad that the Cuyahoga River caught fire on June 23, 1969. Floating oil slicks burned five stories high, making national news, inspiring a song (Randy Newman's "Burn On") and sparking, as it were, public support for clean water. The Cuyahoga drained into Lake Erie, which in 1970 was widely recognized as a dying lake and a symbol of America's ecological crisis.[3]

It was during this point in history that the environmental movement began to organize around issues of environmental quality and human health, including industrial pollution, dangerous chemicals, and toxic wastes. Alarmed at the threats posed by the Cuyahoga fire—as well as the massive Santa Barbara oil spill, the dangers of DDT and other pesticides described by Rachel Carson in her landmark book *Silent Spring*, the oppressive levels of air pollution blanketing America's largest cities, and numerous other pollution problems—millions of working- and middle-class Americans joined the environmental movement. In addition to the growth of traditional conservation organizations such as the

Audubon Society, the Sierra Club, the Wilderness Society, and the National Wildlife Federation that were expanding beyond conservation issues to work on pollution, a host of new nationally based organizations concerned with environmental quality and public health were born. They included the Environmental Defense Fund (now Environmental Defense), the Environmental Policy Institute and Friends of the Earth, Greenpeace, the Natural Resources Defense Council, and Environmental Action.[4] By the time of the first Earth Day on April 22, 1970, some 53 percent of the American people viewed "reduction of air and water pollution" as a national priority (up from only 17 percent in 1965).[5] Today, the environmental health movement has expanded to include citizen–science alliances working on the causes of disease clusters, breast cancer, asthma, Gulf War syndrome, and other health problems related to industrial toxins.[6]

Struggles for Occupational/Consumer Health and Safety

Along with the expansion of environmental organizations concerned with the exposure of community residents to industrial toxins *outside* the factory, the postwar period also witnessed an explosion of labor struggles against the exposure of workers to industrial toxins *inside* the factory.[7] Although there were also attempts to forge organizational links between the largely middle-class environmental health movement and the worker health and safety movement, these branches tended to develop independently of one another. However, led by public health and safety organizations, these worker battles sometimes linked the larger labor and environmental movements into ad hoc coalitions around specific legislative initiatives.[8] Occupational health and safety became primarily a worker rather than union issue but at times was generalized and folded into greater demands by consumer and environmental organizations for protection against toxic chemicals and other "negative externalities" of capitalist production. By the late 1960s and especially in the early 1970s, worker health and safety became a powerful political issue for many politicians in coal, uranium, and other mining states as well as in textile- and chemical-producing regions.[9]

In this limited manner, middle- and working-class concerns coincided over issues of environmental quality and human health. The labor movement's fight against the abuse of workers' health and safety spilled into surrounding communities. Lobbyists for the steelworkers, machinists, autoworkers, and other industrial unions helped shape and pass the 1970 Clean Air Act and the 1972 Clean Water Act amendments. Organizers for the Sierra Club supported the 1973 strike over health and safety issues against Shell by the oil, chemical, and atomic workers. But despite these coalitions, the "jobs versus the environment" disputes slyly promoted by industry would soon sabotage many of the more solid broad-based alliances between the two movements, especially in the face of growing economic problems in the mid- and late 1970s and 1980s.[10] Today, the coalitions are slowly being rebuilt in the form of the Blue-Green Alliance (BGA), an innovative national partnership of the United Steelworkers and the Sierra Club—North America's largest private sector manufacturing union and the nation's oldest environmental organization. This group is focused on promoting environmental programs and policies that result in solutions to global warming solutions, stable jobs, international trade reform, and the promotion of green chemistry to substitute toxics in the workplace and community.

The 1960s and 1970s also saw unionists and environmentalists join consumer rights advocates such as Ralph Nader at Public Citizen to fight the proliferation of dangerous consumer products. Together with public health and safety organizations, the environmental movement helped force an unprecedented outpouring of consumer legislation, such as the Consumer Product Safety Act of 1972. Environmentalists moved naturally into issues concerning pesticides and food additives, dubious baby formulas, and unsafe automobiles while fighting to control hazardous technology and pollution. Their efforts helped create more regulation of food processing, toy manufacturing, drugs, household chemicals, and other consumer goods, although the government stopped short of tracing harmful consumer products back to dangerous production processes and undemocratic economic and regulatory structures.[11] However, these kinds of struggles are emerging today in the form of the Safe Cosmetics Campaign, organizations combating genetic engineering and biotechnology, and the "clean production" movement.[12]

The Emergence of the Modern Environmental Movement

By the mid-1970s, thousands of groups fighting for conservation and preservation of natural resources, local amenities, worker and community health and safety, safe energy sources, consumer product safety, and a toxic-free environment formed a powerful (but loosely organized) social movement. Over 5.5 million people contributed financially to nineteen leading national organizations and perhaps another 20 million people to over 40,000 local environmental groups in 1975.[13] Inspired by a fresh set of environmental disasters like the Three Mile Island nuclear power plant accident and the toxic waste nightmare at Love Canal, old and new local coalitions composed of hundreds of grassroots groups such as Public Citizen, the Citizens Clearinghouse on Hazardous Waste (now the Center for Health, Environment, and Justice), and the National Campaign Against Toxic Hazards continued to grow over the next decade. Environmentalism had arrived as a broad-based social movement.

The ecology movement utilized its growing political muscle to force the establishment of the Environmental Protection Agency, the Occupational Health and Safety Administration, and the Council on Environmental Quality. The creation of these new agencies bypassed traditional natural resource and other agencies long "captured" by corporate interests and introduced a modest modicum of democracy within the state apparatus itself. Although hostile to the movement, President Richard Nixon feared the proenvironmental politics of the Democratic Party challenger Edmund Muskie in the upcoming election. In order to win the support of voters, Nixon agreed to create these agencies. He also signed new legislation into law, including the National Environmental Policy Act (1969) and the Clean Air Act (1970). For its part, worker militancy, combined with a lobbying coalition of more than a hundred labor, consumer, religious, and environmental organizations, managed to put the Occupational Health and Safety Act (1970) in place.

The rush of environmental laws adopted during the 1970s represented a "republican moment"—an outburst of democratic participation and ideological politics—created by widespread and then-rising public demand for environmental protection. Congress passed sweeping laws by overwhelming majorities, as no one from either political party wanted to be punished in a future election for being an enemy of environmental protection.[14] By the end of the so-called environmental decade of the 1970s, Congress had passed twenty-nine major laws regulating consumer products, the environment, and workplace conditions. Despite the presence of significant flaws in much of the legislation, the new federal agencies charged with implementing environmental law, in effect, became weapons of the movement. Under this new *liberal regime of environmental regulation*, the legal framework for environmental protection was transformed from a property and tort system to a specialized branch of federal statutory and administrative law.[15]

Unfortunately, these new federal regulations offered inadequate protection to poor communities of color and working-class neighborhoods. In fact, one of the hallmarks of the liberal regime of regulation is the manner in which it has corrected some single-issue environmental and human health problems for some people (or sector of the environment) by causing industry to transform the ecological hazard into another form that is then displaced onto other members of society and/or another realm of nature. Environmental laws may mandate the "capture" of pollution formerly released in neighborhoods adjacent to the factory but do not halt the disposal of the "captured" pollution in toxic waste dumps or hazardous incinerators in poor communities of color. As stated by one government report, billions of dollars are spent "to remove pollutants from the air and water only to dispose of such pollutants on the land, and in an environmentally unsound manner."[16]

THE RISE OF THE ENVIRONMENTAL JUSTICE MOVEMENT

The displacement of the ecological crisis onto the country's most politically marginalized communities has fueled the rise of America's environmental justice (EJ) movement and efforts to reform traditional policy. Since the early 1980s, a new network of grassroots organizations has developed to challenge the practices of ecological racism on the part of not only capital and the state but also the mainstream environmental movement as well. As seen in the First and Second National People of Color Environmental Leadership summits and other organizing efforts,[17] this growing movement for social and ecological justice seeks to address the connections between poverty, racism, and the ecological problems in America's urban neighborhoods, barrios, Native lands, Chicano farming districts, and poor rural communities of color. Pressing for greater economic equity and political democracy, such as the right to know about hazards facing the community, this movement is mobilizing people of color and the poorest segments of the working class to fight industrial pollution, toxic dumping, uranium mining, and other environmental dangers.

The diversity of people participating in these local, regional, and national organizations is matched by the diversity of political paths and approaches taken to achieving environmental justice. The contemporary EJ movement represents a convergence of seven formerly independent social movements and includes (1) the *civil rights movement*, focused on issues of *environmental racism* and the disproportionate impacts of pollution in communities of color, the racial biases in government regulatory practices, and the glaring absence of affirmative action and sensitivity to racial issues in the established environmental advocacy organizations; (2) the *occupational health and safety movement*, working for the labor rights of nonunion immigrants and undocumented workers; (3) the *indigenous lands movement*, emerging out of the struggles by Native Americans, Chicanos, African Americans, and other marginalized indigenous communities to retain and protect their traditional lands; (4) the *environmental health movement*, which developed largely out of the mainstream environmental movement in general and the antitoxics movement in particular; (5) *community-based movements for social and economic justice* that have expanded their political horizons to incorporate issues such as lead poisoning, abandoned toxic waste dumps, the lack of parks and green spaces, poor air quality, and other issues of environmental justice into their agenda for community empowerment; (6) the *human rights, peace, and solidarity movements*, particularly those campaigns that first emerged in the 1980s around apartheid in South Africa and U.S. intervention in Nicaragua and Central America; and (7) the immigrant rights movements that expand the basic struggle for citizenship to include basic rights of citizenship, including the right to clean air and water.

THE CORPORATE WAR AGAINST THE EJ MOVEMENT

Since the "environmental decade" of the 1970s, the U.S. economy has experienced intensified international competition from foreign capital, especially in East Asia. The United States has lost market after market for mass-produced consumer goods and, increasingly, for many capital goods as well. Furthermore, the U.S. position in the global economy as a competitive producer of some raw materials, foodstuffs, and energy supplies is further eroded by cheaper operations overseas. The renewal of intercapitalist rivalries, higher energy prices, and the decline of Pax Americana (the Iraq War notwithstanding) is slowing the growth rate of U.S. capitalism. In the eyes of American business, the environmental and EJ movements are also implicated. Burdened by costly environmental, consumer, and occupational safety legislation, U.S. capital is seeking ways to reduce the costs of government regulations in order to compete more effectively. As a result, American capital has launched a political counterattack on the liberal regime of environmental regulation as well as environmental and EJ movements.[18]

This book is devoted to explaining the economic, political, and social contours of this corporate assault and the harm it is causing to the American people and environment. Led by America's worst corporate polluters, this offensive is proving to be especially devastating to people of color and working-class families. Five chapters explain how and why America's poorest communities are being selectively victimized by corporate polluters and the state. I also offer a glimpse of the ways in which the EJ movement is fighting back. In the end, this is a hopeful story.

NOT ALL PEOPLE ARE POLLUTED EQUAL: THE ENVIRONMENTAL INJUSTICES OF AMERICAN CAPITALISM

In chapter 1, "Not All People Are Polluted Equal: The Environmental Injustices of American Capitalism," I analyze the global forces currently reshaping the U.S. economy. In order to compete in the world market, American business is looking to become more efficient. As a result, the first imperative of U.S. capital is to lower production costs. In turn, greater cost containment is being achieved through a process of capital restructuring, which includes intensified pressures for the closure of unprofitable businesses; cutting expenses related to environmental protection; reallocating money from less profitable companies that pay workers better wages and do a better job of protecting public health; supplying venture capital to new (often more destructive) businesses, including those practicing acts of environmental racism; and relocating operations to pollution havens in the southern United States or overseas. Simply put, the key to cost containment lies in processes of capital restructuring that have enabled American business to *extract more value from labor power and nature in less time and at less cost*.[19] As a result, the ecological crisis continues to deepen.

Not all citizens are polluted equal in this process of capital restructuring. Instead, it is poor people of color and the white working class, especially the most politically oppressed segments of America's "underclass" (or subaltern peoples), that are being *selectively victimized* to the greatest extent by corporate environmental abuses. The result is increased dumping of ever more toxic pollution into the environment, particularly in poor working-class neighborhoods and communities of color; more destructive forms of natural resource extraction from this country's most unique and treasured landscapes, especially land resources belonging to poor Appalachians and Native Americans; a deterioration in consumer product safety (and attempts to limit corporate liability for defective or damaging products); the disappearance of ever more natural species and habitats; suburban sprawl; and a general assault on those programs and policies designed to protect the environment. In short, to sustain the process of capital accumulation and higher profits in the new global economy, American capital is increasingly relying on ecologically unsustainable forms of production that disproportionately impact communities of color and the working class—sectors that are underrepresented in the traditional environmental movement.

ERODING ENVIRONMENTAL JUSTICE: COLONIZATION OF THE STATE BY THE POLLUTER-INDUSTRIAL COMPLEX

In chapter 2, "Eroding Environmental Justice: Colonization of the State by the Polluter-Industrial Complex," I analyze the political dimensions of corporate America's unrelenting assault on the ecology and EJ movements. As part of a broader "new class war" against popular social movements, this political attack is being spearheaded by the most highly polluting and environmentally destructive sectors of American business as well as important sectors of Wall Street and financial capital that bankroll their activities. Heavily regulated corporate polluters are pouring money into antienvironmental organizations, public relations firms, foundations, think tanks, research centers, and policy institutes as well as the election campaigns of "probusiness" candidates in both major political parties. In fact, the American power structure is now controlled largely by what I term the *polluter-industrial complex*, or those sectors of business that would stand to profit the most from a weakening of the liberal regime of environmental regulation.

In order to roll back environmental regulation and to hold the emerging EJ movement in check, the polluter-industrial complex must engage in a series of maneuvers designed to colonize and restructure the state in its favor—to establish a system of "cooperation" among corporate polluters and the U.S. government at all levels. This chapter focuses on the means by which the corporate power elite in general and the polluter-industrial complex in particular are wielding power over the state apparatus, with a special emphasis on the executive branch and administration of George W. Bush. This focus includes an analysis of the processes by which (1) business-friendly political candidates are selected and financially supported; (2) officials aligned with industry are appointed to administer key government agencies, including those related to environmental protection; (3) corporate lobbyists beholden to the polluter-industrial complex are granted extraordinary influence in the halls of government; (4) a vast policy-making infrastructure favorable to environmentally destructive companies is systematically utilized by both major political parties to roll back ecological protection; and (5) independent scientific investigation of environmental problems is corrupted by corporate polluters. Together, these processes constitute a network of mechanisms that establish and maintain domination of the state by corporate elites, particularly those associated with ecologically destructive companies. It is the hegemony of polluter-industrial complex that is ultimately responsible for the erosion of environmental justice in the United States.[20]

AGAINST OUR NATURE: NEOLIBERALISM AND THE CRISIS OF ENVIRONMENTAL JUSTICE POLICY

In chapter 3, "Against Our Nature: Neoliberalism and the Crisis of Environmental Justice Policy," I outline the political backlash against the liberal regime of environmental regulation. The goal of this assault by American capital is "regulatory reform," including the rollback of President Clinton's executive order for environmental justice, worker health and safety, consumer protection, environmental protection, and other state regulatory "burdens" that impinge on the profits of capital. As part of this offensive, the Bush–Cheney administration has imposed severe cuts in agency staffs and budgets, effectively crippling the research, monitoring, and enforcement activities of the Environmental Protection Agency (and other agencies). Faithfully endorsed by the neoliberals in both the Republican and the Democratic parties, the result has been a worsening of major environmental problems and ecological inequities for working people, communities of color, and the underclass.

Neoliberals are also pushing for the adoption of "free-market" environ-mentalism in state policymaking and enforcement. As a result, many older regulations requiring across-the-board compliance with environmental laws are being replaced with "cost-effective" reforms and "free-market" forms of environmental policy—pollution taxes and credits, effluent charges, subsidies for polluting industries, markets for pollution rights, and bubble schemes—all designed to increase capital's flexibility to meet weaker environmental regulations but continue polluting in a profitable manner. These approaches are allowing the increased displacement of ecological hazards onto commu-nities with less control capacity, namely, poorer communities of color and working-class neighborhoods. As a result, the safeguards won by the EJ and ecology movements over the past twenty years are being systematically dis-mantled.

THE UNFAIR TRADE-OFF: GLOBALIZATION AND THE EXPORT OF ECOLOGICAL HAZARDS

In chapter 4, "The Unfair Trade-Off: Globalization and the Export of Eco-logical Hazards," I show how the worsening ecological crisis in the global South is directly related to a global system of economic and environmental stratification in which the United States and other advanced capitalist nations are able to shift or impose a growing environmental burden on weaker states.

This *export of ecological hazard* from the United States to the less devel-oped countries takes place in the form of (1) foreign direct investment in do-mestically owned hazardous industries as well as destructive investment schemes to gain access to new oil fields, forests, agricultural lands, mining deposits, and other natural resources; (2) the relocation of polluting and en-vironmentally hazardous production processes and polluting facilities owned by transnational capital to the South; (3) the marketing of more profitable but also more dangerous foods, drugs, pesticides, technologies, and other con-sumer/capital goods; and (4) the dumping of toxic wastes, pollution, dis-carded consumer products, trash, and other forms of "antiwealth" produced by northern industry.

Defined in terms of North versus South, corporate-led globalization is magnifying externally and internally based environmental injustices to the advantage of the United States. In much of the developing world, access to natural resources is being restricted by the transformation of commonly held lands (the commons) into capitalist private property, that is, the "commodifi-cation of nature." Those peoples in the global South who draw their livelihood directly from the land, water, forests, coastal mangroves, and other ecosystems are becoming displaced in order to supply cheap raw materials for the dominant classes and foreign capital. Laboring in service of this new global order but receiving few of its benefits, the popular majorities of the developing world—the poor peasants, workers, ethnic minorities, and indigenous peoples who make up the subsistence sector—struggle to survive by moving onto ecologically fragile lands or by migrating to the shantytowns of the cities by the millions to search for employment. Often left with little means to improve the quality of their lives, the world's poor are being forced to overexploit their own limited natural resource base in order to survive. In much of the Third World, these survival strategies by the popular classes in response to their growing impoverishment are resulting in the widespread degradation and ecological collapse of the environment. As a result, globalization-inspired development models are becoming increasingly unviable in the South, giving birth to popularly based movements for social and ecological justice—an *environmentalism of the poor*.[21]

TRANSFORMING GREEN POLITICS: CHALLENGES CONFRONTING THE ENVIRONMENTAL JUSTICE MOVEMENT

In chapter 5, "Transforming Green Politics: Challenges Confronting the Environmental Justice Movement," I explore a new wave of grassroots activism that is building in the United States. In reaction to the economic and ecological injustices accentuated by the rise of neoliberalism and corporate-led globalization as well as the political neglect of the mainstream environmental movement, the EJ movement is forging a deeper shade of green politics. In poor African American and Latino neighborhoods of small towns and the inner cities, depressed Native American reservations, and Hispanic communities all across the country, people who have traditionally been relegated to the periphery of the environmental movement are now challenging the wholesale depredation of their land, water, air, and community health by corporate polluters and indifferent governmental agencies. Combining elements of civil rights, social justice, the struggle for land rights, and respect for the environment, oppressed peoples of color have formed movements for environmental justice to fight the disparate ecological and economic burdens placed on their communities.[22] As such, the continued growth and prosperity of the EJ movement is essential to constructing a more inclusive, democratic, and proactive environmental politics in the United States.

However, there are a number of major challenges confronting the EJ movement as it tries to forge itself into a unified national and international movement. These challenges include the formation of a new master "frame" that allows a wider range of citizens to identify with the goals of the movement, the adoption of suitable organizational structures that will permit the movement to grow and prosper, the availability of sufficient funding necessary to sustain organizations and the utilization of appropriate political strategies and tactics necessary to bring about real social change. These strategies may well include moving beyond approaches aimed at ending the unequal distribution of environmental problems (*distributional justice*) to address the political-economic structures that produce the environmental problems in the first place (*productive justice*).[23] The more radical and far reaching of these alternative visions sublate radical democracy, socialist, and identity politics into a new synthesis. The eventual political necessity is to expand existing EJ coalitions—still in their infancy—to work in harmony with other transnational movements to invent a more transformative political ecology.

WHAT DOES THE FUTURE HOLD?

There are indications that labor, environmentalists, indigenous peoples, women's movements, farmers, consumer product safety advocates, and antiglobalization activists are ready to build a new form of green politics in the United States. The revitalization of grassroots environmental organizations committed to genuine base building and political-economic reform is a reaction to the new challenges posed by neoliberalism and globalization and includes the use of direct action and popular mobilization against indifferent government agencies, timber companies, polluters, the World Trade Organization, and the World Bank and International Monetary Fund as well as criticism toward the "corporatist" and exclusionary approaches of mainstream environmental organizations. Pressing for greater economic equality, smart growth, affordable housing, "fair trade," stricter systems of international environmental regulation and labor rights, greater corporate and government accountability, and more comprehensive approaches to environmental problem solving, the struggle for environmental justice represents the early birth of a *transformative* environmental politics. Understanding the new political-economic terrain of American capitalism is key if this transformation is to ever occur. It is hoped that this book will contribute to the development of such an understanding, and inspire the reader to become involved in the struggle for a more just and sustainable future.

NOTES

1. Jim O'Brien, "Environmentalism as a Mass Movement: Historical Notes," *Radical America* 17, no. 2/3 (1983): 77.

2. Stephen Fox, *The American Conservation Movement: John Muir and His Legacy* (Madison: University of Wisconsin Press, 1985); William K. Wyant, *Westward in Eden: The Public Lands and the Conservation Movement* (Berkeley: University of California Press, 1982); Samuel P. Hays, *Conservation and the Gospel of Efficiency: The Progressive Conservation Movement 1890–1920* (Cambridge, MA: Harvard University Press, 1959).

3. Barry Commoner, *Making Peace with the Planet* (New York: Pantheon Books, 1990), 25–29.

4. Benjamin Kline, *First along the River: A Brief History of the U.S. Environmental Movement* (San Francisco: Acadia Books, 2000), 84–100.

5. Mark Dowie, *Losing Ground: American Environmentalism at the Close of the Twentieth Century* (Cambridge, MA: MIT Press, 1995), 3–5.

6. Phil Brown, *Toxic Exposures: Contested Illnesses and the Environmental Health Movement* (New York: Columbia University Press, 2007).

7. Prior to World War II, labor unions, community-based public health groups, women's organizations, and professional reformers such as Alice Hamilton, the country's first great industrial ecologist and premier investigator of occupational hazards, remained largely detached from the conservation/preservation movements. See Robert Gottlieb, *Forcing the Spring: The Transformation of the American Environmental Movement* (Washington, DC: Island Press, 1993).

8. Charles Noble, *Liberalism at Work: The Rise and Fall of OSHA* (Philadelphia: Temple University Press, 1986), 63.

9. Daniel Berman, *Death on the Job* (New York: Monthly Review Press, 1978)

10. Richard Kazis and Richard Grossman, *Fear at Work: Job Blackmail, Labor and the Environment* (New York: Pilgrim Press, 1982).

11. Joan Claybrook and the Staff of Public Citizen, *Retreat from Safety: Reagan's Attack on America's Health* (New York: Pantheon Books, 1984).

12. Stacy Malkan, *Not Just a Pretty Face: The Ugly Side of the Beauty Industry* (Gabriola Island, BC: New Society Publishers, 2007).

13. Francis Sandback, *Environment, Ideology, and Policy* (Montclair, NJ: Allanheld, Osmun, 1980), 13.

14. Richard J. Lazarus, "A Different Kind of 'Republican Moment' in Environmental Law," *Minnesota Law Review* 87, no. 4 (April 2003): 999–1036.

15. Martin H. Belsky, "Environmental Policy Law in the 1980s: Shifting Back the Burden of Proof," *Ecology Law Quarterly* 12, no. 1 (1984): 12.

16. Lewis Regenstein, *How to Survive in America the Poisoned* (Washington, DC: Acropolis Books, 1986), 160.

17. Held in Washington, D.C., the four-day summit was attended by more than 560 grassroots and national leaders from around the world. On September 27, 1991, delegates

adopted seventeen "Principles of Environmental Justice," which now serve as a common guide for the movement. See Charles Lee, *Proceedings: The First National People of Color Environmental Leadership Summit* (New York: United Church of Christ Commission for Racial Justice, 1992), and Dana Alston, "Transforming a Movement: People of Color Unite at Summit Against Environmental Racism," *Sojourner* 21 (1992): 30–31.

18. Val Burris, "The Political Partisanship of American Business: A Study of Corporate Political Action Committees," *American Sociological Review* 52 (December 1987): 736–37.

19. Daniel Faber, ed., *The Struggle for Ecological Democracy: Environmental Justice Movements in the United States* (New York: Guilford, 1998).

20. Clyde W. Barrow, *Critical Theories of the State: Marxist, Neo-Marxist, Post-Marxist* (Madison: University of Wisconsin Press, 1993), 25–28.

21. Joan Martínez-Alier, *The Environmentalism of the Poor: A Study of Ecological Conflicts and Valuation* (Northampton, MA: Edward Elgar, 2002).

22. Robert D. Bullard, ed., *Confronting Environmental Racism: Voices from the Grassroots* (Boston: South End Press, 1993).

23. Robert Lake, "Volunteers, NIMBYs, and Environmental Justice: Dilemmas of Democratic Practice," *Antipode* 28 (1996): 160–74.

Chapter One

Not All People Are Polluted Equal: The Environmental Injustices of American Capitalism

To be a poor man is hard, but to be a poor race in a land of dollars is the very bottom of hardships.

—W. E. B. Du Bois, American scholar and civil rights leader, 1868–1963

THE ENVIRONMENTAL INJUSTICES OF AMERICAN CAPITALISM

The American people are experiencing an unparalleled assault on the nation's environment. Driven by the thirst for higher profits and the threat of increased international competition in the era of globalization, business elites have initiated a political movement calling for reduced taxes and less government regulation. At the heart of this demand for "regulatory reform" is the rollback of traditional environmental policies, occupational health and safety rules, consumer protection laws, and other regulations seen as impinging on corporate earnings.

Termed *neoliberalism*, this political assault on the regulatory responsibilities and capacities of the state is being spearheaded by the largest and most powerful corporate polluters in the United States. These corporations have created a sophisticated network of think tanks, policy institutes, research centers, foundations, nonprofit organizations, public relations firms, and political action committees. This organizational infrastructure, or what I call the *polluter-industrial complex*, is committed to discrediting the environmental movement and to dismantling state programs and policies that promote environmental justice, protect public health, and safeguard the earth. Corporate polluters are also pouring tens of millions of dollars into the campaigns of

15

candidates for public office who are dedicated to the neoliberal agenda. Thirty years' worth of progress by the environmental movement is being systematically dismantled under the weight of this assault, deepening of the ecological crisis of American capitalism.[1]

While this ecological crisis is impacting everyone, some are more deeply affected than others. As we shall see in this chapter, it is the working class—and especially poorer people of color and the most politically oppressed segments of America's underclass—who are being *selectively victimized* to the greatest extent by corporate environmental abuses. These abuses are manifest in the disparate siting of toxic waste sites, highly polluting factories, and other ecologically hazardous facilities in poor African American communities and low-income neighborhoods across the country. In the hunt for cheaper energy supplies and natural resources, corporate giants are also ravaging landscapes that are home to poor Appalachian whites and isolated Native American tribes in the Southwest. It is the destruction of marshlands surrounding New Orleans and the ecological devastation of the Louisiana coastline by the oil industry that exacerbated the profound human tragedies of Hurricane Katrina.

The neoliberal assault on labor and the civil rights movement is also contributing to the emergence of more dangerous working conditions and occupational hazards for workers of color, particularly for Asian immigrants and undocumented Mexican workers laboring in the pesticide-soaked agricultural fields of California and Florida. Furthermore, the increased geographic mobility of capital is leading corporations to relocate to pollution havens in the Sunbelt, where state environmental laws are weakest. As former governors, Bill Clinton and George W. Bush attracted corporate polluters to Arkansas and Texas, respectively, by dismantling environmental protection and enforcement activities, especially in poorer communities. In short, the concentration of environmental and occupational health hazards among poor people of color and working-class whites is creating ecological sacrifice zones where it is simply dangerous to breathe the air or take a drink of water. These zones allow the polluter-industrial complex to lower the costs of environmental regulation by displacing the ecological crisis onto the least powerful segments of American society—people who are largely outside the traditional environmental movement. In so doing, neoliberals are dividing people of different racial, ethnic, cultural, and class backgrounds against one another and sidestepping demands for a more fundamental transformation of the nation's environmental laws. Under the capitalist system, it pays that not all people are polluted equal.

In summary, the corporate assault on the liberal regime of environmental regulation and the promotion of neoliberal policies (including "free-market" environmentalism) in its place are facilitating a process of economic restructuring by American capital. Absent a system of strong regulatory oversight by the federal government, the profitability of the polluter-industrial complex is dependent on unsustainable forms of production that disproportionately impact oppressed peoples of color and the working poor. Coupled with a corporate assault on labor and the welfare state, it is clear that the health and well-being of ordinary families is being sacrificed for the benefit of industry. The increased economic hardships of the working class and poor people of color and the degradation of the environment in which they "live, work, and play" are two sides of same coin and are deeply interrelated. As a result, issues of social and environmental justice have surfaced together now more intensely than in any period in American history.

NEOLIBERALISM AND THE RESTRUCTURING OF AMERICAN CAPITALISM

Globalization and the U.S. Economy

The business assault on the liberal regime of environmental regulation cannot be understood without reference to the profound changes taking place in the world economy and the advantages and drawbacks it brings for U.S. capital. In the new global economy, multinational corporations and other companies have a newfound ability to locate factories in any part of the world where operations are more profitable. Vast improvements in international communications and transportation systems are giving multinational corporations the freedom to roam the world in search of countries with the most favorable business climate. Once the overseas facilities are up and running, the commodities produced by these ventures are then exported back into the United States. The increased mobility of multinational corporations is consequently eliminating nationally oriented development strategies in favor of export-oriented industrialization in both the North and the global South. It is this internationalization of the productive circuit of capital that distinguishes the current period of corporate-led globalization from any other moment in history. As a result, thousands of American companies are finding themselves embroiled in a life-and-death struggle in the world market. For the less "efficient" producers unable to keep pace, global market forces, especially financial markets, are driving them out of business. Adam Smith's "invisible hand" is baring its knuckles. Now, more than ever, "accumulate or die" has become the sine qua non of American capitalism.

In the United States, corporate-led globalization, facilitated in great part by a host of "free-trade" agreements and policies brokered by neoliberal Democrats and Republicans, benefits many sectors of industry. These sectors include U.S.-based multinational corporations exporting business services, agricultural products, aerospace equipment and parts, pharmaceutical and medical products, financial capital, computer technology, machinery, and other capital goods. The United States exported a whopping $1.3 trillion worth of these goods and services in 2005, according to the Bureau of Economic Analysis. These exports of capital goods and business services are fueling industrialization in the developing nations (as well as the advanced capitalist countries). Semiskilled and highly skilled American workers associated with these industries in the so-called new economy have consequently witnessed strong demand for their services, with substantially higher salaries and benefits and opportunities for advancement.[2]

However, the expansion of global trade is taking a major toll on many sectors of U.S. industry. Not since the pre–World War II period has American business faced such intense international competition from foreign capital. Fueled by innovations in global communication and transportation systems, new production processes and advanced technologies, huge investments in infrastructure, and major improvements in the educational, skill, and productivity levels of labor power, multinational corporations and domestic industries located in China, South Korea, and the newly industrializing countries of the global South are rapidly expanding to capture a growing share of the U.S. and world market. As a result, the U.S. position as a producer of some raw materials and energy supplies is being eroded by more profitable foreign operations. In addition, manufacturers that have traditionally served as the backbone of the U.S. economy, as well as the trade union movement, have also seen their competitive position for mass-produced consumer goods and processed raw materials (such as steel) steadily eroded by lower-cost overseas producers.

American automobile manufacturers make up one such industry now on the defensive. It used to be said that "what is good for General Motors is good for the country," but today the auto giant is reeling. In 2005–2006, General Motors lost a combined $12.4 billion. The automaker is in the midst of a sweeping restructuring plan that aims to reduce costs $9 billion by slashing more than 34,000 jobs and closing twelve plants.[3] In additional to automakers, other American-based industries facing intense import competition with the greatest job losses include the apparel, footwear, electric appliances, plastic products, knitting mills, leather products, textiles, blast furnace, tire, cycle and miscellaneous transport, radio and television, toys, and sporting goods industries. Between 1979 and 1999, 6.4 million U.S. workers were displaced by import-competing industries, representing about 38 percent of the 17 million lost manufacturing jobs. These workers, especially women, the less educated, and older workers, experience great difficulty obtaining new jobs at comparable wages. Among the reemployed, import-competing displaced workers experience sizable average weekly earnings losses of about 13 percent.[4] As a result, living standards are falling for much of the working class displaced by foreign competition and industrial relocation overseas.

The Current Account Deficit and the War against Environmentalism

In the new global economy, foreign capital and multinational corporations operating overseas can avoid paying for environmental safeguards, neglect worker health and safety standards, and exploit cheaper sources of labor. These lower-cost producers are weakening the ability of many U.S. businesses to compete in global export markets. In 2006, the overall U.S. trade deficit in goods and services was $765.3 billion, a fifth consecutive record deficit.[5] China, for example, has one of the fastest-growing economies in the world and is a major trading partner that commits gross abuses of human/labor rights and the environment.[6] In 2006, the U.S. trade deficit with China reached $233 billion. The explosion in cheap Chinese imports has contributed mightily to the loss of some 2.7 million American manufacturing jobs since 2000.[7]

An even more complete view on the state of the U.S. economy can be achieved when analyzing the current account deficit, which includes the difference between U.S. exports and imports of goods and services, income (salaries and investments), and net transfers (workers' remittances, donations, aids and grants and so on). At $875 billion in 2006, the global current account deficit of the United States is the largest in history and now accounts for 7 percent of the country's gross domestic product. Moreover, the deficit has been rising by an average of $100 billion a year since 2002—a trajectory that is clearly unsustainable in the long run.[8] In this respect, the United States is serving as the supermarket for the rest of the world—the primary source of global effective demand in the form of private consumption, investment, and government expenditures.[9] In fact, the expansion of global capitalism is being driven by the debt-ridden U.S. economy, where consumers and businesses have taken advantage of low interest rates to borrow vast sums of money to finance purchases. Along with the record current account deficit, private and public sector debts in the United States have risen to unprecedented levels.[10] Given that these debts must eventually be paid, the foreign debt and current account deficit represent a potential threat to the stability of the U.S. economy and the living standards of the American people.

To contain the current account deficit, the United States must increase exports to the rest of the world. The prospect of achieving monopoly prices for various forms of "intellectual property" and licenses around American culture (songs and movies), biotechnology and genetically engineered (terminator) seeds and other products, nanotechnology, new computers and other forms of high technology, new machinery, and pharmaceuticals offers some of the more promising prospects for U.S. corporations.[11] Many of these new technologies create and/or enlarge demand for affiliated commodities also produced by U.S. manufacturers. For instance, farmers planting Monsanto "Roundup Ready" soybeans genetically altered to withstand the herbicide Roundup use two to five times as many pounds of herbicides (also produced by Monsanto and other pesticide companies) as farmers using conventional systems and ten times as much herbicide as farmers using Integrated Weed Management systems.[12] In order to "grow" markets and expand exports, U.S.-based multinational corporations that make up the polluter-industrial complex are marketing commodities that create a "dependency" among their purchasers for additional (often ecologically destructive) inputs. However, little government support is offered for U.S. capital to manufacture more environmentally friendly and renewable energy technologies, "clean" production processes, and nontoxic substitutes for hazardous chemicals that could be exported to promote more sustainable models of development in the rest of the world.[13]

Regardless of the industry, American capital as a whole must become more efficient in order to compete in the world market. The flood of cheap imports into the country means that U.S. businesses are less able to boost profits by raising the prices of their commodities. To raise prices would drive consumers to purchase low-cost imports manufactured by foreign capital. As a result, the first imperative of U.S.-based capital in the new global economy is to lower production costs. Because domestic and world export markets are becoming both more generalized and more cutthroat, *cost minimization* strategies now lay at the heart of American business strategies for *profit maximization*. Greater cost containment for American capital is being achieved through a process of capital restructuring. The most important goal of this restructuring is to reestablish corporate control over unions and state regulatory agencies that are cutting into profits. Along with labor costs (which include health insurance and other benefits), environmental protection measures are considered by many industries to be some of the most expensive and burdensome. Companies are therefore seeking to protect earnings not only by "downsizing" the labor force but also by cutting investments in pollution control, environmental conservation, and worker health and safety.

To ensure that such discipline is maintained, foreign and domestic sources of finance capital have assumed an even greater role in directing the economy by intensifying pressures for the closure of unprofitable businesses. Finance capital is also compelling companies to reorganize production and cut expenses related to environmental protection, reallocating money from less profitable companies that pay workers better wages and do a better job of protecting public health in favor of nonunion operations. Wall Street is also supplying venture capital to new (often more destructive) businesses, including those practicing acts of environmental racism, and funding the explosion of corporate mergers and acquisitions into larger companies with a greater capacity to dominate the marketplace and/or to exit the economy for pollution havens in the South or overseas. Simply put, the key to cost containment lies in processes of capital restructuring that have enabled American business to *extract more value from labor power and nature in less time and at less cost.*

American business is increasing the rate of exploitation of labor through a general assault on the past gains of the labor movement. This assault takes numerous forms: workforce reductions or so-called corporate downsizing; the business offensive against unions; increased layoffs of permanent workers and the increased use of temporary or "contingent" workers at less pay; greater job insecurity, falling wages, benefits, and living standards; longer hours and a "speedup" of the production process; deteriorating worker health and safety conditions; and a general assault on those private and public programs and policies that serve the interests of working Americans.[14] This assault is proving to be successful from the perspective of industry. According to a 2007 report by the United Nations International Labor Organization, the United States is now the global leader by a considerable amount in terms of labor productivity per person employed in 2006. American workers stay longer each day at the workplace and produce more wealth for business per hour employed than any other workforce in the world.[15]

Economic pressures are especially intense for American workers thrown into direct competition with low-wage labor overseas. American capital is "squeezing" the capacity of labor in the consumer goods industries to organize for higher living standards. With capital's ability to relocate to low-wage havens and utilize "job blackmail" strategies against unskilled or semiskilled industrial workers, the labor movement has been in steady decline. In July 2005, two of the nation's largest and most powerful unions—the 1.7-million-member Service Employees International Union and the 1.3-million-strong International Brotherhood of Teamsters—resigned from the AFL-CIO, fracturing the fifty-year-old federation. Where union membership once comprised 36 percent of all private sector employees in 1953, today the figure has plunged to less than 9 percent. Less educated workers are particularly vulnerable, and are seeing the greatest declines in unionization rates.[16] Union and nonunion workers alike are under increased pressure to accept reduced pay and benefits (including retirement and health care coverage) and to work longer hours. The Economic Policy Institute estimates that "free trade" costs the average American household between $2,000 and $6,000 annually in lost earnings. In fact, 80 percent of all households have seen their pretax incomes decline since 1979.[17]

The business class, which is reaping the benefits of higher labor productivity and increased earnings, are no longer passing along a portion of their profits to workers in the form of higher wages. As stated by Federal Reserve chief Ben Bernanke in June 2006, the absence of "regulations that raise the costs of hiring and firing workers and that reduce employers' ability to change work assignments . . . like those in a number of European countries, for example," further advantage U.S. capital.[18] Combined with monetarist actions of the Federal Reserve to restrict the growth in labor's earnings—which might otherwise cut into corporate profit margins, spark inflation, and ruin the party atmosphere on Wall Street—the effect of the corporate offensive has been to add jobs and increase labor productivity without significantly raising the real wages of workers. From 1980 to 2005, productivity in the manufacturing sector increased 131 percent, while the real median hourly wages for male workers were lower in 2005 than they were in 1973.[19] In contrast, the business class is granting huge rewards to their chief executive officers and top managers (and themselves) in the form of lavish salaries, bonuses, generous stock options, retirement packages, and luxurious perks. Andrew Sum of Northeastern University's Center for Market Labor Studies found that all 93 million of America's nonsupervisory workers had real earnings increases from 2000 to 2006 that were less than half of the combined $36 billion to $44 billion in holiday bonuses awarded by the top Wall Street firms for just one year.[20]

Capital is similarly increasing the rate of environmental exploitation by extracting greater quantities of natural resources more quickly and at less cost. Business is also cutting production costs by spending less on pollution prevention and control and on sound waste disposal methods and environmental restoration. Many sectors of industry are adopting new production processes and technologies (such as biotechnology in agriculture) that increase productivity but are also more polluting or destructive of the environment. American business is producing these results through a general assault on the past gains of the ecology movement and through a general offensive on the policies and programs that make up the environmental protection state. Just as significant, corporations are pursuing strategies that offer the "path of least resistance," which results in the dumping of ever more pollution into working-class neighborhoods and poor communities of color. This corporate offensive is also causing more destructive forms of natural resource extraction from this country's most unique and treasured landscapes, especially lands belonging to Native Americans; a deterioration in consumer product safety and attempts to limit corporate liability for defective or damaging products; the disappearance of ever more natural species and habitats; suburban sprawl; and a general assault on those programs and policies designed to protect the environment. In short, to sustain the process of capital accumulation and higher profits in the new global economy, American capital is increasingly relying on ecologically unsustainable forms of production that disproportionately impact communities of color and lower-income members of the working class—people who are underrepresented in the traditional environmental movement.

In summary, increased profits make up the economic engine pulling the train of American business in the world economy. The increased exploitation of labor and the environment is providing the energy powering the locomotive. As a result, the defining characteristics of liberal capitalism that have traditionally enlisted the mass loyalty of working people—high wages, affordable education, health care insurance plans, retirement benefits, job security and advancement, affirmative action, universal entitlements, civil rights and civil liberties, Medicaid and Medicare (and perhaps Social Security), and other welfare state protections for working families—are being eroded. Instead, under the new bipartisan consensus to increase resources for national security as part of America's War on Terror, trillions of dollars in taxpayer money are being rerouted to the warfare state and major defense contractors. The triumph of the national security state and the "Third Way" neoliberal model of global capitalist integration is undermining the viability of progressive Keynesian economics and New Deal social policy that have been the traditional political foundation of the Democratic Party for the past fifty years. Standing at the controls are neoliberal politicians committed to less public control over corporate behavior. Embodied in the Democratic Leadership Council (Bill Clinton and Al Gore have served in key leadership positions in the council), as well as the Republican Party and President George W. Bush, neoliberals are working with the polluter-industrial complex and American business to engineer a loss of political power by the more progressive sectors of organized labor, environmentalists, environmental justice (EJ) activists, and other social movements.

CAPITALIST STRATEGIES FOR DISPLACING ECOLOGICAL HAZARDS ONTO THE AMERICAN WORKING CLASS AND PEOPLE OF COLOR

Environmental Racism, Selective Victimization, and Capital Restructuring

For the more highly polluting sectors of American business, the costs of complying with various environmental laws are seen as a drain on profits. Since the 1970s, spending for environmental protection has grown three times faster than and constitutes almost 3 percent of the gross domestic product.[21] In contrast to "green chemistry" and "clean" production techniques, the American industrial ecology model favors the adoption of pollution abatement technologies. Unlike new machinery that increases labor productivity and indirectly lowers the costs of wage goods, traditional pollution abatement devices and cleanup technologies usually increase costs. Hence, "end-of-the-pipe" pollution containment and environmental conservation measures are considered to be a luxury that American business is increasingly unwilling to absorb, especially when one considers the advantage enjoyed by foreign competitors with lower labor costs and less stringent regulations.

Without prohibitions and the threat of punitive actions by state regulatory agencies or the courts, it is simply more profitable for corporations to pollute. Rather than spending money for pollution abatement technology, businesses seek to avoid this expense by directly releasing pollution into the environment. So, instead of "internalizing" $10 million in costs for the installation of a "scrubber" to clean the air of chemical pollutants, corporations will "externalize" this expense onto society in the form of air pollution and other environmental health problems. In addition to the over 60,000 Americans killed each year by air pollution, these social losses (or "negative externalities") also take the form of long-term damage to human health, the destruction or deterioration of property values and the premature depletion of natural wealth (such as with acid rain), and the impairment of less "tangible" values associated with environment quality and the loss of community.[22] Thus, pollution control devices and other corporate expenditures to protect environmental quality yield what economists term *nonexcludable benefits*, such as the right of citizens to a toxic-free environment.[23]

With the political ascendancy of neoliberals such as President Bush, the federal government is weakening existing environmental regulations. American business is responding to the state's invitation to more ruthlessly exploit natural resources and cut spending for environmental and consumer protection. But not all Americans are equally impacted by the social and ecological costs of capitalist production. In order to bolster profits and competitiveness, U.S. corporations embrace various strategies for displacing negative environmental externalities that are the most *economically efficient* and *politically expedient*. Most Americans see the act of releasing carcinogens and other dangerous toxins into the air and water as a form of antisocial behavior. Residents will seldom "choose" to see their family members or neighbors poisoned by industrial pollution, especially if they are aware of the dangers. In fact, the successful imposition of such public health dangers by corporations is symptomatic of a lack of economic democracy. Once aware of the dangers, affected residents are likely to mobilize political opposition to the offending facility. Therefore, capital adopts more cost-effective practices for exploiting natural resources and disposing of toxics that offer the path of least political resistance.

In the United States, the less political power a community of people possesses, the fewer resources (time, money, education, and so on) people within have to defend themselves from potential threats; the lower the level of community awareness and mobilization against potential ecological threats; the more likely they are to experience arduous environmental and human health problems at the hands of capital and the state. Only those economically depressed communities burdened by poverty, high unemployment, and a marginal tax base will "choose" to accept hazardous facilities. Such a trade-off is sometimes made because of the potential for job creation, enhanced tax revenues and the provision of social services, and other economic benefits. In contrast, communities with a strong economic base and high degree of *control capacity* over the decision-making processes of local government officials and business leaders are better able to block the introduction of environmental hazards.[24]

Communities that lack control capacity in this country are typically made up of marginalized racial and ethnic minorities as well as the underemployed and poorer segments of the white working class. For those members of the socially and spatially segregated "underclass," powerlessness is even more pervasive. America's undocumented immigrants, Chicano farmers, migrant farmworkers, Indians, and other dispossessed peoples of color are the ones being *selectively victimized* to the greatest extent by corporate environmental health abuses.[25] As part of the country's *subaltern* experiencing multiple forms of political domination, economic exploitation, and cultural oppression, they are effectively denied a voice in American society.[26] However, this process of selective victimization is invoking resistance. A new wave of grassroots activism is building in the United States. In poor African American and Latino neighborhoods of small towns and inner cities, depressed Native American reservations, and Hispanic communities all across the country, people who have traditionally been relegated to the periphery of the environmental movement are now challenging the ruination of their land, water, air, and community health by corporate polluters and indifferent governmental agencies. Combining elements of civil rights, social justice, the struggle for land rights, and respect for the environment, oppressed peoples of color have formed movements for environmental justice to fight the disparate ecological and economic burdens placed on their communities.[27]

That the "disempowered" of America are to serve as the dumping ground for capital is often blatantly advertised. A 1984 report by Cerrell Associates for the California Waste Management Board, for instance, openly recommended

that industry and the state locate waste incinerators (or "waste-to-energy facilities") in neighborhoods of "lower socioeconomic" status because those communities present a much lower chance of offering political opposition. In fact,
the report states,

> Members of middle or higher-socioeconomic strata (a composite index of level
> of education, occupational prestige, and income) are more likely to organize into
> effective groups to express their political interests and views. All socioeconomic
> groupings tend to resent the nearby siting of major [polluting] facilities, but the
> middle and upper-socioeconomic strata possess better resources to affectuate
> their opposition. Middle and higher-socioeconomic strata neighborhoods should
> not fall at least within the one-mile and five-mile radii of the proposed site.[28]

The Cerrell Associates report also makes note of research indicating that
communities made up of residents that are low income, minority, Catholic,
Republican and/or conservative in political affiliation, of a low educational
level (high school degree or less), mostly senior citizens, and/or located the
South and Midwest of the United States tend to exercise less control capacity
over the siting of major polluting facilities. Furthermore, lower taxes and
property values found in these communities offer reduced costs for hazardous
industries.

Despite the profound public health dangers posed by incinerators, government agencies and American business have promoted these facilities as the
optimal low-cost solution to the waste problem (although the growing power
of the EJ and antitoxics movements is helping to reverse this trend).[29] Still,
there are currently 1,900 garbage, hazardous waste, and medical waste incinerators operating in the United States.[30] Heavy metals such as lead, mercury,
arsenic, chromium, and cadmium (as well as dioxins) are released as micro-
scopic particles by the process of incineration and penetrate deep into the
lungs of residents. These particles then enter the bloodstream and are deposited in organs and tissues throughout the body, resulting in increased cancers, nervous system damage, birth defects, respiratory diseases, and other
health problems and are especially dangerous to pregnant women and children. One recent study has found that people living near incinerators show
double the risk of dying from childhood cancer.[31] Federal officials in recent
years have estimated up to 600,000 children may be born in the United States
with neurological problems stemming from mercury exposure in the womb.[32]
Little wonder that government officials are worried about potential opposition to incinerators and hire consultants like Cerrell Associates to help them
figure out a strategy for placing them in unsuspecting neighborhoods.

The state of California has followed the recommendations of the Cerrell report for years, particularly in terms of targeting poorer communities of color.

California now has the nation's highest concentration of racial/ethnic minorities living near incinerators and other commercial hazardous waste treatment, storage, and disposal facilities (TSDFs). In Greater Los Angeles, for instance, some 1.2 million people live in close proximity (less than two miles) to seventeen such facilities, and 91 percent of them (1.1 million) are people of color.[33] Of course, the question remains, Which came first, the city's (Los Angeles) most polluted neighborhoods or minority residents? Studies sponsored by the California Policy Research Center looked at the character of an area before a TSDF siting and the demographic and other shifts that occurred in the years after a siting. The findings indicate that since the 1970s, the neighborhoods targeted to house toxic storage and disposal facilities have more minority, poor, and blue-collar populations than areas that did not receive TSDFs.[34]

Residential Segregation, Racial and Ethnic "Churning," and Environmental Injustice

California is not alone when it comes to concentrating environmental problems in racially segregated communities. All across the United States, communities of "lower socioeconomic status" are routinely targeted by corporate executives and state officials for the siting of incinerators and other ecologically hazardous facilities.[35] Neighborhoods undergoing rapid ethnic, racial, and class-based transitions (or "churning") are often the most vulnerable.[36] Towns experiencing "white flight" to the suburbs and a corresponding demographic shift toward newly arrived Latino or Asian immigrants, for instance, often lack the tight community networks, political connections, and social capital necessary to mobilize residents to oppose ecologically hazardous facilities.[37] Communities highly fragmented by peoples of different racial, ethnic, religious, national-origin identities, class backgrounds, and languages can also be more vulnerable to the "divide-and-conquer" strategies of capital. In contrast, poor but homogeneous communities of color often have strong cultural institutions (such as the Church) that build social solidarity and support long histories of struggle on behalf of civil rights. As such, they can pose formidable opposition to corporate polluters.[38]

In Massachusetts, the city of Lawrence fits the Cerrell Associates report profile. Formerly a white working-class mill town located in the Merrimack Valley, Lawrence has been in transition to a poor immigrant community for nearly three decades. Roughly 60 percent of the population is of Hispanic or Latino descent (especially Dominican and Puerto Rican). The household median income of just $27,983 is among the lowest in the state, and almost two-thirds of the residents do not speak English as their first language. The state approved the siting of both the Ogden-Martin (RDF) trash incinerator and the

Stericycle incinerator in Lawrence during the height of the transition. Before closing, the Odgen-Martin (RDF) facility was permitted to burn 600 to 700 tons of trash per day and was responsible for thousands of pounds of mercury, lead, and dioxin pollution. In addition, the Wheelabrator incinerator in North Andover and the Ogden-Martin Haverhill MSW incinerator were also built within four miles of the Lawrence border. Furthermore, the Safety-Kleen hazardous waste storage and sorting facility was located in downtown Lawrence on the Merrimack River.[39]

The siting of four major incinerators within a twelve-mile area of downtown Lawrence—in contrast to the high-rent districts of downtown Boston—is a powerful example of the manner in which capital and the state are displacing environmental health problems onto politically marginalized communities. The methylmercury released from these incinerators has the ability to build up in the body of animals over time (bioaccumulation) and increase in concentration as one organism eats another organism lower on the food chain (biomagnification). The metal eventually builds up in larger fish at the top of the food chain, including yellow perch, largemouth bass, and other freshwater fish frequently eaten by Lawrence residents (especially among the immigrant population). According to a study by the Biodiversity Research Institute, the Lower Merrimack River watershed (including the city of Lawrence) has been identified as a mercury "hot spot"—one of nine areas of concern in the northeastern United States where mercury levels in biota exceed levels at which adverse impacts occur.[40]

Lawrence is one of hundreds of poorer communities where daily struggles over the preservation of environmental quality are taking place. The weight of the ecological burden on a community is dependent on the balance of power and level of struggle between capital, the state, and social movements responding to the needs and demands of the populace. And in the United States, working-class neighborhoods and poor communities of color often experience the worst environmental problems. This is not to say that the white middle class is not also being significantly harmed by industrial pollution and other abusive corporate practices because it too is impacted. But in contrast to the working poor, wealthier citizens exercise greater control over community planning processes, including the "exclusionary zoning" of dirty industries and other locally unwanted land uses. The white middle class can also better afford to move and purchase homes in communities with nicer neighborhoods, better schools and housing, ecological amenities, and a cleaner environment.[41]

In contrast, people of color are denied the same opportunities to escape environmental hazards. There is a disturbing pattern of mortgage lending in the United States that serves to reproduce highly segregated patterns of residential location by race/ethnicity.[42] Just a handful of town and cities in Massachusetts, for instance, account for the majority of loans given to African Americans and Latinos. Just four communities (Brockton, Randolph, Lynn, and Lowell) typically receive more than half of all home-purchase loans to African Americans, while five other communities (Lawrence, Lynn, Chelsea, Brockton, and Revere) receive more than half of all home-purchase loans for Latinos.[43] With the exception of Randolph, every one of these communities is ranked as among the thirty most environmentally overburdened communities in Massachusetts.[44] In addition, African Americans and Latinos *at all income levels* are more than twice as likely to be rejected for a home-purchase mortgage loan than are white applicants *at the same income levels*. It is clear that racial and ethnic minorities are being tracked into the most distressed neighborhoods, or what may be termed *ecological sacrifice zones*.

Racial discrimination of this sort has severely restricted home-ownership opportunities for people of color throughout the nation. Racial residential segregation also reserves additional neighborhoods in which the white working class and salariat may desire to move and thus facilitates the upward geographic (and class) mobility for most white Americans out of the more economically and ecologically distressed areas.[45] Ecological sacrifice zones also serve as convenient locations where polluting corporations can substantially lower the costs of compliance with environmental regulations.

Racial and ethnic segregation in the United States is not only a product of racial discrimination by the banking, real estate, and insurance industries but also due to government housing, welfare, immigration, and transportation policies.[46] More specifically, real estate developers, bankers, industrialists, and other sectors of capital work in coalition with government officials (at all levels) to form policy and planning structures that promote community development conducive to these business interests, that is, local growth machines.[47] Growth machines function to create favorable conditions for capital investment and accumulation, especially in terms of the commodification and reconstruction of space as desired by industry and real estate interests. This includes the creation of housing, industrial parks, roadways and infrastructure, and other conditions of production. Growth machines also create residential and occupational enclaves through zoning practices and labor market segmentation, often along racial/ethnic lines.[48] These class-based and racialized territories serve to reproduce various kinds of labor power for capital, including the concentration of highly skilled workers and managers residing in "pristine" suburbs or gated communities. Semiskilled blue-collar workers may be channeled to live in row homes near industrial zones, while unskilled, underemployed members of the "underclass" are pushed into distressed inner-city neighborhoods and serve as a reserve army of cheap labor for capital in periods of rapid job growth and economic expansion. Regardless, the power of local growth machines is critical in determining the patterns of residential and industrial development.

With the neoliberal assault on the welfare state, there is now significantly less investment of public and private money for education, job training, housing, mass transportation, health care services, and other programs in distressed communities. It pays capital and the state to displace environmental health problems onto these communities where most residents lack health care insurance, possess lower incomes and property values, and are more easily replaced in the labor market if they become sick or die. Both the siting of ecologically hazardous industrial facilities in communities of color and "minority move-ins" to already heavily polluted areas are governed by the systemic logic of capitalist accumulation.[49] Such acts of environmental racism are perfectly rational from the perspective of capital and the power structures that govern local growth machines. Only strong government policies informed by popular mobilization can deter the various ecological manifestations of racial, ethnic, gender, and class-based disparities in a capitalist economy.

Dirty Air and Environmental Health

Over the past decade, the balance of state power has shifted dramatically in favor of big business, leading to the increased production of ecological hazards. Coupled with the assault on the regulatory capacities of the federal government by the polluter-industrial complex (see chapter 2), business is now externalizing more social and ecological costs onto the American people, spending less on the prevention of health and safety problems inside and outside of the factory as well as on reducing pollution and the depletion of natural resources. *Tens of billions of pounds* of toxic chemicals have been dumped into the nation's air, water, and land over the past ten years alone by America's largest industrial facilities. In 2004, for instance, self-reporting by industry to the federal government's Toxics Release Inventory program revealed over 1.8 billion pounds of toxic pollutants released to the air and water alone, including more than 70 million pounds of carcinogens (cancer-causing substances) and over 134 million pounds of chemicals linked to developmental and reproductive problems (such as birth defects and learning disabilities). An additional 608 million pounds of carcinogens and developmental and reproductive toxins were released onto the land by U.S. corporations, particularly in the mining industry.[50]

Again, it is important to remember that not all people are polluted equal. In order to cut costs related to environmental protection and at the same time sidestep the capacity for political mobilization by the white middle class around perceived health hazards, American business is increasingly concentrating its pollutants in poorer communities of color and working-class neighborhoods. In December 2005, the Associated Press released an analysis of a little-known Environmental Protection Agency (EPA) research project revealing that black Americans are 79 percent more likely than whites to live in neighborhoods where industrial pollution is suspected of posing the greatest health danger. The residents of neighborhoods with the highest pollution scores are also poorer and less educated and suffer unemployment rates 20 percent higher than the national average. In many states, blacks, Hispanics, and Asians are more than twice as likely as whites to reside in neighborhoods where air pollution poses the greatest health dangers. For instance, more than half the blacks in Kansas live in the worst 10 percent of the state's neighborhoods.[51]

Industrial air pollution is a serious problem in the United States. According to the EPA, "millions of people live in areas where air toxins may pose potentially significant health concerns."[52] Automobile and industrial air pollution combine to kill tens of thousands of Americans each and every year. In fact, half a million people living in the most polluted areas in 151 cities across the country face a risk of death which is some 15 to 17 percent higher than in the least polluted areas.[53] Over 164 million Americans are now at risk for respiratory and other health problems from exposure to excessive air pollution. But this is only part of the story. Clearly, Asians, African Americans, Hispanics, and the working poor are bearing the greatest health risks from air pollution coming from nearby industrial facilities, highways, and transportation infrastructure.[54] According to the EPA, 57 percent of all whites nationwide live in areas with poor air quality, compared to 80 percent of all Latinos.[55] In Los Angeles, where organizations such as the Labor/Community Strategy Center, Mothers of East Los Angeles, and Communities for a Better Environment have come to the forefront to challenge environmental racism, 71 percent of the city's African Americans and 50 percent of the Latinos live in what are categorized as the most polluted areas, compared to 34 percent of whites.[56]

The Quadruple Exposure Effect, Liberal Environmental Policy, and Environmental Injustice

As in the case of industrial pollution in the United States today, the working class in general and poorer people of color in particular face a greater "quadruple exposure effect" to environmental health hazards. This takes the form first of higher rates of "on-the-job" exposure to toxics used in the production process and second as greater neighborhood exposure to toxic pollutants emitted from nearby factories, toxic waste dumps, agricultural fields, transportation systems, and hazardous waste facilities.[57] In addition, unequal exposure to ecological hazards takes the form of faulty cleanup efforts implemented by the government or the waste treatment industry, such as through the increased use of permanent or mobile incinerators that burn these wastes in the community. A 2005 study finds that Superfund sites in low-income and high-minority areas now take significantly longer to be cleaned up than in the early 1990s.[58] The final piece to the quadruple exposure effect comes in the form of greater exposure to toxic chemicals in the household (such as lead paint), commercial foods, and a variety of consumer products. For example, lead poisoning continues to be a leading health threat to children, particularly poor children and children of color living in older, dilapidated housing. Black children are now five times more likely than white children to have lead poisoning.[59] Taken together, it is clear that people of color experience a disparate exposure to environmental hazards where they "work, live, and play."[60]

As is evident from the growing toxic waste problems, pollution, and other social/environmental costs of capitalist production, the liberal regime of environmental regulation is insufficient when it comes to halting capital's displacement of environmental harm onto people of color and the working poor. In fact, many liberal policy initiatives are actually intensifying the problems they were designed to cure. Most environmental laws require capital to *contain* pollution sources for more proper treatment and disposal. Once the pollution is "trapped," the manufacturing industry pays for its treatment and disposal. The waste, now commodified, becomes mobile, crossing local, state, and even national borders in search of low-cost areas for treatment, incineration, and/or disposal.[61] More often than not, the waste sites and facilities themselves are hazardous and located in communities with less control capacity. As stated by one government report, billions of dollars are spent "to remove pollutants from the air and water only to dispose of such pollutants on the land, and in an environmentally unsound manner."[62] The result has been the explosion of environmental hazardous waste facilities in poor working-class neighborhoods and communities of color.

By emphasizing less costly pollution capture and relocation techniques over pollution prevention, the liberal regime of environmental regulation is assisting capital in the displacement of the ecological crisis onto the underclasses of American society. In Sierra Blanca, Texas, for instance, the local economy has collapsed. Underemployment is so pervasive that 40 percent of the population lives below the poverty line. Since 1992, New York City and a company called Merco have shipped roughly 200 tons of processed sewage sludge *a day* to the small town. Once dumped into the Atlantic Ocean before Congress banned the practice in 1988, the sludge is now transported by rail to be applied (in what industry terms "beneficial land applications" of "biosolids" as "fertilizer") to nearly 200 square miles of land around this mostly Latino community. Because of concerns that the sludge is poisoned with heavy metals, petroleum, pathogens, and other hazardous substances, community residents see this act of environmental racism as posing a significant health threat. Despite the adverse environmental impacts and human health problems (including deaths) linked to the application of toxic municipal sewage sludge, the EPA and the wastewater treatment industry have worked with Congress to promote land application projects against the wishes of local governments.[63] There are more than 200 other such sewage sludge sites in Texas alone, many of which were established when George W. Bush was governor.

The failure of traditional environmental policy to significantly reduce the creation of pollution and hazardous waste is magnifying problems of environmental racism. In 2001, U.S.-based industry generated more than 41 million tons of hazardous wastes in the United States, according to the EPA. Under the Resource Conservation and Recovery Act of 1976, the waste is sent to various TSDFs that include incinerators and landfills. More than 9.2 million people now live less than two miles away from the nation's 413 commercial hazardous waste facilities. Again, in order for capital to cut costs and lessen the potential for political opposition, these facilities are disproportionately sited in poorer communities of color. More than 5.1 million racial and/or ethnic minorities live in neighborhoods with one or more TSDFs. Despite the declaration of President Clinton's executive order for environmental justice in 1994, which mandated federal agencies to incorporate environmental justice into their work and programs, the displacement of ecological problems onto minority neighborhoods is intensifying.[64] In fact, for the first time in history, people of color now make up the majority of the population living near the nation's commercial hazardous waste facilities.[65]

The lack of enforcement of federal environmental laws is also resulting in a failure to halt the widespread practices of illegal hazardous waste dumping.[66] The higher costs arising from the EPA's regulations of toxic wastes (based on the agency's authority under the Resource Conservation and Recovery Act) is leading some companies to "hide" externalities by employing organized crime and other "shady" businesses to handle their wastes. The Mafia, active in garbage hauling and the landfill industry, is historically one of the largest toxic waste disposers in the country.[67]

As in the case with "legitimate" businesses, organized crime also targets communities with less control capacity. Aided by the outright bribery of local government officials to look the other way, thousands of tons of debris were illegally dumped in Chicago's West Side Latino and African American communities during the 1990s. Pervasive poverty and lack of political influence made these neighborhoods easy targets. An investigation by the Chicago Department

of Streets and Sanitation found that all ten city neighborhoods with the most illegal dumping of garbage were at least 60 percent African American and/or
Latino. In fact, 79 percent of all illegal dumping in Chicago occurred in wards
where people of color are the majority of the population.[68] Only after years of
political mobilization were these neighborhoods able to initiate government action, including a Federal Bureau of Investigation sting named Operation Silver
Shovel against corrupt aldermen, to halt the dumping and initiate a cleanup.[69]

Chicago is not alone. In thousands of communities across the United States,
ranging from Love Canal, New York, to Houston, Texas, to Times Beach, Mis-
souri, billions of pounds of highly toxic chemicals, including mercury, dioxin,
polychlorinated biphenyls, arsenic, lead, and heavy metals such as chromium,
have been dumped or left behind in unsuspecting neighborhoods. These sites
poison the land, contaminate drinking water, and potentially cause cancer,
birth defects, nerve and liver damage, and other illnesses. The U.S. Government Accountability Office (GAO; formerly the U.S. General Accounting Office, an independent and nonpartisan investigative agency of Congress) estimates that there are between 130,000 and 450,000 abandoned waste sites (or
brownfields). A disparate proportion of these sites are located in or near poorer
working-class neighborhoods and communities of color.[70] In Massachusetts,
for instance, communities of color average over forty-eight hazardous waste
sites per square mile, a rate that is *more than twenty-three times greater* than
the average of two sites in predominantly white communities.[71] Meanwhile,
Chemical Waste Management Inc. and other toxic waste handlers have been at
the center of a number of controversial plans in recent years to use poverty-
stricken Native American reservations as alternative sites for toxic and radioactive waste disposal.[72] America's communities of color are the new low-
cost dumping grounds for capital and the state.

ENVIRONMENTAL JUSTICE, OCCUPATIONAL HEALTH AND SAFETY, AND THE RESTRUCTURING OF WORK

Death on the Job for the American Working Class

The colonization of the state by the polluter-industrial complex is having a
profound impact on the lives of working-class families in the United States.
Since the election of George W. Bush to the presidency, the Occupational
Safety and Health Administration (OSHA) has issued the fewest significant
worker health and safety standards in its history. Instead, political appointees
at OSHA—often former chief executive officers, lawyers, and lobbyists representing the very industries they now oversee—have weakened regulations

and the enforcement of rules designed to protect labor. Industry-friendly appointees to OSHA have killed dozens of existing and proposed safety regulations and delayed the adoption of many others. Instead of tougher regulations and stricter enforcement of the law, OSHA has favored a "voluntary compliance strategy," reaching agreements with industry associations and companies to police themselves. However, voluntary programs tend to have little focus on specific hazards, have no enforcement power, and carry little weight among the business class. Since only companies with strong safety records are eligible, voluntary programs do not address the worst corporate offenders to improve their workplaces.

Opposition by the business community and its political allies to OSHA is grounded in the fact that most worker health and safety programs add to the construction and production costs of capital; restrict or prevent the use of more profitable (and more hazardous) chemical substances, materials, and production processes; mandate periodic breaks and "rest times" for workers; and/or lower the flexibility of capital to appropriate labor power in the most profitable manner possible. As such, many safety rules lower labor productivity and drive up expenses. Industries under stronger competitive pressures from low-cost operations overseas are especially eager to avoid "internalizing" costs on such "unproductive expenditures" as worker health and safety and will instead displace (or "externalize") these costs onto their labor force in the form of dangerous working conditions and exposure to health hazards.[73] According to Liberty Mutual, the nation's largest workers' compensation insurance company, the direct cost of occupational injury and illness is $48.6 billion (nearly $1 billion per week), with another $145 billion to $290 billion in indirect costs.[74] Indeed, corporations use a variety of tactics to obscure the dangers associated with their products or production processes. These tactics involve the corruption of scientific testing of various chemicals of potential danger to workers, including the manipulation of data presented to state officials and the larger court of public opinion. The purpose of these actions is to secure the least restrictive regulations and to avert or limit legal liability in order to maximize profits.[75]

Since 2001, when the Bush administration took office, the OSHA budget has been cut by $24 million in real-dollars terms. Federal OSHA enforcement staff levels have been reduced from 1,683 to 1,543 positions.[76] The impact of the neoliberal offensive against the regulatory capacities of OSHA is that capital is now spending less on the prevention of health and safety problems and American workers are being exposed to greater hazards at the point of production. Some 16,000 workers are injured on the job *every day*, of which about seventeen will die. Another 135 workers die *every day* from diseases caused by exposure to toxins in the workplace.[77] Between 400,000 and 3 million workers alone suffer from occupationally induced asthma.[78] In fact, if occupational injuries and diseases were classified as a separate cause, they would be the eighth-leading cause of death in the United States—just between diabetes and motor vehicle accidents.[79]

In the context of the current War on Terror, no politician would tolerate the killing of thousands of Americans at the hands of a foreign adversary. Yet the actions of American business routinely result in the deaths of 70,000 workers each and every year, and there is hardly a regulatory peep from the halls of power in Washington, D.C. In the neoliberal age, death on the job is an acceptable trade-off that capital is all too often willing to make in order to boost profits and economic performance.

Accidents Will Happen in Periods of Capital Restructuring

Given the neoliberal assault on OSHA and the labor movement, high "accident" rates are inevitable. Almost 6 million injuries occur each year as a result of dangerous working conditions. In 2006, however, there were only 818 federal OSHA inspectors and just 1,294 state OSHA inspectors responsible for protecting 131 million workers at approximately 8 million workplaces. At its current staffing and inspection levels, it would take OSHA 133 years to inspect each workplace under its jurisdiction just once.[80] This is a grossly inadequate number of OSHA staff. The International Labor Office recommends that at least 13,090 OSHA inspectors are necessary to ensure adequate oversight of the American workforce.[81]

Under President Bush, the number of citations assessed by an understaffed OSHA against solid waste companies went down 42 percent in 2006, the lowest number for at least a decade (the average OSHA penalty issued to a solid waste employer in 2006 was $840).[82] A 2007 government report found that OSHA failed to inspect plants with enough care and frequency to prevent an accident like the March 23, 2005, explosion at BP's Texas City refinery that killed fifteen people and injured 170, the worst U.S. industrial accident since 1990. The report specifically blames the London-based oil giant BP for a series of cost-cutting measures, particularly in the area of process safety, that left the plant vulnerable to catastrophe. Even though the plant had several fatal accidents over the past three decades, OSHA conducted only one process safety management inspection at the refinery in 1998.[83] Furthermore, the hazards faced by workers inside the refinery were shared by residents living outside the factory in adjacent neighborhoods. BP's refinery, one of the largest in the country, released more recognized carcinogens into the air and water than any other facility in 2004.[84] These releases included more than 1.9 million pounds of formaldehyde. Notably, Texas City is a racially mixed working-class community where 15 percent of the population lives below the poverty line.

Tragic "accidents" like that at the BP Texas City refinery are all too common in the oil and gas industry. Over the past decade and more, the fantastic profits of the largest oil companies in the United States have been augmented by what the trade paper *Oil Daily* calls "massive cost-cutting," including large layoffs; cuts in pollution prevention, worker health and safety measures, and oil recovery programs; and less maintenance and repair of decaying equipment and infrastructure.[85] A recent congressional committee investigating the spills from BP's Alaska North Slope pipelines, which caused the shutdown of Prudhoe Bay oil production in the summer of 2006, revealed that anticorrosion programs that could have prevented the accidents were repeatedly targeted for cost-cutting measures. The cuts were made even though the London-based BP PLC made more than $106 billion in profits from 1999 through 2005.[86] These cuts at BP are typical of capital's counterattack on organized labor, as oil and petrochemical companies have increasingly replaced more highly trained and well-paid union workers with less costly contingent laborers—many of whom lack the knowledge and experience of their union counterparts. Some 30 percent of the hours worked in the petrochemical industry are logged by contract employees.[87] As a result, the rate of job-related deaths in the oil and gas industry has worsened in recent years and now stands at approximately one fatality every 4.3 days. This rate is over eight and a half times higher than the average fatality rate for all industries in the United States.[88]

Rising industrial accident rates are no accident but rather a product of growing corporate control over the state, labor unions, and local communities. Since the initiation of the neoliberal counterassault on the labor movement under President Reagan, the frequency of *major* chemical accidents in the United States has increased tenfold.[89] It has been estimated that there are as many as 240,000 chemical industry accidents per year in the United States—some 658 per day.[90] Risk Management Plan data collected in 2001 by the EPA found that over 1,200 chemical-related facilities reported accidents between 1994 and 1999. These accidents caused in excess of $1 billion in property damage. Over 200,000 community residents impacted by the accidents were forced to evacuate their homes and/or take shelter.[91] Not coincidentally, African Americans face much greater risks for living in much closer proximity (location risk) to the most accident-prone facilities (operations risk). America's highest-risk facilities are found in counties with sizable poor and/or minority populations. It is these communities that disproportionately bear the collateral environmental, property, and health impacts of industrial accidents.[92]

Capital, the State, and the Killing of Coal Miners

The assault of the polluter-industrial complex on the regulatory capacities of OSHA is having an especially devastating impact in the coal mining industry.[93] A series of deadly coal mining accidents in West Virginia, Kentucky, and other states claimed the lives of forty-seven coal miners in 2006. Sixteen West Virginia miners were killed in a number of "accidents" in the month of January alone, compelling Governor Joe Manchin to shortly thereafter call for a voluntary shutdown of all coal companies in the state for safety checks. The largest of these accidents in West Virginia involved the death of a dozen nonunion miners from carbon monoxide poisoning on January 2 at the Sago mine.

In 1968, an explosion at a coal mine in Farmington, West Virginia, killed seventy-eight miners and prompted Congress to approve the Mine Health and Safety Act of 1969. The law required the federal government to inspect underground coal mines four times a year. This legislation, combined with the more recent shift toward cheaper and more environmentally destructive forms of strip mining (mountaintop removal methods pose fewer hazards to workers), dramatically reduced the numbers of mining deaths. For instance, 260 miners died in 1970, compared to twenty-two deaths in 2005. After President Bush took office in 2001, however, the administration dropped or postponed eighteen health and safety regulations proposed by President Clinton to improve mine-worker safety, including the requirement to upgrade miners' emergency respiratory devices and to add more emergency-response mine rescue teams.[94] The Bush administration also scaled back enforcement and fines and in 2005 called for significant budget cuts to the Mine Safety and Health Administration. By 2006, the year of the Sago mine disaster, the agency had been forced to shed about 120 coal-industry enforcement jobs.[95]

Even when inspections do occur, government penalties for violations are not strong enough to deter companies from endangering workers. In 2006, *serious* violations of the Federal Coal Mine and Safety Act carried an average penalty of only $881—a rate below 1990 levels. A violation is considered "serious" if it poses a substantial probability of death or serious physical harm to workers.[96] A *New York Times* investigative series in 2003 revealed that prosecutions of recklessly negligent employers are extremely rare. Of the 170,000 workplace deaths since 1982, only sixteen convictions involving jail time have resulted, even though 1,242 cases of worker deaths were determined by OSHA to involve "willful" violations by employers (violations in which the employer knew that workers' lives were being put at risk). The *Times* also found that "companies whose willful acts kill workers face lighter sanctions than those who deliberately break environmental or financial laws." Under increased industry pressure to further reduce fines, OSHA has steadily downgraded more and more cases from willful to less serious violations (in 2001, 60 percent of all cases were downgraded).[97]

In 2005, federal officials cited the Sago mine's owners, Internal Coal Group, for alleged shortcomings in safety planning, including allegations of inadequate safeguards against cave-ins and an insufficient ventilation plan to control methane and breathable coal dust. Both conditions can cause explosions. While the expectation is that gross violations of safety rules would be met with substantial penalties by the federal government, this was not the case. Of the 208 citations issued by the Mine Safety and Health Administration at the Sago mine, nearly half carried the minimum fine of $60 (a total of $24,000 in fines were assessed the owners in 2005).[98] In fact, over a period of twenty-three months prior to the disaster, two dozen miners were hurt in a string of accidents at the Sago mine. Despite this terrible safety record, government regulators never publicly discussed shutting down the mine and never sought criminal sanctions. The biggest fine was $440, a paltry 0.0004 percent of the $110 million net profit reported in 2005 by the mine's owner, International Coal Group Inc., which acquired Sago in November 2005.[99] At that level, the fines become a minor cost of doing business.[100]

The Sago mine disaster is a prime example of a long-standing flaw in the enforcement of federal mining regulations. Severe violations of safety standards rarely translate into serious fines. In the first five years of the Bush administration, the number of mines referred to the Justice Department for criminal prosecution dropped from thirty-eight to twelve. When inspectors do step forward to impose large penalties on coal owners, government officials and industry-friendly administrative law judges reduce the fines. In 2001, thirteen miners died at an Alabama coal mine. In 2005, the fine against the owners was reduced from $435,000 to a measly $3,000.[101] Even these small fines are not paid by many companies and are essentially voluntary in the eyes of business. The Mine Safety and Health Administration was owed more than $16 million in delinquent fines at the end of 2005—more than $11 million was for safety violations at coal mines.

Many of the government officials responsible for collecting fines and enforcing worker safety laws come from industry. Three of the four members of a federal panel that currently settles disputes involving mining safety are former executives of mining companies or trade associations and are predictably hostile to strict penalties. As a result, the number of mines referred to the Justice Department for criminal prosecution dropped from thirty-nine in 2000, the last year of the Clinton administration, to twelve in 2005. Even before the recent accidents, the administration policy of light enforcement of violations drew criticism. In 2003, the GAO took the Mine Safety and Health Administration to task for its lack of follow-up in safety violation cases. The report found the agency's top management to be seriously at fault for not providing "adequate oversight" to guarantee safety compliance from mining capital. As argued in a *Boston Globe* editorial, if Congress had acted after the GAO report recommendations toward stricter regulation and enforcement, the Sago deaths and others might have been avoided.[102]

Race, Class, and Dying for Work in America

Not all workers face the same level of health threats on the job as America's coal miners. Highly skilled workers are more essential to many businesses and are therefore provided greater protection by industry. These workers are typically more difficult to replace if they become sick, die, or leave the firm because of poor pay or working conditions. Since companies often invest significant resources in the training of skilled workers to perform highly specialized tasks, lost work days and productivity declines due to occupational illness or death can lower labor productivity and significantly impact profits. Skilled workers also have medical insurance and other programs that are partially financed by companies, and higher premiums can result for the company if there are recurrent safety problems. Furthermore, highly educated and highly skilled workers can more easily move to other jobs if they perceive working conditions to be unsafe.

Unskilled and semiskilled blue-collar workers involved in mining, manufacturing, construction, logging, and agriculture face greater occupational hazards on the job.[103] Workers in these industries are more "expendable," as they are more easily replaced by other people if an injury or death occurs. In fact, economic damages awarded in tort law are in large part based on wage loss. A timber worker earning $10 an hour is simply "worth" far less than a highly experienced and well-paid company manager. Since the usual penalty for inflicting environmental and/or occupational disease is the "restitution" of the injured through the payment of compensatory fines rather than criminal penalties or confiscatory fines, the costs almost never approach the economic advantages that accrue to companies that perpetrate injury and death on American workers. In other words, it is cheaper to use unsafe technology, poisonous chemicals, and dangerous production processes that kill or maim unskilled workers than to make the workplace safe.[104]

Occupational dangers are more profound for unskilled or semiskilled laborers lacking the protections afforded by unions. Organized labor is now on the defensive in the United States. Union membership has declined from its high-water mark of 35 percent in 1954 to only 12.9 percent of the workforce. Private sector union membership is even lower, at 8.2 percent, a level not seen since the 1920s.[105] Absent union rules, most U.S. laws that ensure worker safety are inadequate and weakly enforced. Meatpacking and chicken-processing plants, which are among the fastest-growing industries in a number of "right-to-work" (antiunion) southern states, provide such an example. The reported injury and illness rate for meatpacking in Nebraska is a staggering 20 percent of all full-time workers, almost four times higher than the overall rate for private industry.[106] Again, the state is largely ignoring the hazards faced by such workers, often with tragic consequences. On September 3, 1991, a fire ripped through the nonunion Imperial Food Products poultry processing plant in Hamlet, North Carolina, killing twenty-five and injuring another fifty-five workers. According to the Government Accountability Project, because the plant had never been inspected in eleven years of operation, safety violations were rife. Emergency doors were locked from the outside to prevent theft, thus trapping workers inside during the fire.[107]

Occupational exposures to cancer-causing substances, toxic chemicals, and dangerous working conditions are especially prevalent for people of color. In California, for instance, Hispanic men have a two-and-a-half-times-greater risk of occupational disease and injury than white men. Despite the implementation of affirmative action programs and other gains by the civil rights movement over the past three decades, the racial segmentation of labor persists. The continued implementation of informal "job closure" practices by business (and some unions) restricts occupational mobility for racial and ethnic minorities into safer and better-paying jobs. Business owners and managers regularly rank people of differing racial and ethnic backgrounds for specific job categories. White workers are typically placed at the head of the line for the most desirable jobs, especially those offering better working conditions, higher pay, and opportunities for advancement. People of color and ethnic minorities are typically placed at the end of the line.

The racial segmentation of labor by this method is functional for capital in that the "racialization" of certain occupations depresses wages/benefits, divides labor against itself and inhibits unionization, and provides a large pool of unemployed/underemployed workers that industry can draw from in periods of rapid economic expansion. Just as important, the racial segmentation of labor inhibits the ability of minorities to escape dangerous jobs for safer occupations. Knowing that such mobility is limited, capital can place greater demands on workers of color and also slash costs related to health and safety programs.[108] Hispanic workers are now among the most occupationally restricted ethnic groups in America and subject to some of the worst working conditions. Occupational injuries and illnesses among Hispanic workers have now increased to 13.1 percent (compared to 9.4 percent in 1995).

In the same manner that capital is responding to government regulations by displacing ecological hazards onto poor communities of color, businesses are displacing occupational hazards onto poorer workers of color. In this respect, racial forms of ecological stratification and occupational stratification are mutually reinforcing processes beneficial to American industry. The restructuring of American capitalism is facilitating the increased displacement of both environmental hazards into racially segregated areas (or ecological sacrifice zones) and workplace hazards into racially segregated job categories (or occupational sacrifice zones).[109] This process is enhancing the ability of business to sidestep those government regulations and established norms of behavior that cut into profits. As a result, African American, Latino, Asian, Pacific Islander, Caribbean, and Native American workers throughout the country face a significantly higher risk of experiencing job-related health problems.[110]

Blacks and Latinos are especially overrepresented in hazardous jobs that place them at higher risk for serious occupational diseases, injuries, and muscular-skeletal disabilities.[111] Moreover, the fatality rate among Latino workers in 2005 was 23 percent higher than the fatal injury rate for all U.S. workers. At the same time that people of color are being channeled into more dangerous occupations, the lack of inspections and enforcement actions by OSHA is allowing for these hazardous jobs to become even more dangerous for workers of color than for whites. Businesses assign the most dangerous tasks within the more dangerous occupations to racial and ethnic minorities. This is especially true for people of color employed in construction, agriculture, manufacturing, and the service sector.[112] Construction workers of color have, on average, a fatal occupational injury rate that is 27 percent higher than for white construction laborers.[113]

Occupational dangers are even more profound for those unskilled or semiskilled immigrants and undocumented workers that lack the formal legal protections afforded by U.S. citizenship. As the U.S. economy continues to integrate into the global economy, American capital is once again becoming increasingly reliant on cheap foreign-born workers. New immigrant and migrant workers in the United States now make up 14 percent of the workforce. Lacking the legal protections afforded by U.S. citizenship and often desperately poor, immigrant labor is almost always relegated to the most difficult and dangerous jobs *within* the most difficult and dangerous occupations. As a result, immigrant workers are at far greater risk of being killed or injured on the job than native-born workers. Although the share of foreign-born employment increased by 22 percent between 1996 and 2000, the share of fatal occupational injuries for this population increased by 43 percent.[114]

Immigrant labor is fueling the revival of "home work" and new industrial "sweatshops" where health and safety conditions are more or less unregulated. Sweatshops regularly violate both health and safety laws as well as wage and child labor laws and are common in the clothing and textile, meat-packing and processing, electronics, food, and other labor-intensive indus-tries. The growth of sweatshops is accelerating on a scale that, in the words of former Secretary of Labor Robert Reich, we have not "seen since the turn of the [last] century."[115] The General Accounting Office estimates that at least 2,000 of New York City's 6,000 garment factories (employing 70,000 work-ers, mostly Latino and Chinese immigrants) are sweatshops—defined as ap-parel makers that systematically violate labor laws.[116]

Hispanics are among the largest pool of highly exploited immigrant work-ers. These workers are less likely to speak English, understand the worker compensation system, be aware of health and safety regulations, have access to health care and the legal system, belong to a union, earn decent wages with good benefits, or gain access to more highly skilled and safer positions in the company.[117] Of the 1,035 foreign-born workers who were fatally injured at work in 2005, 62 percent were Hispanic or Latino (since 1992, the number of fatalities among Hispanic workers has increased by 73 percent).[118] "Dying for a job" is particularly prevalent among Mexican immigrants. Under President Bush, Mexicans are about 80 percent more likely to die on the job than na-tive-born workers (compared to 30 percent in the mid-1990s). Often in the country "illegally" and reluctant to complain about poor working conditions for fear of deportation or being fired, Mexicans are nearly twice as likely as the rest of the immigrant population to die at work (representing about one in twenty-four workers in the United States, Mexican immigrants make up one in fourteen workplace deaths).[119] Mexicans also make up the largest segment of migrant farmworkers. Over 313,000 of the 2 million farm workers in the United States—90 percent of whom are people of color and most of whom are undocumented immigrants—suffer from pesticide poisoning each year. Of these, between 800 and 1,000 die.[120] However, these fatality rates capture only a fraction of the actual deaths occurring on the job.[121]

Tragically, many farmworker families live in close proximity to the agri-cultural fields and receive significant pesticide exposure.[122] In fact, Mexican and Hispanic immigrant workers are much more likely than whites to live in polluted communities and experience community-based environmental injus-tices, especially along the U.S.–Mexico border.[123] The plight of such undoc-umented workers is spurring new coalitions between associations such as the United Farm Workers and the Farmworker Network for Economic and Envi-ronmental Justice, immigrant rights and consumer groups, environmental or-ganizations, labor, and the EJ movement. The Immigration and Environment Campaign of the Political Ecology Group in San Francisco, which helped or-ganize the participation of numerous EJ and immigrant rights groups in the Immigration and Environment National Strategy Meeting in March 1996, is an example of one such coalition. Despite some important victories for these workers, it still remains true that neoliberalism is resulting in more and more immigrants "dying for a job."

ENVIRONMENTAL INJUSTICE AND
THE NEW NATURAL RESOURCE WARS

America's Ravaged Environment

A key component of the neoliberal offensive against the environmental movement involves efforts to contain and roll back policies establishing national parks as well as protections for wilderness, forests, wild rivers, wetlands, wildlife, and endangered species. The reason is that capital restructuring is facilitating a much more aggressive and destructive scramble by American business for cheaper sources of renewable and nonrenewable natural resources. These include efforts to exploit the majestic old-growth forests in Alaska's Tongass National Forest and the ancient redwoods in the Pacific Northwest, habitat of the endangered spotted owl; the rich deposits of low-sulfur coal that lie underneath the Black Mesa homelands of the Hopi and Navajo Indians in the Four Corners region of the American Southwest; and the vast oil and natural gas reserves that lay in the Arctic National Wildlife Refuge in Alaska as well as along the southern, western, and New England coastlines of the continental United States. These also include efforts to hold down grazing fees for ranchers on environmentally sensitive federal lands and to open up more wetlands and fragile ecosystems to agricultural, commercial, and residential developers.[124] Such schemes to exploit new resource reserves are motivated less by timber, oil, and coal shortages than by the drive of American corporations to bring in lower-cost oil, coal, timber, and other fuels and raw materials to more effectively compete in the global economy as well as to lower the cost of inputs utilized by capital as a whole in the production process. The result has been the growth of more destructive mining operations, offshore oil drilling, and destructive timber harvests with all the attendant adverse social and environmental consequences.

Hurricane Katrina, Environmental Injustice, and
the Oily Mess of New Orleans

New resource wars are consequently developing in every corner of the country, particularly around oil. American oil companies have seen their dominance over the world's oil reserves steadily decline over the past two decades.

Today, ExxonMobil produces less than 3 percent of world output of oil, while the seven largest oil companies control less than 5 percent of world reserves.[125] As a result, oil capital is looking to open up the country to greater oil exploration and development, including in ecologically vulnerable areas under government protection. The 2005 energy bill pushed through Congress by President Bush and the polluter-industrial complex, for instance, imposed limits on states' power to influence decisions about offshore drilling projects in order to facilitate easier access to coastal waters by the big oil companies. Furthermore, the law exempts the oil industry from numerous environmental regulations embedded in the Clean Water Act and the Safe Drinking Water Act, allowing even the most profitable companies to pollute the nation's waterways and drinking water. The law also suspends the payment of royalties for publicly owned oil and gas from offshore leases in the deeper waters of the Gulf of Mexico and allows the oil industry to forgo royalty payments to the federal treasury for oil drilled in areas of Alaska's coastline.[126]

In May 2007, the Interior Department announced a major expansion of offshore oil and gas development, with proposed lease sales covering 48 million new acres off Alaska, in the eastern Gulf of Mexico, and in the central Atlantic off the coast of Virginia. The Interior Department estimates that the leases over the next five years could produce 10 billion barrels of oil and 45 trillion cubic feet of natural gas. A year earlier, Congress directed the Interior Department to make available 8.3 million acres in the east-central Gulf that long had been off limits and to begin issuing leases within a year. The Interior Department's five-year plan mirrors essentially the congressional directive in the Gulf of Mexico but promises that no drilling will take place within 125 miles of the Florida coast (there is substantial opposition to oil drilling in Florida for fear that a major "Santa Barbara–like spill" would harm the tourist industry). In January 2007, President Bush also lifted a ban on drilling in Bristol Bay, Alaska, home to one of the largest wild salmon runs in the world as well as the habitat of an array of marine life from Steller sea lions to endangered whales.[127] In each of these cases, the economic and environmental integrity of local communities is being sacrificed for the sake of Big Oil and the polluter-industrial complex.

Perhaps nowhere else has this sacrifice been greater than for the people of New Orleans. Prior to the arrival of Hurricane Katrina in late August 2005, the oil industry had been busy at work destroying the city's natural defenses against major storms. As stated by Joel Bourne Jr., these defenses include "the hardest working wetlands in America, a water world of bayous, marshes, and barrier islands that either produces or transports more than a third of the nation's oil and a quarter of its natural gas, and ranks second only to Alaska in commercial fish landings."[128] The oil and natural gas comes from deep offshore wells as well as

a series of platforms anchored eighteen miles off the coast. Together these facilities form the state's Offshore Oil Port and service a steady stream of super-
tankers. To deliver the oil to the refineries and petrochemical plants that occupy
"Cancer Alley" between Baton Rouge and New Orleans, Big Oil carved more
than 8,000 miles of oil pipeline canals out of Louisiana's coastal wetlands.
These canals destroyed the marshes that provide invaluable protection against
the "storm surge" associated with major hurricanes. Prior to Katrina, these wetlands disappeared at the rate of *thirty-three football fields a day*. In fact, since
the arrival of the oil industry, the state has lost 1,900 square miles of wetlands—
a vast area nearly the size of Delaware.

The construction of river levees along the Mississippi River further degraded the marshes. Intended to guard against potential river flooding, the
levees denied the usual flow of vital nutrients and sediments into coastal wetlands (without the sediment, delta soils naturally compact and sink and eventually give way to the ocean). Finally, the U.S. Army Corps of Engineers
dredged fourteen major ship channels through the swamps to inland ports,
damaging the protective ring of wetlands around the city. The Corps also constructed the Mississippi River Gulf Outlet (MR-GO), a 620-foot-wide canal
designed to provide a shipping shortcut for freighters between New Orleans
and the Gulf of Mexico. When Katrina slammed into New Orleans on August
29, 2005, the degraded wetlands and barrier islands provided little protection
against the storm surge (each kilometer of wetlands reduces a storm surge by
about a foot). In fact, MR-GO channeled the rising ocean waters directly into
the city, making the surge 20 percent higher and up to 200 percent faster than
it would have been without the channel.

The storm surge that pushed up MR-GO breached the protective levees in
approximately twenty places, flooding much of east New Orleans and the east
bank of Plaquemines Parish. As is the case with most disasters, the poorer and
more politically marginalized segments of the New Orleans area were most
vulnerable to the flooding.[129] The white working-class community of St.
Bernard Parish, just south of the canal, was practically annihilated. Most of
the parish's housing was destroyed. Even today no hospitals or public li-
braries have reopened, and only 20 percent of its schools are operating.[130] Adjacent to St. Bernard Parish in the Lower Ninth Ward, where the flooding was
worst, the national media relayed shocking images of people trapped on
rooftops or in their attics by the rising water with no place to escape (unless
they could cut through their roofs). More than 98 percent of the residents in
the Lower Ninth Ward were African American, with an average annual household income below $27,5000, not even half the national average. A quarter of
the population lived in extreme poverty (earning less than $10,000) and
lacked the necessary resources to flee the storm.[131]

The flood protection system in New Orleans and along Lake Pontchartrain also failed in fifty-three different places, a problem compounded by the fact that some 80 percent of the city and the metropolitan area on the southern shore is below sea level. Major levee breaches in New Orleans occurred along the 17th Street Canal, London Avenue Canal, and the navigable Industrial Canal, leaving 80 percent of the city flooded. These levees failed because they were poorly built. The National Science Foundation concluded that the conception, design, construction, and maintenance of the region's flood control systems were known by the Army Corps of Engineers to be inadequate. Likewise, an Independent Levee Investigation Team concluded that "safety was exchanged for efficiency and reduced costs" in building the levees.[132] The Bush administration's spending squeeze that delayed the strengthening of the levees in New Orleans—despite repeated warnings from knowledgeable experts—reflects the skewed political priorities of neoliberals: money for the war and occupation in Iraq (but not for protection of life at home), tax cuts that have redistributed billions to the rich and corporate America, and a willingness to serve the interests of Big Oil and the polluter-industrial complex at the expense of the environment. The result was a grossly negligent government response to the potential for natural disaster.

This was clearly a disaster waiting to happen.[133] In 2001, a Federal Emergency Management Agency (FEMA) report ranked a major hurricane striking New Orleans as one of the three most likely potential disasters—after a terrorist attack on New York City and an earthquake in San Francisco. The report concluded that a major storm could cause massive flooding that would lead to thousands of drowning deaths as well as many more suffering from disease and dehydration as the floodwater receded from the city. The Bush administration ignored the warnings and then failed to respond to the crisis when the disaster did materialize. In February 2006, the GAO blamed Homeland Security Secretary Michael Chertoff for failing to efficiently mobilize disaster resources despite sufficient warning that Hurricane Katrina would be devastating. The GAO especially faulted Chertoff and FEMA Director Michael D. Brown for failing to designate Hurricane Katrina as a "catastrophic event," which would have allowed the federal government to take proactive measures rather than waiting for state and local agencies to request assistance.

The disaster in New Orleans was an inevitable by-product of neoliberal politics—a willful disregard for investing state resources in the protection of the environment and public infrastructure. Instead, the poor of New Orleans were left to sink or swim on their own. Over 1,460 people were immediately killed by Katrina in Louisiana (nearly half were African American). Another 2,358 deaths attributed to the storm occurred in New Orleans in the first six months of 2006.[134] The storm is estimated to have caused $81.2 billion in damage, making it the costliest natural disaster in U.S. history. As of early July 2006, there were still about 100,000 people living in 37,745 FEMA provided trailers. In Greater New Orleans, about 125,000 homes remain damaged and unoccupied.[135] As a result of the exodus of those rendered homeless by the storm, the black population of the New Orleans metropolitan area has fallen 42 percent.[136] In short, Bush administration policies have resulted in the selective victimization of those people most vulnerable to the disaster—poorer people of color and the white working class.[137]

In the aftermath of the storm, the Bush administration has sided with the region's large real estate developers, bankers, Big Oil, and other corporate interests to oppose reconstruction efforts that prioritize the building of affordable housing, neighborhood relief, and bringing the displaced back to the city. Instead, resources are being channeled to promote gentrification and reconstruction by politically allied firms like Halliburton subsidiary KBR (Dick Cheney was chief executive officer of Halliburton before becoming vice president) and the Shaw Group, which enjoy the services of lobbyist Joe Allbaugh, a former FEMA director and Bush's 2000 campaign manager. As stated by Republican Congressman Richard Baker from Baton Rouge to the *Wall Street Journal* less than two weeks after Katrina, "We finally cleaned up public housing in New Orleans . . . we couldn't do it, but God did."[138] Congress cut out $250 million allocated to combat coastal erosion[139] and provided inadequate funding for the cleanup of tens of thousands of tons of hazardous waste left strewn across the landscape.[140] For the cost of about two weeks of warring in Iraq, both the levees and the wetlands could be restored. Clearly, the deeper structures of neoliberal policies are at the root of the travesty in New Orleans.

King Coal's Devastation of the American Landscape

As part of the corporate war against nature, the U.S. government is allowing mining companies access to some of this country's most pristine landscapes. For instance, the Northern Dynasty Minerals' Pebble project in Alaska threatens to destroy the world's most valuable wild salmon run by digging North America's largest open-pit gold and copper mine. Near the headwaters of Bristol Bay, an earthen dam to hold back the mining wastes (or tailings) would be 4.3 miles long and more than 700 feet high—larger than the Three Gorges Dam in China. Actively supported by the Bush administration, the dam, as well as the pollutants released by the project, would destroy fish spawning waters. Bristol Bay produces 30 percent of all Alaskan wild salmon, with a value of $216 million in 2006.[141] Mining operations such as these typically result in massive contamination of the surrounding environment. In 2004, it is conservatively estimated that U.S. mining facilities released more than 485 million pounds of carcinogens, developmental toxins, and reproductive toxins.[142]

Expressing concern for the America's "addiction" to oil, the Bush administration has also enabled an expansion of coal mining. The Energy Policy Act of 2005, for instance, repeals the 160-acre cap on coal leases and requires an assessment of potential coal resources on federal lands. One hundred tons of coal are now extracted every two seconds in the United States. Most of the coal is destined for America's power plants, which burn over a billion tons of coal annually and provide over 50 percent of this country's electricity use.[143] But coal is an extremely "dirty" source of energy and is a major source of air pollution.[144] To stave off challenges from the environmental movement, the Bush administration is offering $1.6 billion of incentives to invest in dubious "clean coal" technologies, which further promote the consumption of coal (between 2003 and 2005, the demand for coal increased by 2.6 percent in the United States).[145] In concert with its political allies in the polluter-industrial complex, the administration has failed to make any environmental regulatory improvements that would impact the way that coal is mined. In fact, since the passage of the Surface Mining Control and Reclamation Act in 1976, coal mining has become even more ecologically devastating. In short, neoliberals are supplementing America's addiction to oil with that of an even more "destructive" fossil fuel—coal.

The restructuring of the coal industry is facilitating a turn toward more surface mining, which accounts for 67 percent of U.S. coal production. Capital favors surface, or opencast, mining because it recovers a higher proportion of coal deposits (90 percent more) and is cheaper than underground mining.[146] Furthermore, surface mining operations require fewer workers and offer significantly lower labor costs per ton of extracted coal. Since the early 1980s, the number of surface mines has grown as earthmoving machines have become sophisticated. Surface mines have also grown in sheer size and become much more ecologically destructive, particularly with the development of more aggressive forms of strip mining and mountaintop removal. To maximize profits, the industry has turned from surface excavation techniques to simply blasting away the tops of the mountains. Large areas of forests, topsoil, and underlying rocks covering hillsides are blown up by explosives. Bulldozers and front-end loaders then push this material, or overburden, off the edge of the mountains into the valleys below in order to exposure the underlying seams of coal. Some 6,700 coal company "valley fills" were approved by the state in central Appalachia between 1985 and 2001 alone.[147]

The growth in surface mining is turning vast areas of the Appalachian Mountains and the western United States into desolate landscapes. Although the 1977 Surface Mining Control and Reclamation Act requires that mine operators replace vegetation and "restore the land" to its original contours, the law is weak and regularly violated. Surface mining denudes hillsides, causes landslides, and destroys the watershed's ability to absorb moisture, resulting in severe flooding during storms (and problems of drought when conditions are dry). Soil erosion, overburden, and coal wastes from mine operations also destroy fish and wildlife habitat and ruin water supplies. In May 2003, a study by five government agencies calculated that over 724 miles of healthy perennial and intermittent streams are buried by mountaintop removal in Appalachia.[148] Thousands more are seriously damaged. Mountaintop removal has also destroyed over 300,000 acres of forests and is accelerating. The deforestation is expected to double over the next decade.[149] Sedimentation and mineral wastes from mine sites in water supplies are also causing outbreaks in parts of Appalachia of "baby blue syndrome"—a children's health condition characterized by nausea, diarrhea, vomiting, and shortness of breath. Long-term effects of the condition may also include liver, kidney and spleen failure, bone damage, and cancers of the digestive tract.[150]

The federal government is currently ignoring thousands of acres that have not been reclaimed (the GAO estimates that some 560,000 abandoned mines now sit on federal lands). But instead of offering tougher regulations to correct the problem, the Bush administration pressured the EPA in 2002 to ease rules on mountaintop removal mining, streamlined the review process for new mining permits, and revised the Clean Water Act to legalize the already common practice of dumping "fill" directly into waterways.[151] As a result of these rollbacks in environmental law, King Coal is creating yet another type of ecological sacrifice zone.[152] Every day the mostly white working class of Appalachia experiences devastating ecological violence yet receives scant attention from the national media. As stated by Eric Reece, "Those who live in the path of the coal industry—beneath sheared-off mountains, amid unnatural, treeless landscapes, drinking poisoned water and breathing dirty air—are fighting their own civil-rights battle."[153] Despite the enormous wealth generated by the coal industry, few people in the region share the economic benefits. The poverty rate in central and southern Appalachia stands at 30 percent, right where it did in 1964.[154]

Plagued by an ideology of liberal reform, with an emphasis on regulatory and technical solutions, mainstream environmentalism is implicated in the current tragedy. In the 1960s and early 1970s, the people of Appalachia were calling for the outlawing of strip mining because of the severe damage it was doing to their communities, farms, and water supplies. Despite the rise of mass protests and use of civil disobedience, opposition to King Coal failed. With the support of many in the mainstream environmental movement, Congress passed and President Jimmy Carter signed the Surface Mining Control and Reclamation Act. However, the legislation was a defeat for those popular forces looking to abolish strip mining. Instead, a state–federal control system inferior to the program being voiced from below prevailed. If the environmental movement had supported efforts to outlaw strip mining, a method of coal mining that was clearly devastating to the natural environment would have been stopped. They would have also supported labor and campaigns for economic justice by eliminating one part of coal operators' drive to reduce labor costs by finding ways to mine coal with fewer workers, a primary reason they were shifting away from underground (or deep) mining.[155]

Under the Clean Air Act, power plants are compelled to reduce sulfur dioxide emissions that cause acid rain and other major and related health problems. The utilities are responding in part by blending high-sulfur coal with low-sulfur coal. As a result, the demand for low-sulfur coal is rapidly increasing, especially from coal fields underlying Native American reservations in the West. The Native American land base alone amounts to 100 million acres and is equivalent in size to all "wilderness lands" in the national wilderness preservation system. In fact, Native lands in the lower forty-eight states are larger than all of New England. The Navajo Reservation alone is five times the size of Connecticut and twice the size of Maryland. Two-thirds of the uranium and one-third of all low-sulfur coal reserves lie on Native lands. In an attempt to gain control over and exploit the low-cost energy resources on these lands, the polluter-industrial complex has launched a nationwide corporate attack on Native Americans, including calls for the termination of treaty rights.[156]

CAPITAL MOBILITY AND THE DISPLACEMENT OF ENVIRONMENTAL INJUSTICES TO THE SUNBELT

Under policies of "new federalism" and the rhetoric of "states' rights," environmental responsibilities are being shifted from the federal government to the states, many of which are financially strapped by fiscal crises and capital disinvestment. The neoliberal hope is that many states will engage in bidding wars with other states to attract capital to their home regions by offering more favorable investment conditions, including less worker and environmental regulation. One such business haven is the state of Arkansas, which had one of the highest rates of mostly low-paying job creation in the 1980s and early

1990s under then Governor Bill Clinton. He attracted factory farming, chemical plants, and other businesses to Arkansas by supporting a number of antiunion (or "right-to-know") legislation initiatives while giving numerous tax breaks to businesses and raising regressive taxes on the working and middle classes. Clinton also sold out on pledges to improve the workers' compensation process and clean up the state's environmental problems. Furthermore, the Arkansas Pollution Control and Ecology Department permitted companies to boost profits through the improper disposal of toxic chemicals. As a result, the health of the huge Sparta aquifer, a supply tapped by community water districts and industry throughout southern Arkansas, is now threatened.

In the 1990s, the state of Texas came to symbolize the lax environmental enforcement that neoliberals had brought to the south. With generous campaign contributions and political resources provided by the polluter-industrial complex, George W. Bush was able to capture the governorship in 1994. During his nearly six years in the governor's mansion, Bush ignored calls for more environmental protection. In fact, Texas possessed five of the ten most polluted ZIP code areas in the country and led the nation in total air, water, and land releases of carcinogenic pollution. Texas also ranked as the country's worst for the number of hazardous waste incinerators, total toxic releases to the environment, and mercury emissions from industry. Furthermore, Texas ranked next to last on state spending for environmental cleanup.[157] Refineries in Texas were also the nation's most environmentally inefficient (in terms of pollution releases and waste produced per barrel of oil refined per day). In contrast, refineries in northern states such as New Jersey, which has some of the country's toughest pollution laws, are among the best.

Polluting industries are attracted to southern states such as Texas, Arkansas, South Carolina, Alabama, Florida, and Louisiana by cheaper sources of labor as well as by lower taxes, generous government subsidies, efficient infrastructure, close proximity to natural resources and transportation routes, and the dominance of neoliberal politicians committed to promoting capital investment and economic growth. Home to more than 300 chemical facilities; forty pulp, paper, and paperboard mills; and ninety petroleum refining facilities, these states continue to attract industries in search of weaker environmental regulations.[158] Louisiana's chemical plants, especially those located in the small and poor African American communities in the corridor between New Orleans and Baton Rouge known as Cancer Alley, release nearly ten times as much pollution per worker as such plants in New Jersey and California, where law enforcement and industry spending for pollution control and abatement are greater. In fact, the twenty-five states currently handing out the largest subsidies to polluting industries are the very same states that have the weakest environmental protection policies and the most polluted environments. All but five of these states are in the Sunbelt, with Louisiana being the nation's worst offender.[159]

In May 2007, for instance, the Belcher Corporation, one of the oldest foundries in the country, announced it was moving from Massachusetts to Alabama. As stated by Joseph Dynof, the company's chief financial officer, "The environmental regulations aren't as stringent in Alabama as they are in Massachusetts." Specializing in the outsource manufacturing of gas fittings, hand tools, and valves for companies such as Ford and General Motors, the foundry has for years drawn criticism from neighbors and environmental groups for what they say are undue dust, odors, and noise. In 2004, the company's excessive pollution problems resulted in a "Dirty Dozen Award" from the Toxics Action Center, a regional environmental watchdog group. In 2006, the State Department of Environmental Protection fined the company $210,000, of which $30,000 was paid. The rest was suspended with the condition that the firm meet deadlines for installing air pollution control equipment. As a result of the decision to close the facility, however, the company will not pay the remainder of the fine.[160]

By exercising a stranglehold over state and local governments in the Sunbelt, the polluter-industrial complex is able to promote weaker environmental regulations and enforcement. Under legislation such as the Texas Environmental, Health, and Safety Audit Privilege Act (Audit Act), polluters are encouraged to perform their own assessment and compliance of environmental laws, regulations, and permits for their own facilities. This "honor" system invites widespread abuses by industry. In fact, the Texas Commission on Environmental Quality has only "guidelines" for 2,500 pollutants, a legal ambient air quality standard that is not enforceable.[161] In this manner, Texas and other southern states function as domestic "pollution havens" for U.S. industry. Areas occupied by poor people of color and working-class whites serve as the ecological sacrifice zones within these pollution havens. These zones are not hard to identify. In 2004, roughly a quarter of all air and water releases of carcinogens occurred within just twenty U.S. counties. Thanks to the Audit Act and other weak regulations, four Texas counties—Harris, Galveston, Brazoria, and Jefferson—have the most carcinogenic emissions in the United States.[162] The pollution from these industrial facilities is taking a terrible toll on local residents. In the poor, mostly Hispanic community of Corpus Christi, Texas, for instance, the overall rate of birth defects is 84 percent higher when compared to the rest of the state of Texas. Corpus Christi ranks number one in the state for pollution containing benzene, a potent cancer-causing agent.[163]

The creation of pollution havens and ecological sacrifice zones is not restricted to the southern United States. Aided by recent "free-trade" initiatives, such as the North American Free Trade Agreement, the movement of dirty industry is moving beyond the American South to Mexico and other parts of the world where environmental standards are lax, unions are weak, and worker health and safety issues are ignored.[164] Similar to the displacement of ecological hazards onto working-class families and people of color *inside* the country, American business is also displacing externalities onto marginalized communities *outside* the United States. Both practices are integral to the profit-making schemes of the polluter-industrial complex and the economic restructuring of American capitalism.

LOOKING AHEAD

In communities all across the United States, a vibrant grassroots environmental politics is developing. Led by multiracial organizations grounded in local communities as well as regional and national networks led by people of color, the EJ movement is challenging environmental racism and the dis parate exposure to ecological hazards.[165] Acting in coalition with the rise of new forms of working-class environmentalism, antitoxics activism, and the clean production movement, the EJ movement is slowly but surely developing networks and long-term strategies for arresting the ecological crisis.[166] As such, the continued growth and prosperity of these community-based EJ organizations and networks is essential to constructing a more inclusive, democratic, and proactive environmental politics in the United States.

To achieve its goal, the EJ activists are employing a variety of tactics. The EJ movement is making extensive use of direct action, civil disobedience, grassroots organizing, and popular protests to draw attention to the differential enforcement and disparate treatment received by the working poor and people of color. The EJ movement is also participating in government advisory bodies, assisting in the drafting of prospective rules and regulations, conducting scientific research, and undertaking litigation and lobbying activities to eliminate environmental inequities. In this respect, the EJ movement is coupling political "outsider" and "insider" strategies to place political pressure on abusive oil and mining companies, corporate polluters, hostile state agencies, and indifferent environmental organizations. As stated in *Toxic Wastes and Race at Twenty*, a report by a group of leading EJ scholars,

> The movement set out clear goals of eliminating unequal enforcement of environmental, civil rights and public health laws. It also targeted differential exposure of vulnerable populations to harmful chemicals, pesticides and other toxins in the home, school, neighborhood and workplace—and challenged faulty assumptions in calculating, assessing and managing risks, discriminatory zoning and land-use practices, and exclusionary policies and practices that limit low-income persons and people of color from participation in decision making. Many of these prob-

lems could be eliminated if current environmental, health, housing, land use and civil rights laws were vigorously enforced in a nondiscriminatory way.[167]

To end environmental injustice, the report offers a series of recommendations that call for better enforcement of existing environmental and civil rights laws as well as institutional reforms at the EPA. Such reforms include the development of a clear vision and comprehensive plan for integrating EJ considerations into the day-to-day operations of the EPA. The report calls on industry to adopt clean production principles and methods that would include the use of renewable energy sources and the phaseout of toxic chemicals in favor of nontoxic materials, renewable energy sources. By adopting the Louisville Charter, industry could also invest in the development of sustainable chemicals, products, materials, and production processes. Corporations especially need to eliminate the use of persistent, bioaccumulative, or highly toxic chemicals that cause the most damage to public health.

Bringing about these changes is a tall order. Nevertheless, important progress is being made. In the final analysis, only by gaining greater democratic governance over community planning and national economic development can a potentially divisive "not-in-my-backyard" politics oriented to equitable distribution of environmental risks be replaced with a truly transformative "not-in-anyone's backyard" politics oriented to eliminating the production of environmental risks. Central to this endeavor is the struggle to wrest control of the federal government away from the polluter-industrial complex.

As we shall see in the following chapter, the largest and most powerful corporate polluters in the country have colonized the state and are leading the charge against the environmental and EJ movements. The historic task confronting activists is to build a larger mass movement capable of democratizing the state and moving the country forward into a more just and sustainable future. To do so will require the construction of a coherent national strategy that is more considerate of the class, gender, and international inequalities inherent in American capitalism. This requires that the EJ movement eventually build an indigenous base of support that is inclusive of working-class and middle-class whites.[168] Otherwise, the comprehensive set of recommendations outlined in *Toxic Wastes and Race at Twenty* and by other EJ organizations may never be realized.

NOTES

1. Joel Kovel, *The Enemy of Nature: The End of Capitalism or the End of the World?* (New York: Zed Books, 2002).

2. Edward T. Gullason, "The Dynamics of the U.S. Occupational Structure during the 1990s," *Journal of Labor Research* 21, no. 2 (April 2000): 363–75.

3. Associated Press, "Toyota Unseats King GM: Firm Is Tops in Sales in Quarter for 1st Time," *Boston Globe* (April 25, 2007), C2.

4. Lori G. Kletzer, "Measuring the Costs of Trade-Related Job Loss," testimony prepared for the Committee on Finance, United States Senate (July 20, 2001), available at http://www.iie.com/publications/print.cfm?doc=pub&Research ID=418 (accessed May 16, 2007).

5. Associated Press, "Oil Imports Push Up US Trade Gap: Retailers Post Weak Sales Figures in April," *Boston Globe* (May 11, 2007), C2.

6. Vaclav Smil, *China's Environmental Crisis: An Inquiry into the Limits of National Development* (New York: M. E. Sharpe, 1997).

7. Pete Engardio and Dexter Roberts, "The China Price," *BusinessWeek* (December 6, 2004), 102–12.

8. C. Fred Bergsten, "The Current Account Deficit and the US Economy," testimony before the Budget Committee of the United States Senate (February 1, 2007), 1–5, available at http://www.iie.com/publications/prinit.cfm?doc=pub&ResearchID= 705 (accessed May 16, 2007).

9. Stephen Roach, "Global: Do Imbalances Matter?," Morgan Stanley Global Economic Forum (September 2, 2003), http://www.morganstanley.com/GEFdata/digests/latest-digest.html, cited in Minq Li, "After Neoliberalism: Empire, Social Democracy, or Socialism?," *Monthly Review* 55, no. 8 (January 2004): 22.

10. Li, "After Neoliberalism," 22; Bergsten, "The Current Account Deficit and the US Economy," 1–5; Cletus C. Coughlin, Michael R. Pakko, and William Poole, "How Dangerous is the US Current Account Deficit?," *The Regional Economist* (2006), available at http://www.stlouisfed.org/publications/re/2006/b/pages/account_deficit (accessed May 20, 2007).

11. Li, "After Neoliberalism," 22.

12. Rachel Massey, "Biotech—The Basics, Part 3," *Rachel's Environment and Health News* 718 (February 15, 2001), 1–2.

13. Ken Geiser, *Materials Matter: Toward a Sustainable Materials Policy* (Cambridge, MA: MIT Press, 2001).

14. Lawrence Mishel, Jared Bernstein, and Sylvia Allegretto, *The State of Working America, 2006–2007* (Ithaca, NY: Cornell University Press, 2007).

15. The UN report titled *Key Indicators of the Labor Market* (5th ed.), found that the average U.S. worker produces $63,885 of wealth per year. This figure beats all twenty-seven nations in the European Union, Japan, and Switzerland in the amount of wealth created per hour of work, a key measure of productivity.

16. Robert E. Baldwin, *The Decline of US Labor Unions and the Role of Trade* (Washington, DC: Institute for International Economics, 2003).

17. Lawrence Mishel, "Viewpoints: Globalization That Works for Working Americans," testimony presented to the U.S. House of Representatives Committee on Ways and Means (January 30, 2007), http://www.epi.org/content/cfm/webfeatures_viewpoints_globalization.htm (accessed June 5, 2007), 1–4.

18. Kim-Mai Cutler, "Fed Chief Sees Growth Ahead: Technology to Spur Further Productivity Gains, Bernanke Says," *Boston Globe* (June 10, 2006), B8–B9.

19. Mishel, "Globalization That Works," 1.

20. Cited in William K. Tabb, "Wage Stagnation, Growing Insecurity, and the Future of the US Working Class," *Monthly Review* 59, no. 2 (June 2007): 20–30, 23.

21. Roger H. Bezdek, "The Net Impact of Environmental Protection on Jobs and the Economy," in *Environmental Justice: Issues, Policies, and Solutions*, ed. Bunyan Bryant (Washington, DC: Island Press, 1995), 86–106.

22. K. William Kapp, *The Social Cost of Private Enterprise* (New York: Schocken Books, 1950), 13.

23. Richard Cornes and Todd Sandler, *The Theory of Externalities, Public Goods, and Club Goods* (New York: Cambridge University Press, 1986), 6.

24. Kenneth A. Gould, "The Sweet Smell of Money: Economic Dependency and Local Environmental Political Motivation," *Society and Natural Resources* 4, no. 2 (April/June 1991): 133.

25. Barbara Rose Johnston, *Who Pays the Price? The Sociocultural Context of Environmental Crisis* (Washington, DC: Island Press, 1994).

26. Laura Pulido, *Environmentalism and Economic Justice: Two Chicano Struggles in the Southwest* (Tucson: University of Arizona Press, 1996), 4–5, 12–13, 127–28.

27. Robert D. Bullard, ed., *Confronting Environmental Racism: Voices from the Grassroots* (Boston: South End Press, 1993).

28. California Waste Management Board, *Political Difficulties Facing Waste-to-Energy Conversion Plant Siting* (Los Angeles: Cerrell Associates, 1984), 42–44, C1–C4.

29. David Naguib Pellow and Robert J. Brulle, "Poisoning the Planet: The Struggle for Environmental Justice," *Contexts* 6, no. 1 (Winter 2007): 37–41.

30. National Research Council, *Waste Incineration and Public Health* (Washington, DC: National Academy Press, 2004).

31. Pat Thomas, "The Lethal Consequences of Breathing Fire," *The Ecologist* 36, no. 7 (September 2006): 44–48.

32. California Waste Management Board, *Political Difficulties Facing Waste-to-Energy Conversion Plant Siting*, 29–30, 65.

33. Robert D. Bullard, Paul Mohai, Robin Saha, and Beverly Wright, *Toxic Wastes and Race at Twenty: 1987–2007—Grassroots Struggles to Dismantle Environmental Racism in the United States*, a report prepared for the United Church of Christ Justice and Witness Ministries (March 2007), 58–60.

34. Manuel Pastor Jr., Jim Sadd, and John Hipp, "Which Came First? Toxic Facilities, Minority Move-In, and Environmental Justice," *Journal of Urban Affairs* 23, no. 1 (2001): 1–21; Manuel Pastor Jr., Rachel Morello-Frosch, and James L. Sadd, "The Air Is Always Cleaner on the Other Side: Race, Space, and Ambient Air Toxics Exposures in California," *Journal of Urban Affairs* 27, no. 2 (2005): 127–48; Manuel Pastor Jr., James L. Sadd, and Rachel Morello-Frosch, "Waiting to Inhale: The Demographics of Toxic Air Release Facilities in 21st-Century California," *Social Science Quarterly* 85, no. 2 (2004): 420–40.

35. Pat Costner and Joe Thornton, *Playing with Fire* (Washington, DC: Greenpeace, 1990); Joe Thornton, *Pandora's Poison: Chlorine, Health and a New Environmental Strategy* (Cambridge, MA: MIT Press, 2000), 277–94.

36. Jennifer McNulty, "Unfair Exposure: Seeking Justice for Neighborhoods Bearing the Brunt of Toxic Hazards," *US Santa Cruz Review* 41, no. 4 (March 2004): 18–22; Pastor, Sadd, and Hipp, "Which Came First?," 1–21.

37. Rachel Morello-Frosch, Manuel Pastor, and James Sadd, "Environmental Justice and Southern California's Riskscape: The Distribution of Air Toxics Exposures and Health Risks Among Diverse Communities," *Urban Affairs Review* 36, no. 4 (2001): 551–78.

38. Evan J. Ringquist, "Equity and the Distribution of Environmental Risk: The Case of TRI Facilities," *Social Science Quarterly* 78 (1997): 811–18.

39. Daniel R. Faber and Eric J. Krieg, *Unequal Exposure to Ecological Hazards 2005: Environmental Injustices in the Commonwealth of Massachusetts*, a report by the Philanthropy and Environmental Justice Research Project, Northeastern University (Boston, October 12, 2005), 20–25.

40. David C. Evers, *Mercury Connections: The Extent and Effects of Mercury Pollution in Northeastern North America*, a report by the BioDiversity Research Institute (Gorham, ME, 2005), 1–28.

41. Scott J. South and Kyle D. Crowder, "Escaping Distressed Neighborhoods: Individual, Community, and Metropolitan Influences," *American Journal of Sociology* 102, no. 4 (January 1997): 1040–84.

42. Melvin L. Oliver and Thomas A. Shapiro, *Black Wealth/White Wealth: A New Perspective on Racial Inequality* (New York: Routledge, 1995).

43. Jim Campen, "The Color of Money in Greater Boston: Patterns of Mortgage Lending and Residential Segregation at the Beginning of the New Century," a report prepared for the Metro Boston Equity Initiative of the Harvard University Civil Rights Project (January 2004), 3–8.

44. Faber and Krieg, *Unequal Exposure to Ecological Hazards 2005*, 51–53.

45. Laura Pulido, "Rethinking Environmental Racism: White Privilege and Urban Development in Southern California," *Annals of the Association of American Geographers* 90, no. 1 (2000): 12–40.

46. Douglas Massey and Nancy Denton, *American Apartheid: Segregation and the Making of the Underclass* (Cambridge, MA: Harvard University Press, 1993).

47. John Logan and Harvey Molotch, *Urban Fortunes* (Berkeley: University of California Press, 1987).

48. Rachel Morello-Frosch, "Discrimination and the Political Economy of Environmental Inequality," *Environment and Planning C: Government and Policy* 20 (2002): 477–96.

49. Laura Pulido, "A Critical Review of the Methodology of Environmental Racism Research," *Antipode* 28, no. 2 (1996): 149–62.

50. Alison Cassady and Alex Fidis, *Toxic Pollution and Health: An Analysis of Toxic Chemicals Released in the Communities across the United States* (Washington, DC: U.S. PIRG Education Fund, March 2006), 1–65.

51. David Pace, "AP: More Blacks Live with Pollution," *Aberdeen News.com* (December 13, 2005), 1–4.

52. U.S. Environmental Protection Agency, *National-Scale Air Toxics Risk Assessment* (May 2002); *Technology Transfer Network National Air Toxics Assessment,*

Frequently Asked Questions, available at http://www.epa.gove/ttn/atw/nata/natsafaq .htmul#B1.

53. A study conducted by researchers at the Harvard School of Public Health, Brigham Young University, and the American Cancer Society (released March 10, 1995, in the *American Journal of Respiratory and Critical Care Medicine*) estimated some 60,000 annual air pollution deaths. Another study by the Natural Resources Defense Council released in 1996 that analyzed air quality in 239 cities across the country estimated some 64,000 Americans to be dying each year from air pollution, even at levels the federal government considers to be safe.

54. Rachel Morello-Frosch, Manuel Pastor, Carlos Porras, and Jim Sadd, "Environmental Justice and Regional Inequality in Southern California: Implications for Future Research," *Environmental Health Perspectives* 110, Supplement 2 (2002): 149–54; Manuel Pastor, Jim Sadd, and Rachel Morello-Frosch, "Who's Minding the Kids? Toxic Air, Public Schools, and Environmental Justice in Los Angeles," *Social Science Quarterly* 83, no. 1 (2002): 263–80; Robert D. Bullard, Glenn S. Johnson, and Angel O. Torres, *Highway Robbery: Transportation Racism and New Routes to Equity* (Boston: South End Press, 2004).

55. D. R. Wernette and L. A. Nieves, "Breathing Polluted Air: Minorities Are Disproportionately Exposed," *EPA Journal* (March/April 1992), 16.

56. Eric Mann with the Watchdog Organizing Committee, *L.A.'s Lethal Air: New Strategies for Policy, Organizing, and Action* (Los Angeles: Labor/Community Strategy Center, 1991).

57. Rachel Morello-Frosch, "Environmental Justice and California's 'Riskcape': The Distribution of Air Toxics and Associated Cancer and Non-Cancer Health Risks among Diverse Community" (PhD diss., University of California at Berkeley, 1997).

58. Sandra George O'Neil, "Environmental Justice in the Superfund Clean-Up Process" (PhD diss., Boston College, April 2005).

59. Peter Montague, "Pediatricians Urge a Precautionary Approach to Toxic Lead," *Rachel's Democracy and Health News* 827 (September 29, 2005), 1–2, cited in Benjamin Goldman and Laura Fitton, *Toxic Waste and Race Revisited: An Update of the 1987 Report on the Racial and Socioeconomic Characteristics of Communities with Hazardous Waste Sites* (New York: United Church of Christ Commission for Racial Justice, 1994).

60. Dana Alston, *We Speak for Ourselves: Social Justice, Race, and Environment* (Washington, DC: The Panos Institute, 1990).

61. Rodger C. Field, "Risk and Justice: Capitalist Production and the Environment," in *The Struggle for Ecological Democracy*, ed. Daniel Faber (New York: Guilford Press, 1998), 81–103.

62. Lewis Regenstein, *How to Survive in America the Poisoned* (Washington, D.C.: Acropolis Books, 1986), 160.

63. Caroline Snyder, "The Dirty Work of Promoting 'Recycling' of America's Sewage Sludge," *International Journal of Occupational and Environmental Health* 11, no. 4 (October/December 2005): 437–43.

64. United Church of Christ Commission for Racial Justice, *Toxic Wastes and Race in the United States: A National Report on the Racial and Socioeconomic Characteristics*

of Communities Surrounding Hazardous Waste Sites (New York: United Church of Christ, 1987); U.S. General Accounting Office, *Siting of Hazardous Waste Landfills and Their Correlation with Racial and Economic Status of Surrounding Communities* (Washington, DC: U.S. Government Printing Office, 1983).

65. Bullard et al., *Toxic Wastes and Race at Twenty*.

66. Mary Clifford, ed., *Environmental Crime: Enforcement, Policy, and Social Responsibility* (Gaithersburg, MD: Aspen Publishers, 1998).

67. Donald Rebovich, *Dangerous Ground: The World of Hazardous Waste Crime* (New Brunswick, NJ: Transaction Publishers, 1992); Russel Mokhiber, *Corporate Crime and Violence: Big Business Power and the Abuse of the Public Trust* (San Francisco: Sierra Club Books, 1989); Alan A. Block and Frank R. Scarpitti, *Poisoning for Profit: The Mafia and Toxic Waste in America* (New York: William Morrow, 1982).

68. David N. Pellow, "The Politics of Illegal Dumping: An Environmental Justice Framework," *Qualitative Sociology* 27, no. 4 (Winter 2004): 511–25.

69. David Naguib Pellow and Robert J. Brulle, "Poisoning the Planet: The Struggle for Environmental Justice," *Contexts* 6, no. 1 (Winter 2007): 37–41.

70. Renee Twombly, "Urban Uprising," *Environmental Health Perspectives* 105, no. 7 (July 1997): 696–701.

71. Low-income towns average 19.2 sites (per square mile). See Faber and Kreig, *Unequal Exposure to Ecological Hazards 2005*, 12–19.

72. Political Ecology Group, *Toxic Empire: The WMX Corporation, Hazardous Waste and Global Strategies for Environmental Justice* (San Francisco: Political Ecology Group, 1995).

73. Vernon Mogensen, *Worker Safety under Siege: Labor, Capital, and the Politics of Workplace Safety in a Deregulated World* (Armonk, NY: M. E. Sharpe, 2006).

74. AFL-CIO, *Death on the Job: The Toll of Neglect*, 16th ed. (Washington, DC: AFL-CIO, April 2007).

75. Susanna Rankin Bohme, John Zorabedian, and David S. Egilman, "Maximizing Profit and Endangering Health: Corporate Strategies to Avoid Litigation and Regulation," *International Journal of Occupational and Environmental Health* 11, no. 4 (October/December 2005): 338–48; Michael F. Jacobson, "Lifting the Veil of Secrecy from Industry Funding of Non-Profit Health Organizations," *International Journal of Occupational and Environmental Health* 11, no. 4 (October/December 2005): 338–48, 349–55.

76. AFL-CIO, *Death on the Job*, 1–5.

77. Charles Levenstein and John Wooding, "Dying for a Living: Workers, Production, and the Environment," in Faber, *The Struggle for Ecological Democracy*, 60–80; Philip Landrigan and Steven Markowitz, "Current Magnitude of Occupational Disease in the United States: Estimates from New York State," *Annals of the New York Academy of Sciences* 27, no. 27 (1989): 572.

78. Stuart M. Brooks, "Occupational and Environmental Asthma," in *Environmental and Occupational Medicine*, 2nd ed., ed. William N. Rom (Philadelphia: Lippincott-Raven, 1992), 393–94.

79. Paul A. Schulte, "Characterizing the Burden of Occupational Injury and Disease," *Journal of Occupational Medicine* 47, no. 6 (2005): 607–22.

80. AFL-CIO, *Death on the Job*, 1–5.

81. International Labor Office, *Strategies and Practice for Labor Inspection*, G.B .297/ESP/3 (Geneva, November 2006); Department of Labor, Bureau of Labor Statistics, *Employment and Wages, Annual Averages* (Washington, DC: The United States Department of Labor, 2005); U.S. Department of Labor, OSHA, *Summary of Federal CSHO Totals by State FY 2007 and Summary of State Safety and Health Compliance Staffing, FY 2007* (Washington, DC: The United States Department of Labor, 2007). The total number of inspectors does not include fifty-six inspectors in Puerto Rico and the Virgin Islands.

82. David Biderman, *Waste Age Magazine* (April 1, 2007).

83. James Baker, Frank L. Bowman, Glenn Erwin, Slade Gorton, Dennis Hendershot, Nancy Leveson, Sharon Priest, Isadore Rosenthal, Paul V. Tebo, Douglass A. Wiegmann, and L. Duane Wilson, *The Report of the BP US Refineries Independent Safety Review Panel* (Washington, DC: U.S. Chemical Safety and Hazard Investigation Board, January 2007), 1–335.

84. Cassady and Fidis, *Toxic Pollution and Health*, 8.

85. Eyal Press, "Almighty Oil," *The Nation* (May 9, 1994), 61 /; Jack Doyle, *Crude Awakening* (Washington, DC: Friends of the Earth, 1994).

86. Associated Press, "Budget Cuts by BP Cited in Spills," *Boston Globe* (May 17, 2007), D3.

87. Michael Tanzer, "Growing Instability in the International Oil Industry," in *Instability and Change in the World Economy*, ed. Arthur MacEwan and William K. Tabb (New York: Monthly Review Press, 1989), 225–40.

88. See C. K Curlee, S. J. Broulliard, M. L. Marshall, T. L. Knode, and S. L. Smith, *Upstream Oil and Gas Fatalities: A Review of OSHA's Database and Strategic Direction for Reducing Fatal Accidents*, a report presented at the Society of Petroleum Engineers, Environmental Protection Agency, and Department of Energy Exploration and Production Environmental Conference, Galveston, Texas (March 7–9, 2005), available at http://www.spe.org/jpt.

89. Nicholas A. Ashford et al., *The Encouragement of Technological Change for Preventing Chemical Accidents: Moving Firms from Secondary Prevention and Mitigation to Primary Prevention* (Cambridge, MA: MIT Press, 1993), iii–vi.

90. *Rachel's Environmental and Health Weekly* 408 (September 22, 1994), 1–2.

91. Paul R. Kleindorfer, James C. Belke, Michael R. Elliott, Kiwan Lee, Robert A. Lowe, and Harold I. Feldman, "Accident Epidemiology and the US Chemical Industry: Accident History and Worst-Case Data from RMP* Info," *Risk Analysis* 23, no. 5 (2003): 865–81, esp. 871.

92. M. R. Elliott, Y. Wang, R. A. Lowe, and P. R. Kleindorfer, "Environmental Justice: Frequency and Severity of US Chemical Industry Accidents and the Socioeconomic Status of Surrounding Communities," *Journal of Epidemiology and Community Health* 58 (2004): 24–30.

93. Curlee et al., *Upstream Oil and Gas Fatalities*.

94. Editorial, "When Lax Rules Are Deadly," *Boston Globe* (March 9, 2006), A14.

95. Rick Klein and Susan Milligan, "12 Miners Reportedly Found Alive: 1 W.Va. Man Dies in Tragedy," *Boston Globe* (January 4, 2006), A1, A16.

96. Nicholas A. Ashford, et al., *The Encouragement of Technological Change for Preventing Chemical Accidents: Moving Firms from Secondary Prevention and Mitigation to Primary Prevention* (Cambridge, MA: Massachusetts Institute of Technology, 1993), vi–1; AFL-CIO, *Death on the Job*, 1–5.

97. David Barstow, "When Workers Die: US Rarely Seeks Charges for Deaths in Workplace," *New York Times* (December 22, 2003), A1.

98. Klein and Milligan, "12 Miners Reportedly Found Alive," A1, A16.

99. Joby Warwick, "Sago Mine Safety Declined Sharply: Stiff Sanctions Are Seen as Rare," *Boston Globe* (January 9, 2006), A4.

100. Samira Jafari, "Ky. Mine Was Cited 41 Times in 5 Years: Probe Targets Gases and Seals," *Boston Globe* (May 25, 2006), A2.

101. Warwick, "Sago Mine Safety Declined Sharply," A4.

102. Editorial, "When Lax Rules Are Deadly," A14.

103. AFL-CIO, *Death on the Job*, 3–6.

104. David S. Egilman and Susanna Rankin Bohme, "Over a Barrel: Corporate Corruption of Science and its Effects on Workers and the Environment," *International Journal of Occupational and Environmental Health* 11, no. 4 (October/December 2005): 331–37.

105. Vernon Mogensen, "Introduction," in *Worker Safety under Siege*, xiii–xxix.

106. Human Rights Watch, *Worker Health and Safety in the Meat and Poultry Industry* (New York: January 2005), available at http://www.hrw.org/reports/2005/usa 0105/4.htm. (accessed May 5, 2007).

107. Community Environmental Health Program, *Environment and Development in the USA: A Grassroots Report for UNCED* (New Market, TN: Highlander Research and Education Center, 1992).

108. Beverly Hendrix Wright, "The Effects of Occupational Injury, Illness and Disease on the Health Status of Black Americans: A Review," in *Race and the Incidence of Environmental Hazard: A Time for Discourse*, ed. Bunyan Bryant and Paul Mohai (Boulder, CO: Westview Press, 1992).

109. Judith T. L. Anderson, Katherine Hunting, and Laura S. Welch, "Injury and Employment Patterns among Hispanic Construction Workers," *Journal of Occupational and Environmental Medicine* 42, no. 2 (February 2000): 176–86.

110. George Friedman-Jimenez, "Achieving Environmental Justice: The Role of Occupational Health," *Fordham Urban Law Journal* 21 (1993–1994): 605–31.

111. James C. Robinson, "Racial Inequality and the Probability of Occupational-Related Injury or Illness," *Milibank Quarterly* 62 (1984): 567–90; James C. Robinson, "Trends in Racial Inequality and Exposure to Work-Related Hazards," *Milibank Quarterly* 65 (1987): 404–19; James C. Robinson, "Exposure to Occupational Hazards Among Hispanics, Blacks and Non-Hispanic Whites in California," *American Journal of Public Health* 79 (1989): 629–30.

112. Friedman-Jimenez, "Achieving Environmental Justice."

113. Anderson et al., "Injury and Employment Patterns among Hispanic Construction Workers."

114. AFL-CIO, *Immigrant Workers at Risk: The Urgent Need for Improved Workplace Safety and Health Policies and Programs* (August 2005), http://www.aflcio.org/ issues/safety/upload/immigrant_risk.pdf (accessed May 7, 2007).

115. Cited in Fred Kaplan, "The Fruit of Their Labor Is Misery," *Boston Globe* (July 12, 1996), 1, 12.

116. Kaplan, "The Fruit of Their Labor Is Misery," 1, 12.

117. Anderson et al., "Injury and Employment Patterns among Hispanic Construction Workers."

118. AFL-CIO, *Death on the Job*, 1–6.

119. Justin Pritchard, "AP Investigation: Mexican Worker Deaths Rise Sharply Even as Overall US Job Safety Improves," Associated Press,http://fmmac2.mm.ap.org/polk_awards_dying_to_work_html/DyingtoWork.html (accessed May 6, 2007).

120. Ivette Perfecto, "Farm Workers, Pesticides, and the International Connection," in Mohai and Bryant, *Race and the Incidence of Environmental Hazards*, 177–203.

121. J. Leigh, P. James, J. Marcin, and T. R. Miller, "An Estimate of the US Government's Undercount of Nonfatal Occupational Injuries," *Journal of Occupational and Environmental Medicine* 46, no. 1 (January 2004); K. D. Rosenman, A. Kalush, M. J. Reilly, J. C. Gardiner, M. Reeves, and Z. Luo, "How Much Work-Related Injury and Illness Is Missed by the Current National Surveillance System?," *Journal of Occupational and Environmental Medicine* 48, no. 4 (April 2006): 357–67.

122. Linda McCauley, Michael Lasarev, Gregory Higgins, Joan Rothlein, Juan Munox, Caren Ebbert, and Jacki Phillips, "Work Characteristics and Pesticide Exposures among Migrant Agricultural Families: A Community-Based Research Approach," *Environmental Health Perspectives* 109, no. 5 (2001): 533–38.

123. Katherine Loh and Scott Richardson, "Foreign-Born Workers: Trends in Fatal Occupational Injuries, 1996–2001," *Monthly Labor Review* (June 2004): 42–54.

124. William R. Freudenburg and Robert Gramling, *Oil in Troubled Waters: Perceptions, Politics, and the Battle over Offshore Drilling* (Albany: State University of New York Press, 1993).

125. William K. Tabb, "Resource Wars," *Monthly Review* 58, no. 8 (January 2007): 32–42, esp. 38.

126. Allison Cassady, *Big Money to Big Oil: How ExxonMobil and the Oil Industry Benefit from the 2005 Energy Bill*, a report by the U.S. PIRG Education Fund (August 2005), 1–17.

127. H. Josef Hebert, "US Expanding Offshore Drilling: Congress Not Moving to Life Moratorium," *Boston Globe* (May 1, 2007), A5.

128. Joel K. Bourne Jr., "Gone with the Water," *Natural Geographic* (October 2004): 88–105, 96. This article correctly predicts and analyzes the impact that a major hurricane would have on New Orleans and was published just months prior to the arrival of Katrina.

129. Chester Hartman and Gregory D. Squires, *There Is No Such Thing as a Natural Disaster: Race, Class, and Hurricane Katrina* (New York: Routledge, 2006).

130. Adolph Reed Jr., "Undone by Neoliberalism: New Orleans Was Decimated by an Ideological Program, Not a Storm," *The Nation* 283, no. 8 (September 18, 2006), 26–30.

131. Eric Alterman, "Found in the Flood," *The Nation* 281, no. 9 (September 26, 2005), 11.

132. Reed, "Undone by Neoliberalism," 26–30.

133. Betsy Reed, ed., *Unnatural Disaster: The Nation on Hurricane Katrina* (New York: Nation Books, 2005).

134. In testimony before the House Committee on Energy and Commerce Subcommittee on Oversight and Investigations on March 13, 2007, Dr. Kevin Stephens Sr., director of the New Orleans Health Department, reported an increase of 2,358 deaths over the baseline in the post-Katrina period (even though the city's population had declined by 50 percent following the storm).

135. Mike Davis, "Who Is Killing New Orleans?," *The Nation* 282, no. 14 (April 10, 2006), 11–20.

136. Gary Younge, "New Orleans Forsaken," *The Nation* 283, no. 8 (September 18, 2006), 17–21.

137. Michael Eric Dyson, *Come Hell or High Water: Hurricane Katrina and the Color of Disaster* (New York: Basic Civitas, 2006).

138. Younge, "New Orleans Forsaken," 17–21.

139. Davis, "Who Is Killing New Orleans?," 11–20.

140. Beverly Wright and Robert D. Bullard, "Wrong Complexion for Protection: Will the 'Mother of All Toxic Cleanups' in Post-Katrina New Orleans Be Fair?," in Bullard et al., *Toxic Wastes and Race at Twenty*, 124–33.

141. Editorial, "Protect Alaska's Wild Salmon," *Boston Globe* (April 2, 2007), A10.

142. Cassady and Fidis, *Toxic Pollution and Health*, 5.

143. Erik Reece, "Moving Mountains: Mountaintop-Removal Mining Is Devastating Appalachia, but Residents Are Fighting Back," *Orion Magazine* (January/February 2006), 1–10, available at http://www.grist.org/news/maindish/2006/02/16/reece (accessed May 10, 2007).

144. Martha Keating, *Cradle to Grave: The Environmental Impacts from Coal*, a report by the Clean Air Task Force (Boston, June, 2001), 1–9.

145. World Coal Institute, *The Coal Resource: A Comprehensive Overview of Coal* (London: WCI, May 2005).

146. World Coal Institute, *The Coal Resource*, 10–15.

147. Reece, "Moving Mountains," 1–10.

148. Environment2004, *Putting Polluters First: The Bush Administration's Environmental Record*, a report by Environment2004 (June 2004), 17.

149. Jennifer Hattam, "Dethroning King Coal: A Miner's Daughter Stands Up for Appalachia's Mountains," *Sierra Magazine* (November/December 2003), available at http://www.sierraclub.org/sierra/200311/profile.asp (accessed May 10, 2007).

150. Reece, "Moving Mountains," 1–10.

151. Erik Reece, *Lost Mountain: A Year in the Vanishing Wilderness; Radical Strip Mining and the Devastation of Appalachia* (New York: Riverhead, 2006).

152. Hattam, "Dethroning King Coal," 1–2.

153. Reece, "Moving Mountains," 1–10.

154. Reece, "Moving Mountains," 1–10.

155. Chad Montrie, *To Save the Land and People: A History of Opposition to Surface Coal Mining in Appalachia* (Chapel Hill: University of North Carolina Press, 2003).

156. Winona LaDuke, *All Our Relations: Native Struggles for Land and Life* (Boston: South End Press, 1999); Jane Weaver and Russell Means, eds., *Defending*

Mother Earth: Native American Perspectives on Environmental Justice (Maryknoll, NY: Orbis Books, 1996); Donald A. Grinde, Howard Zinn, and Bruce Elliott Johansen, *Ecocide of Native America: Environmental Destruction of Indian Lands and Peoples* (Santa Fe, NM: Clear Light Publishers, 1998).

157. Ken Silverstein, "The Polluters' President," *Sierra Magazine* (November/December 1999); http://www.sierraclub.org/sierra/199911/bush.asp (accessed May 10, 2007).

158. Cassady and Fidis, *Toxic Pollution and Health*, 9–17.

159. Paul H. Templet, *Defending the Public Domain: Pollution, Subsidies, and Poverty*, Political Economy Research Institute Working Paper no. DPE-01-03 (Amherst: University of Massachusetts, 2001); Paul H. Templet, "Energy Price Disparity and Public Welfare," *Ecological Economics* 36 (2000): 443–60; Beverly Wright, "Living and Dying in Louisiana's 'Cancer Alley,'" in Bullard, *The Quest for Environmental Justice*, 87–105.

160. Erin Conroy, "Foundry Will Move South, with 78 Jobs," *Boston Globe* (Mary 3, 2007), GS1, GS4.

161. Suzie Canales, *Criminal Injustice in an All-American City: Toxic Crimes, Race Zoning and Oil Industry Pollution Cover-Up* (Corpus Christi, TX: Citizens for Environmental Justice, and Global Community Monitor, 2006), 1–12.

162. Cassady and Fidis, *Toxic Pollution and Health*, 5.

163. Corpus Christi is 54 percent Hispanic, and 17.6 percent of the population lives below the poverty line. See Canales, *Criminal Injustice in an All-American City*, 1–12.

164. Barry Castleman and Vicente Navarro, "International Mobility of Hazardous Products, Industries, and Wastes," *Annual Review of Public Health* 8 (1987): 1–19.

165. Bullard, *The Quest for Environmental Justice*.

166. Thomas Estabrook, *Labor-Environmental Coalitions: Lessons from a Louisiana Petrochemical Region* (Amityville, NY: Baywood Publishing, 2007).

167. Bullard et al., *Toxic Wastes and Race at Twenty*, 152.

168. Robert J. Brulle and David Naguib Pellow, "The Future of Environmental Justice Movements," in *Power, Justice, and the Environment: A Critical Appraisal of the Environmental Justice Movement*, ed. David Naguib Pellow and Robert J. Brulle (Cambridge, MA: MIT Press, 2005), 293–300.

Chapter Two

Eroding Environmental Justice: Colonization of the State by the Polluter-Industrial Complex

To put the environmental lobby out of business. . . . There is no greater imperative . . . If the petroleum industry is to survive, it must render the environmental lobby superfluous, an anachronism.

—Bob Williams, an oil industry consultant and author of *US Petroleum Strategies in the Decade of the Environment*[1]

COLONIZATION OF THE STATE BY THE POLLUTER-INDUSTRIAL COMPLEX

The American power structure has long been dominated by the wealthiest members of the capitalist class. Rooted in the ownership and control of large corporations, the business class "governs" the political system through a leadership group (or *power elite*) at the national level.[2] The power elite is made up of members of the capitalist class who have assumed important positions of authority in the country's major public and private institutions. It also includes high-level corporate directors, managers, academics, lawyers, and politicians who work on behalf of these business owners. The power elite exercise control over the state through interlocking networks of foundations, think tanks and policy institutes, research centers, public opinion–shaping organizations, nonprofits, and strategy groups in the Democratic and Republican parties.[3] These organizations work with elected government officials to enact policies and programs that are favorable to corporate America.

Although the business class shares certain material interests around the defense of private property, the American power structure is not homogeneous. In the 1960s and 1970s, for instance, the social mobilization of oppressed racial minorities, trade unionists, feminists, environmentalists, students, and peace activists placed the corporate power structure on the defensive. To alleviate social disruption and political conflict, centrists in the business community sought "accommodation" with the liberal–labor political coalition as well as the civil rights, antiwar, student, and women's movements. Centrists were especially concerned about the growing power of the environmental movement. By 1975, some 5.5 million people contributed financially to nineteen leading national environmental organizations and perhaps another 20 million to over 40,000 local groups.[4] Capable of swinging significant numbers of middle-class voters, the movement successfully enacted over twenty pieces of major environmental legislation during the "environmental decade" of the 1970s. Although the legislation supported by the corporate centrists (along with Presidents Richard Nixon and Jimmy Carter) during this period was generally weak and preemptive in nature—designed to head off more significant policy proposals from below—some of the adopted reforms imposed serious costs on American business and resulted in significant improvements in environmental quality.

The age of compromise ended rather quickly once popular mobilization waned. Over the past three decades, the ultraconservative wing of the business class has gone on the offensive in an attempt to roll back the gains made by America's popular social movements. Utilizing hot-button wedge issues like abortion and gay rights to tap into more socially conservative and economically insecure white voters, ultraconservatives among the power elite have reassumed the political initiative against liberalism and the welfare state.[5] Creating a strong base of support among southern Democrats (or "Dixiecrats") and uncompromising Republicans, the ultraconservatives are teaming with corporate centrists in pursuit of their political agenda. Now largely in control of the federal government, this agenda includes major tax cuts for the rich and large corporations. It also entails assaults on affirmative action and labor rights, a rollback of civil liberties and legal protections in the name of "homeland security" and the fight against terrorism, a more aggressive foreign policy, and a general dismantling of welfare state programs that redistribute wealth from capital to working families.[6]

The broader aim of the power elite is the promotion of neoliberal economic policy, especially in terms of pushing for governmental deregulation of industry and reprivatization schemes aimed at "freeing" corporations from "excessive" state intervention. These efforts are complemented by neoconservative social policy, which emphasizes a greater reliance on religious organizations, charities, foundations, nonprofit organizations, and individual volunteers to assume the roles previously performed by the welfare state. By subordinating the regulatory capacities of the state to the economic imperatives of capital and by dismantling the human welfare capacities of the state in favor of the charitable impulses of private institutions, the power elite is reasserting their own interests over those of the labor, civil rights, women's, antiwar, and other social movements.

Acting on the perception that strong environmental regulations are detrimental to the competitiveness of U.S. capital in the new global economy, America's power elite have also unleashed an unrelenting assault on the ecology and environmental justice (EJ) movements. As part of a broader "new class war" against popular social movements, this political attack is being spearheaded by the most environmentally destructive sectors of American business. These corporate polluters and their financial supporters on Wall Street are pouring money into old and new antienvironmental organizations, public relations firms, foundations, think tanks, research centers, and policy institutes as well as the election campaigns of "probusiness" candidates in both major political parties. In fact, the American power structure is now largely controlled by the polluter-industrial complex, or those sectors of business that would stand to profit the most from a weakening of the liberal regime of environmental regulation. These sectors include chemical companies and agribusiness firms seeking to relax rules governing the use of pesticides; logging, oil, and mining companies wanting to open up protected wilderness areas to resource exploitation; and auto manufacturers and big utilities seeking exemptions for clean air regulations. As we shall see, these segments of the polluter-industrial complex are overrepresented among America's ultraconservative power elite.

In order to weaken environmental regulation and to hold the emerging EJ movement in check, the polluter-industrial complex must engage in a series of maneuvers designed to colonize and restructure the state in its favor—to establish a system of "cooperation" among corporate polluters and the U.S. government at all levels. The process of state restructuring has been based on a number of administrative strategies designed to bypass more democratic elements in Congress, the courts, various regulatory agencies, and the larger arena of public opinion. This is being achieved, in large part, by centralizing power in the hands of the executive branch and industry-friendly political appointees at the Environmental Protection Agency (EPA) and the Department of the Interior. In short, the political power of the polluter-industrial complex is being elevated by the evolving structure of the contemporary state, especially the emergence of "independent" regulatory agencies and the reemergence of the imperial presidency.

This chapter focuses on the means by which the corporate power elite in general and the polluter-industrial complex in particular are wielding power over the state apparatus, with a special emphasis on the presidency of George W. Bush.

More specifically, I analyze the processes by which (1) business-friendly political candidates are selected and financially supported; (2) officials aligned with industry are politically appointed to administer key government agencies, including those relating to environmental protection; (3) a vast policymaking infrastructure favorable to environmentally destructive companies is systematically utilized by both major political parties to roll back ecological protection; (4) corporate lobbyists beholden to the polluter-industrial complex are granted extraordinary influence in the halls of government; and (5) the independent scientific investigation of environmental problems has been corrupted by corporate polluters. Together, these processes constitute a network of mechanisms that establish and maintain domination of the state by the power elite, particularly those associated with ecologically destructive corporations. It is the hegemony of the polluter-industrial complex that is responsible for the erosion of environmental justice in the United States.

BUYING ELECTIONS: SUPPORTING CANDIDATES OPPOSED TO ENVIRONMENTAL JUSTICE

The High Costs of Campaigning for Political Office

It is extremely expensive to run for political office in the United States, especially at the federal level. Moreover, these costs are escalating at an alarming rate. Some $4.2 billion was spent in the 2004 federal election, a billion dollars more than was raised in the 2000 election cycle. The 2004 election also saw the cost of winning a House seat average more than a million dollars for the first time in history, while the price of a Senate victory was 50 percent higher than in 2002.[7] And in 2006, New York Senator Hillary Clinton broke fund-raising records by bringing in well over $37.8 million for her successful reelection bid—the equivalent of raising $121,325 every week of the year for six straight years.[8] Similarly, Republican George W. Bush brought in $294 million for his 2004 presidential campaign, while Democratic contender John Kerry raised $252 million. In comparison, George W. Bush accumulated less than half that amount ($126 million) in the 2000 election, while Democrat Al Gore raised a "paltry" $49 million.[9]

The high costs of campaigning mean that gaining access to sufficient financial resources is often the determining factor in whether an individual can even entertain the notion of running for office, let alone win an election. It also translates into political death for most progressive, third-party, and independent candidates who cannot compete at the federal level against the iron triangle of the two-party system, self-funded campaigns by multimillionaires, incumbent self-subsidies, and money provided by wealthy individuals and corporations. As stated by the noted environmental journalist Philip Shabecoff, "Money, more than issues, ideology, the personality or record of candidates and even party affiliation most often determines the victor in electoral campaigns. In a majority of elections, the winner is the candidate who outspends his or her opponent."[10] For instance, in the 2000 Senate races, only two seats were won by lower-spending candidates and just three in 2002.[11] Only in cases where there is deep disapproval of a particular candidate and/or political party is the capacity of such money to tip elections significantly reduced. The 2006 elections were such an instance, where the failures of the Bush administration and the Republican Party with respect to the Iraq War and the fiasco around the government response to Hurricane Katrina in New Orleans and the Gulf coast (as well as a series of other scandals and policy failures) resulted in numerous victories for the Democratic Party.

The Growing Power of Corporate Money in Federal Elections

The soaring costs of elections magnify the political power of corporate capital over that of progressive social movements and popular citizen campaigns that, with the exception of labor, lack similar financial resources. According to the Center for Responsive Politics, the top 100 "organizational" donors provided just over $1 billion to federal candidates and the national political parties from 1989 to 2002. At least 132 candidates received a combined total of $1 million each from this list of contributors. Among these top donors, fifty-one were corporations or business-related political action committees (PACs) or trade associations, including tobacco companies such as Philip Morris and energy giants such as ChevronTexaco and ExxonMobil. Some seventeen of the top donors were also trade and professional associations (representing mostly real estate agents, trial lawyers, and doctors), while twenty-seven donors were made up of large labor unions (such as the United Auto Workers and the International Brotherhood of Electrical Workers). Although the majority of corporate donations went to the Republican Party, 94 percent of the money from labor went to Democratic candidates and party committees. In times of significant mass mobilization, the liberal–labor alliance can serve as a crucial counterbalance to the dominance of corporate cash.[12]

Just below this layer of top 100 donors lay a vast number of other corporate contributors and wealthy individuals whose influence in federal elections is even more pervasive. Although individual contributions accounted for only 34 percent of Al Gore's funds and 52 percent of Bush's funds in the controversial 2000 elections, in 2004 these figures doubled to 69 percent for Democratic candidate John Kerry and accounted for 74 percent of Bush's second war chest. The majority of these individual contributors are conservative, white, wealthy, and male. Roughly 90 percent of the total individual contributions to both Bush and Kerry in the 2004 election came from non-Hispanic white areas, and more than 50 percent of total contributions came from wealthy areas. Communities of color provided only 8.3 percent of Bush contributions and 10.7 percent of Kerry contributions. High-poverty areas fared even worse: 3.6 percent total contributions for Bush and 4.5 percent for Kerry. The statistics demonstrate, as stated by William E. Spriggs of the National Urban League Institute for Opportunity and Equality, "that communities of color and the poor are severely under-represented because of their inability to keep pace with the campaign contributions from wealthier, non-minority communities."[13] Financial disparities of this sort help to explain why elected officials devote so much energy on implementing tax cuts for the wealthy and so little attention to issues of affordable housing, decent jobs, and environmental justice for working-class whites and people of color.

The jump in contribution dollars from wealthy individuals is attributable to a number of loopholes recently created by the Bipartisan Campaign Reform Act of 2002, better known as the McCain-Feingold Reform Act. Under this legislation, "hard-money" limits on individual contributions to candidates were raised from $1,000 to $2,000 per election (primary and general, or $4,000 total), effectively doubling the influence of wealthy donors. Individuals are now allowed to contribute as much as $95,000 per election cycle. Up to $57,500 per election cycle can be donated to all national party committees and PACs.[14] "The dirty little secret" of American politics in 2004 was the increased importance of the "big-dollar check writers" to the fortunes of both the Republican and the Democratic parties. For instance, in the 2000 election, small donors (those giving $200 or less) gave $58.8 million out of a total $110.8 million raised from individuals by the Democratic National Committee. In 2004, however, small donors provided $165.2 million out of $356.6 million in total contributions to the Democratic National Committee. In other words, even though the overall amount of small contributions went up, they declined in importance relative to those of wealthy donors.[15] This growing influence of the wealthy was jokingly acknowledged by George W. Bush during the 2000 election at the Alfred E. Smith memorial dinner, a high-society fund-raiser for Catholic charities, when he stated, "This is an impressive crowd—the haves and have-mores. Some people call you the elite. I call you my base."[16]

Under the current electoral system, therefore, the public and private discourses around various election issues, policy debates, and the platforms of candidates and parties themselves are skewed in favor of those corporate executives and wealthy elites that fund campaigns. As the premier investors in American politics, they enjoy greater political access (meetings with candidates at fund-raising dinners) and special privileges (overnight stays in the Lincoln Bedroom of the White House) that are denied to ordinary citizens. As a result, the power elite largely dominates the political agendas of both the Republican and the Democratic parties.

The Polluter-Industrial Complex and Funding Antienvironmental Candidates

The biggest corporate contributors to elections are those dependent on government contracts or those who want to protect profits by minimizing the impacts of costly government regulations, "like the securities and energy sectors, as well as everyone from tobacco to those on the receiving end of asbestos lawsuits."[17] Among the larger and more important corporate contributors were companies associated with the polluter-industrial complex—including electric utilities, oil and gas companies, airline and automobile industries, crop production, and chemical manufacturers. These industries provided $41.5 million to congressional candidates during the 2005–2006 election cycle.[18] As stated in a recent U.S. PIRG Education Fund report,

> Under current campaign finance laws, the most direct and effective strategy to influence the political process, for those who can afford it, is to help elect politicians who are receptive to one's interests. While campaign contributions may provide access to and influence over decision-makers, they more importantly help determine who is elected in the first place. Thus it is not simply a matter of electric utilities, the oil industry, manufacturers, and other polluters influencing the decisions that politicians make, but these interests increasingly ensure that politicians who are elected agree with, and actively support, their agendas.[19]

To combat the rise of the environmental and EJ movements, individual owners and company executives, PACs, and corporations affiliated with the polluter-industrial complex channel their enormous resources into the campaigns of favored candidates. Some 267 of the "dirty-water PACs"—so named because of their antienvironmental agenda—contributed $57 million to political candidates between 1989 and 1994. Dow Chemical (and its subsidiaries Destec and Dowelanco) and Dow Corning alone had a total of fourteen affiliated PACs, which gave over $1.2 million to congressional candidates.[20] Moreover, the influence of these "polluter PACs" has grown in recent years, especially in Congress. Since 2000, PACs have consistently provided around 40 percent of the total contributions in the House of Representatives and just under a quarter of total campaign funds in the Senate. In the 2004 election alone, PACs donated over $310 million to federal candidates.[21] Environmentally oriented PACs spent just a little over $2 million between 2000

and 2006—an average of only \$333,400 a year. In contrast, the polluter-
industrial complex has donated at least \$49 million in each election cycle
since 2000, with 70 percent of that money going to Republican candidates.[22]

A recent U.S. PIRG Education Fund report exposes the true extent of the assault on public health and environmental protection by the polluter-industrial
complex. Each of the eighteen trade associations analyzed in the report are
core organizational components of the polluter-industrial complex and include
the National Association of Manufacturers, the U.S. Chamber of Commerce,
the Alliance of Automobile Manufacturers, the American Chemistry Council,
the American Forest and Paper Association, the National Mining Association,
and the National Petrochemical and Refiners Association. Each trade association actively supports the rollback of one or more key air quality regulations.
To achieve this goal, the report finds that the associations and select member
companies made \$53 million in PAC contributions to federal candidates in the
three election cycles between 1997 and 2002.[23] The largest campaign contributors were also among the country's worst polluters.

A top recipient of these campaign funds in the House is Representative
John Dingell, the highest-ranking Democrat and current chairman of the powerful House Energy and Commerce Committee. This committee is responsible for energy and environmental policy. Dingell is a longtime champion of
the automobile industry who has vehemently opposed higher fuel standards
and other pollution/safety controls on industry. The Michigan Democrat is
also an outspoken opponent of the new House Select Committee on Energy
Independence and Global Warming created by House Speaker Nancy Pelosi
in 2007. Pelosi initiated the new committee in order to circumvent the power
of Dingell and a committee "captured" by the polluter-industrial complex to
thwart the regulatory progress. Interestingly, Dingell's wife, Deborah, is a top
lobbyist for General Motors. The new committee is expected to push for
tougher regulations on auto emissions, higher fuel economy standards,
mandatory emission caps on U.S. industry, and new approaches to slowing
the pace of global warming. In a concession to the power of the polluter-
industrial complex, however, the new committee will not have the power to
draft legislation, which means that all the panel's recommendations must
work their way through other committees (including Dingell's) before they
can reach the House floor.

Another top recipient of these campaign funds is Senator James M. Inhofe,
an Oklahoma Republican. As Chair of the Environment and Public Works
Committee, Inhofe received the second-largest amount of money of any Senate member. A staunch antienvironmentalist who recently dismissed global
warming as "the greatest hoax ever perpetrated on the American people," Inhofe has attempted to use his power as committee chair to discredit and in-

timidate scientists and environmental officials. On January 26, 2005, John Paul testified before the committee on behalf of the State and Territorial Air Pollution Program Administrators, representing forty-eight state air pollution control agencies, as well as the Association of Local Air Pollution Control Officials, which represents about 165 local agencies. Paul's testimony was critical of a Bush administration initiative (inappropriately termed "Clear Skies") that would significantly compromise the EPA's ability to regulate air pollution from power plants. Paul stated that the proposal "fails on every one of our associations' core principals," was "far too lenient" on polluters, and would undermine "states' abilities to protect air quality." Inhofe retaliated against Paul for his testimony by taking the unprecedented step of demanding the financial statements, membership lists, and tax returns of both groups for the previous six years.[24] More recently, in a dismissal of EJ considerations, Inhofe also introduced his "Domestic Fuels Security Act" amendment to a bill on the Senate floor in March 2007. The amendment promotes the development of a highly profitable domestic coal-to-liquids industry (which "squeezes" oil from coal) by providing loan guarantees and encouraging the construction of environmentally damaging refineries on lands occupied by Indian tribes.

As demonstrated previously, campaign funds distributed by the polluter-industrial complex are done so strategically, targeting industry enemies for defeat and allies for victory (especially those sitting on key regulatory committees).[25] While corporate polluters will support neoliberals in Congress from both political parties, George W. Bush and the Republican Party are clearly favored as being more "probusiness" and "anti–environmental regulation."[26] As uncovered in a recent Earthjustice/Public Campaign report, one out of every three dollars contributed by the polluter-industrial complex (mining, oil and gas, timber, chemical companies, coal-burning utilities, and manufacturers) to all federal candidates and party committees between 1999 and 2002 was invested in the Bush–Cheney ticket and the Republican National Committee. This is more money than was contributed to all federal Democratic candidates and party committees combined. In all, the Bush–Cheney 2000 campaign and the Republican National Committee received more than $44 million in contributions from the polluter-industrial complex, including $16.97 million from the oil and gas industry and $18.61 million from the chemical and manufacturing industries.[27] In stark contrast to the millions of dollars received by the Bush campaign, the 2000 presidential campaign of self-described environmentalist Al Gore received just $309,575 from agribusiness, $340,114 from energy and natural resources, and only $337,705 from transportation-related PACs and wealthy individuals.[28] George W. Bush was clearly the favored candidate of America's worst polluters.

Corporate Polluters and the Bush–Cheney Campaign

The election and reelection of President Bush illustrates the effectiveness of the candidate selection process as a tool employed by the power elite to colonize the state. In many ways, this was a process of self-selection, as both Bush and Dick Cheney themselves were important players *within* America's polluter-industrial complex. Bush utilized his family connections to enter the oil business. In 1989, he invested $606,000 in part of a syndicate that bought the Texas Rangers baseball team by borrowing and repaying the loan with money earned from selling shares of his Harken Energy Company stock for a handsome price shortly before the company's financial collapse. Bush later convinced the city of Arlington to build the Rangers a new stadium with public funds, and his popularity as owner allowed him to run for governor of Texas and win (after his election, Bush sold his share in the Rangers for $14.9 million).[29] As governor, Bush worked to continually weaken state environmental laws to the benefit of Texas industry, particularly the oil companies. In fact, Texas was the worst state in the nation for total air, water, and land releases of carcinogenic pollution.[30]

Similarly, prior to becoming vice president, Dick Cheney was chief executive officer of Halliburton Inc., a giant oil field services firm. One of the worst violators of environmental health in the United States, Halliburton was forced to settle 207,000 asbestos-related claims between 1976 and 2002 at a cost of $162 million. The cost of resolving future claims is expected to be hundreds of millions of dollars. Asbestos fibers can lead to respiratory diseases and various types of cancer, including mesothelioma, a deadly type of cancer that affects the area around the lungs and abdomen.[31] As Halliburton's chief executive officer, Cheney earned $45 million in just five years, with at least another $18 million in stock options.

Cheney was also a board member of Hunt Oil Company, Procter & Gamble, and TRW. After becoming vice president, Cheney and his wife held assets of at least $20 million and possibly as much as $69 million. Lynne Cheney works at the American Enterprise Institute, a right-wing Washington think tank promoting less environmental regulation, and sits on several corporate boards, including American Express. Among the provisions in the Bush–Cheney 2004 energy bill is an environmental exemption for a method of gas drilling invented by Halliburton that prevents the EPA from regulating it under the Safe Drinking Water Act. The exemption overturned a federal appeals court decision in Alabama that stated that hydraulic fracturing should be regulated under the Safe Drinking Water Act. In hydraulic fracturing, chemicals, diesel fuel, hydrochloric acid, and other agents are injected into the ground in order to more cheaply extract oil and gas. This process can also result in the contamination of drinking water. Halliburton is a major beneficiary of Cheney's proposal since about 5 percent of the company's $12 billion total business is done by hydraulic fracturing.[32]

It is not surprising then that the Bush–Cheney administration would select oil company executives to fill out the president's cabinet. Prior to her selection as national security adviser and then secretary of state, Condoleezza Rice served on Chevron's board and was a policy expert on securing oil from the Caspian Sea region. For her service to the company, a 130,000-ton oil tanker was named the *Condoleezza Rice*. Rice's financial assets at the time of her appointment included $240,000 in Chevron stock. Kathleen B. Cooper, undersecretary of commerce for economic affairs, was formerly the chief economist and manager of the economic and energy division of ExxonMobil, while Nicholas Calio, assistant to the president for legislative affairs, was a former lobbyist for Arco, an oil company that recently merged with BP. Patrick H. Wood III served as chairman of the Federal Energy Regulatory Commission and worked for Arco Indonesia until 1995.[33]

The Bush–Cheney campaign tapped into their networks within the polluter-industrial complex to secure additional campaign funds through *bundling*. Encouraged by the McCain-Feingold Reform Act, bundling is the practice whereby an individual "bundler" sympathetic to the campaign solicits and pools together a large number of contributions from other individuals and PACs. For instance, Bush–Cheney raised $262 million in the 2004 primary elections. Of this total, between $76.5 and $100 million came from just 548 bundlers—221 "Rangers" (individuals who raised at least $200,000 each from other sources) and 327 "Pioneers" (individuals who raised at least $100,000 each).[34] Many of those individuals pledging to raise money for Bush's Pioneer or Ranger programs in the 2000 and 2004 presidential campaigns were representatives of some of the worst-polluting utilities and energy companies in the country.

According to a recent report from the Environmental Integrity Project and Public Citizen, the thirty largest utility companies owning the majority of the eighty-nine dirtiest power plants in the country have contributed $6.6 million into the coffers of the Bush presidential campaigns and the Republican National Committee. Since 1999, these companies and one of their trade associations, the Edison Electric Institute, have also produced ten Rangers and Pioneers. In addition, these companies hired at least sixteen lobbying or law firms with twenty-three Rangers or Pioneers (who raised a total of a least $3.4 million for the Bush campaigns). These firms, together with the private utility industry's trade associations, eventually met with Vice President Cheney's secret energy task force at least seventeen times to help formulate the country's energy and pollution policies. The recommendations of that task force led directly to the EPA's reassessment and rewriting of the Clean Air Act rule that the utilities had been accused of violating.[35] As the nation's top polluters as measured in terms of mercury, sulfur dioxide, and carbon dioxide emissions, the owners of these power plants have a significant financial stake in weakening environmental regulations.[36] A recent study estimated that 30,000 people die prematurely because of pollution from power plants. Some 18,000 of these deaths could be prevented if these plants installed costly but effective pollution control systems.[37]

One of these Bush bundlers was Southern Company Executive Vice President Dwight Evans. As a member of President Bush's Ranger program, Evans pledged to raise $200,000 for Bush in the 2004 election cycle. In 2002, Southern's plants emitted nearly 1 million tons of soot-forming sulfur dioxide, 300,000 tons of smog-forming nitrogen oxide, and more than 165 million tons of carbon dioxide (the equivalent of what 24.5 million cars would produce in a year) and was among the country's worst polluters. Another utility executive, Thomas Kuhn, president of the Edison Electric Institute, was a Pioneer for the Bush campaign in 2000 and 2004. Edison Electric Institute is the most prominent trade association representing the electric utility sector, including the five biggest polluters—American Electric Power, Southern Company, Cinergy, Xcel, and TXU. As a reward for his fund-raising efforts, Kuhn was granted a position on the Bush 2000 transition team that formulated the incoming administration's energy policy. He met at least fourteen times with Vice President Cheney's secret energy task force. The Cheney task force eventually proposed policies that have undermined the public health and environmental safeguards in the Clean Air Act to the benefit of the companies that Kuhn represents. In all, nine out of ten of Bush's bundlers are associated with corporate interests, with many of them having a major stake in decisions made by the federal government around environmental policy, including agency appointments, regulatory actions, contracts, and legislative proposals.[38]

By channeling significant resources to key neoliberal candidates opposed to government regulation, the polluter-industrial complex has now achieved a level of political influence that is perhaps unmatched by any other sector of capital in the United States. Polluting industries are strategically spreading money into all sorts of key races, helping to determine who runs for office in the first place as well as who wins and what issues come up for debate. And although these funds have gone to members of both political parties, it is clear that the two-time election of President Bush represents the culmination of such efforts. The industry patronage has paid off handsomely, resulting in the "buying" of elections. Accordingly, the Bush administration has remolded the state in a manner that increases corporate accessibility and reduces public accountability and has resulted in scores of policies designed to cripple environmental protection, public health, and social justice. Attempts to weaken environmental safeguards are so pervasive, concludes an association of public research interest groups, "that it can only be accounted for by a conscious administration-wide intent to enrich corporations at the expense of ordinary citizens and the environment."[39] The Bush administration is devoted to weakening environmental laws to reward those industries that paid to put it in office.

APPOINTING CORPORATE POLLUTERS TO ADMINISTER ENVIRONMENTAL AGENCIES

Corporate Foxes Guarding the Environmental Henhouse

The neoliberal assault on environmental regulation is predicated on the ability of the capitalist class to gain positional control of the state, especially to the degree that the power elite associated with polluting industries gains decision-making authority over key environmental agencies and offices. The polluter-industrial complex has established such control not only by supporting "business-friendly" political candidates but also by ensuring that politicians, once elected, select industry-related "political appointees" to run government agencies. Out of 1.8 million federal employees, there are some 3,000 political appointees running the federal bureaucracy.[40] These appointees include not only the owners and chief executive officers of environmentally destructive corporations and financial institutions but also those lawyers, lobbyists, policy analysts, academics, and other officials working on behalf of these same companies.[41] Colonization of these "independent" administrative and regulatory agencies is especially important, as these institutions are capable of exerting broad authority in the drafting, implementation, and enforcement of preexisting and/or new environmental policy initiatives. It is also the most "fail-safe" manner of colonizing the state. As stated by the late journalist Molly Ivins, "Why hire lobbyists when your CEOs [chief executive officers] and board members are running the show?"[42]

Corporate control over the executive branch is especially important since the president is responsible for selecting government appointees (including federal judges). And perhaps no other president in recent history owes as much of their political success to the support provided by the polluter-industrial complex as does President Bush. The Bush administration is clearly committed to weakening environmental laws in order to help those industries that paid to put it in office. The administration has filled key behind-the-scenes jobs with lawyers and lobbyists plucked from the industries they now regulate. Long-serving civil servants have been pushed aside by having their traditional roles redefined as "political jobs" and embedding hidden political appointees in their career slots. Bush has also demoted or excluded civil servants from decision making on an unprecedented scale. By junking a 100-year-old system of merit-based hiring for career bureaucrats, entire generations of government managers and staff loyal to their agency's mission are being systematically replaced. People who have spent their professional careers seeking to dismantle or circumvent environmental rules on behalf of the polluter-industrial complex are now overseeing the nation's most powerful environmental agencies. The corporate foxes are in charge of guarding the government henhouse and are leading the assault on environmental/EJ policy.

Perhaps the most valuable henhouse is the Department of the Interior, the federal government's principal conservation agency. This department manages over 500 million acres, about one-fifth of the land in the United States. It houses the U.S. Fish and Wildlife Service, the National Park Service, the U.S. Geological Survey, the Bureau of Reclamation, the Bureau of Land Management, the Bureau of Indian Affairs, the Office of Surface Mining, and the Minerals Management Service.

Under President Bush, industry "foxes" are running the Interior Department and its various services. In July 2001, for instance, the administration selected Stephen Griles to serve as deputy interior secretary. Prior to joining Interior as second in command, Griles was a coal company executive and lobbyist for mining and energy interests. Despite an obvious conflict of interest, Deputy Secretary Griles continued to receive hundreds of thousands of dollars in "compensation" from National Environmental Strategies, his former lobbying firm that represents mining interests. As the point man for the industry, Griles spearheaded the effort to weaken environmental enforcement at Interior. After leaving the office in January 2005, he returned to work as an oil and gas lobbyist.

In response to allegations of ethics violations around Griles, the House Oversight and Government Reform Committee initiated an investigation in February 2007. The investigation focused on the government's top environmental prosecutor, Sue Ellen Wooldridge; Griles; and a major lobbyist for ConocoPhillips, Vice President Donald R. Duncan. Griles began dating Wooldridge while working as her boss at Interior. Wooldridge was later appointed by President Bush as Interior's top lawyer in June 2004 and then as head of the Justice Department's environment division. Representing virtually every federal agency, Woodridge assumed the most important environmental enforcement position in the government. In November 2005, Griles, Duncan, and Wooldridge bought a $1 million vacation home together on Kiawah Island, South Carolina. Nine months prior to the joint purchase of the home, Wooldridge signed two proposed consent decrees with ConocoPhillips, one delaying the installation of $525 million in pollution controls at nine refineries as required under the Clean Air Act. The other decree dealt with a Superfund toxic waste cleanup in Elkton, Maryland. Wooldridge resigned shortly thereafter in January 2007.[43]

The Bush administration also appointed Gale Norton to serve as secretary of the interior. Norton's career started in 1979 when she was hired by the Mountain States Legal Foundation, an antienvironmental group funded by oil, gas, coal, and utility companies with major holdings in the West and leases on federal resources. In 1983, Norton transferred to the Hoover Institution, a right-wing policy center at Stanford University, where she advocated for market-based approaches to controlling air pollution. She also served on the advisory boards of two other right-wing organizations pushing for a rollback of federal environmental laws—the Defenders of Property Rights and the Washington Legal Foundation.

Between 1991 and 1998, Norton served as Colorado attorney general, and she pushed programs of "voluntary compliance" with environmental safeguards for industrial polluters. An active advocate for capitalist "property rights" and "takings" legislation, whereby government agencies compensate developers and industries when environmental laws and regulations limit their real or future profits, Norton opposed the Endangered Species Act and led efforts to promote the access of large agribusiness operations to cheap federal water. After leaving office, she founded a national group called the Council of Republicans for Environmental Advocacy (CREA), an organization designed to enhance the public image of Republicans with bad environmental voting records. The formation of CREA undercut Republicans for Environmental Protection, which was considered by ultraconservatives among the power elite to be too accommodating of environmentalism. As national chairwoman of the CREA, Norton lobbied for a weakening of national environmental laws. The council was funded by such corporate entities as the American Forest Paper Association, Amoco, Arco, Ford, and the Chemical Manufacturers Association.

In 1999, Norton went to work for Brownstein, Hyatt, Farber & Strickland, a Denver-based law firm representing a range of antienvironmental clients, including the probusiness Colorado Civil Justice League, which seeks to protect builders of defective houses from home-owner lawsuits. The law firm was also listed with Congress as a lobbyist for NL Industries (formerly known as National Lead), which is named as a defendant in suits involving several dozen toxic waste sites. NL is being sued by parents of lead-poisoned children in Cleveland, New Orleans, New York, and other cities. As a lobbyist with the firm, Norton worked to "immunize" NL Industries against lead paint issues. Lead exposure is one of the most significant EJ issues in the nation.

Children who are exposed to lead through paint dust or who ingest it by eating paint chips can suffer brain damage and sometimes blindness and hearing loss. Since 1989, New York City and other cities have tried to get NL to pay for removing lead paint from various housing projects.[44] In 2001, Norton's law firm lobbied in Washington for forty-five other clients, including a number of oil and chemical companies involved in direct dealings with the Interior Department. Norton also helped Alaska challenge an Interior Department fisheries law, publicly declared the Endangered Species Act to be unconstitutional, wrote legal opinions against the National Environmental Policy Act, and unsuccessfully argued that the Surface Mining Control Law—a piece of legislation protecting communities from the hazards of coal mining—was unconstitutional.

Norton was sworn in as interior secretary on January 2001 and resigned on March 16, 2006. Her time at Interior was marked by constant controversy, given her brazen attempts to benefit industry at the expense of the environment. Norton even went so far as to post a propaganda piece developed by Arctic Power, a group that lobbies for oil drilling in the Arctic Refuge, on the agency's website and distribute it to network television anchors.[45] Only a few months after her resignation, Norton accepted an offer to serve as counsel for Royal Dutch Shell's unconventional resources division (unconventional resources pertains to emerging technology that targets such resources as oil shale and extra-heavy oil). The Colorado plateau—much of it on land administered by Interior—contains one of the world's largest deposits of oil shale. During Norton's tenure at Interior, rules pertaining to the permitting of oil and gas were eased, allowing the Bureau of Land Management to speed up the leasing process for natural gas extraction in controversial areas like the Jonah Field and Pinedale Anticline in the upper Green River basin of Wyoming. Despite record profits for the oil companies, Interior also waived royalty payments assessed against private oil companies for two years running pertaining to oil leases in the Gulf of Mexico, where Shell is a major player. The Government Accountability Office reported that lost royalties amounted to $10 billion for American taxpayers.[46] In recent years, Shell has recorded record profits—$22.9 billion in 2005 alone—yet has drawn condemnation from poor communities of color for refusing to address the myriad social and environmental problems created by its operations.[47]

The Revolving Door at the EPA

Key political appointments to the EPA are also dominated by lobbyists, lawyers, politicians, or scientists who have worked for the polluter-industrial complex. In fact, there has been a continuous "revolving door" between the polluter-industrial complex and the leadership of the EPA since the formation of the agency. For instance, William Ruckelshaus served as the first EPA administrator under President Nixon (1971–1973) and once again under President Ronald Reagan (1983–1985). After leaving the EPA in 1973, Ruckelshaus became senior vice president and director of Weyerhaeuser, the giant timber company and common foe of the environmental movement.

Ruckelshaus served as director for a number of other highly polluting companies between and after his two terms at the EPA, including Monsanto, Cummins Engine Company, Pacific Gas Transmission, and the American Paper Institute. He also formed a consulting firm after leaving the Reagan administration called William D. Ruckelshaus Associates. This firm was soon hired by the industry-funded Coalition on Superfund to "weaken the Superfund law by absolving polluters of strict legal liability for their actions. The coalition included such Superfund polluters and their insurers as Monsanto, Occidental Petroleum, Alcoa, Flow Chemical, AT&T, DuPont, Union Carbide, Aetna Insurance, and Travelers Insurance."[48] The head of the Conservation Foundation, William Reilly, received funding (with the help of Ruckelshaus) to produce studies in support of the Coalition on Superfund. He would be rewarded for his services by being selected to serve as EPA administrator under President George H. W. Bush from 1989 to 1992. Former Ruckelshaus Associate Vice President Henry Habicht was selected to serve as deputy EPA administrator. Under the leadership of Reilly and Habicht at the EPA, gross racial disparities with respect to the enforcement of Superfund regulations were rampant. Government penalties for violations of hazardous waste laws in communities of color were only one-sixth ($55,318) the average fine ($335,566) in white communities. Dumps in communities of color also took 20 percent longer to make the National Priorities List, or Superfund list.[49] The EPA attempts to undermine Superfund by Bush appointees continue in the new millennium.

As chief executive officer of Browning-Ferris Industries (BFI) from 1988 to 1995, Ruckelshaus earned a salary of more than $1 million a year. One of the largest waste management companies in the United States at the time of his hiring, BFI was earning enormous profits (more than $1.6 billion alone in 1986) through an industry-wide modus operandi described by environmentalists to be "based on bribery, pricefixing, political payoffs, back door campaign contributions, the intimidation and suppression of business competition, the distortion and manipulation of technical data, and the systematic violation of environmental laws and regulations."[50] In 1987, for instance, government investigators reported more than 2,800 violations of the Resource Conservation and Recovery Act at a BFI hazardous waste facility in Livingston, Louisiana.[51] Under the leadership of Ruckelshaus, BFI kept costs

down and profits high by locating the more dangerous facilities in neighborhoods of color within such cities as Birmingham,[52] San Antonio, Houston,
and other poor communities.[53] Practices of "environmental racism" by BFI,
Chemical Waste Management, and other "titans of waste" became rampant in
the 1980s and 1990s and fueled the growth of the EJ movement.[54] The environmental injustices perpetuated by these corporations were made easy by the
placement of company officials at key positions throughout the entire EPA
bureaucracy.[55]

President George W. Bush selected Christine Todd Whitman to serve as his
first EPA administrator. Although portrayed by herself and in the media as a
strong advocate for traditional environmental policy,[56] Whitman was a key
point person in the corporate attack on environmentalism. As governor of New
Jersey, Whitman eviscerated environmental protection efforts in that state. In
her first three years in office, Whitman dismantled state environmental regulations, decreased the state Department of Environmental Protection staff by
738 employees, eliminated fines on polluters as a source of department revenue, and made large cuts in the agency's budget. An extensive investigation
of her administration by the Bergen County *Record* detailed dozens of cases in
which Whitman's policies circumvented laws designed to protect the environment, particularly those affiliated with big campaign contributors.[57]

As EPA administrator, Whitman continued her efforts to rewrite the rules
and weaken the agency's capacity to address environmental injustices. Nevertheless, she did lock horns with the ultraconservatives of the power elite in
the Bush administration around some issues, including global warming. She
eventually resigned from the administration to become cochair of the Clean
and Safe Energy Coalition, an industry front group that raises "awareness of
the benefits of clean and safe nuclear energy" and builds "policymaker and
public support for nuclear energy as a component of a comprehensive plan
to meet America's future electricity needs."[58] Despite her support for nuclear
power as an alternative to fossil fuels and a "solution" to global warming,
Whitman owns 853 acres of oil-producing property in Jim Hogg County,
Texas, and Hunt Oil Company oil wells. While serving as EPA administrator, she had tens of thousands of dollars of investments in BP Amoco,
Chevron, ExxonMobil, Halliburton, Newmont Mining, Phillips Petroleum,
and other members of the polluter-industrial complex. In summary, virtually
every high-level environmental appointee in the Bush administration is in-
tertwined with America's polluter-industrial complex.

Appointees Wrecking Environmental Policy "under the Radar"

Beyond the selection of more highly visible figures to serve as agency heads,
antienvironmentalists are also appointed to key "under-the-radar" positions

within the federal bureaucracy.[59] These appointees are often tied directly to major campaign contributors from polluting industries and can have a profound impact on the day-to-day operations of regulatory agencies. As such, these appointees owe their careers as corporate executives, lawyers, and lobbyists to the same polluter-industrial complex that they are now charged with regulating. As second-tier appointees working in the lower rungs of power as deputy secretaries and assistant administrators, however, they often have a deeper understanding of which rules and regulations need to be weakened or eliminated. This is because they have been fighting these same rules on behalf of industry for many years. A 2004 study by the Center for American Progress and OMB Watch found that "executives from a wide spectrum of industries and trade associations now hold powerful, policy-setting positions throughout the Bush Administration—positions they have quickly turned to the benefit of the industries and corporations they previously managed." The result? Relaxed enforcement of regulations; greatly increased government secrecy, including a clampdown on granting public and congressional requests for information; and the suppression and distortion of scientific information whenever it appears at odds with the administration's goals.[60]

Jeffrey Holmstead was such a lower-level appointee. Before becoming the EPA's assistant administrator of air and radiation under President Bush, Holmstead worked for Lathan & Watkins, a Washington corporate law firm specializing in representing environmental polluters. His clients included Sempra Energy and Clean Air Future, an industry group advocating for a weakening of clean air laws. As a government official, Holmstead worked to weaken EPA rules and enforcement to the benefit of business. He even gave false testimony to Congress about the EPA's assessment on how new air pollution rules adopted by the administration would hamper government lawsuits against corporate polluters. The companies targeted under the old rules were the same polluters his firm used to represent. Holmstead was joined at the EPA by two colleagues from his old firm. William Wehrum, a leading architect of the newly weakened air pollution rules, formerly specialized in "clean air matters" at Latham & Watkins. So did Linda J. Fisher, who became the deputy administrator of the EPA. Wehrum replaced Holmstead in 2005 when he resigned and was the lead author of the ill-fated "Clear Skies" legislation designed to weaken air pollution controls on industry.

President Bush also selected Mark Rey for the job of undersecretary of natural resources and environment at the U.S. Department of Agriculture, a position responsible for the management of 156 national forests, twenty national grasslands, and fifteen land utilization projects on 191 million acres in forty-four states. For almost two decades, Rey had worked for a number of timber trade associations, including the National Forest Products Association, the American Paper Institute, and the American Forest Resources Alliance. In fact, Rey was the timber industry's lead lobbyist in fighting the creation of the Northwest Forest Plan as well as in fending off legislative efforts to protect old growth in the region.[61] At the same time, Rebecca Watson was selected as assistant secretary for land management at Interior. Watson was a partner in a Montana law firm that represented mining interests, coming from a previous job with the American Forest and Paper Group. In the mid-1990s, she represented a Montana business group fighting an initiative requiring mining companies to remove carcinogens from their discharges. She also represented Montana businesses (unsuccessfully) in a 1999 court case that challenged language in the state constitution guaranteeing a clean and healthy environment.

Representatives of chemical companies and pesticide manufacturers also typically hold a number of powerful positions within federal environmental regulatory agencies. Prior to serving in the EPA's number two position, for instance, EPA Deputy Administrator Linda Fisher was Monsanto's vice president for government and public affairs and managed the company's PAC and political contibution funds. Another official, Adam Sharp, the associate assistant administrator in the Office of Prevention, Pesticides, and Toxic Substances, previously worked for the American Farm Bureau Federation, where he challenged EPA programs assessing pesticide risks for children.[62] Furthermore, a lawsuit launched by environmentalists in 2004 asserted that the Bush administration allowed a special chemical industry task force to lobby secretly and illegally inside the EPA in order to circumvent current protections for endangered species. The lawsuit alleged that the task force, known as the FIFRA Endangered Species Task Force, representing Monsanto and thirteen other agrochemical companies, met regularly in secret with EPA officials in violation of the Federal Advisory Committee Act. The industry strategy, according to internal documents obtained through the Freedom of Information Act, was to eliminate the role of biologists with the U.S. Fish and Wildlife Service and NOAA Fisheries to serve as oversight experts in determining whether a pesticide poses a risk to wildlife.[63]

The prevalence of Monsanto officials in the federal government is symptomatic of the manner in which the polluter-industrial complex has colonized the state bureaucracy under the administration of President Bush. Larry Thompson, the deputy attorney general, had previously served as Monsanto's in-house counsel. Ann M. Veneman served as secretary of agriculture and was formerly a lawyer with a firm specializing in representing agribusiness giants and biotech corporations. She was also on the Board of Directors of Calgene Inc., a subsidiary of Monsanto, a maker of polychlorinated biphenyls (one of the most damaging chemical pollutants ever created), bovine growth hormone, terminator seeds (which prevent farmers from growing their own seed stocks), and questionable genetically altered food products. The secretary further participated in the International Policy Council of Agriculture, Food, and Trade, funded by Monsanto, Cargill, Archer Daniels Midland, Kraft, and Nestlé (Perrier). Even Supreme Court Justice Clarence Thomas was a former lawyer for Monsanto Corporation. Under the Bush administration, it appears that working for Monsanto is the best way of being appointed to an important position in the federal government.

BUILDING A MOVEMENT FROM THE TOP DOWN: CREATING A POLICY INFRASTRUCTURE THAT PAYS FOR THE POLLUTER-INDUSTRIAL COMPLEX

Reshaping Public Opinion

Over the past three decades, the political capacity of the polluter-industrial complex has grown through the expansion of a sophisticated national public policy infrastructure made up of think tanks, research centers, policy institutes, foundations, academic institutions and training programs, media and judicial watchdogs, and public relations firms. This infrastructure works to reshape public opinion from the top down and provide policy recommendations and political strategies to government officials, recruit and train new leaders and intellectuals for the conservative movement, and mobilize core constituencies to influence policy. It also serves to apply sustained political pressure on the media, colleges and universities, the federal judiciary, foundations and state funding agencies, scientific organizations, and other social institutions.[64] The interconnected organizations that make up this network are united in their demands for neoliberal economic policies designed to deregulate and reprivatize the economy ("liberalize" or "free" the market of costly state regulation of industry) in the hope of boosting economic growth and profits. Walter Dean Burnham terms this political moment the hegemony of market theology.[65]

In the United States, corporate-sponsored think tanks and policy institutes play a particularly important role in moving international, national, and state public policy priorities to the right. In contrast to lobbying efforts by individual companies or specific trade associations, policy planning institutions serve as the place where various owners and chief executive officers of corporate America in general and the polluter-industrial complex in particular transcend their narrower interest-group approaches to develop a fuller conception of their overall class interests.[66] Enlisting the services of academic advisers, conservative intellectuals, scientists and lawyers, and other "technical" experts, these think tanks bring together the inner circles of the capitalist and manage-rial classes to serve as a leadership group (or power elite) on behalf of Amer-ican capital. As a result, there are extensive interlocking members among the boards, trustees, directors, and other key positions in large polluting corpora-tions, think tanks, foundations, research centers, policy planning groups, banks and financial institutions, and federal advisory committees.[67] ExxonMobil, for instance, has numerous officials serving in this policy infrastructure.[68] A report by the Union of Concerned Scientists shows that between 1998 and 2005, ExxonMobil donated $16 million to a mixture of think tanks and opinion-in-fluencing organizations with the expressed goal (as stated in internal company memos) of casting doubt on the claims of the scientific community that fossil fuels cause global warming. Many of the organizations funded by ExxonMo-bil have overlapping boards of directors that are part of the corporate elite.[69] In fact, well over 80 percent of the nearly 300 directorships for business pol-icy organizations and think tanks such as the American Enterprise Institute, the Brookings Institute, the Business Roundtable, and the Hoover Institute are cor-porate leaders.[70]

The influence of these think tanks is heightened by the fact that the Dem-ocratic and Republican parties do not have their own policy research units. In contrast to much of Europe and other advanced industrial nations, where pol-icy research and advocacy functions are undertaken by organized political parties, politicians in the United States are almost completely dependent on the expertise provided by private policy institutions and networks. In addi-tion, think tanks serve as a "revolving door" for the power elite and polluter-industrial complex—providing the personnel for the rush of political ap-pointments that come with each new administration and also providing a refuge for discarded government officials.[71] Policy institutes are a frequent meeting point for the power elite—a place where past, present, and future policy analysts, high-ranking government officials, business leaders and chief executive officers, intellectuals, journalists, and conservative activists come together to develop a political vision and strategy.

Although there are a small number of liberal think tanks in the United States, their influence has waned in recent years in comparison to corporate-supported neoliberal institutions serving both the Democratic and Republican Party establishments. For instance, the Democratic Leadership Council (DLC) has included Al Gore, Joseph Lieberman, and cofounder Bill Clinton and is at the center of a web of think tanks, lobbying groups, and electoral activity de-signed to create a more business-friendly Democratic Party. The DLC-tied Progressive Policy Institute has become a prime proponent of the U.S. Cham-ber of Commerce line on globalization and a cheerleader for the World Trade Organization and efforts to discredit critics of corporate-designed trade liberalization.[72] Think tanks committed to neoliberal economic policy and neoconservative social policy have also proven instrumental to the rise of the New Right and Republican Party in recent years. This conservative policy infrastructure is firmly anchored in sectors of capital represented by the National Association of Manufacturers, the U.S. Chamber of Commerce, and many smaller and medium-sized corporations and family businesses. It is especially supported by those polluting corporations most deeply impacted by environmental regulations.

Think Tanks and Policy Institutes against Environmental Justice

The corporations that make up the polluter-industrial complex have utilized think tanks to further their neoliberal political agenda in a number of different ways. For instance, think tanks serve as a repository for "experts" and dissident scientists to cast doubt on the existence and magnitude of various environmental problems, including global warming, ozone depletion, and species extinction. These "greenwashing experts" produce a steady stream of books, reports, magazine articles, and newspaper editorials that argue that many ecological problems are not all that serious (or do not exist at all) and that if government would just get off the backs of industry and offer the proper incentives, the marketplace would solve the ecological problems that do exist. Self-described "experts" belonging to major think tanks or policy centers regularly appear in the media to minimize concern for the ecological crisis.[73] This strategy aims to weaken public pressure for governmental action to solve these environmental problems—potential action that might adversely affect corporate profits.

The Competitive Enterprise Institute (CEI) illustrates this point. A think tank established in 1984 by Fred Smith Jr., an ex-EPA employee, CEI is devoted to advancing the principles of free enterprise and limited governmental regulation of industry. Much of CEI's support comes from corporations opposed to the liberal regime of environmental regulation, including Dow Chemical, General Motors, Ford, Amoco, Coca-Cola, Pfizer Inc., Philip Morris, and Texaco Inc.[74] Since its formation, CEI has carried on a relentless campaign attacking the science on global warming. In 2007, for instance, Christopher C. Horner, an attorney and fellow at CEI, published *The Politically Incorrect Guide to Global Warming and Environmentalism*,[75] one of many in a long line of CEI publications denouncing environmentalists and the widely accepted science showing that human activities are causing global warming.

Similarly, the American Enterprise Institute (AEI) is one of several other influential Washington think tanks funded by ExxonMobil that have challenged the science around global warming and whether governmental efforts to address climate change (if it did exist) would be effective. In the summer of 2006, AEI went so far as to offer $10,000 to any scientist who would oppose the UN's Intergovernmental Panel on Climate Change report that says global warming is "unequivocal" and likely to have dire ecological impacts on the planet.[76] Lynne Cheney, the wife of Vice President Cheney and a global warming skeptic, is an AEI fellow. The AEI is also one of the major think tanks and research institutes funded by the polluter-industrial complex that is leading the charge against the legitimacy of the EJ movement. For example, David Friedman, writing for the AEI, argues that despite "sensational charges of racial 'genocide' in industrial districts and ghastly 'cancer alleys,' health data doesn't show minorities being poisoned by toxic sites" and that environmental injustice is "an 'outrage' that doesn't exist." Instead, "the success of the environmental justice movement . . . shows just how much a handful of ideological, motivated [EPA] bureaucrats and their activist allies can achieve in contemporary America unfettered by fact, consequence, or accountability."[77] Likewise, Brookings Institute fellow Christopher H. Foreman Jr. states that though "activists have a hard time accepting it, racism simply doesn't appear to be a significant factor in our national environmental decision-making."[78]

If efforts to delegitimate the existence or seriousness of a particular environmental problem(s) or EJ issue is unsuccessful, and government action appears inevitable, think tanks and policy institutes associated with the polluter-industrial complex will work to weaken or scale back proposed regulations as much as possible. This is accomplished by arguing that the regulations are (1) too expensive and/or too difficult to implement and would damage the competitiveness of industry and/or (2) too burdensome on consumers, workers, and/or the larger public and could result in higher prices, taxes, or unemployment. In place of traditional "command-and-control" legislation associated with the liberal regime of environmental regulation, conservative think tanks propose alternative neoliberal approaches that utilize cost-benefit analyses and risk assessments in order to reduce the economic burden to industry or seek to compensate polluting companies and property owners with taxpayer money for the costs of complying with the legislation.

Conservative think thanks also promote free-market techniques such as tradable property and pollution rights, pricing mechanisms, tax incentives, and voluntary agreements for dealing with environmental degradation. They argue that there is little incentive to protect environmental resources that are not privately owned by corporate interests, neglecting the manner in which corporations maximize profits by cutting expenses related to environmental protection and restoration. Instead, conservative think tanks propose the creation of property rights over parts of the environment that are currently free.[79]

These policy instruments, such as tradable pollution rights, for example, create the right for corporations to use environmental resources or to pollute the environment up to a predetermined limit. Quantities of pollution below these predetermined limits can be traded or sold to other corporations that exceed such limits. As stated by Sharon Beder, these proposals "have been taken seriously by government and in some cases accepted by [conventional] environmentalists as a valid alternative to tougher legislation."[80]

The Heritage Foundation is one such policy institute that has exerted enormous political influence on behalf of the polluter-industrial complex. Formed in 1973, early support for Heritage came from conservative beer magnate Joseph Coors and petroleum tycoon Edward Noble. Under President Ronald Reagan, an "unofficial" 1,093-page report completed by the Heritage Foundation titled *Mandate for Leadership: Policy Management in a Conservative Administration* was adopted and widely utilized by the administration to weaken traditional environmental policy on behalf of industry. In fact, nearly two-thirds of the recommendations made by the report were adopted by the Reagan administration after only two years.[81] The Heritage Foundation has been at the center of the corporate attack on environmentalism ever since, singling out the environmental movement in its *Policy Review* magazine as "the greatest single threat to the American economy."[82]

Conservative foundations like the Heritage Foundation and the Cato Institute promote government deregulation of industry, particularly in the area of environmental policy, as well as the sell-off of public lands to corporate interests. A common goal of free-market environmentalism and related policy devices at Cato is the transfer of decision-making authority over environmental quality from the state to those private interests most able to pay, that is, corporate America. Pollution rights and credit schemes result in pollution becoming a commodity that is bought and sold on the stock market or "traded" between companies. Clean air and water is no longer a fundamental human right guaranteed to every American. The Cato Institute receives the majority of its budget from private grants and gifts from foundations, individuals, and corporations, including the American Farm Bureau Federation, the American Petroleum Institute, ExxonMobil, the Ford Motor Company, Monsanto, and the Procter & Gamble Fund.[83]

The Strategic Philanthropy of Conservative Foundations and Corporate Polluters

As seen in the case of the Cato Institute, the financial resources necessary to sustain the infrastructure of think tanks, research centers, policy institutes, media and judicial watchdogs, and public relations (or educational) campaigns are provided largely by a network of private foundations linked to the polluter-industrial complex.[84] These private foundations include corporate foundations, many of which are large polluters (the nation's 2,170 corporate foundations distributed an estimated $3.4 billion to various causes in 2002 alone). However, independent grant makers in the form of conservative family foundations (where the board is created and controlled by direct donors and family members) are even more significant to the New Right.[85] These private family foundations are created by the wealth coming from family-owned companies and often play a pivotal role in financing the neoliberal policy infrastructure. In their role as businessmen, many of these family members have a history of confrontation with environmental regulations. For instance, the Smith Richardson Foundation, administered by the son of the founder of the Vicks Chemical Company, is a key conservative grant maker. So is the Olin Foundation (founded by Olin Chemical Company money) and the Scaife Foundation (whose fortune is derived from Gulf Oil).[86]

Conservative foundations engage in a form of *strategic philanthropy* whereby the translation of conservative ideals are converted into specific policy products by think tanks and research centers and then marketed to government officials and the media. The financial resources provided by these foundations is substantial. In fact, the top twenty think tanks funded by conservative foundations spent over $1 billion on "ideas" over the course of the 1990s.[87] These ideas included the rollback of environmental and consumer protection laws, as well as occupational health and safety regulations; the reduction of government spending on public education and other programs serving the poor and the middle class; huge tax cuts for the wealthy; and the privatization of public goods and services, including Medicare and Social Security.[88] Some seventy-nine foundations awarded $254 million to 350 distinct conservative policy grantees between 1999 and 2001, including $3.25 million to organizations working exclusively for "free-market" environmentalism. Most of the money, however, was funneled to the Heritage Foundation, the AEI, the Free Congress Research and Education Foundation, the Cato Institute, Citizens for a Sound Economy, and other major multi-issue think tanks. Moreover, the top five grant-making institutions—Sarah Scaife, Lynde and Harry Bradley, John M. Olin, Shelby Cullom Davis, and Richard and Helen DeVos Foundations—accounted for just over 50 percent of total conservative public policy funding during this time frame.

Foundations associated with Koch Industries provide tens of millions of dollars for these policy initiatives. David H. Koch also sits on the boards of the Cato Institute and the Reason Foundation and is a cofounder and chairman of Citizens for a Sound Economy. Each of these policy organizations seeks to limit government regulation of industry, particularly with respect to environmental policy. For instance, Citizens for a Sound Economy subsidized the creation of amici briefs providing reason to proclaim the Clean Air Act unconstitutional. Deeply embedded in the polluter-industrial complex, Koch Industries is the nation's second-largest privately owned company and the largest privately owned energy/chemical company. In September 2000, the U.S. Department of Justice charged the company with ninety-seven counts of defying federal hazardous waste and clean air acts when it knowingly emitted benzene fumes into the environment (and then lied about its actions). In April 2001, Koch agreed to pay $20 million in fines for these crimes, making it (at the time) the fifth-largest sum of money ever reached in a case related to environmental crime. This fine came on the heels of a $30 million settlement in January 2000 stemming from civil lawsuits involving more than 300 oil spills from Koch facilities in six states.

Putting Pressure on the Courts to Roll Back Environmental Policy

Along with Castle Rock, the John M. Olin Foundation, and other conservative grant makers, the Koch family foundations are also major supporters of the Foundation for Research on Economics and the Environment (FREE). Multinational corporations such as ExxonMobil, General Electric, General Motors, Merck, Shell, and Temple also provide substantial funding to FREE, which is an organization devoted to "educating" the judiciary as to the detrimental impacts of environmental law on industry. FREE accomplishes this by providing publications, such as the *Federal Judge's Desk Reference on Environmental Economics*, as well as all-expenses-paid trips for federal judges to attend educational "seminars" at luxurious retreats. A report issued by the Community Rights Counsel found that 137 federal judges reported 194 trips to FREE seminars over a six-year period during the 1990s (FREE claims that nearly one-third of the federal judiciary has either attended or requested enrollment in a FREE seminar). These seminars present a one-sided view on the so-called evils of current environmental legislation and regulations.[89]

FREE efforts to influence the judiciary produces results. In 1993, Circuit Judge Stephen Williams of the Court of Appeals for the District of Columbia Circuit sided with the majority in a two-to-one vote in the case of *Sweet Home v. Babbit*, which upheld the government's authority to prohibit modification of the environment that could harm an endangered species. Two weeks after the ruling, Williams attended a FREE seminar in Idaho. When he returned, the circuit panel reheard the case, and in 1994 Williams changed his vote and struck down the regulations in favor of the timber companies. Similarly, Ed Warren, a lead attorney pressing a legal attack by industry against pending federal air pollution regulations, had social contacts with two federal appellate judges at a guest ranch before they decided a 1999 case. The meetings came as part of a series of FREE expense-paid seminars for judges. The case—*American Trucking Association v. Environmental Protection Agency*—was one of the biggest environmental cases of the 1990s. The appeals court struck down new EPA regulations on soot and smog, claiming that Congress had never delegated the authority to the EPA (the U.S. Supreme Court later rejected the lower court's decision, upholding the EPA's right to tighten such regulations under the Clean Air Act). While the case was pending, U.S. Circuit Judge Douglas Ginsburg and Judge David Sentelle attended the retreat seminars, including one given by Warren, a partner in the Chicago-based firm Kirkland and Ellis.[90]

FREE is part of a much larger effort by the polluter-industrial complex to move the judiciary to the right on environmental policy. The Center for Regulatory Effectiveness, an industry-funded public policy group, and the U.S. Chamber of Commerce, for instance, have launched a propaganda campaign arguing that lawsuits by environmentalists are creating a de facto regulatory process. The purpose of the campaign is to create pressure for increased White House oversight over settlements resulting from lawsuits. The polluter-industrial complex is also aggressively pursuing an antitort agenda, often termed "tort reform." Toxic torts provide remedies for personal injuries resulting from exposure to hazardous waste or products as well as predatory business behavior. As stated by sociologists Thomas Koenig and Michael Rustad, "Tort reform has become the rallying cry of powerful corporations who wish to shift costs back to the injured victim, the victim's family and to the taxpayer."[91] Ever since serving as governor of Texas, one of George W. Bush's highest priorities was the enactment of tort "reforms" that undermined the ability of individuals to receive compensation for corporate wrongdoing.

The public relations infrastructure pushing for tort reform asserts that firms are being bankrupted by "frivolous" environmental lawsuits based on the logic of "phantom risk" and/or that toxic injury lawsuits are often frivolous litigation based on "junk" science. Public relations and legalistic ploys of this sort displace public attention from the often devastating harm stemming from environmental abuses to the extremely difficult task of establishing a causal connection between an injury and a particular toxic exposure. As a result of pressure tactics such as these, the courts are making it more difficult to introduce expert testimony on the causal connections between environmental abuses and public harm. As a result, the American legal system is placing an increasingly cruel and almost insurmountable burden on the small, individual plaintiff in toxic torts litigation. Environmental justice requires judgments that force the polluter to pay instead of the injured victim, the community, and the taxpayer.[92]

The courts are important in other ways as well. Liberal judges often uphold the validity of existing environmental laws and regulations and thwart the introduction of neoliberal policy initiatives. The corporate colonization of the judiciary, including the appointment of more conservative judges, is therefore essential to the push for "free-market" environmentalism. A recent report of federal rulings from 1991 to 2001 found that a group of highly ideological judges—most appointed by former Presidents Ronald Reagan and George H. W. Bush—has disregarded norms of judicial conduct to shape a new judicial philosophy that threatens core environmental laws. The analysis, conducted by the Alliance for Justice, the Community Rights Counsel, and the Natural Resources Defense Council, finds a decade-long pattern of judicial activism by judges ideologically opposed to environmental protection. According to the report, the judges in question have consistently ignored basic principles of judicial fairness to shut citizens out of the courthouse and create new rights for polluters.[93]

The appointment of judges sympathetic to the interests of the polluter-industrial complex includes the nation's highest court. Over the past decade, the Supreme Court has sharply limited the intervention rights of citizen's groups such as the Sierra Club, Friends of the Earth, and the National Wildlife Federation to file suit to force corporations to obey or the EPA to enforce environmental standards.[94] In 2003, for instance, Supreme Court Justice Roberts cast doubt on the constitutionality of sweeping federal environmental laws and wrote that the Endangered Species Act cannot protect "a hapless toad that, for reasons of its own, lives its entire life in California" because the Constitution allows only the regulation of matters involving more than one state. Supreme Court Justice Antonin Scalia has also joined with some judges presiding in various lower federal courts to invoke more limited definitions of "standing" (or rights to sue) for citizen groups. On the other hand, Scalia has left more accessible rights to timber companies, mining conglomerates, and manufacturers to challenge environmental regulations. For instance, Scalia authored an opinion that the National Wildlife Federation, a group with a long-standing interest in protecting the environment, had no standing to intervene in filing litigation challenging the opening up of public lands to mining. In fact, a series of opinions written by Scalia has distinguished between the object of regulation (e.g., a corporate polluter) and the beneficiary (e.g., a citizen trying to stop pollution) and used this distinction to exclude environmental plaintiffs from court.[95]

That Scalia should side with corporate polluters is no surprise. In January 2003, Scalia and Vice President Cheney went on what became a controversial duck hunting trip together in Louisiana. The trip took place just three weeks after the Supreme Court had agreed to take up the vice president's appeal of lawsuits over his handling of the administration's secret energy task force. A lower court had ruled, over the vice president's objections, that Cheney was to turn over documents revealing who met with the task force. The task force created an energy policy blueprint that included significant rollbacks of federal environmental rules. The Sierra Club and Judicial Watch had contended that Cheney and his staff had violated the open-government measure known as the Federal Advisory Committee Act by meeting behind closed doors with outside lobbyists for the oil, gas, coal, and nuclear industries, including Enron chairman Kenneth Lay. On the duck hunting trip, Cheney and Scalia were guests of Wallace Carline, the owner of Diamond Services Corporation, an oil services company. Scalia refused to recuse himself from hearing the case or to opt out of the vacation with the vice president.

The family connections of conservative Supreme Court justices to the Bush administration are quite revealing of the political influence exerted by the policy infrastructure of the polluter-industrial complex. For instance, Virginia Thomas, the wife of Supreme Court Justice Clarence Thomas, is director of executive branch relations at the Heritage Foundation and was part of the foundation's "Mandate for Leadership 2000" program to help transition the Bush administration after the 2000 election. Similarly, Eugene Scalia, the son of Supreme Court Justice Antonin Scalia, is known as the "godfather of the antiergonomics movement" for his work as a lawyer and lobbyist with the National Coalition on Ergonomics, an industry-funded group devoted to repealing legislation designed to prevent repetitive-motion injuries among workers.[96] The coalition tries to cast doubt on the existing science that shows that repetitive motion is a serious and sometimes debilitating form of injury.[97]

LOBBYING AGAINST THE ENVIRONMENT: THE SPECIAL-INTEREST PROCESS FOR CORPORATE POLLUTERS

Corporate Investments in the American Political System

In the United States, political candidates are largely responsive to the blocs of "investors" that support their campaigns. Large corporations, trade associations, and wealthy individuals constitute the most powerful set of investors, although unions are also a key source of financial support for liberal Democrats. Once elected to office, these politicians know "not to bite the hand that feeds them" and make appointees to various government positions that will meet the approval of such supporters. They also draw on the policy infrastructure of the power elite to advance the general interests of these investors. In this respect, public policy is shaped by the interplay and jockeying of these blocs, although politicians will sometimes act in opposition to their backers on various issues in periods of heightened public attention or outrage.[98]

The polluter-industrial complex constitutes one such bloc of pragmatically bipartisan investors in the American political system. As we have just seen, an interlocking system of think tanks, policy institutes, and research centers is working to implement neoliberal economic policies that are largely supportive of the *general* interests of the corporations that make up the polluter-industrial complex. In contrast, the special interest process involves the actions of formal lobbying organizations of *individual* companies, wealthy families, specific industries, and trade associations within the polluter-industrial complex. These lobbying organizations strive to obtain government contracts and subsidies, secure tax breaks, thwart the actions of regulatory agencies that are viewed as costly or a threat to private control over investment decisions, funnel self-serving advice and information to state officials, and secure favorable legislation for a particular company or industry. The sum of these lobbying actions constitute another manner by which the polluter-industrial complex colonizes the state.

Political lobbying by big business is now a big business in and of itself. Some 90,000 people are currently engaged in or supporting lobbying activities in Washington, D.C., alone. The amount of lobbying money spent to influence federal lawmakers since 1998 is double the amount of money spent to elect them and continues to skyrocket.[99] Lobbying expenses by corporations, trade associations, and other "interest" groups rose to a record $2.4 billion in 2005, some 14 percent higher than the $2.1 billion spent in 2004 (and 50 percent higher than the $1.6 billion spent in 2000). Corporations affiliated with the polluter-industrial complex are among the biggest spenders. In the last half of 2005, over $200 million a month was spent on lobbying, including a total of $92.5 million by industries involved in energy and natural resources. The transportation industries also spent $90.6 million.[100]

The quantities of money spent on an army of well-paid lobbyists by the polluter-industrial complex obviously dwarf the financial resources of environmentalists and the EJ movement. It also tends to cast a shadow on other sectors of capital as well. In 2002, for instance, some ninety-eight trade associations and member companies spent more than $173 million on in-house lobbyists.[101] More than $96 million of this total came from associations and companies in the electric utility and oil and gas sectors. In comparison, the entire banking industry spent only $26 million on lobbying in 2002, while the defense sector spent $60 million. In fact, the five largest oil companies spent well over $175 million on lobbying activities from 1998 to 2004, just behind the U.S. Chamber of Commerce at $204.6 million. During this time frame, huge sums of money were also spent by other sectors of the polluter-industrial complex, including auto manufacturers such as General Motors ($48.2 million) and Ford ($41.35 million); aerospace and technology companies such as General Electric ($94.1 million) and Northrop Grumman ($83.4 million); timber interests such as the American Forest and Paper Association ($20.5 million) and International Paper ($18.97 million); chemical companies and trade associations such as the American Chemistry Council ($27 million), Monsanto ($22.5 million), Johnson & Johnson ($21.76 million), and the Asbestos Study Group ($21.9 million); and the National Association of Manufacturers ($29.56 million).

The Energy Lobby and Environmental Injustice

The infusion of such enormous sums of money into the lobbying process buys corporate polluters disproportionate access to governmental officials and exerts a corrosive effect on American democracy. Industry lobbyists are now integrated so extensively into the environmental agency rule-making and legislative processes that their recommendations are frequently adopted with little modification. In some cases, corporate lobbyists are the ones actually writing the new rules and regulations word for word.

The Bush administration's Department of Energy transition team provides a good example. Responsible for designing the administration's energy policy strategy after the 2000 election, it included officials from Edison Electric Institute, Southern Company, FirstEnergy, and Dominion. These utilities are among the country's worst producers of air pollution and cause devastating health problems in working-class towns and communities of color across the United States (nationwide, 68 percent of African Americans live in close proximity to a coal-fired power plant).[102] They are also among the most powerful corporate lobbies in Washington opposing environmental regulation, with Edison ($82.87 million) and Southern ($34.9 million) being among the largest spenders on lobbying between 1998 and 2003, according to the Center for Public Integrity.[103] Two corporate lobbyists from the Electric Reliability Coordinating Council (an industry-funded front group working for weaker clean air regulations) were also a members of the transition team. Each of these lobbyists had experience fighting environmental laws on behalf of industry. Scott Segal was a partner at Bracewell & Patterson, a law firm that has represented BP Amoco, Shell Oil, and Valero Energy. C. Boyden Gray played a chief role in the formation of the Air Quality Standards Coalition, an industry front group dedicated to fighting against the strengthening of clean air standards in the mid-1990s and whose largest contributing members in 1997 were Ford Motor Company and the American Petroleum Institute. Gray was also legal counsel to Vice President George H. W. Bush from 1981 to 1989 and served as counsel to President Bush from 1989 to 1993.[104]

The energy transition team was the precursor to Vice President Cheney's secretive Energy Task Force that developed the blueprint for the energy package that was sent to Congress in 2003. The energy bill constitutes a blatant example of the excessive power waged by the polluter-industrial complex lobby. According to a special investigation by the *Boston Globe*, the federal energy bill became a cash bonanza for corporate interests in and out of the energy arena. Lobbying records show that companies and trade associations with a stated interest in energy policy spent a whopping $387.8 million lobbying Washington in 2003 alone. The money was well spent. These corporations were eventually rewarded in the bill with billions of dollars in tax breaks, massive government contracts and subsidies, and significant rollbacks in government regulation. For instance, the nuclear industry spent some $71.4 million on lobbying Capitol Hill but received $7.37 billion in tax breaks and project monies, including federal funds to construct a $1 billion nuclear plant in Idaho. Massey Energy of West Virginia—whose director, James H. "Buck" Harless, was a major Bush fund-raiser—also received hundreds of millions of dollars in loan guarantees for a coal gasification plant. Harless served on the Energy Department's transition team.[105]

As additions to the Energy Department's transition team, corporate lobbyists were also integrated into the energy task force led by Vice President Cheney. A 2003 study by the nonpartisan General Accounting Office found that the energy task force received advice from many private "energy stakeholders" in the petroleum, coal, nuclear, natural gas, and electricity industries. For instance, members of the American Petroleum Institute interacted with the energy task force six times and in 2003 spent $3.14 million lobbying around the bill. In exchange, the oil industry received billions in tax breaks and subsidies to encourage domestic oil production. In contrast, environmentalists were locked out of the meetings and achieved little success in their lobbying efforts around the bill.

In the summer of 2005, President Bush signed into law the new energy bill. By that time, lobbyists had included such massive subsidies for the oil industry that the legislation had become a public embarrassment and sparked outrage among environmentalists, public interest organizations, and the general population. Despite obscene profits for the oil giants—ExxonMobil, for instance, brought in $24 billion in profits in 2004 and a record-breaking $15 billion in the first half of 2005—the energy bill allocated at least $4 billion in subsidies and tax breaks for the oil industry. Furthermore, as documented by the report *Exxpose Exxon*, the new energy law exempts "the oil industry from several environmental laws, including the Clean Water Act and the Safe Drinking Water Act, allowing even the most profitable companies to pollute our waterways and drinking water." The law also suspends the payment of royalties for publicly owned oil and gas from offshore leases in the deeper waters of the Gulf of Mexico and allows the oil industry to forgo royalty payments to the federal treasury for oil drilled in areas of Alaska's coastline.[106]

The Bush–Cheney energy bill is illustrative of the manner in which corporate lobbyists, elected officials, and appointed heads of government agencies are now working together in such a symbiotic fashion to roll back the nation's environmental laws that is often difficult to tell them apart. In early January 2004, for instance, Bush administration officials and members of Congress hosted dozens of industry leaders at a Phoenix golf resort to discuss the rewriting of environmental legislation and federal energy policy. Advertised as a "mulligans and margaritas" event, corporate leaders paid $3,000 for the privilege of having a private dinner and golf game with fifteen Republican members of Congress, including Senator Pete Domenici, chairman of the Senate Energy and Natural Resources Committee. The money was divided among the campaign committees of participating members of Congress. This event was part of the "Roundtable Summit of the West," with members of the Western Business Roundtable and U.S. Chamber of Commerce, which includes chief executive officers and leaders of the oil and gas, mining, coal, and chemical industries. Industry officials also paid to attend sessions with members of Congress, Senate staffers, and EPA officials on "How the West Should Prepare for the Upcoming Re-Write of the Clean Air Act" and "Building a Top Ten 'To Do' List for the Congress." The keynote speaker was J. Steven Griles, then acting deputy secretary of the Interior Department and a former coal industry lobbyist. No environmentalists were invited to attend the event.

Griles is not the exception to the rule. More than 2,200 former federal employees registered as lobbyists between 1998 and 2004, according to the Center for Public Integrity. Many of these employees formerly worked at the EPA but left to work for the polluter-industrial complex. In 2003, for instance, the Southern Company, which owns coal-fired power plants in the Southeast, hired John Pemperton, the chief of staff for the EPA office in charge of air pollution programs. Southern was one of the companies most active in lobbying the EPA to change the "new source review" provision of the Clean Air Act, which determines when a facility must install pollution control equipment. Pemberton was hired one week after the EPA announced it was easing an important air pollution control program beneficial to the company. The company was the subject of a pending EPA lawsuit over noncompliance with the rule (the EPA was suing Southern Company for violations at eight of its plants). At the same time, Ed Krenik, the associate administrator for congressional and intergovernmental relations at EPA, left the agency for the law firm of Bracewell & Patterson to lobby on behalf of industries regulated by the EPA (Southern Company is also a client of the firm).[107] Southern Company spent $34.9 million on lobbying between 1998 and 2004 and is "one of the most outspoken members" of the electric utility industry, opposing a wide range of environmental and public health protections.[108]

Ethics and the Corruptive Influence of the Polluter-Industrial Complex

There are a hundred or more high-level officials in the Bush administration regulating industries that they once represented as lobbyists, lawyers, or company advocates.[109] As former lobbyists for the polluter-industrial complex, they exert control over federal regulators who are supposed to control the companies they used to represent. The free rein granted to these former lobbyists is crippling the ability of the EPA and Interior Department to safeguard the nation's environment. In February 2007, the U.S. Interior Department's inspector general, Earl E. Devaney, testified before the House Natural Resources Committee that the department was plagued by problems that were "deep and wide," including ineffective law enforcement, inadequate protection of some national parks' resources, a failure to follow funding and procurement laws, and an unethically cozy relationship among senior officials and companies seeking government contracts. Furthermore, Devaney complained that officials at the Interior Department received free golf outings, dinners, hunting trips, and box seats at sporting events from companies they monitored but were rarely punished for the ethics violations. Devaney further testified that "throughout the department, the appearance of preferential treatment in awarding contracts and procurement has come to our attention far too frequently, and the failure of department officials to remain at arm's length from prohibited sources is pervasive."[110]

From 2003 to 2006, investigations by Interior's inspector general identified seventy-one employees whose actions triggered ethics probes. The vast majority of those penalized were low- to midranking employees. Of the twenty-one senior officials whose ethical behavior was reviewed, more than half were not disciplined by the administration. The remaining received a reprimand that often involved a two-hour course on ethics, a transfer, or the option to resign. Devaney's office is also investigating the broader issue of whether the Interior Department has been properly collecting money from its oil and gas contracts with energy companies (the *New York Times* first reported the omission of royalty payments during the late 1990s). Robin M. Nazzaro, director of the Government Accountability Office's Natural Resources and Environment, told the same house panel that the royalty mismanagement could cost taxpayers as much as $10 billion for 576 active leases granted during 1998 and 1999 under the Clinton administration. Nazzaro also identified the

Interior Department's inadequate land appraisals as also resulting in the loss of millions of dollars in revenue.

The ethics problems associated with corporate lobbyists are not restricted to the Interior Department—they are pervasive throughout the federal government. From January 2000 through June 2005, members of Congress and their aides took at least 23,000 trips—valued at almost $50 million—financed by private sponsors, many of them corporations, trade associations, and nonprofit groups with business on Capitol Hill. Records reviewed by the Center for Public Integrity show that Representative Tom DeLay, who resigned as House majority leader in January 2006 after being indicted on charges of violating campaign finance laws, and his staffers accepted about half a million dollars in trips during the period, although the office of Representative Don Young was only about $8,000 behind (like DeLay, Young is a virulent opponent of environmental regulation and was among the most powerful members of Congress). DeLay took a now-infamous $28,000 golf trip to Scotland in the spring of 2000 that was sponsored by Jack Abramoff, the lobbyist who pleaded guilty in January 2006 to charges of fraud, conspiracy, and tax evasion regarding his extensive lobbying activities. The Scotland trip was later found to have violated House ethics rules.

Abramoff secretly routed his clients' funds through tax-exempt organizations with the acquiescence of those in charge. Among the organizations used by Abramoff was prominent conservative activist Grover Norquist's Americans for Tax Reform, which served as a "conduit" for funds that flowed from Abramoff's clients to surreptitiously finance grassroots lobbying campaigns. Another Norquist-related group, Council of Republicans for Environmental Advocacy (CREA), received about $500,000 in Abramoff client funds. Abramoff often used the CREA's president to lobby former Deputy Secretary of the Interior J. Steven Griles. CREA was founded in 1998 by Gale Norton, and received support from the mining and chemical industries. Beginning early in 2001, Indian tribes represented by Abramoff gave more than $250,000 to CREA. The suggestions for donations had come from staffers of Representative Tom DeLay, who were advising Abramoff on how to gain influence with Norton. On September 24, 2001, at a private fund-raising dinner arranged by CREA, Coushatta tribal chairman Lovelin Poncho and Abramoff sat at Norton's table while tribal attorney Kathy Van Hoof sat at another table with Norton's top deputy, Steven Griles. Griles eventually pleaded guilty to felony charges of lying to investigators about his relationship to Abramoff lobbying activities. Lobbying records obtained by the Associated Press show that Abramoff's lobbying team met nearly 200 times with administration officials during the first ten months of Bush's presidency on behalf of just one of his clients, the Northern Mariana Islands.[111]

"TOXIC SLUDGE IS GOOD FOR YOU": THE PRODUCTION OF IDEOLOGY AS ENVIRONMENTAL SCIENCE

The Ideological Control of State Officials

As we have seen, owners, chief executive officers, lobbyists, lawyers, and other "representatives" of the polluter-industrial complex occupy key positions of power in the federal government and exert decisive influence over most policy battles. Nevertheless, the state bureaucracy, including those agencies charged with protecting the environment, are staffed with thousands of lower- and middle-level career state managers that operate with a significant degree of autonomy from the governing power structure. These government officials are often dedicated to fulfilling the mission of the agency and experience a high degree of public scrutiny and legal oversight in the performance of their duties. Hence, it is of the utmost importance to create public and private ideological mechanisms for socializing state employees to act in accordance with the predilections of capital.

Perhaps the most important mechanism for exercising ideological control over state managers, as well as policymakers, involves the production of scientific knowledge and information. Government regulators establish various regulatory controls and standards for industry based on scientific studies of the health dangers posed by various pollutants and toxic substances as well as by conducting environmental impact reviews of business and state projects. Wresting control away from ecologically minded "independent" scientists in favor of industry-sponsored researchers is key if government regulations are to be thwarted, weakened, or overturned. The corporate production of science is also key to the public relations campaigns waged by the polluter-industrial complex to convince the American people that environmental problems are imagined or overblown or even that "toxic sludge is good for you."[112]

Over the past three decades and more, the polluter-industrial complex has utilized a wide variety of tactics to obscure the dangerous effects of their products to government agencies. These tactics include contracting outside scientists to conduct research designed to show that a particular production process or product is safe or to organize groups of industry-friendly "third-party" scientists in the form of scientific advisory boards. Such boards work in coordination with neoliberal policy institutes and think tanks, industry "front groups," corporate lobbyists, and public relations firms to support industry assertions in the regulation-setting and policymaking processes and in the courts, where they testify as expert witnesses in tort litigation lawsuits. Scientific advisory boards also launch attacks in the press on scientists and scientific work that claim environmental harm is resulting from corporate practices. The Public Relations firm Burson-Marsteller, for instance, has organized a number of phony grassroots (Astroturf) organizations to battle the genuine "grassroots" movements.[113] Dow Chemical, for instance, has contributed to the formation of ten "greenwash" front groups, including the Alliance to Keep Americans Working, the Alliance for Responsible CFC Policy, the American Council on Science and Health, Citizens for a Sound Economy, and the Council for Solid Waste Solutions.[114]

Astroturf front groups and closely related policy institutes often rely on the work of "scientific" writers hostile to liberal environmental regulation and science, such as Elizabeth Whelan, *Toxic Terror: The Truth behind the Cancer Scare*; Dixie Lee Ray, *Environmental Overkill*; Michael Fumento, *Science under Siege*; and Dennis Avery of the Hudson Institute, *Saving the Planet with Pesticides and Plastic.* Whelan, for example, incorrectly argued that the EPA's experts did not think that Uniroyal Corporation's pesticide Alar posed a threat to human health. However, the EPA's Carcinogen Assessment Group labeled Alar a "probable human carcinogen"—a judgment reiterated by the U.S. National Toxicology Program. Whelan, who has received support from Monsanto, is what *Consumer Reports* labels a "public interest pretender"—one that publishes deceptive or misleading information around the true hazards posed by the polluter-industrial complex.[115] The aim of these actions by such writers is to produce enough "doubt" in order to thwart regulatory action by state officials and secure the least restrictive possible regulatory environment as well as to avert legal liability for resulting deaths or injuries. Scientific advisory boards and corporate-sponsored "researchers" are often effective because they provide an appearance of "scientific legitimacy" in support of industry claims.

Manufacturing "Junk" Science in Support of the Polluter-Industrial Complex

As part of the liberal regime of environmental regulation, the polluter-industrial complex has been especially successful in creating a "risk paradigm" approach. The risk paradigm focuses on the regulation of individual pollutants at "acceptable levels" of public exposure utilizing a variety of scientific and engineering tools, including risk assessment, toxicological testing, epidemiological investigations, and so forth. This risk paradigm assumes that scientists can know "safe" exposure doses to toxins and that public exposure rates can be controlled. Magnified by industry pressures to make speedy regulatory and policy decisions with inadequate information, however, a lack of data showing any "harmful" impact is typically misconstrued by state officials as evidence of safety. Most chemicals are approved without any restrictions.

In the United States, the lack of government health data on chemicals is startling. The vast majority of the 70,000 and more chemicals registered for use by industry have not undergone adequate long-term testing for their health and environmental impacts. A recent study by the Environmental Defense Fund found that 75 percent of the high-profile, high-volume chemicals used by industry lack even the most minimal health testing information.[116] The regulation of toxic substances is instead based on permitting the use and release of toxic substances in "amounts that the producers and users claim are essential for them" to be profitable. Only in a few nightmare cases, where the obvious health and environmental impacts of the substance in question has resulted in a large public outcry, have much stricter regulations or the banning of a specific chemical (such as DDT) actually occurred.[117]

Most toxicity testing and health research on chemicals is initially conducted by the manufacturer and then submitted to the government. In addition, with deeper and deeper cuts in government research budgets becoming more profound in the new millennium, the EPA and other agencies are increasingly forced to rely on regulated companies and industry-affiliated institutions instead of their own scientists to supply data. The reports coming out of these industry investigations have a profound impact in shaping the "understanding" and behavior of government policymakers and regulators, including EPA staff.[118] However, as has been documented in recent years in countless investigations, corporations that make up the polluter-industrial complex have repeatedly withheld, falsified, or altered their own internal studies that show their products to be harmful. The suppression of such research includes the true health dangers posed by polyvinyl chloride plastic, lead, tobacco, silicon dust, asbestos, and many other substances. In fact, as in the case of lead and vinyl—two substances causing devastating health impacts among workers and EJ communities throughout the country—entire industries have banded together to deny and suppress information about the toxic nature of their products. The studies conducted by industry are clearly not reliable, yet the government continues to utilize these studies to the detriment of public health.[119]

The corruptive impacts of the polluter-industrial complex extends to America's universities. A recent study of corporate funding of academic research reveals that more than half of the university scientists who received gifts from drug or biotechnology companies admitted that the donor expected to exert influence over their work. The concern is so widespread that many scientific journals, including the prestigious *New England Journal of Medicine*, now require that the source of support for the investigator's research be clearly identified.[120] For instance, an influential study published in the *Journal of Occupational and Environmental Medicine* exonerating hexavalent chromium from causing high rates of cancer in five villages in northeastern China was re-tracted in 2006 (hexavalent chromium, also known as industrial chromium or chromium-6, is classified by the EPA as a known carcinogen). The retraction occurred when the *Wall Street Journal* revealed that the article was conceived, drafted, and edited by consultants for Pacific Gas and Electric (PG&E), which was embroiled in toxic-tort litigation over hexavalent-chromium contamination in California. The PG&E consultants submitted the 1997 article for publication without disclosing their own or PG&E's involvement to the journal.[121] PG&E had a major stake in overturning the science on the harmful impacts of hexavalent chromium. It was during the 1990s that law firm employee Erin Brockovich put together the cancer cluster stories from over 600 plaintiffs from Hinkley, California, in a successful multi-million-dollar lawsuit against PG&E.

The polluter-industrial complex is also attempting to undermine the ability of independent and government-sponsored scientists and institutions to conduct research that may prove damaging to capital, including efforts to fire or blackball researchers.[122] With the Republican takeover of Congress in the mid-1990s, industry pressure resulted in the dismantling of the Office of Technology Assessment (OTA). Serving as perhaps the most important scientific advisory office in the country, OTA's twenty-three-year body of work included some 750 reports and assessments on subjects ranging from acid rain to climate change. Created in 1972 during the Nixon administration, OTA was politically "neutral," serving to provide technical studies and scientific information in an accessible manner to both sides of aisle. However, the OTA drew increased opposition over the years from the polluter-industrial complex because the analyses provided by the office often revealed dangers associated with pollution.[123]

As reported in the *Washington Post*, the Bush administration also initiated a "broad restructuring of the scientific advisory committees that guide federal policy" in order to serve the interests of capital. These largely anonymous committees of scientists, lawyers, and academics make recommendations vital to determining health and environmental risks.[124] In 2002, for instance, the Department of Health and Human Services retired two expert committees before their work was completed, including one that recommended the Food and Drug Administration expand its regulation of the increasingly lucrative genetic testing industry (the other committee was rethinking federal protections for human research subjects). Yet another committee, which had been assessing the health impacts of low-level exposure to environmental chemicals, had fifteen of its seventeen members replaced by people with links to the industries that make those chemicals. One new member was a California toxicologist, Dennis Paustenbach, who helped defend PG&E against Erin Brockovich in the Hinkley case.[125]

Under the administration of George W. Bush, nominees for federal scientific advisory committees were routinely screened for their political views and corporate connections over their professional qualifications. As a result, the findings and recommendations of these newly reconstituted committees—which frequently form the basis for environmental regulation—tilted sharply in favor of the polluter-industrial complex. For instance, Dr. Michael Wetzman, a leading expert on lead poisoning, was not reappointed to the Centers for Disease Control Committee on Childhood Lead Poisoning by the administration. Instead, the Centers nominated Dr. William Banner, who had a record of serving as an expert witness for the lead industry in downplaying the effects of lead on children, and Kimberly Thompson, who was affiliated with the Harvard Center for Risk Analysis, which had twenty-two corporate funders with a financial interest in the deliberations of the lead advisory committee.[126] In short, the Bush administration systematically turned the government's production of science over to industry-friendly scientists and contracted out thousands of science jobs to compliant consultants already in the habit of massaging data to support corporate profits. As stated by Robert F. Kennedy Jr., "The Bush Administration has so violated and corrupted the institutional culture of government agencies charged with scientific research that it could take a generation for them to recover their integrity."[127]

The Scientific Backlash against the Bush Administration

The colonization of scientific institutions by the polluter-industrial complex under the guidance of the Bush administration has sparked a backlash of sorts. In November 2001, the *Chronicle of Higher Education* ran a lengthy article on "the waning influence of scientists on national policy" and cited the already dramatic rifts between the Bush administration and the majority of scientists on climate change, toxic chemicals, reproductive health, stem cells, and missile defense. In 2004, the Union of Concerned Scientists issued a report, *Scientific Integrity in Policymaking*, signed by sixty-two of the nation's preeminent scientists, including twenty Nobel laureates, charging the Bush administration with widespread manipulation of science and egregious conflicts of interest in policymaking. The document analyzes the White House manipulation of science in areas such as climate change, mercury emissions, air pollution, breast cancer, endangered species, forest management, workplace safety, and childhood lead exposure.[128] The following year, scientists at the National Oceanic and Atmospheric Administration Fisheries Service made similar charges—that agency science is suffering as a result of political manipulation and the inappropriate influence of special interests, rendering the agency increasingly unable to carry out its charge of protecting imperiled fish, seal, and whale populations from extinction.[129] Nevertheless, the corporate assault on environmental science continues to move forward.

The actions of the Bush administration around climate change provide a further illustration of this assault. Instead of positioning the United States as a world leader in the international fight to curb global warming, the Bush administration adopted a position of the Global Climate Coalition by repeatedly denying and then underplaying the problem. The Bush administration actively suppressed the science around global warming and distorted the economic consequences of taking action.[130] The Global Climate Coalition is made up of dozens of U.S. trade associations and private companies representing oil, gas, coal, automobile, and chemical interests. It resists international agreements (such as the Kyoto Protocols) to reduce greenhouse emissions because of claims of scientific "uncertainty" and the potential economic harm such a treaty would cause to industry.

Faithfully serving his coal, oil, and auto industry constituencies, President Bush rejected the scientific consensus articulated by the Intergovernmental Panel on Climate Change and other studies showing that greenhouse gases are accumulating in the earth's atmosphere as a result of human activities, causing surface air temperatures and subsurface ocean temperatures to rise.[131] When the National Academy of Sciences came to Bush in 2001 with a report saying that global warming was real, serious, and human caused, he ignored it. When the EPA sent a 2002 report to the United Nations saying that global warming will result in "rising seas, melting ice caps and glaciers, ecological system disruption, floods, heat waves and more dangerous storms," Bush rejected it as a document "put out by the bureaucracy."[132] The following year, the White House ordered the EPA to delete from its *State of the Environment Report* references showing that global temperatures have risen sharply and that such warming is at least partially caused by industrial emissions.[133]

Philip Cooney was one of those charged by a whistle-blower with changing the language in several 2002 and 2003 government reports, including the *Strategic Plan for the United States Climate Change Science Program*. Before joining the White House Council on Environmental Quality as chief of staff, Cooney was a lobbyist for the American Petroleum Institute, which is the largest trade association affiliated with the oil and gas industry, a member of the Global Climate Coalition, and a key player in the fight against the regulation of greenhouse gases. Cooney and the White House edited the section on global warming in the EPA's *State of the Environment Report* by replacing data showing increases in greenhouse gas emissions in the late 1990s with references to a different report funded by the American Petroleum Institute, among others.[134] Trained as a lawyer and not a scientist, Cooney was accused by Rick Piltz, a senior associate of the U.S. Climate Change Science Policy

Office and former associate director of the U.S. Global Change Research Program, of altering the reports. Piltz resigned from the Climate Change Science Program in protest of the politicization of his science program.

Besides watering down research documents and stacking scientific advisory panels with ideological allies, the polluter-industrial complex has applied direct political pressure on the Bush administration to terminate government scientists. One of those targeted early on was the world-renowned climatologist Dr. Robert Watson, chair of the Intergovernmental Panel on Climate Change (IPCC). A joint project of the United Nations and the World Meteorological Association, the IPCC is made up of 2,500 researchers and other climate experts and has led international efforts to assess the science behind global climate change. Under Watson's tenure, the IPCC produced its third comprehensive assessment of the state of climate science in 2001, concluding that "there is new and stronger evidence that most of the warming observed over the last 50 years is attributable to human activities," especially the burning of fossil fuels. Among those calling for Watson's replacement was Exxon-Mobil, which sent a confidential memo to the White House in the spring of 2002 urging the Bush administration to replace Watson. Lobbyists for the coal industry, electric utilities, and automakers joined in the request (the energy industry had been quietly pressing for the removal of Watson from the helm of the IPCC since the Bush administration took office in January 2001). Exxon-Mobil's efforts were rewarded on April 19, 2002, when Watson was replaced by Dr. Rajendra Pachauri, an official with two PhDs in economics and industrial engineering but none in atmospheric science.

In January 2006, the top climate scientist at the National Aeronautics and Space Administration (NASA), James E. Hansen, went public in the *New York Times* with claims that the Bush administration tried to stop him from speaking on climate change since he gave a lecture calling for prompt reductions in emissions of greenhouse gases. Hansen, longtime director of the agency's Goddard Institute for Space Studies, said that officials at NASA headquarters had ordered the public affairs staff to review his lectures, papers, and postings on the Goddard website and requests for interviews from journalists. In addition, internal memorandums circulated in the Alaskan division of the federal Fish and Wildlife Service directed government biologists and other employees in the Arctic region to not discuss climate change, polar bears, or melting sea ice. During this period, the Bush administration faced a deadline under a suit by environmental organizations to list polar bears under the Endangered Species Act because global warming is causing a retreat of the sea ice that polar bears use for seal hunting during the summertime. The memorandum came on the heels of news reports showing that political appointees at NASA had canceled journalists' interview requests with climate scientists and discouraged news releases on global warming.[135] Only recently has President Bush responded to growing national and international criticism and acknowledged the role of industrial emissions in contributing to climate change.

RECLAIMING THE STATE

As we have seen, the power elite is carrying out a profound assault on the gains won by environmentalists, civil rights activists, feminists, trade unionists, EJ activists, and other progressive social movements over the past three decades. At the forefront of this corporate assault is the polluter-industrial complex, which is wielding enormous power over the state apparatus. In fact, under President Bush, the executive branch of the federal government has been colonized by the largest and most powerful corporate polluters in the world. Through the financing of congressional and presidential candidates opposed to strong environmental regulations and the appointment of its own corporate officials to key government agencies (including those relating to environmental protection), the polluter-industrial complex has successfully assumed direct control over numerous leadership positions in the federal government. Moreover, corporate lobbyists and a vast policymaking infrastructure supported by environmentally destructive companies are being utilized by these same politicians and appointees in both major political parties to roll back ecological protection. Along with the corruption of independent scientific investigation of environmental problems by corporate polluters, these processes have resulted in the colonization of the state by the polluter-industrial complex and the erosion of environmental justice in the United States. In the age of neoliberalism, corporate polluters dominate the U.S. government agencies that regulate them.

The impact of this political assault is profound. The environmental/EJ movements as well as labor, immigrant rights, civil rights, women's, peace, and other social movements committed to economic and social justice are largely unable to advance their policy agendas in relation to the state. Many of these movements are in retreat and rapidly losing their capacity to bring about meaningful social change, particularly at the national level. Moreover, most of the major national organizations representing progressive movements remain locked into "policy silos" that are narrowly focused on categorical programs and policies.[136] As a result, these movements have been ineffective at building a broader political vision capable of building common ground between working- and middle-class whites and people of color. Absent the joining of movements around more "universalistic" sets of demands pertaining to rights of citizenship and popular class interests, these fragmented movements are more easily "divided and conquered" by the power elite. The election of a few liberals and progressive Democrats to Congress and even the presidency will not in and of itself change the structural features of the power exerted by corporate elites over the American political system from behind the scenes.

The absence of a united left-of-center power structure to combat the sophisticated infrastructure of the ultraconservatives and corporate centrists enables the hegemony of the polluter-industrial complex. As we shall see in chapter 3, the political dominance of these corporate polluters is responsible for a profound weakening of policies and programs designed to ensure environmental justice and protection of the earth. To halt this assault and chart a new course with respect to environmental policy and social justice concerns will ultimately require the American people to reclaim the state.

NOTES

1. Bob Williams, *US Petroleum Strategies in the Decade of the Environment* (Tulsa, OK: PennWell Books, 1991).

2. G. William Domhoff, *Who Rules America? Power and Politics* (Boston: Mc-Graw-Hill, 2002), 72.

3. G. William Domhoff, *The Power Elite and the State: How Policy Is Made in America* (New York: Aldine de Gruyter, 1990), 17–25.

4. Francis Sandbach, *Environment, Ideology, and Policy* (Montclair, NJ: Allanheld, Osmun, 1980), 13.

5. Thomas Frank, *What's the Matter with Kansas?: How Conservatives Won the Heart of America* (New York: Metropolitan Books, 2004); Barbara Ehrenreich, *Fear of Falling: The Inner Life of the Middle Class* (New York: Perennial, 1990).

6. Robert O. Bothwell, "Up against Conservative Public Policy: Alternatives to Mainstream Philanthropy," in *Foundations for Social Change: Critical Perspectives on Philanthropy and Popular Movements*, ed. Daniel Faber and Deborah McCarthy (Lanham, MD: Rowman & Littlefield, 2005), 115–47.

7. Nick Nyhard, "The Myth of Small-Donor Clout: Large Contributors' Importance Grew in 2004, Contrary to Popular Perception," *The Nation* 280, no. 25 (June 27, 2005): 25–27.

8. The top fund-raiser for a House candidate in 2006 was Democrat Robert Menendez of New Jersey with more than $10.8 million. See "Candidate Money Leaders," *PoliticalMoneyLine from Congressional Quarterly*, http://www.tray.com/cgi-win/x_webl_all.exe?DoFn=&sYR=2006 (accessed November 7, 2006).

9. Nyhard, "The Myth of Small-Donor Clout," 25–27.

10. Philip Shabecoff, *A Fierce Green Fire: The American Environmental Movement* (Washington, DC: Island Press, 2003), 280.

11. http://www.opensecrets.org/bigpicture/bigspenders.asp?Display=A&Memb=S&Sort=A (accessed April 26, 2006).

12. Overall, Democrats collected 60 percent of the money from these top 100 donors, largely because of the financial power of the unions and their strong preference for Democratic candidates. See http:www.opensecrets.org/pubs/toporgs/intro.asp (accessed April 26, 2006).

13. A wealthy area is defined as a place where more than 24.6 percent of households make $100,000 per year or more—twice the national average. A high-poverty area is where more than 23.5 percent of households are in poverty—twice the national average. See *The Color of Money 2003: Campaign Contributions, Race, Ethnicity, and Neighborhood*, a report by Public Campaign, the Fannie Lou Hamer Project, and the William C. Velasquez Institute (December 2003), 1–48, and *The Color of Money: The 2004 Presidential Race—Campaign Contributions, Race, Ethnicity, and Neighborhood*, a report by Public Campaign, the Fannie Lou Hamer Project, and the William C. Velasquez Institute (October 2004), 1–36.

14. Maria Weidner and Nancy Watzman, *Paybacks—Policy, Patrons, and Personnel: How the Bush Administration Is Giving Away Our Environment to Corporate Contributors*, a report by Earthjustice and Public Campaign (September 2002), 1–27.

15. Nyart, "The Myth of Small-Donor Clout," 25–27.

16. Robert McNatt, "Up Front," *BusinessWeek* (November 6, 2000), 12, cited in William K. Tabb, "The Power of the Rich," *Monthly Review* 58, no. 3 (July–August 2006): 6–17.

17. Tabb, "The Power of the Rich,"13.

18. Center for Responsive Politics, "Top Industries Giving to Members of Congress: 2006 Cycle," available at http://www.opensecrets.org/industries/mems.asp (accessed November 3, 2006).

19. Brandon Wu, *Paying to Pollute: Campaign Contributions and Lobbying Expenditures by Polluters Working to Weaken Environmental Laws*, a report by the U.S. PIRG Education Fund (April 2004), 1–45.

20. Louise Levathes, "Easy Money: How Congressional Candidates Are Cleaning Up with the Dirty Water PACs," *Audubon* 97, no. 6 (November–December 1995): 16–22.

21. See http://www.opensecrets.org/pubs/toporgs/intro.asp (accessed April 26, 2006).

22. See http://www.opensecrets.org/pacs/industry.asp?txt=Q11&cycle=2000 (accessed April 26, 2006).

23. Wu, *Paying to Pollute*, 17.

24. Alan C. Miller and Tom Hamburger, "Records Sought for Two Groups Opposed to Bush Clean-Air Plan," *Boston Globe* (February 20, 2005), A18.

25. Wu, *Paying to Pollute*, 19.

26. Brad Heavner and Ellen R. Montgomery, *America's Environment at Risk*, a report by the Frontier Group, a policy center of the national association of state Public Research Interest Groups (2003), 19.

27. Weidner and Watzman, *Paybacks*, 2.

28. "Al Gore: Contributions by Sector," and "President George W. Bush: Contributions by Sector," at http://www.opensecrets.org/2000elect/sector/P80000912.htm (accessed November 2, 2006).

29. Tabb, "The Power of the Rich," 6–17.

30. Ken Silverstein, "The Polluters' President," *Sierra Magazine* (November/December 1999), available at http://www.sierraclub.org/sierra/199911/bush.asp (accessed May 10, 2007).

31. Matt Kelly, "Halliburton Should Repay Overcharges on Gas, Bush Says," *Boston Globe* (December 13, 2003), A11.

32. "Bush-Cheney Energy Bill Includes Gift to Halliburton," *BushGreenwatch* (January 9, 2004), 1–3.

33. Heavner and Montgomery, *America's Environment at Risk*, 23.

34. Public Citizen, "The Importance of Bundlers to the Bush and Kerry Campaigns: Post-Election Summary of Findings," *Public Citizen's Congress Watch* (2005): 1–23.

35. Ilan Levin and Conor Kenney, with Neal Pattison and Dan Himmelsbach, *America's Dirtiest Power Plants: Plugged into the Bush Administration*, a report by the Environmental Integrity Project and Public Citizen's Congress Watch (May 2004), 1–17.

36. Levin et al., *America's Dirtiest Power Plants*, 1–17.

37. Wu, *Paying to Pollute*, 7–9.

38. Public Citizen, "The Importance of Bundlers to the Bush and Kerry Campaigns."

39. Weidner and Watzman, *Paybacks*, 24.

40. Dan Zegart, "The Gutting of the Civil Service," *The Nation* 283, no. 17 (November 20, 2006): 24–30.

41. George A. Gonzalez, *Corporate Power and the Environment: The Political Economy of US Environmental Policy* (Lanham, MD: Rowman & Littlefield, 2001).

42. Molly Ivins, "This Cabinet Is Full of Corporate America," *Boston Globe* (February 10, 2001). Ivins died in late January 2007 at the age of sixty-two after a long battle with breast cancer.

43. John Heilprin, "ConocoPhillips' Lobbyist's Real Estate Deal Probed," Associated Press (February 15, 2007); Margie Burns, "Despite Cheney's Absence, His Influence Looms over Complex CIA Leak Trial," *Washington Spectator* 33, no. 4 (February 15, 2007), 1–5.

44. Emily Gest and Corky Siemaszko, "W Interior Pick Panned on Paint: Lobbies for Firm in Lead-Poisoning Suits," *Daily News* (January 12, 2001), 4–5.

45. Miguel Lianos, "Does Arctic Refuge Video Break the Law?," MSNBC (April 12, 2002).

46. For more information on the control of federal lands by the polluter-industrial complex, see Environmental Working Group, *Who Owns the West? Oil and Gas Leases*, available at http://www.ewg.org/oil_and_gas/execsumm.php (accessed February 8, 2007).

47. Shell Accountability Coalition, *Use Your Profit to Clean Up Your Mess: Report on How Shell Should Fund Local Solutions for Environmental and Social Destruction Caused by Its Projects* (February 2007), 5–58.

48. William Sanjour, "In Name Only," *Sierra Magazine* (September/October 1992), 1–8, and "What's Wrong with the EPA?," *Synthesis/Regeneration* 7–8 (Summer 1995): 1–7.

49. Marianne Lavelle and Marcia Coyle, "Unequal Protection: The Racial Divide in Environmental Law," *National Law Journal* (September 21, 1992), 2–12.

50. Peter Montague, "What We Must Do: The Moral Issue of the '80s," *Rachel's Environment and Health News* (July 31, 1988), 1–2.

51. Peter Montague, "Feds Seeking $2.2 Billion Fine from Browning-Ferris Industries," *Rachel's Hazardous Waste News* 27 (June 1, 1987), 1–2.

52. Laura Westra, "The Faces of Environmental Racism: Titusville, Alabama, and BFI," in *Faces of Environmental Racism: Confronting Issues of Global Justice*, 2nd ed., ed. Laura Westra and Bill E. Lawson (Lanham, MD: Rowman & Littlefield, 2001), 113–40.

53. Robert D. Bullard, *Dumping in Dixie: Race, Class, and Environmental Quality* (Boulder, CO: Westview Press, 1994).

54. Political Ecology Group, *Toxic Empire, the WMX Corporation, Hazardous Waste and Global Strategies for Environmental Justice* (San Francisco: Political Ecology Group, 1995).

55. "EPA's Revolving Door" provides a partial list of EPA officials who found subsequent employment in the waste management industry in the 1970–1980s at http://pwp.lincs.net/sanjour/Revolving.htm (accessed May 20, 2007).

56. Christine Todd Whitman, *It's My Party Too: The Battle for the Heart of the GOP and the Future of America* (New York: Penguin, 2005).

57. Doug Ireland, "Whitman: A Toxic Choice," *The Nation* 272, no. 4 (January 29, 2001): 18.

58. Christine Todd Whitman and Patrick Moore, "Nuclear Should Be a Part of Our Energy Future," *Boston Globe* (May 15, 2006), A9.

59. Reece Rushing, *Special Interest Takeover: The Bush Administration and the Dismantling of Public Safeguards*, a report by the Center for American Progress and OMB Watch on behalf of Citizens for Sensible Safeguards (May 2004).

60. Rushing, *Special Interest Takeover*, 1–4.

61. Weidner and Watzman, *Paybacks*, 8.

62. Rebecca Clarren, "Fields of Poison: While Farmworkers Are Sickened by Pesticides, Industry Writes the Rules," *The Nation* 227, no. 22 (December 29, 2003): 23–25.

63. "Chemical Industry Given Private Access to EPA; Seeks Approval of Pesticides at Expense of Wildlife," *BushGreenwatch* (January 23, 2004), 1–2.

64. Sally Covington, "Moving Public Policy to the Right: The Strategic Philanthropy of Conservative Foundations," in *Foundations for Social Change: Critical Perspectives on Philanthropy and Popular Movements*, ed. Daniel R. Faber and Deborah McCarthy (Lanham, MD: Rowman & Littlefield, 2005), 89–114.

65. Walter Dean Burnham, "The 1996 Elections: Drift or Mandate?," *The American Prospect* 27 (July–August 1996): 43–49.

66. Clyde W. Barrow, *Critical Theories of the State: Marxist, Neo-Marxist, Post-Marxist* (Madison: University of Wisconsin Press, 1993), 25–28, 33.

67. Gwen Moore, Sarah Sobieraj, J. Allen Whit, Olga Mayorova, and Daniel Beaulieu, "Elite Interlocks in Three US Sectors: Nonprofit, Corporate, and Government," *Social Science Quarterly* 83 (2002): 726–44.

68. Greenpeace has developed an interactive tool for researching these interlocking directors that are related to ExxonMobil and the polluter-industrial complex policy infrastructure. See *Exxonsecrets.org: How ExxonMobil Funds the Climate Change Skeptics* at http://www.exxonsecrets.org (accessed May 4, 2007).

69. Seth Shulman, with Kate Abend and Alden Meyer, *Smoke, Mirrors, and Hot Air: How ExxonMobil Uses Big Tobacco's Tactics to Manufacture Uncertainty on Climate Science* (Cambridge, MA: Union of Concerned Scientists, 2007).

70. J. Craig Jenkins and Craig M. Eckert, "The Right Turn in Economic Policy: Business Elites and the New Conservative Economics," *Sociological Forum* 15 (2000): 307–38.

71. Sharon Beder, *Global Spin: The Corporate Assault on Environmentalism* (White River Junction, VT: Chelsea Green, 1997), 83–84.

72. John Nichols, "Behind the DLC Takeover," *Progressive* 64, no. 10 (October 2000): 28–30.

73. For critiques that expose the many falsehoods of such "greenwashing" works, see Tom Athanasiou, "The Age of Greenwashing," *Capitalism, Nature, Socialism* 7, no. 1 (March 1996): 1–36; and Tom Athanasiou, *Divided Planet: The Ecology of Rich and Poor* (New York: Little, Brown, 1996), and "How They Lie" (parts 1–2), in *Rachel's Environment and Health Weekly*, no. 503–04 (July 18–25, 1996), 1–2; and no. 437 (April 13, 1995), 1–2.

74. Beder, *Global Spin*, 91.

75. Christopher C. Horner, *The Politically Incorrect Guide to Global Warming and Environmentalism* (Washington, DC: Regnery, 2007).

76. Ellen Goodman, "No Change in Political Climate," *Boston Globe* (February 9, 2007), A19.

77. David Friedman, "The 'Environmental Racism' Hoax," *The American Enterprise* 9, no. 6 (November–December 1989): 75–78.

78. Christopher H. Foreman Jr., *The Promise and Peril of Environmental Justice* (Washington, DC: Brookings Institute, 1998).

79. Ken Silverstein and Alexander Cockburn, "Easterbrook's Moment: Dr. Pangloss Goes Corporate," *CounterPunch* 2, no. 9 (May 1, 1995): 1–2.

80. Beder, *Global Spin*, 24–25, 91–106.

81. Michael Kraft, "A New Environmental Policy Agenda: The 1980 Presidential Campaign and Its Aftermath," in *Environmental Policy in the 1980s*, ed. Norman J. Vig and Miachel E. Kraft (Washington, DC: Congressional Quarterly Press, 1984), 38.

82. David Helvarg, *The War against the Greens: The "Wise Use" Movement, the New Right, and Anti-Environmental Violence* (San Francisco: Sierra Club Books, 1994), 20–21.

83. Beder, *Global Spin*, 77–79, 91–106.

84. Rachel Egen, *Buying a Movement: Right-Wing Foundations and American Politics*, a report by the American Way (1996), 1–43.

85. Daniel Faber and Deborah McCarthy, "Foundations for Social Change: Critical Perspectives on Philanthropy and Popular Movements," in *Foundations for Social Change: Critical Perspectives on Philanthropy and Popular Movements*, ed. Daniel Faber and Deborah McCarthy (Lanham, MD: Rowman & Littlefield, 2005), 14–15.

86. Beder, *Global Spin*, 83.

87. David Callahan, *$1 Billion for Ideas: Conservative Think Tanks in the 1990s* (Washington, DC: National Committee for Responsive Philanthropy, 2001), 5.

88. Jeff Krehely, Meaghan House, and Emily Kernan, *Axis of Ideology: Conservative Foundations and Public Policy* (Washington, DC: National Committee for Responsive Philanthropy, March 2004), 4–8; Rick G. Cohen, "Introduction: The State of Philanthropy 2002," in *The State of Philanthropy 2002* (Washington, DC: National Committee for Responsive Philanthropy, 2002), v.

89. Kreheley et al., *Axis of Ideology*, 40–42.

90. John J. Fialka, "Lawyer Who Challenged EPA Case Had Social Contacts with Judges," *Wall Street Journal* (March 23, 2004), A4.

91. Thomas Koenig and Michael Rustad, "Toxic Torts, Politics and Environmental Justice: The Case for Crimtorts," *Law and Policy* 26, no. 2 (April 2004): 189–207.

92. Thomas Koenig and Michael Rustad, *In Defense of Tort Law* (New York: New York University Press, 2001).

93. Sharon Buccino, Tim Dowling, Doug Kendall, and Elaine Weiss, *Hostile Environment: How Anti-Environmental Federal Judges Threaten Our Air, Water, and Land*, a report by the Alliance for Justice, Community Rights Counsel, and the Natural Resources Defense Council (July 2001), available at http://www.nrdc.org/legislation/hostile/execsum.asp (accessed June 12, 2007).

94. Koenig and Rustad, "Toxic Torts, Politics and Environmental Justice," 189–207.

95. Buccino et al., *Hostile Environment*.

96. Molly Ivins and Lou Dubose, *Bushwhacked: Life in George W. Bush's America* (New York: Vintage, 2004).

97. SourceWatch, "Eugene Scalia," a Project of the Center for Media and Democracy, available at http://www.sourcewatch.org/index.php?title=Eugene_Scalia (accessed April 2, 2007).

98. Center for Public Integrity, "Lobbyists Double Spending in Six Years" (April 7, 2005), available at http://www.publicintegrity.org, cited in Tabb, "The Power of the Rich," 8–10.

99. Center for Public Integrity, "Lobbyists Double Spending in Six Years," in Tabb, "The Power of the Rich," 8–9.

100. See the "Money and Politics Databases" at http://www.politicalmoneyline.com/cgi-win/lp_sector.exe?DoFn=ye&Year=05 (accessed May 1, 2007). PoliticalMoneyLine is a Washington, D.C.-based organization that tracks lobbying based reports to Congress.

101. Wu, *Paying to Pollute*, 20.

102. Martha H. Keating and Felicia Davis, *Air of Injustice: African Americans and Power Plant Pollution,* a report by the Black Leadership Forum, Clear the Air, Georgia Coalition for Peoples' Agenda, and the Southern Organizing Committee for Economic and Social Justice (October 2002), 4.

103. Center for Public Integrity, "Lobbyists Double Spending in Six Years," 8–10.

104. Wu, *Paying to Pollute*, 20–25.

105. Susan Milligan, with Marc Schechtman, Maud S. Beelman, Kevin Baron, and Samiya Edwards, "Energy Bill a Special-Interests Triumph: Closed, for Business Deals but No Debate in Congress," *Boston Globe* (October 4, 2004), A1, A10–A11.

106. Allison Cassady, *Big Money to Big Oil: How ExxonMobil and the Oil Industry Benefit from the 2005 Energy Bill*, a report by the U.S. PIRG Education Fund (August 2005), 1–17.

107. Elizabeth Shogren, "Senior EPA Official to Become Lobbyist," *Los Angeles Times* (September 4, 2003).

108. Wu, *Paying to Pollute*, 21–22.

109. Emily Cousins, Robert Perks, and Wesley Warren, *Rewriting the Rules: The Bush Administration's First-Term Environmental Record*, a report by the Natural Resources Defense Council (January 2005), v.

110. John Donnelly, "Interior Ethics Lapses Rarely Punished: IG—Royalty Loss Could Cost US Tens of Billions," *Boston Globe* (February 17, 2007), A2.

111. Mark Sherman, "Group Sues to Get White House Logs on Lobbyist's Visits," *Boston Globe* (March 1, 2006), A16.

112. John Stauber and Sheldon Rampton, *Toxic Sludge Is Good for You: Lies, Damn Lies, and the Public Relations Industry* (Monroe, ME: Common Courage Press, 1995).

113. Susanna Rankin Bohme, John Zorabedian, and David S. Egilman, "Maximizing Profit and Endangering Health: Corporate Strategies to Avoid Litigation and Regulation," *International Journal of Occupational and Environmental Health* 11, no. 4 (October/December 2005): 338–48.

114. Beder, *Global Spin*, 27.

115. Peter Montague, "How They Lie, Parts 1–2," *Rachel's Environment and Health Weekly*, nos. 503 and 504 (July 18–July 25, 1996), 1–2.

116. David Roe, William Pease, Karen Florini, and Ellen Silbergeld, *Toxic Ignorance: the Continuing Absence of Basic Health Testing for Top-Selling Chemicals in the United States* (New York: Environmental Defense Fund, 1997).

117. Mary H. O'Brien, "When Harm Is Not Necessary: Risk Assessment as Diversion," in *Reclaiming the Environmental Debate: The Politics of Health in a Toxic Culture*, ed. Richard Hofrichter (Cambridge, MA: MIT Press, 2000), 113–34.

118. Devra Davis, *When Smoke Ran Like Water: Tales of Environmental Deception and the Battle Against Pollution* (New York: Basic Books, 2002), 89–122.

119. Gerald Markowitz and David Rosner, *Deceit and Denial: The Deadly Politics of Industrial Pollution* (Berkeley: University of California Press, 2002).

120. Linda Rosenstock, "Global Threats to Science: Policy, Politics, and Special Interests," in *Contributions to the History of Occupational and Environmental Prevention*, ed. A. Grieco, S. Iavicoli, and G. Berlinguer (London: Elsevier Science, 1999), 113, cited in Markowitz and Rosner, *Deceit and Denial*, 4.

121. Peter Waldman, "Publication to Retract an Influential Water Study," *Wall Street Journal* (June 2, 2006), A10.

122. Elihu D. Richter, C. Soskolne, J. LaDou, and T. Berman, "Whistleblowers in Environmental Science, Prevention of Suppression Bias and the Need for a Code of Action," *International Journal of Occupational and Environmental Health* 7 (2001): 68–71.

123. Chris Mooney, *The Republican War on Science* (New York: Basic Books, 2006).

124. Glenn Scherer, "Religious Wrong: A Higher Power Informs the Republican Assault on the Environment," *E Magazine* 14, no. 3 (March/April 2003): 2–6.

125. Rick Weiss, "HHS Seeks Science Advice to Match Bush Views," *Washington Post* (September 17, 2002), A1.

126. OMB Watch, "Administration Stacks Scientific Advisory Panels," http://www.ombwatch.org/article/articleview/1384/1/39 (accessed March 4, 2006).

127. Robert F. Kennedy Jr., "The Junk Science of George W. Bush," *The Nation* 278, no. 9 (March 8, 2004): 11–18.

128. Seth Shulman, *Scientific Integrity in Policy Making: An Investigation of the Bush Administration's Misuse of Science*, a report by the Union of Concerned Scientists (March 2004), and *Scientific Integrity in Policy Making: Further Investigation of the Bush Administration's Misuse of Science*, a report by the Union of Concerned Scientists (July 2004).

129. "Political Appointees Pollute Waters at Ocean Agency: Survey Shows Special Interest Influence and Altered Scientific Findings," (June 28, 2005), available at http://www.ucsusa.org/news/press_release.cfm?newsID=491 (accessed June 28, 2005).

130. Environment2004, *Putting Polluters First: The Bush Administration's Environmental Record*, a report by Environment2004 (June 2004), 21–24.

131. National Research Council, *Climate Change Science: An Analysis of Some Key Questions*, a report for the National Research Council's Division on Earth and Life Studies, Committee on Science of Climate Change (2001), 1.

132. Scherer, "Religious Wrong."

133. Statement of Scientists, *Restoring Scientific Integrity in Policymaking* (February 18, 2004), http://www.ucsusa.org/global_environment/rsi/page.cfm?pageID=1320 (accessed March 12, 2007).

134. Elizabeth Kolbert, "Getting Warmer," *New Yorker* (November 10, 2003) 1–2, accessed at http://www.newyorker.com/archive/2003/11/17/031117ta_talk_kolbert (accessed March 2, 2008).

135. Andrew C. Revkin, "Memos Tell Officials How to Discuss Climate," *New York Times* (March 8, 2007).

136. Bothwell, "Up against Conservative Public Policy," 115–20.

Chapter Three

Against Our Nature: Neoliberalism and the Crisis of Environmental Justice Policy

Social injustice, growing inequality, and a looming environmental crisis are the greatest threats facing the global community as we enter the twenty-first century. We have little chance of seriously solving our global environmental problems . . . unless we also address global and local inequality. Ultimately, this will entail profound economic and cultural change, particularly for the privileged of the world.

—Laura Pulido, American scholar and environmental justice advocate[1]

THE ECOLOGICAL CRISIS AND THE CRISIS OF ENVIRONMENTALISM

Over the course of the past four decades, environmentalists have built one of the largest and most powerful social movements in the history of the United States. There are over 10,000 Internal Revenue Service–registered environmental organizations, with an overall membership between 19 million and 41 million people.[2] The thirty largest national environmental organizations alone possess 7.8 million members.[3] In addition, tens of thousands of more "informal" environmental groups work out of schools and college campuses, neighborhoods and local communities, and the workplace. These vital organizations have won many important victories resulting in the protection of endangered species, wildlife habitats, parks, and wilderness; reductions in some types of air, noise, land, ocean, and water pollution; and some key improvements in public, consumer, and worker health safety, including reductions in human exposure to highly dangerous substances such as lead, asbestos, DDT, and other toxic chemicals. Furthermore, movement mobilization since the 1970s has spurred the creation of a vast *liberal regime of environmental regulation*,

119

during which dozens of major environmental statutes costing business hundreds of billions of dollars have been passed into law. As a result, U.S. governmental policies for protecting the environment and worker/human health are among the most stringent in the world.

Still, the news is not good. Although many important battles have been won over the years, it is now apparent that the contemporary environmental movement is losing the war for a healthy planet. Despite a governmental pledge at the 1992 Earth Summit in Rio to reduce emissions of greenhouse gases, the United States is generating ever-greater quantities. In 2006, the United States produced 5.8 billion metric tons of carbon dioxide, a 20 percent increase since 1990. Air pollution is also contributing to an asthma epidemic in the United States. According to the American Lung Association, more than 6 million children have asthma, which can be life threatening if not properly managed. It is the leading cause of school absenteeism due to chronic conditions and the leading cause of hospitalizations in children under age fifteen. Astonishingly, over 60,000 Americans continue to die each year from air pollution alone. Half a million people living in the most polluted areas in 151 cities across the country face a risk of death some 15 to 17 percent higher than those living in the least polluted areas.[4]

Water pollution is another serious environmental problem. While more than $100 billion has been spent as a result of Clean Water Act regulations, the water quality of most major rivers is poor. A growing number of water tables are being poisoned or depleted, while more agricultural soil is being eroded or rendered unproductive because of salinization, chemical contamination, and other problems. Pesticides linked to cancer, birth defects, and neurological disorders contaminate virtually all rivers and streams. In fact, the U.S. National Geologic Survey reports that more than 80 percent of America's urban streams contain pesticide concentrations that exceed safe water quality benchmarks for aquatic life.[5] Most environmental regulations also fail to solve problems related to urban/suburban sprawl or to halt the ecological destruction of watersheds and wildlife habitats by logging and strip mining activities.

Meanwhile, nearly half the American people live within ten miles of at least one of the nation's 1,623 highly dangerous Superfund toxic waste sites. The landmass of these sites is twice the size of Los Angeles, New York City, and Chicago combined.[6] Among people who live near these sites, the National Research Council has found a disturbing pattern of elevated health problems, including heart disease, spontaneous abortions, genital malformations, and death rates, while infants and children are found to suffer a higher incidence of cardiac abnormalities, leukemia, kidney–urinary tract infections, seizures, learning disabilities, hyperactivity, skin disorders, reduced weight, central nervous system damage, and Hodgkin's disease.[7] Although these dumps are the worst of the worst, the Office of Technology Assessment estimates that there are as many as 439,000 other illegal hazardous waste sites in the country.[8] Exposure to industrial chemicals is also contributing to the dramatic increases since the 1950s in cancer of the testis, prostate gland, kidney, and breast as well as malignant myeloma, non-Hodgkin's lymphoma, and numerous childhood cancers—a cancer epidemic that kills half a million Americans each year. And, by most reliable accounts, these and other environmentally related health problems are growing worse.[9] In the United States, men now have about a one-in-two lifetime risk of developing cancer; for women, the lifetime risk is slightly more than one in three.[10]

Given the magnitude of these and other ecological problems, it is evident that many environmental policies are not adequate to the task. In this respect, a major paradox confronts environmental activists—namely, that despite the creation of broad-based movement and a vast federal bureaucracy devoted to environmental protection, the ecological crisis continues to deepen. Most environmental laws are poorly enforced and overly limited in their application, emphasizing, for instance, *pollution control* measures that aim to limit public exposure to specific industrial pollutants at "tolerable" levels (a very difficult and uncertain task) over *pollution prevention* measures that prohibit whole families of dangerous pollutants from being produced in the first place. The U.S. system of environmental regulation may have at one time been the best in the world, but it is not adequate for safeguarding human health and the integrity of nature. And while there is no doubt that ecological problems would be much worse absent the environmental movement and current system of regulation, it is also clear that the traditional political strategies and policy solutions embraced by the mainstream of the environmental establishment are proving to be increasingly ineffective and even contradictory to their intended purposes. The liberal regime of environmental regulation is in deep crisis.

POLITICAL OPPOSITION TO THE LIBERAL REGIME OF ENVIRONMENTAL REGULATION

The Environmental Justice Critique of Traditional Policy Approaches

The contradictions inherent in traditional American environmentalism are revealed in new forms of political opposition on both the left and the right. The liberal regime of environmental regulation has initiated some improvements in environmental quality as sought by broad sectors of the population, particularly the white middle class (or salariat). But because liberal environmental policies are not embedded in popular democratic control over capitalist accumulation and state administration of society, such approaches often neglect (or even worsen) problems for other sectors of the population that possess less political-economic power to defend themselves. In fact, one of the hallmarks of the liberal regime of regulation is the manner in which it has corrected some single-issue environmental and human health problems for some people by causing industry to transform the ecological hazard into another form, which is then displaced into another realm of nature and/or onto other members of society, especially the working class or poor people of color. For instance, when the Sierra Club and other environmentalists were successful in getting the pesticide DDT banned for use in the United States in order to protect wildlife (such as the bald eagle) and public health in the early 1970s, agribusiness firms in California switched to more toxic pesticides, such as methyl parathion. Because the DDT ban did not address pesticide abuses in general, acute health problems and poisoning deaths went up dramatically among immigrant farmworkers exposed to the replacement chemicals in the fields.

Environmental regulations relating to industrial pollution also serve to displace ecological hazards. By requiring manufacturers to *contain* pollution sources for more proper treatment and disposal, the liberal regime of regulation promotes the commodification of pollution by the waste treatment industry, hence a new source of profit. With the expansion of the waste circuit of capital, pollution becomes geographically mobile as corporations search for ever more "efficient" (low-cost and politically feasible) disposal sites. The places in which these environmental hazards become relocated are increasingly distant from the industrial facilities in which they are produced and typically wind up in politically marginalized communities. Hence, the liberal regime of regulations has contributed to an explosion of toxic waste sites and other ecological hazards in poor communities of color and working-class communities since the 1980s. In 2001, for instance, U.S.-based industry generated more than 41 million tons of hazardous wastes. Under the Resource Conservation and Recovery Act of 1976, hazardous waste is managed by specially designed facilities referred to as treatment, storage, and disposal facilities, which include incinerators and landfills. More than 5.1 million people in racial and/or ethnic minority groups nationwide now live in neighborhoods with one or more such facilities.[11]

The displacement of the ecological crisis onto the disenfranchised has fueled the rise of the environmental justice (EJ) movement. In Latino and Asian-Pacific neighborhoods in the inner cities, small African American townships, depressed Native American reservations, Chicano farming communities, and white working-class districts all across the country, peoples traditionally relegated to the periphery of the ecology movement are now also challenging the wholesale degradation of their land, water, air, and community health by corporate polluters and indifferent governmental agencies and nongovernmental organizations. At the forefront of this new wave of grassroots activism are hundreds of community-based organizations working to reverse the disproportionate social and ecological hardships borne by people of color and poor working-class families. These community-based organizations, as well as regional EJ networks and national constituency–based EJ networks, are all united against environmental racism, poverty and social inequality, and political disempowerment.

In addition to challenging the distributional impacts of environmental policy, many EJ activists are beginning to contest production-related policy flaws. For instance, it is now clear that the "risk paradigm" approach employed by the Environmental Protection Agency (EPA) is largely incapable of accurately determining "acceptable levels" of public exposure to industrial toxins. What have been assumed to be safe levels of exposure in the past have been proven time and again to be dangerous levels of exposure. Furthermore, industry regularly violates such standards once they are established by the government.[12] In fact, chemicals routinely approved for commercial use are tested solely by the manufacturers with virtually no governmental oversight.[13] A recent study by the Environmental Defense Fund found that three-quarters of the high-profile, high-volume chemicals used by industry lack even the most minimal health testing information.[14] Only after severe health and environmental impacts occur have much stricter regulations or the banning of a specific chemical (such as lead paint and DDT) actually occurred.[15]

The liberal regime of regulation and standard risk assessments also assume that "dilution is the solution"—that pollutants emitted from industrial facilities will be dispersed over a wide area and cause minimal or "acceptable rates" of harm to the general population. A recent study by the Institute of Medicine found that low-income families and people of color are exposed to higher levels of pollution than the rest of the nation and that these same populations experience many diseases in greater number than the white salariat.[16] As a result, dangerous levels of industrial chemicals permeate the environments where poor people live, work, and play. These substances also contaminate much of the country's food supply, cleaning agents, household and personal care products, and other consumer goods.[17] In fact, Americans carry a toxic "body burden" of dozens (and perhaps hundreds) of synthetic chemicals and other contaminants, according to a new study by the Centers for Disease Control and Prevention.[18] Nevertheless, recent polling data show that most Americans mistakenly believe that the U.S. government routinely tests chemicals used in consumer products to make sure they are safe.[19]

Standard environmental policy approaches are further problematic in that they take single-issue policy approaches to what are often highly complicated, interrelated problems; divorce issues of the environment from larger social issues (such as jobs or housing); promote *risk avoidance* strategies whereby those being harmed by pollution are asked to alter their behavior (such as asking Native Americans to stop eating mercury-contaminated fish) rather than promoting *risk reduction* strategies (whereby industry is required to clean up, reduce, or prevent mercury contamination of waterways); and focus on single species rather than the health of entire ecosystems. As stated by Dr. Robert Bullard,

> The dominant paradigm exists to manage, regulate, and distribute risks. As a result, the current system has institutionalized unequal enforcement of safety precautions; traded human health for profit; placed the burden of proof on the victims and not the polluting industry; legitimated human exposure to harmful chemicals, pesticides, and hazardous substances; promoted risky technologies such as incinerators; exploited the vulnerability of economically and politically disenfranchised communities; subsidized ecological destruction; created an industry around risk assessment; . . . delayed cleanup actions; and failed to develop pollution prevention as the overarching strategy.[20]

These inadequacies exacerbate antagonisms between people of color and the mainstream environmental movement. Such tensions are grounded not only in the contradictions of current environmental policy but also in the fact that too many mainstream environmental organizations neglect concerns held by poor people of color and white working-class families. This conflicted relationship first boiled over in March 1990, when the Southwest Organizing Project—a major EJ organization—sent a letter to ten of the largest national environmental organizations (at that time referred to as "the Group of Ten"), stating,

> There is a clear lack of accountability by the Group of Ten environmental organizations towards Third World communities in the Southwest, in the United States, and internationally. Your organizations continue to support and promote policies which emphasize the clean-up and preservation of the environment on the backs of working people in general and people of color in particular. In the name of eliminating environmental hazards at any cost, across the country industrial and other economic activities which employ us are being shut down, curtailed or prevented while our survival needs and cultures are ignored. We suffer from the results of these actions, but are never full participants in the decision-making which leads to them.[21]

Despite these past tensions, new coalitions of EJ advocates and grassroots environmental activists on the left are now coming together to promote more holistic solutions. To combat the "toxic trespass" of industrial poisons, for instance, the "clean production" wings of the environmental/EJ movements are working to promote pollution prevention strategies, safer substitutes for toxic chemicals, and a more precautionary approach to environmental policy that shifts the burden onto industry to prove that a given chemical is safe before it can be used (rather than placing that burden on the public to prove that a given chemical is dangerous after being introduced into the marketplace). As seen with the Alliance for a Healthy Tomorrow (AHT) in Massachusetts, where a coalition of more than 160 organizations representing labor, health professionals, environmentalists, public health advocates, EJ organizations, parents, scientists, and academics have come together to push for the required commercial phaseout of the most dangerous chemicals, these new coalitions offer the promise of transforming environmental policy at the state and, eventually, federal levels.[22]

The Neoliberal Critique of Traditional Policy Approaches

The liberal regime of environmental regulation is also invoking a profound political backlash on the right, spearheaded by corporations that make up the polluter-industrial complex. Even though traditional policies fail to establish popular democratic control over the process of capital accumulation (investment, production, and distribution), they do sometimes impose significant regulatory costs and inflexibilities that impinge on the profits of capital. Liberalist "command-and-control" approaches to regulation, including policies that restrict the amount of specific pollutants that industry can release into the workplace or environment, typically add to the costs of capital but not to revenues. Most pollution control devices in the United States are added on to existing plants and equipment, such as the installation of a "scrubber" designed to help "clean" polluted air coming from a smokestack, and fail to make industry more cost efficient. Unlike "productive expenditures" on machinery that increase labor productivity and indirectly lower the unit costs of capital/wage goods, pollution abatement devices and cleanup technologies usually increase costs and hence, everything else being the same, reduce profits or increase prices. In short, "end-of-the-pipe" pollution containment and environmental conservation measures are viewed as "unproductive expenditures" that American business is increasingly unwilling to absorb, especially when one considers the advantages enjoyed by foreign competitors with lower labor costs and less stringent regulations.

These costs and other *inflexibilities* in the deployment of capital funds and labor create a widespread perception in the business community that the liberal regime of environmental regulation is a major obstacle to corporate profitability. In the current period of increased foreign competition and the pressure to cut costs and defend market share that goes with the globalization of capital, this has prompted a profound corporate assault on the liberal environmental establishment. The alternative proposal on behalf of business is for the adoption of neoliberal forms of "free-market" environmentalism in state policymaking and enforcement.[23] Neoliberals are committed to deregulation and reprivatization of the economy—to "liberalize" or "free" the market of costly government regulations. Free-market economists see liberalist "command-and-control" kinds of policies, where the state imposes standards of behavior on industry under the threat of punitive sanctions, as inefficient and counterproductive. Such an approach limits the flexibility of corporations to find creative solutions to ecological problems, provides no incentive to improve environmental performance beyond the limits set by the government, and is often extremely expensive.[24]

Neoliberals strive to reduce the costs of environmental regulations to industry and to increase the flexibility of capital to appropriate labor power and natural resources in the most profitable manner possible by transferring power from the state to private institutions under the control and domination of capital. In this respect, the political relations of liberal democracy, which vest social rights of citizenship in persons, are contradictory to the economic relations of capitalism, which vest private property rights in owners. The rights of citizens to clean air, water, and other elements of nature necessary for human survival often stand in the way of business owners making use of their private property in the most profitable manner. An owner or chief executive officer of a major corporation working to maximize one's self-interest by releasing large quantities of polychlorinated biphenyls (PCBs) and other toxic chemicals into the Hudson River is violating the individual and collective rights of citizens who depend on the same river for safe drinking water and recreation. Neoliberals seek to privilege the economic rights of the capitalist class over social and environmental rights or ordinary citizens. The corporate war on the environment is also a war against democracy.

NEOLIBERALISM AND THE CORPORATE ASSAULT AGAINST THE ENVIRONMENTAL MOVEMENT

Acting on the perception that the liberal regime of environmental regulation is a detriment to the competitiveness of U.S. capital in the new global economy, the polluter-industrial complex has unleashed an unrelenting assault on the ecology movement. This political attack is being spearheaded by the more heavily regulated companies, especially those involved in energy, electric utilities, real estate, industrial manufacturing, construction, petrochemicals, mining, timber, agribusiness and biotechnology, and large-scale ranching. As we saw in chapter 2, these corporations are pouring money into antienvironmental organizations, public relations firms, think tanks, research centers, and policy institutes as well as the election campaigns of neoliberal candidates in both major political parties. The neoliberal reforms exercised by both of these business-dominated political parties are aimed at lessening the economic impact of environmental regulations on industry. In particular, free-market environmentalism and government deregulation are allowing for a greater displacement of ecological hazards onto poor communities of color and working-class neighborhoods. In this respect, the aims of the EJ movement are seen by neoliberals as contradictory to the needs of capital in general and the polluter-industrial complex in particular.

Neoliberals in Direct Confrontation with the Environmental Movement, 1981–1992

There are three different political approaches utilized by neoliberal politicians in the rollback of environmental law and EJ policy. The first approach initially implemented by President Ronald Reagan (1981–1988), as well as the administration of George H. W. Bush (1989–1992), reflects a strategy of *direct confrontation* with the environmental movement in order to achieve a *wholesale rollback* of existing environmental laws, regulations, and programs considered to be detrimental to business. Bolstered by a host of reports produced by right-wing corporate think tanks and policy institutes, such as the Heritage Foundation, this strategy attempts to publicly discredit and delegitimate the environmental movement by convincing the American public that most ecological problems are not serious (or do not exist at all) and that the costs of regulations to American business, taxpayers, and workers are excessive.

The Reagan–Bush administration appointed James Watt as secretary of the interior and Ann Gorsuch as head of the EPA. Both openly ridiculed environmental sensibilities and soon became provocative symbols of the radical antienvironmentalism of the corporate neoliberals. Watt even likened environmentalists to "Nazis" impinging on the freedom of American capital. Both were eventually forced to resign in separate scandals. Nevertheless, the Reagan–Bush administration worked closely with Watt and Gorsuch to exercise stronger oversight of the EPA and the Interior Department. Reagan issued Executive Order 12291 in 1982, which required that all environmental and health agencies conduct cost-benefit analyses of new rules, policies, and regulations before their submission to the Office of Management and Budget (OMB) for review. David Stockman, director of the OMB, supervised the regulatory impact review process through the newly created Office of Information and Regulatory Affairs and cut off many environmental policy proposals on behalf of the administration before they could become public discussion.[25]

The reorganization of authority within the federal bureaucracy was also coupled with efforts to weaken the regulatory capacity of the EPA and other agencies. After the election, President Reagan fired the entire staff of the Council on Environmental Quality and eliminated 25 percent of the EPA's workforce. In fact, during Reagan's first term in office, the EPA's operating budget (adjusted for inflation) declined by about one-third, while its research funding was cut by more than one-half. Overall, spending for all federal programs that dealt with natural resources and environmental protection dropped from a 1981 Carter proposal of $16.2 billion budget for fiscal year 1984 to $8.9 billion under Reagan. As Watt declared in 1981, "We will use the budget system" as the "excuse to make major policy decisions."[26] These cuts in staff and budgets greatly reduced the government's ability to monitor, investigate, and enforce environmental laws.[27]

The basis for assessing the desired changes in policy under Reagan was provided by the Presidential Task Force on Regulatory Relief. Chaired by Vice President George H. W. Bush, the task force quickly compiled a hit list of "burdensome" regulations that it had solicited from businesses, trade associations, state and local governments, and other organizations. In fact, the largest number of industry requests for policy changes focused on EPA regulations, particularly in the automobile, chemical, and pesticide industries.[28] The recommendations of this task force outlined the attack on liberal environmental policy that would be continued by his son, George W. Bush, in the new millennium. Once George H. W. Bush was elected president, Vice President Dan Quayle headed a similar body called the Council on Competitiveness.

In 1994, Newt Gingrich and his House Republicans rode into power determined to weaken the Clean Water Act and the EPA Superfund program. Their bold verbal assaults against environmentalists were aimed at discrediting government regulation.[29] Tom DeLay, as the Republican majority whip (and former bug exterminator), once called the EPA "a Gestapo organization." Even before the emergence of Gingrich and DeLay to leadership positions in Congress, public denouncements of environmentalists and ecological concerns were proving to be counterproductive, provoking a political backlash by the American people. As a result, the memberships of most major environmental organizations increased dramatically. At the beginning of the 1980s, the nation's ten leading environmental organizations had a combined membership of 3.3 million people. By the end of the decade, they boasted 7.2 million members. The perception that the Reagan administration was attacking federal environmental laws also boosted movement fund-raising efforts. In 1985, the ten leading environmental organizations had combined donations of $218 million per year; by 1990, those donated sums had more than doubled to over half a billion dollars.[30]

The growing political capacity of the movement initiated a retreat by centrist politicians, creating a type of regulatory stalemate. In 1992, Democratic Party presidential contender Bill Clinton would capitalize on the aroused ecological concerns of the populace and strength of the environmental and EJ movements by selecting the self-described environmentalist Al Gore as his vice-presidential running mate. Together they would defeat President George H. W. Bush in the 1992 election.

Neoliberals Co-Opting and Accommodating the Environmental Movement, 1993–2000

The second neoliberal approach, as utilized by the Clinton–Gore administration (1993–2000), is characterized by attempts to *co-opt* the mainstream environmental movement and engage in preemptive "containment" of more costly environmental laws with weaker policy approaches. Rather than embracing Reagan's politics of confrontation, the Clinton–Gore approach sought *accommodation* with the environmental and EJ movements. Clinton's strategy was to enlist the support of the business-friendly organizations in the ecology movement around a number of highly symbolic policy proposals and give the administration the *appearance* of being proenvironment. The more progressive segments of the movement were split off from the administration. For instance, the President's Council on Sustainable Development was stacked with executives from some of the worst polluters in the country along with conservative environmentalists such as Jay Hair of the National Wildlife Federation, Fred Krupp of the Environmental Defense Fund, John Sawhill of The Nature Conservancy, and John Adams of the Natural Resources Development Council. Are all noted for their cooperation with industry and support for the North American Free Trade Agreement, which most of the environmental and EJ movements opposed.[31]

In exchange for allowing the administration its high-profile environmental victories, the polluter-industrial complex was rewarded with weaker regulations and other concessions—often at the expense of other battles being waged by grassroots environmental organizations. In August 1996, for instance, the Clinton–Gore administration brokered a highly public gold mine deal with Crown Butte Mines, a Montana subsidiary of a Toronto-based company, in which the company agreed to give up its interests to mine a site in a national forest just north of Yellowstone National Park. Many environmentalists who had mounted a strong campaign against the project applauded the announcement, arguing that toxic wastes from the site would threaten the region's waterways and wildlife habitats. But in exchange for giving up efforts to mine gold, silver, and copper in the area—an event the courts would most likely not have allowed to occur because of the severe damage it would have caused—Clinton–Gore quietly pledged the company tens of millions of dollars worth of other mineral-rich federal property as compensation. Despite decades of court rulings finding that corporations and private property owners are not entitled to such an award, the Clinton–Gore administration embraced the *takings compensation* principles (paying companies for any "lost" profits resulting from environmental regulations) as embodied in free-market theology. One day after pleasing environmentalists by blocking the mine project, Clinton also signed major legislation dramatically easing government regulations (and rents, royalties, taxes, and other costs) for companies drilling for oil and gas on federal lands.

By manipulating the movement, the Clinton–Gore administration operated in concert with a conservative Congress and the polluter-industrial complex to slash twenty-five years of environmental progress. The attack under Clinton was at times stealthlike, with new and weaker rules hidden away in various riders, amendments, and appropriations bills. In this respect, the Clinton–Gore administration strategically instituted what Ryan Delcambre, Dow Chemical's director of environmental and health regulatory affairs, called "surgical fixes" to each environmental statute. The strategy was to help industry meet more "reasonable" environmental standards in more "cost-effective and more compliance-assisted" manners (i.e., incentives) rather than through "gotcha" governmental enforcement typical of the liberal regime of regulation.[32] As a result, many older regulations requiring across-the-board compliance with environmental laws were replaced with "cost-effective" reforms—the EPA's new Project XL, pollution taxes and credits, effluent charges, markets for pollution rights, and bubble schemes—all designed to increase capital's flexibility to meet regulation requirements but continue polluting in a profitable manner. As a result these efforts to weaken policy and the administrative capacities of the EPA and other environment-related agencies, more progressive environmental leaders, such as David Brower, endorsed Ralph Nader in the 1996 presidential elections.

The "Orwellian" Face of Neoliberalism toward the Environmental Movement, 2001 to 2008

Since the rise of George W. Bush to the White House, the corporate war against the liberal regime of environmental regulation has intensified. Like the Reagan–Bush administrations of the 1980s, which made regulatory reform a priority, officials under the Bush–Cheney administration have introduced new rules to ease or dismantle existing regulations they see as cumbersome to industry. Sweeping measures aimed at delaying and/or dismantling programs and policies designed to protect public health and the environment are being implemented. President Bush has reneged on a campaign promise to curb U.S. emissions of greenhouse gases, blocked efforts to protect a third of national forests from roads and logging, and repealed tough scientific-based standards for removing poisons in drinking water, among other assaults on environmental protection. The administration, at the request of lumber and paper companies, has also given Forest Service managers the right to approve logging in federal forests without the usual environmental reviews.[33] In 2004, using a backdoor route to deregulation, the Bush administration removed clean water protections for 20 million acres of American wetlands and tens of thousands of miles of streams, lakes, and ponds. This action was in line with a 2003 federal policy directive encouraging regulators to routinely avoid enforcing Clean Water Act protections for American waterways unless otherwise directed by national headquarters in Washington, D.C.[34]

The Bush–Cheney rollbacks are the latest manifestation in a relentless campaign by the polluter-industrial complex to weaken America's environmental safeguards. However, the tactics are now more sophisticated. Aware of the powerful backlash created by strategies of direct confrontation in the 1980s, the Bush–Cheney administration has incorporated elements of the Clinton–Gore approach to pay "lip service" to environmental concerns and rhetoric and to create a public image of caring about the environment. Taking a lesson from Reagan's experience with Gorsuch and Watt, the Bush administration realized that it would be a mistake to appoint abrasive persons with outspoken anti-environmental views to the most visible government posts. Administration officials also recognized that proposed bills that overtly attacked environmental protection laws stood little chance of surviving in Congress.

Adopting tactics aimed at the *covert rollback* of the liberal regime of environmental regulation, the Bush White House has quietly initiated fundamental regulatory and procedural changes that are unraveling decades of progress in protecting human health, wildlife, and natural places. In the words of Robert F. Kennedy Jr., "Aware of past failures to overrun environmental safeguards, the Bush Administration and its cronies in industry are using stealth and outright deceit to mask their agenda."[35] Knowing that the vast majority of Americans favor strong protection measures by the federal government, the administration aims to slip through potentially unpopular proposals with minimal fanfare (although the administration tactics have periodically received the condemnation of environmentalists, the protest of leaders in the Democratic Party, and the attention of the national news media).[36] For example, "instead of pushing legislation, Bush/Cheney have pursued their goals through obscure administrative actions and in closed-door settlements with industry," notes Kennedy. Assaults on regulations (rather than laws) are less visible to the public. While the Bush administration can write or revise regulations largely on its own, Congress must pass new laws. And since assuming office, the Bush administration has often been stymied in some of its efforts to pass major domestic environmental initiatives through the Congress.[37] Instead, they have introduced new rules to ease or dismantle existing regulations seen as cumbersome to industry.

As part of this offensive, the Bush administration adopted the Data Quality Act. Written by an industry lobbyist and slipped into a giant appropriations bill without congressional discussion or debate in 2000, the Data Quality Act is a below-the-radar legislative device that polluters have increasingly relied on to attack scientific studies on the dangers of global warming, exposure to cancer-causing chemicals, and other environmental impacts. In the words of Chamber of Commerce Vice President William Kovacs, the act allows industry to bog down the rule-making process from the "very beginning" by requiring a government-wide, industry-friendly "peer review" system for scientific information. The Data Quality Act's overarching strategy—dubbed "paralysis by analysis"—is to make the rule-making fight turn on the validity of information.[38] A 2004 analysis by the *Washington Post* and OMB Watch shows that the act is overwhelmingly used by industry groups to thwart new government rules. The most heavily petitioned are the EPA, the Fish and Wildlife Service, the National Institutes of Health, and the Consumer Product Safety Commission.[39] As stated by a Natural Resources Defense Council report, "In sabotaging them [rules], even while leaving the statutes themselves unchanged, federal agencies threaten to render these laws mere words on paper, irrelevant to what polluters and developers do in the real world."[40]

The president's political appointees at the Interior Department, the EPA, the Department of Agriculture, and the OMB carry out this agenda through behind-the-scenes legal settlements and obscure rule changes. For instance, when political appointees in the administration stepped away from actively defending those rules protecting roadless areas in national forests, both the chief and the deputy chief of the Forest Service resigned in protest. The administration has attempted to disguise the nature and impact of its actions by cynically assigning its ecologically devastating initiatives such Orwellian-sounding names as "Healthy Forests" (which increases logging in national forests) and "Clear Skies" (a rollback of the Clean Air Act) while also "arguing that its elixir of market-based mechanisms, voluntary programs, and supposedly local solutions will heal what ails the environment."[41]

In short, the Bush presidency has been the most antienvironmental administration in the modern era. In partnership with neoliberals in the Congress, it is busily dismantling the traditional framework of environmental laws, standards, and enforcement.[42] In addition to undermining pollution and public safety standards, the Bush administration is systematically cutting critical funding for enforcement agencies and programs and nominating agency and judicial appointees who are openly hostile to environmental and public health protections. As a result, Bush has managed to "effect a radical transformation of the nation's environmental laws, quietly and subtly, by means of regulatory changes and bureaucratic directives."[43] As we shall see, this general attack on the liberal regime of environmental regulation extends to the EJ movement and federal initiatives to address racial and class-based disparities in the production and distribution of ecological hazards in the United States.

THE RISE AND FALL OF FEDERAL ENVIRONMENTAL JUSTICE PROGRAMS AND POLICIES

The Creation of a Federal Apparatus to Address Environmental Injustice

The election of Bill Clinton to the White House in 1992 created fresh opportunities for the EJ movement to institutionalize EJ policy and programs in the federal government. On the heels of the First National People of Color Environmental Leadership Summit and the formation of new regional and national constituency-based EJ networks, the Clinton administration was compelled to respond more forcefully to the movement. Seeking accommodation, the new head of the EPA, Carol Browner, changed the name of the Office of Environmental Equity to the Office of Environmental Justice. She also created the National Environmental Justice Advisory Council (NEJAC) as an advisory body to the EPA. Comprised of twenty-five stakeholders from the movement as well as government, industry, and academia, NEJAC "raised the stature of the EJ movement to new heights and institutionalized the movement's transformative power over agency policy."[44]

The influence of the movement was further elevated when, on February 11, 1994, President Clinton signed Executive Order 12898, "Federal Actions to Address Environmental Justice in Minority Populations and Low-Income Populations," which directed federal agencies, including the EPA and the departments of Housing and Urban Development, Interior, and Transportation, to develop strategy "that identifies and addresses disproportionately high and adverse human health or environmental effects of its programs, policies, or activities on minority populations and low-income populations."[45] In a memorandum issued contemporaneously with the executive order, the president further emphasized the opportunities provided by Title VI of the Civil Rights Act of 1964 for federal agencies to address environmental racism. For instance, federal agencies are required to ensure that their funding recipients comply with Title VI by conducting their programs and implementing policies in a nondiscriminatory manner. Advocates of EJ have attempted to use this nondiscrimination provision to remedy environmental injustices by suing in federal court or by filing administrative actions with the EPA.[46] To help accomplish the objectives of the executive order, Clinton established the Interagency Working Group on Environmental Justice composed of agency representatives and chaired by the EPA administrator.[47]

Unlike Title VI, Clinton's executive order did not create legally enforceable rights or obligations. Nevertheless, it represented a significant victory for EJ activists. The order and the formation of NEJAC integrated the EJ perspective into the institutional culture of the EPA and other agencies. The order also provided invaluable support to the efforts of agency staffers who had tried, unsuccessfully, to bring EJ concerns to the fore of their work. As noted by EJ advocates Luke Cole and Sheila Foster, the impact of this transformation in the federal government was sudden and unexpected, when the Nuclear Regulatory Commission cited the executive order as the basis for its denial of a permit for a uranium enrichment facility in rural Louisiana. This was the first permit ever denied by the commission because of questions raised over siting a plant in an African American community.[48]

The polluter-industrial complex became alarmed by the decision. Represented by industry "front groups" like the Business Network for Environmental Justice, corporate polluters began mobilizing to undermine the executive order. In February 1998, for instance, the EPA issued its interim guidance for addressing complaints of discrimination filed under Title VI of the 1964 Civil Rights Act. The largest group to file comments with the EPA's Office of Civil Rights were individual corporations and industry associations representing the nation's biggest polluters that opposed the EPA interim policy.[49] Despite the work of dedicated EPA staff around environmental injustice, it was obvious to many activists that Clinton was not going to stand up to business and initiate more fundamental reforms that would halt the displacement of ecological hazards onto America's communities of color. A crisis in "institutional" EJ politics had emerged.

The Crisis of Federal EJ Policy and Programs

In December 2000, frustrations among EJ activists boiled over when members of NEJAC lambasted President Bill Clinton, Vice President Al Gore, and the EPA for failing to aggressively combat the scourge of "environmental racism." The charges came as the NEJAC board met with EPA officials in Arlington, Virginia, to discuss the agency's EJ guidance document. A central complaint was that the document was secretly drafted by high-ranking EPA officials who "completely ignored" the recommendations of the NEJAC panel. Instead, the NEJAC board was treated like "window dressing." The administration was also sharply criticized for failing to develop a proactive, affirmative analysis of how to use EJ concepts in the courts.[50] The honeymoon between the EJ movement and the Clinton–Gore administration was over.

After the 2000 presidential election, it soon became clear that the Bush–Cheney administration would make things worse. It was not surprising then to many EJ advocates when a 2002 report for the National Black Environmental Justice Network found that the EPA was failing to enforce Title VI of the Civil Rights Act of 1964.[51] According to the report, the EPA consistently ignored complaints by African Americans and other people of color and had dismissed nearly 70 percent of the complaints filed without any clear criteria for doing so. The report noted that not a single case of racially disparate impact had been found among the 129 Title VI complaints filed with the EPA.[52] In 2001, a separate survey was launched of several federal agencies to determine what actions they had undertaken in response to the executive order and to offer a preliminary assessment of their compliance. The law professors conducting the survey discovered that all agencies had an initial outburst of energy on issuance of the executive order but that carry-through was inconsistent among agencies. These problems were rooted in a lack of commitment to the executive order by high-level officials within the agency.[53]

Thwarting the Civil Rights Act and EJ Policy: The *Sandoval* Case

The opposition offered by the Bush administration and the polluter-industrial complex to EJ policy has culminated in a crisis for the movement. A limited number of options are now available to EJ activists. One option involves utilizing citizen suits, constitutional claims, common law actions, and Title VI of the Civil Rights Act of 1964 in the battle against environmental injustices. Section 602 of Title VI authorizes federal agencies to adopt regulations that prohibit recipients of federal funds from engaging in racial discrimination.[54] Unfortunately, private legal actions utilizing Title VI are encountering significant bottlenecks, including the growing presence of conservative judges in the federal courts.

In 2001, the Supreme Court ruled in *Alexander v. Sandoval* that disparate impact lawsuits under Section 602 could not be brought directly by private citizens and that citizens had standing to sue only for *intentional* discrimination under Section 601. Instead, private citizens alleging disparate impact could send a complaint to a federal agency that funded the recipient who was allegedly discriminating. The funding agency could then launch an investigation, and, if a violation of their disparate impact regulations was found and not remedied, the federal agency could terminate funding of the discriminating recipient.[55]

The *Sandoval* case was a major blow to the EJ movement by the conservative court. While citizens may demonstrate that the siting and operation of an ecologically hazardous facility will *result* in disproportionate impacts in a specific community of color, *proving* that such a facility was sited in the community so as to intentionally *cause* discrimination is an almost impossible task. Unfortunately, the language of Title VI drafted by Congress does not consider discrimination arising from disparate impact.[56] The ruling also reveals the limitations of using equal protection and Title VI claims as a legal "basis" to correct environmental injustices. Described as "certain losers," civil rights laws have not successfully aided plaintiffs with their claims around environmental racism.[57] In fact, the dependency of civil rights law on the "bad actor" model, which recognizes environmental racism only when an actor engages in the intentional act of discrimination, is extremely narrow and self-limiting.

When a corporation looks to locate an incinerator or hazardous waste site in a community of color, it can do so ostensibly for "nonracist" economic reasons. As stated by Alex Sugarman-Broza,

> A neighborhood where low-income people of color live is a desirable location for such a facility for numerous self-reinforcing reasons: that neighborhood has been redlined by banks, reducing home ownership; educational segregation has undereducated the neighborhood's residents, producing not just "white flight" but "class flight" as well and leaving those remaining behind much less equipped to challenge such a siting; economic discrimination has forced residents into low-wage service jobs, requiring many to work multiple jobs and thus reducing overall civic and community involvement that forms the basis of any community efforts to resist a toxic hazard; economic deprivation further makes the promise of a handful of (dangerous) new jobs in the neighborhood difficult to resist; racist voter redistricting and gerrymandering has robbed the neighborhood of political power; and racist law enforcement and prosecution has incarcerated a whole generation who would otherwise have the energy and drive to oppose such predations on their homes and families. For these and a thousand other reasons, it is logical for a company to pollute such a neighborhood and possible for them to do so without overt racism.[58]

Motivated purely by economic practicality, the polluter-industrial complex can site ecologically hazardous facilities in communities of color without a legal "whiff" of conscious or intentional racism. Nevertheless, the effect is racist in that people of color are disproportionately exposed to greater health threats and obnoxious land uses. In this respect, the siting of facilities occurs in the context of the capitalist system and a legacy of racial oppression and segregation that gives the decision a larger racial impact. As a consequence, environmental racism will not be solved by civil rights law until the larger social injustices endemic to American capitalism are addressed and resolved.

Because of the *Sandoval* decision, a plaintiff seeking to bring a Title VI suit directly against a polluter is confronted by an "intent" hurdle in equal protection cases. This can be overcome by filing an administrative complaint with an appropriate federal agency. Such administrative actions or complaints filed with the EPA or other federal funding agencies are now the primary means for citizens to seek redress of potential Title VI violations.[59] Many of these complaints are made to the EPA's Office of Civil Rights by EJ activists attempting to remedy discrimination by state environmental agencies. However, with the colonization of the state by the polluter-industrial complex, citizen complaints to EPA are having little impact. From 1993 through 2005, the agency received 164 complaints alleging civil rights violations in environmental decisions and accepted only forty-seven for investigation. Twenty-eight of these forty-seven cases were quickly dismissed, while the remaining nineteen were left pending.[60] Another recent study revealed that after ten years of receiving, evaluating, and investigating complaints (1993–2003), the EPA has never made a formal finding that a federally funded entity has violated Title VI, nor has the EPA imposed a sanction of any kind against any entity.[61]

The Breakdown of the Executive Order for Environmental Justice

Since the *Sandoval* ruling, the Office of the General Council of the U.S. Commission on Civil Rights has found significant delays in the EPA's issuance of final guidance to investigate claims, while procedural delays in investigating and ruling on complaints have left communities continually exposed to harmful pollutants.[62] Furthermore, the EPA's Office of the Inspector General has faulted the EPA for making "slow progress in implementing environmental justice" and further concludes that the EPA has not developed a clear vision or comprehensive strategic plan and has not established values, goals, expectations, and performance measurements for integrating environmental justice into the agency's operations.[63] Furthermore, the Government Accounting Office has condemned the EPA for sidelining EJ issues in drafting rules, conducting economic reviews, and considering public comments relating to clean air rules.[64]

Rather than instituting significant reforms to address environmental disparities, the EPA has moved in the opposite direction. More specifically, the

EPA is proposing a major change to its Environmental Justice Strategic Plan by adopting "color-blind" language. Designed by Bush administration officials to weaken the executive order, the agency's new plan defines environmental justice as "the fair treatment and meaningful involvement of all people *regardless* of race, color, national origin, or income, with respect to development, implementation, and enforcement of environmental laws, regulations, and policies." Although reasonable at first glance, the draft plan's use of the term "regardless" effectively removes race and income from receiving any special consideration and makes the EJ policy meaningless. In effect, the Bush administration's proposal allows the "EPA to shirk its responsibility for addressing environmental justice problems in minority populations and low-income populations and divert resources away from implementing Executive Order 12898."[65]

The Bush administration's position that it cannot consider race in furthering environmental justice echoes the position taken by lobbyists working for the Business Network for Environmental Justice. The EPA's Office of Environmental Justice has responded to a barrage of criticism of the draft plan by claiming that recent Supreme Court affirmative action rulings would create "significant legal issues" if the agency continued to stress race in EJ policy. The agency states that socioeconomic and racial factors can still be taken into account but that race cannot be used as a sole decision-making factor because doing so would be inconsistent with Supreme Court rulings on affirmative action. Advocates of EJ respond that the policy shift is unjustified. The EPA is citing affirmative action rulings by the Supreme Court in the 2003 University of Michigan case *Grutter v. Bollinger* and the 1995 *Adarand Constructors v. Pena*, both of which said that the government must demonstrate that its use of racial classifications is "narrowly tailored" to achieve a "compelling governmental interest," according to an EPA memo circulated to parties who commented on the new policy.

Advocates of EJ dispute that the affirmative action cases apply to the agency's EJ policy. Instead, they claim that the policy is based on Title VI of the Civil Rights Act, which the Supreme Court has upheld and which requires federal agencies to develop regulations prohibiting actions that have a disproportionate impact on racial minorities. Advocates of EJ point to the 2001 Supreme Court ruling in *Alexander v. Sandoval*, which rejected a private right of action under Title VI but did not question that the law was intended to prevent discrimination in federally funded activities.[66] On July 15, 2005, the National Association for the Advancement of Colored People (NAACP) Legal Defense and Educational Fund and a coalition of civil rights and environmental nonprofit organizations sent a comment letter objecting to the EPA draft Environmental Justice Strategic Plan. That same month, nearly eighty legislators also signed a letter denouncing the draft plan as a step backward and urged EPA Administrator Stephen Johnson to "take real steps to combat the environmental injustices" that afflict communities throughout the nation."[67]

More recently, the EPA's Office of the Inspector General (OIG) has issued a new report criticizing the agency for failing to "conduct environmental justice reviews of its programs, policies, and activities."[68] More specifically, the inspector general charged the EPA with failing to identify those populations at a disproportionately high level of risk from environmental contaminants. The response of the Bush administration officials at EPA to the OIG was that it does not need to do so because its goal of the agency is to provide "environmental justice for everyone." In turn, the OIG response to the EPA was that the agency was not at liberty to reinterpret the order. In 2007, the U.S. General Accountability Office (GAO) condemned the EPA's handling of toxic contaminates in post-Katrina New Orleans and the Gulf coast.[69] As all these reports indicate, federal policies and programs designed to bring about environmental justice are in shambles. In short, the Bush administration is looking for any kind of excuse to avoid doing what the inspector general, Congress, and EJ community has demanded of them.

GETTING AWAY WITH MURDER: THE FAILURE OF THE STATE TO ENFORCE ENVIRONMENTAL LAWS

The crisis of EJ policy is intimately linked to the larger neoliberal assault on the liberal regime of regulation. The goal of this assault by American capital is "regulatory reform"—the rollback of Clinton's executive order and other EJ policies, worker/consumer health and safety, consumer protection, environmental protection, and other state regulatory "burdens" that impinge on the profits of capital. Severe cuts in the budgets and staffs of federal agencies that enforce and prosecute environmental laws are part of the plan. The lack of enforcement of federal environmental policy by both Democratic and Republican administrations alike is seriously compromising the health of all Americans, especially those living in working-class neighborhoods and poor communities of color.

From Bad to Worse: Environmental Enforcement under the Bush–Cheney Administration

Lax enforcement is a critical tactic that the White House employs to undercut popular environmental policies without having to openly attack them.[70] According to an investigation by the *Sacramento Bee* newspaper, EPA inspections of polluting businesses dipped 15 percent during the first two years of the Bush administration in comparison to the last two years of the Clinton–Gore administration. Criminal cases referred for federal prosecution also dropped 40 percent, and the amount of pollution reduced or prevented as a result of the agency's legal actions—the bottom line in environmental enforcement—plummeted from 7.5 billion pounds to only 921 million pounds. Meanwhile, total inspections of businesses dropped 15 percent (from 41,533 to 35,480), while the EPA's criminal referrals fell 40 percent (from 564 in 1999 to 341 in 2002). Declines in the enforcement of the Toxic Substance Control Act (down 80 percent), the Clean Air Act (down 54 percent), and the Clean Water Act (down 53 percent) were even more profound. The *Sacramento Bee* also found that in reports to Congress and the press, the EPA had puffed up the number of criminal investigations it initiated and overreported the number of cases it referred to federal prosecutors. The EPA also padded the length of prison terms served for environmental crimes, all in an effort to mask "a significant drop-off in the federal government's pursuit of criminal polluters."[71]

A 2004 report by the EPA's OIG similarly accused EPA officials of misleading Americans about improvements in the quality of America's tap water.[72] The report documents a pattern of false statements released by the EPA to the media. Between 1999 and 2002, the EPA publicly boasted that it met its goal of supplying safe tap water to 94 percent of U.S. residents—up from 79 percent in 1993. However, the OIG report asserts that the EPA's conclusion was based on "flawed and incomplete" information, especially since 35 percent of known health standard violations nationwide were not entered into the EPA's compliance database. In fact, overall toxic releases to U.S. waterways increased 10 percent between 2003 and 2004.[73] During this time, more than 3,700 facilities across the United States violated the Clean Water Act. On average, these facilities exceeded their permit limits by an average of 275 percent, or about four times the allowed amount.[74] In total, U.S. facilities released more than 4.25 billion pounds of toxic chemicals into the air, water, and land in 2004.[75] In some instances, EPA officials would even notify potential polluters of impending inspections, giving corporations the opportunity to temporarily mask potential violations from visiting officials. In September 2003, for instance, the Refinery Reform Campaign found that the EPA had violated its own protocols by apparently warning polluters that the environmental testing was about to be done at facilities in the poor minority community of Port Arthur, Texas.

Because of inadequate enforcement and prosecution of environmental wrongdoing, it often makes economic sense for a company to intentionally violate the law. Such environmental crime is now a pervasive feature of American capitalism. A survey by the *National Law Journal* and Arthur Anderson Environmental Services found that two-thirds of the corporate lawyers representing manufacturers, mining companies, insurance and real estate firms, and other industries acknowledged that their companies had violated environmental laws during the preceding year.[76] For instance, in 1988 when an estimated 730,000 gallons of diesel oil leaked from an Ashland Oil Inc. tank into the Monongahela River near Pittsburgh and then into the Ohio River, other industries took advantage of the spill to dump cancer-causing industrial solvents (chloroform and methylene chloride) into the Ohio River in the hope that the spill would disguise their own illegal dumping.[77] An internal EPA study recently uncovered by the *Washington Post* finds that about a quarter of the nation's largest industrial plants and water treatment facilities are in serious violation of pollution standards at any one time but that only a fraction of them face formal enforcement actions. When formal disciplinary actions are taken, fewer than half result in any fines, which average a paltry $6,000. Furthermore, the study found that 50 percent of those companies in noncompliance are at least 100 percent over the limit for toxics pollution and that 13 percent are at least 1,000 percent over.[78]

When fines are assessed on corporate violators, they often go unpaid. A 2006 Associated Press investigation found that corporations regularly avoid large penalties for wrongdoing in areas of environmental protection and worker health and safety. In fact, the government was owed more than $35 billion in fines and other payments from criminal and civil cases in 2006—almost five times higher than the amount uncollected ten years ago.[79] A key explanatory factor is that the many government appointees at the Treasury Department responsible for collecting such penalties come from the polluter-industrial complex. Treasury head Paul O'Neill, for instance, used to be chief executive officer of the aluminum mining and manufacturing giant Alcoa as well as the International Paper Company. Alcoa is the world's largest aluminum manufacturer and one of the biggest polluters in Bush's home state of Texas. In 1996, Alcoa enjoyed profits of $339 million and paid nothing in federal taxes. In fact, Alcoa collected a rebate of $17.6 million from the federal government (Alcoa was one of forty-one companies, including Enron, Weyerhaeuser, General Motors, and CSX, that paid nothing on their collective $25.8 billion in profits while receiving $3.2 billion in rebates).[80] Knowing that the Bush administration will not pursue the payment of these fines (and taxes), American business is getting away with murder. It is little wonder that 77 percent of all American citizens want tougher environmental laws and stricter enforcement.[81]

Power Plant Pollution, Environmental Injustice, and New Source Review

The 1977 amendments to the Clean Air Act required that modifications made to existing power plants would be subject to the strict standards imposed under

New Source Review (NSR)—standards that usually necessitated the installation of sulfur dioxide scrubbers, electrostatic precipitators, and other relatively
expensive air pollution control technology. From the late 1970s through the
early 1990s, the EPA did little to enforce NSR requirements against electric utilities. In the mid-1990s, however, Bruce Buckheit, a Department of Justice attorney, was appointed to be director of the Air Enforcement Division in the Office of Enforcement and Compliance Assurance. Buckheit launched a massive
investigation of the electric utility industry that revealed that approximately 70
percent of all coal-fired electricity-generating stations across the United States
were in violation of NSR standards. In 1999, on the basis of these findings, the
EPA referred to the Department of Justice nine lawsuits against some of the
largest electric utility companies in the country. In response, the utilities devised
a massive political lobbying strategy to derail the suits and avoid liability. These
companies also made huge campaign contributions to George W. Bush, who
defeated Al Gore in the controversial 2000 presidential election. Once in office,
Bush implemented new EPA regulations that permitted the utilities to spend as
much as 20 percent of generating unit replacement costs on plant upgrades each
year before NSR standards could be applied.[82] This new rule effectively destroyed the foundation of the government's lawsuits against these major polluters and let the utilities off the hook.

These and other administrative roadblocks raised by the Bush–Cheney administration are having a profound impact. For instance, the Department of
Justice was able to conclude fewer than 160 enforcement actions in 2004, the
lowest by far in the 10 years such data have been tracked (the Clinton administration averaged only 230 settlements per year). According to the Environmental Integrity Project, headed by Eric Schaeffer, the civil penalties for
enforcement of the Clean Air and Clean Water acts dropped to a paltry $57
million that same year—the lowest in the 15 years of recorded data. Overall,
the number of complaints filed by the Justice Department declined 75 percent
between 2001 and 2004.[83] Prior to his work with the Environmental Integrity
Project, Eric Schaeffer served as director of regulator enforcement for the
EPA. In February 2002, he resigned from his EPA position to protest the obstacles to enforcement of the Clean Air Act and other laws created by the
Bush administration. In his letter of resignation, Schaeffer referred to the nine
EPA lawsuits against the utilities that were being held up by the Bush administration.[84] In addition to Schaeffer, a number of other high-ranking EPA officials also resigned or retired during this time frame out of frustration with
the Bush administration's "Clear Skies" initiative.[85]

The current head of the Office of Enforcement and Compliance Assurance
at the EPA is Granta Nakayama, a former partner in the Kirkland & Ellis law
firm. The firm has a long record of battles fought against the EPA on behalf

of companies that use toxic materials and chemicals. The fights include defending W. R. Grace & Company against multiple criminal charges alleging that the company and seven of its current or former executives knowingly put their workers and the public in lethal danger through exposure to vermiculite ore contaminated with asbestos from the company's mine in the white working-class community of Libby, Montana (18 percent of the adult population in Libby have signs of asbestos-related lung abnormalities resulting from occupational and environmental exposures to tremolite produced at the W. R. Grace facility).[86] Nakayama attended George Mason University School of Law, which is one of the leading recipients of conservative foundation money and a training ground for conservative intellectuals opposed to the liberal regime of environmental regulation.[87]

Some of the largest and most successful agreements are obtained only after the Justice Department has taken polluters to court and, in some cases, obtained favorable decisions on the law. However, with Department of Justice and EPA officials such as Nakayama muzzling the EPA's career staff and refusing to take polluters to court, the nation's biggest corporations seem to be enjoying an extended vacation from enforcement actions. Refineries and large coal-fired power plants—major contributors to the Bush campaign—appear virtually immune from prosecution.[88] In September 2005, the EPA's OIG confirmed that the regulatory rollbacks of the Clean Air Act so beneficial to these utilities and energy companies had not only seriously harmed enforcement but also cost the agency a historic opportunity to reduce several million tons of pollutants linked to acid rain, smog, asthma attacks, and heart and lung diseases.[89] These rule changes were particularly devastating to poor communities of color located near power plants. Nationwide, over two-thirds of all African Americans live within thirty miles of a coal-fired power plant. This is the distance within which the maximum health impact of the smokestack plume occurs.[90]

SUPERFUND: A SUPER FAILURE IN ADDRESSING ENVIRONMENTAL INJUSTICE

The Disintegration of Superfund

Some of the most glaring injustices associated with the nonenforcement of environmental regulations concerns the Comprehensive Environmental Response Compensation and Liability Act (CERCLA) of 1980. The role of CERCLA was to create funding for cleaning up the thousands of major toxic waste dump sites across the country, punish those parties who dump toxic waste illegally, and deter, with the threat of lawsuits, other potential dumpers from doing the same. The sites perceived to be the most threatening to both surrounding populations and the environment are placed on the National Priorities List (or Superfund). This "listing" makes the site eligible for federal cleanup. There are now 1,623 Superfund sites in the United States. One in four Americans, including 10 million children, live within four miles of one or more Superfund sites. Groundwater contamination is a problem at over 85 percent of the nation's Superfund sites—a particularly alarming statistic given that over 50 percent of the American people rely on groundwater sources for drinking. These residents are often found to have a host of health problems, including cardiac abnormalities, leukemia and other cancers, kidney–urinary tract infections, seizures, learning disabilities, and central nervous system damage.[91]

Superfund was originally financed by a tax levied on the petroleum and chemical industries, which created a pool of money used to pay for the cleanup of sites whose polluters were unknown or unable to finance the work. In response to the growing power of the antitoxics movement, Superfund was reauthorized, and its funds were increased when the Superfund Amendments and Reauthorization Act was passed by Congress in 1985. However, in 1995, this "polluter-pays" tax was allowed to expire. Consequently, the financial reserves in the Superfund trust have declined from a surplus of $3.8 billion in 1996 to levels that approach or reach zero at the end of each fiscal year, forcing ordinary American taxpayers to shoulder more of the cost for toxic waste cleanups. Since the depletion of the trust, Superfund has relied on the annual appropriation of $1.3 billion or less in tax dollars and the money recovered by the EPA from companies linked to the sites.[92]

Under Superfund, the EPA is supposed to look for "potentially responsible parties" to either clean up a site or pay for the cleanup. However, Bush appointees have successfully reduced such funds recovered by the state from corporate polluters from a peak of about $320 million in 1998–1999 to only $60 million per year in 2000–2006. Where no responsible party can be found, cleanups are often paid for entirely by taxpayers. In alliance with his corporate sponsors, the Bush administration opposes reinstatement of the fees. As a result, the cost to taxpayers to clean up the toxic waste sites increased by 427 percent between 2004 and 2006. Superfund's financial demands now outstrip federal appropriations and cost recovery efforts from responsible parties, leading to program funding shortfalls that slow or stop site cleanups and hinder the EPA's ability to address the backlog of contaminated sites.[93] Denied the income provided by these fees on corporate polluters, appropriations for critical cleanup actions have declined by 32 percent. Funding shortfalls now range from $100 million to $300 million per year. As a result, cleanups have fallen by 50 percent, compared with the pace of cleanups between 1997 and 2000.[94] Since the program started in 1980, fewer than one out of five sites has been cleaned up enough to be removed from the list.[95] In short, the slow pace of these cleanups has rendered Superfund a "super failure."

Superfund Injustices Past and Present

The "super failure" of Superfund is especially evident in regard to EJ policy. Prior to President Clinton's executive order for environmental justice, federal government enforcement action appeared uneven with regard to the class and racial composition of the impacted community. Superfund toxic waste sites in communities of color were likely to be cleaned 12 to 42 percent *later* than sites in white communities. Lacking the capacity to participate in the regulatory process, communities of color also witnessed government penalties for violations of hazardous waste laws that were on average only one-sixth ($55,318) of the average penalty in predominantly white communities ($335,566). Furthermore, it took an average of 20 percent longer for the government to place toxic waste dumps in minority communities on the National Priorities List for cleanup than sites in white areas.[96] And despite the fact that the 1986 amendments to CERCLA authorized the EPA to provide technical assistance grants to impacted communities, EPA administrative barriers limited the number of minority and/or working-class communities that could receive the grants and use them effectively.[97]

A more recent 2005 study by sociologist Sandra George O'Neil confirms that a site in a low-income or high-minority area is less likely to make the Superfund list and takes significantly longer to reach the National Priorities List if it is listed. Despite their overrepresentation in proximity to environmental hazards, communities of color remain underrepresented in environmental cleanup programs like the EPA Superfund program.[98] This finding is somewhat surprising in that many EJ advocates expected that the implementation of Clinton's 1994 executive order for environmental justice would lessen the degree to which demographic factors could be associated with the chance of listing. However, these results show the opposite. In fact, the study found that racial disparities in the Superfund program have actually *worsened* since Clinton's executive order.

The numbers speak for themselves. Since 1994, toxic waste sites discovered in minority communities have been 21 percent less likely to be listed as Superfund sites than similar sites in nonminority areas. This disparity was only 3 percent in the early 1990s. The discovery os such a site in a Native American area reduces its chance of being listed by almost 80 percent. These figures show that sites recently proposed for the Superfund in an area with a high percentage of racial minorities (with the exception of foreign-born populations) have a much lower chance of listing than in "pre-1994" Superfund era. Poorer, less educated populations (as denoted by poverty and lack of a high school diploma) are even more strongly associated with a lower chance of listing in sites discovered since 1994 than they were in the initial decade of the Superfund program. Despite their overrepresentation in proximity to environmental hazards, people of color and the poor continue to be underrepresented in the Superfund cleanup program.

The Corporate War against Superfund

The failure of the Superfund program to address environmental injustices and clean up the nation's worst toxic waste sites is no accident. Instead, the polluter-industrial complex has successfully mobilized its economic and political power to orchestrate a weakening of the program. According to an investigation by the Center for Public Integrity, some 100 companies and federal agencies are connected to 700 (or 40 percent) of America's worst toxic waste sites.[99] Between 1998 and 2005, seventy-one of these companies disclosed spending more than $1 billion to hire a total of nearly 550 lobbying firms to influence government officials. They also donated more than $120 million to candidates for Congress and the White House, especially those candidates willing to weaken Superfund and other environmental programs.[100]

These corporations are among the giants of American industry. At least sixty of the companies are listed among the Fortune 1000 and Global 500, with revenues of more than $2.8 trillion in 2006 alone, including nearly $190 billion in profits. They are also among the most "politically connected" corporations. For instance, Halliburton (and one of its former subsidiaries) is one of the EPA's biggest contractors, yet it is connected to at least twenty-five Superfund sites. In addition, Dresser Industries, a company also identified by the EPA as a subsidiary to Halliburton, is linked to twenty-four Superfund sites (adding another fourteen to Halliburton's total).[101] Before becoming vice president, Dick Cheney served as the chief executive officer of Halliburton, earning $63 million in salary and stock options from the company over a five-year period. Since 1998, corporations associated with the polluter-industrial complex have hired at least 100 former government employees who worked on environmental issues, including thirty-three former EPA officials. According to a Center for Public Integrity report, "The objective of the companies through lobbying is to influence and to channel regulation to win government contracts or get out of liabilities."[102]

Bringing Bad Things to Light: General Electric and the Subversion of Superfund

General Electric (GE) is among the most active opponents of the Superfund program. The world's second-largest company by market value, GE is connected to more Superfund sites than any other corporation in the country. In order to minimize its financial responsibility for cleaning up its toxic waste sites and win other concessions from the state, GE has spent more than $116 million on political lobbying since 1998. This sum is about four times what three of the nation's largest environmental groups—the Environmental Defense, the Sierra Club, and the National Environmental Trust—collectively spent to lobby during the same time. In exchange for this lobbying investment, GE has also received $3.8 billion in federal contracts during the two years ending September 20, 2004.[103]

GE is responsible for the nation's largest toxic waste site, in the upper Hudson River, where two of its capacitor plants discharged PCBs, considered to be among the most dangerous carcinogens of any chemical manufactured by industry today, directly into the river for decades. In 1983, the EPA declared 200 miles of the majestic river—from the two plants south to New York Harbor—a Superfund site. Since that time, the New York State Health Department has advised women of childbearing age and children under age fifteen not to eat any fish from this entire stretch of the river, where the cancer risk from such consumption is 700 times the EPA protection level. Some 100,000 pounds of PCBs in the sediment continue to poison fish, wildlife, and humans. GE freely dumped PCBs into the Hudson for more than twenty-five years before obtaining a state permit in 1973, four years before the federal ban on PCBs forced the company to stop polluting.[104]

To escape the costs of cleaning up the river, GE asked a federal court to declare the Superfund law unconstitutional in November 2000, calling it a violation of due process (GE's main attorney in the suit against the Superfund law, Laurence Tribe of Harvard University Law School, was simultaneously representing Vice President Al Gore in the presidential election recount case before the U.S. Supreme Court). By their own admission, GE did indeed discharge about 1.3 million pounds of PCBs into the Hudson River over a thirty-year period, although Eliot Spitzer, then attorney general and later governor for the state of New York, has publicly charged that the actual figure exceeds 100 million pounds. The action was unsuccessful. In October 2005, more than twenty years after the EPA designated the Hudson River a Superfund site, GE finally agreed in a settlement to begin dredging the river of the contaminated sediment at a cost of $700 million. However, the agreement negotiated by the Bush administration obligates GE for costs incurred only in the first year, which could allow the company to avoid $600 million in cleanup costs. This case is part of a larger pattern in which responsible parties—even the wealthiest corporations in the world—are escaping the majority of the costs associated with environmental cleanup. In yet another form of environmental injustice, American taxpayers are instead absorbing a growing share of these costs. The EPA has recovered only 18 percent of the money it has spent on all Superfund and similar pollution cleanups since 1998.[105]

GE is one of a number of companies making up the polluter-industrial complex that have formed organizations such as the Superfund Action Alliance and the Superfund Settlements Project to challenge the Superfund program. These organizations also push a larger antienvironmental agenda in Congress and the media as well as the courts. At least ten of these companies have hired firms that employ former EPA employees to lobby their former agency on behalf of industry. For instance, Kin Gump Strauss Hauer & Feld is a firm representing polluting companies that has hired former EPA employees as lobbyists, including Sheila D. Jones. Jones is a partner at the firm and is head of the environmental litigation group. She was formerly assistant chief of the Environmental Enforcement Section in the Department of Justice, where she worked on cases involving Superfund, the Clean Air Act, and the Clean Water Act. GE has employed at least eleven in-house lobbyists and outside lobbyists who are former EPA employees. The lobbyists held high-level positions at the EPA, such as deputy general counsel and regional counsel.

Besides the Hudson River, GE has created yet another PCB pollution nightmare in New England. In the white working-class community of Pittsfield, Massachusetts, a GE plant manufacturing electrical transformers polluted the Housatonic River with millions of pounds of PCBs. The deadly chemicals are now found in the river from western Massachusetts to its mouth in the Long Island Sound some 100 miles away. To insulate the company from the costs of a potential cleanup, GE hired Stephen Ramsey away from his job as head of the environmental enforcement section of the Department of Justice. In his new capacity as vice president for environmental programs, Ramsey coauthored a ten-page manual on how to stymie government efforts to hold companies accountable for pollution. Widely circulated among industry, the Ramsey manual included advice on how to flood the government with paperwork by using the Freedom of Information Act "broadly and often." It also recommends making creative use of the "book-of-the-month-club" response: "If we don't hear from you, we assume you agree with us." In the words of investigative journalist Eric Goldscheider, "The advice in Ramsey's manual, based on his intimate knowledge of how the government works, was so worrisome to David Buente, Jr., his successor at the Justice Department, that Buente distributed a memo warning colleagues about it. That was before Buente himself became part of GE's team."[106]

RACE, CLASS, AND THE ENVIRONMENTAL INJUSTICES OF "FREE-MARKET" ENVIRONMENTALISM

For almost three decades, the state has utilized "command-and-control" regulation of industry to address environmental problems. Under the liberal regime of environmental regulation, the federal government establishes uniform national pollution limits ("command") that the federal or state governments impose on individual polluters through a system of permits or other regulatory devices ("controls").[107] Although the established standards are often weak and inadequate when it comes to protecting public health, the command-and-control approach has reduced many of the most prolific sources of pollution in the United States. It has also raised construction and operating costs for American capital and precipitated a call by the polluter-industrial complex for new market-based approaches, especially those that make use of economic incentives to reward rather than punish capital in order to spur improved environmental performance.

Since the late 1990s, neoliberals in both the Republican and the Democratic parties have introduced over 100 different economic incentive mechanisms to address environmental problems. The most important of these instituted market-based approaches are pollutant-trading programs that allow corporations sell "pollution rights" to other companies unwilling to buy expensive pollution control equipment. It also involves government subsidies and "takings" policies whereby the state compensates corporations for lost profits associated with halting destructive practices and/or making environmental improvements. Finally, free-market environmentalism also emphasizes regulatory waivers or variance programs that allow capital to avoid some command-and-control requirements in favor of more cost-effective alternatives. As we shall see, the polluter-industrial complex is utilizing these neoliberal policy initiatives to further exploit the environment and displace the social and ecological costs of production onto poor communities of color and working-class neighborhoods. In effect, neoliberalism is deepening the environmental injustices of American capitalism.

Trading Away the Rights of Citizens to Clean Air and Water

Among the most problematic approaches to "free-market" environmentalism is emissions trading, whereby the state gives a corporation the "right" to discharge a set amount of pollution. These pollution rights can then be bought and sold by other companies. In theory, this approach provides incentives to capital to reduce their pollution discharges beyond the levels allowed by law in order to sell their unused pollution "credits" to other corporations. Companies unwilling to reduce profits by making significant investments in pollution abatement technology may instead exceed federal environmental standards by purchasing excess pollution rights from another, less polluting company. Under the Clean Air Act of 1990, for instance, power plants are compelled to reduce sulfur dioxide emissions that cause acid rain and other major and related health problems. Cosponsored by Al Gore as a then senator from Tennessee, the act promotes the commodification of pollution (which can be bought and sold on the stock market) and allows enterprises such as the Tennessee Valley Authority to buy millions of dollars worth of pollution credits from Wisconsin Power and Light. These pollution credits allow the Tennessee Valley Authority to exceed federal limitations on sulfur dioxide and other toxic emissions in older facilities, including facilities located in poor working-class communities of color. Under this program, capital is granted flexibility to utilize the most cost-effective means for reducing (or maintaining) pollution levels.

Pollution-trading policies fall under three broad categories termed *emissions offset programs*, *cap and trade programs*, and *open market trading*. The first two strategies involve the placement of a regulatory "bubble" over a specific facility and a geographic region. If only one facility is involved, it can trade emissions among units within the facility. Firms within a regional market program can trade emission credits to other facilities as long as the overall pollution load remains the same. The third strategy, open market trading, allows firms to use emission reduction credits from past reductions in lieu of installing equipment that may be required under the law. All these market strategies have their problems with respect to environmental justice, namely, that those citizens living in close proximity to companies purchasing the "right" to release greater quantities of pollutants are having their health placed at a much higher risk than other citizens.

On March 16, 1995, President Clinton and Vice President Gore announced their ambitious plans for the "re-invention of environmental regulation," with open market trading being listed as the top priority. This announcement signaled that previous efforts to balance traditional command-and-control policies and market-based approaches were at an end. Free-market environmentalism would become deeply entrenched under Clinton and Gore, including emissions trading, which was used to delay rather than accelerate compliance with the Clean Air Act's requirements.[108] In their eagerness to pursue this neoliberal agenda, however, the White House overrode the EPA's OIG, which had identified a host of problems with the plan. These problems included a general inability on behalf of the EPA to verify and enforce the equal trading of emissions credits. In addition, it is much more difficult for residents in poorer communities to find the time, money, expertise, and political access necessary to adequately monitor pollution rates and serve as a watchdog in support of EPA enforcement. Furthermore, trading programs do not require capital to compensate residents living near the offending facilities for harms that are caused by the trades or allow them to bargain with the trading partners to prevent the harm from being created in the first place. In the final analysis, pollutant-trading schemes are fundamentally undemocratic.

Another set of potential problems with regional trading programs is that they carry a substantial risk of creating toxic "hot spots" in poor communities of color and working-class neighborhoods.[109] When several industrial facilities purchase pollution credits in one geographic area and use these credits to maintain or increase releases of the most dangerous chemical pollutants, toxic hot spots are created. Older industries may find it more cost effective to buy pollution rights rather than install expensive pollution abatement technologies. The communities surrounding those industries will thus be exposed to higher levels of pollution than other communities. Older and more hazardous industrial facilities most likely to *purchase* pollution credits (rather than re-selling them) are often located in poorer communities, where there is less political pressure on firms to clean up their operations.

California provides an example of the potential problems associated with emissions trading. In Los Angeles, 71 percent of the city's African Americans and 50 percent of the Latinos live in what are categorized as the most polluted areas, compared to 34 percent of whites.[110] Refineries in southern California have avoided the costs of installing vapor recovery systems by purchasing pollution reduction credits in exchange for ridding themselves of 17,000 older, highly polluting automobiles under a vehicle-scrapping program. The bulk of the credits were bought by three refineries located in lower-income Latino communities.[111] Citizens for a Better Environment and the NAACP Legal Defense Fund recently challenged this auto scrapping program by the South Coast Air Quality Management District on the grounds that it discriminates against minorities in violation of federal civil rights laws by concentrating previously dispersed pollutants in the Latino community.

Again, these innovations in program design tend to be industry friendly and offer few protections to the more heavily impacted communities. To the extent that firms purchasing excess pollution rights are disproportionately located in poorer host communities, pollution trading poses greater health risks for people of color and the white working class than for the general population.[112] The EPA's OIG has found the potential for toxic hot spots to be an even greater concern with open market trading programs, as they lack the protection of a regulatory cap. Furthermore, the EPA's focus on market trading schemes that allow facilities to maintain or increase their current levels of "smokestack" pollution by eliminating mobile pollution sources (such as from old cars) has dealt a significant blow to air pollution control plans for all federally designated "nonattainment areas." Nonattainment areas experience much more dangerous pollution levels because polluting facilities are more heavily concentrated in the region.[113]

In addition, under "cross-pollutant-trading" schemes, a corporation is permitted to increase its emissions of a highly toxic chemical (such as benzene) if another company decreases its emissions of a relatively nontoxic chemical (such as nitrogen oxide). Thus, more deadly pollutants could remain unabated or increase in poor communities of color in return for reductions of chemicals with little direct results for public health. There is now overwhelming evidence that highly polluting and ecologically hazardous industrial facilities are clustered in poor communities of color and white working-class neighborhoods. In Massachusetts, communities of color receive ten times as many pounds of pollutants per square mile as white communities. Even more striking is the fact that communities of color received 38 percent of all carcinogens, 33 percent of all persistent bioaccumulative toxins, and 37 percent of all reproductive toxins (chemicals that cause damage to the reproductive system, including potential birth defects and sterility), even though they make up only 9.4 percent of all towns in the state.[114]

These and other problems associated with the Clinton administration's plans to permit the trading of pollution rights encountered a great deal of opposition from EJ advocates inside and outside the state bureaucracy. In December 1999, after a series of embarrassing leaks of internal assessments regarding the potential effects of the administration's plans on poor and minority communities, the EPA's Office of Civil Rights issued a "gag order" warning employees of possible criminal prosecution or disciplinary action for the disclosure of nonpublic information. Playing hardball with EJ advocates and progressive environmentalists, the Clinton–Gore administration allowed the policy debate to be hijacked by the polluter-industrial complex. Framed as having to choose between two mutually exclusive approaches—command and control on one side and free-market environmentalism on the other— Congress relented. The Clean Air Act and other policies were turned over to "the market"—setting aside requirements based on public health in favor of economic efficiency and capital accumulation.[115]

There is yet another set of unintended consequences related to pollutant trading and the Clean Air Act. A preliminary investigation of the Acid Rain Program has not yet uncovered evidence that the allowance trading systems has transferred additional sulfur dioxide pollution to poor communities of color.[116] Those rates are already very high. Instead, the increased availability of inexpensive low-sulfur coal has resulted in reductions in sulfur dioxide emissions at many plants and limited the utility of emissions trading. However, the act has made a major EJ impact with respect to the mining of low-sulfur coal. In 1985, the Acid Rain Roundtable, a corporatist group representing select environmental organizations, utilities, coal companies, and state officials, formulated recommendations for burning more low-sulfur coal. The recommendations were incorporated into the Clean Air Act of 1990. The utilities are responding by blending high-sulfur coal with low-sulfur coal. As a result, unionized labor working the high-sulfur coal mines have seen significant declines in employment. Similarly, the strip mining of low-sulfur coal is equally devastating to the landscape and public health in the mountains of Appalachia.[117]

These same air pollution protection regulations are pushing coal companies to develop low-sulfur coal deposits through the strip mining of western lands, including the fragile desert regions home to Indian and Latino communities. One-third of all low-sulfur coal reserves in the United States lie on Native lands. In an attempt to gain control over and exploit the low-cost energy resources on these lands, the polluter-industrial complex has launched a nationwide corporate attack on Native Americans, including calls for the termination of treaty rights.[118] The solutions embraced in the legislation fractured the mainstream environmental movement from grassroots environmentalists, labor, EJ activists, and the indigenous land rights movements. It is in this political context that the Navajo–Hopi controversy with the Peabody Coal Company at Big Mountain and other resource wars against Native peoples must be interpreted.[119] As such, the Clean Air Act is a powerful reminder of how neoliberal environmental policy is likely to exacerbate rather than resolve the profound social and environmental injustices fostered by traditional regulatory approaches over the past thirty years.

Federal Government Subsidies for Exploiting the Environment under Clinton and Gore

In contradiction of their publicly stated ideology calling for more limited government, neoliberals are providing billions of dollars in corporate welfare and state subsidies for environmentally destructive activities. These subsidies include tax breaks and government research money for dirty forms of energy production and use (oil shale, coal gasification, and oil refining), questionable biotechnology projects and chemical-intensive forms of agriculture, tax exemptions for extracting natural resources from public lands, and insurance schemes that cap the fiscal liability of the nuclear power industry in the case of an accident. The U.S. Forest Service, for instance, loses billions of dollars subsidizing destructive logging practices in the national forests. Through the Purchaser Road Credit program, the Forest Service has paid for the construction of over 381,000 miles of logging roads for the timber industry in the national forests—more than ten times the U.S. interstate highway system and enough to circle the earth seventeen times. Under the Clinton administration, the Forest Service spent $387 million alone on new timber road construction, engineering, and design between 1992 and 1997. Taking into account other subsidies, the GAO estimates that the Forest Service's commercial timber program lost more than $2 billion during this time frame. Meanwhile, the lumber companies are reaping enormous profits from these handouts. Boise Cascade generated a $1.6 billion in profit in 2003, while Weyerhaeuser generated a $3.9 billion profit in 2002.[120]

Historically, the U.S. welfare state has served to redistribute wealth from the capitalist class to working families, especially those families living in poverty, via higher taxes on corporate earnings and the wealthy. However, the reinvention of the federal tax code under President Bush has cut taxes on the wealthy and major corporations and instead shifted the tax burden onto the American middle class. According to the Citizens for Tax Justice, millionaires received 62 percent of the reduced tax rates on long-term capital gains and dividends granted by the 2003 tax law. In fact, a mere 11,433 of 134 million taxpayers reaped 28 percent of the total investment tax cuts, saving $21.7 billion in taxes.[121] At the same time, neoliberals have successfully expanded the size and scope of the corporate welfare state, effectively redistributing hundreds of billions in dollars from middle- and working-class families into the pockets of this country's largest and most profitable corporations. Similarly, during the Clinton administration, an estimated $150 billion annually—in the form of direct federal subsidies and tax breaks that specifically benefited capital—was funneled to American companies. This was more than the $145 billion paid out annually for the core programs of the social welfare state: Aid to Families with Dependent Children, student aid, housing, food and nutrition, and all direct public assistance (excluding Social Security and medical care).[122]

One of the worst abuses of power by the polluter-industrial complex with respect to government subsidies is connected to Vice President Al Gore. Under the auspices of his National Performance Review (NPR), also known as the "reinventing government" initiative, the Clinton administration sold valuable federal properties and natural resource assets to capital at bargain-basement prices. The sale of the Elk Hills petroleum reserve to Occidental Petroleum represents such a rip-off of the American people. Elk Hills was a huge oil field outside Bakersfield, California, set aside long ago as a strategic reserve for the U.S. Navy. It is estimated to contain over 1 billion barrels of oil. In 1998, the Occidental Petroleum Company orchestrated a deal with the active support of Vice President Gore to buy 78 percent of Elk Hills for $3.65 billion—one of the largest privatization acts in U.S. history. Elk Hills is the home of the Kitanemuk Indians, who opposed the sale of the land. The field proved sensationally profitable because of lower-than-expected oil extraction costs for Occidental, leading many analysts to conclude that the bidding had not occurred on a level playing field. These suspicions were well founded.

Within weeks of the announced purchase, Occidental stock rose 10 percent. As it turned out, Gore controlled between $250,000 and $500,000 of Occidental stock (after the sale, Gore began disclosing between $500,000 and $1 million of his significantly more valuable stock).[123]

Gore's direct financial interest and his close relationship with Occidental Petroleum dates back to his father, Al Gore Sr., who sat on Occidental's board of directors. Throughout his political life, Al Gore Jr. received the favor of patronage from Occidental and its chief executive officer, Ray Irani (Irani was one of the contributors who slept in the Lincoln Bedroom in "exchange" for a $100,000 check to the Democratic National Committee). From 1972 to the time of the sale, Irani contributed $470,000 in soft money to Clinton, Gore, and the Democratic Party. Occidental bought the Elks Hill region from the federal government for $3.7 billion. The sale represented a tripling of the company's U.S. oil reserves. To complete the sale, the Energy Department hired a private company to complete the necessary environmental impact statement. The company was ICF Kaiser International, and on its board of directors sat Democratic Party super-fund-raiser Tony Cohelo, who would later become Gore's campaign manager. The Elk Hills sale was quickly approved.

This pattern of political favoritism was repeated around a controversial proposal to locate a major incinerator in the depressed white working-class community of East Liverpool, Ohio, where more than 25 percent of the population lives below the poverty line. Owned and operated by Waste Technologies Industries, the large incinerator was located just 320 feet from the nearest homes and 1,100 feet from an elementary school containing hundreds of children and was slated to burn more than 70,000 tons of hazardous waste each year. In 1992, when plans to build the incinerator were announced, then vice-presidential candidate Al Gore blasted the incinerator as an "unbelievable idea" and promised outraged environmentalists that he would "be on your side for a change." However, a key financier and original partner in the company that developed the incinerator plan was Jack Stephens. An investment banker from Little Rock, Arkansas, and a key donor to Bill Clinton's campaigns for governor, Stephens also gave $100,000 to the Clinton presidential campaign in 1992. Worthen Bank, which is partly owned by the Stephens family, even extended the Clinton–Gore campaign a $3.5 million credit line. The Clinton campaign likewise deposited up to $55 million in federal election funds in this bank.[124]

Not surprisingly after the election, the Clinton–Gore administration refused to shut down the incinerator, even though EPA Ombudsman Robert Martin released a report stating that the facility posed significant dangers to community residents. Despite strong protests, Clinton and Gore sided with EPA Deputy Administrator Robert Sussman in approving of the incinerator. A key government official overseeing the WTI–East Liverpool controversy, Sussman was a law school classmate of Bill and Hillary Clinton. He also previously served as legal counsel to the Chemical Manufacturers Association at a time when two of its biggest clients—DuPont and BASF—were negotiating contracts to supply two-thirds of the waste to WTI. In fact, Hillary Clinton helped incorporate WTI while at the Rose Law Firm and served on the board of LaFarge Cement, which operates a cement kiln in Alpena, Michigan, on Lake Huron that switched from natural gas to burning hazardous wastes (used motor oil and solvents) in the mid-1980s. In short, Bill and Hillary Clinton and Al Gore owed a substantial part of their political souls to the polluter-industrial complex. It is little wonder that they betrayed their pledge to the environmental movement and people of East Liverpool.

State Subsidies for the Corporate Assault on Mother Earth under Bush and Cheney

To subsidize the exploitation of the country's natural wealth, the federal government doles out billions of dollars in handouts to the polluter-industrial complex.[125] In the summer of 2005, for instance, President Bush signed into law the new energy bill that included massive subsidies for the oil industry. Despite record-setting federal budget deficits and outrageous profits for the oil giants—ExxonMobil, for instance, brought in $24 billion in profits in 2004—the energy bill allocated at least $4 billion in subsidies and tax breaks for the oil industry. In addition, the bill exempts the oil industry from several environmental laws, including the Clean Water Act and the Safe Drinking Water Act, allowing even the most profitable companies to pollute waterways and drinking water. The law also suspends the payment of royalties for publicly owned oil and gas from offshore leases in the deeper waters of the Gulf of Mexico and allows the oil industry to forgo royalty payments to the federal treasury for oil drilled in areas of Alaska's coastline.[126]

The energy bill is exemplary of the manner in which the state is subsiding the destructive behavior of U.S. corporations, often in ways which contradict established environmental/EJ policy. Every year, the United States burns more than 900 million tons of coal, releasing more than fifty-one tons of mercury and 2 billion tons of carbon dioxide into the air. The bulk of government assistance in the energy sector has been directed to the nation's most profitable and dirtiest energy sources. Yet, as reported in the *New York Times* in late January 2006, the Interior Department undervalues the natural gas royalties collected from the oil companies by $700 million per year. The 1872 Mining Law also allows companies to take more than $245 billion worth of precious minerals from public lands without paying a dime in royalties to taxpayers. The 131-year-old law allows a mining company to patent, or buy, mineral-rich public land worth billions of dollars for $5 an acre or less. Even more scandalous is the fact that taxpayers have been left with a $32 billion to $72 billion cleanup bill for the half a million contaminated mine sites, more than seventy of which have been designated Superfund sites.[127]

Besides providing direct subsidies to capital, the U.S. Forest Service and the Bureau of Land Management frequently swap federal land for privately owned land. However, these exchanges have created a furor over the appraisal and environmental review processes conducted by federal agencies. In June 2000, the GAO released a report charging that the Forest Service and the Bureau of Land Management have undervalued federal land and overvalued land the government has obtained in trades from private interests. The report concluded that, too often, these land exchanges benefit large corporations at the public's expense. For example, when companies exchange their exploited lands with the federal government, they avoid environmental obligations, thus sticking taxpayers with the cost of decommissioning logging roads and restoring damaged lands. In early February 2006, the Bush administration announced its proposal to sell more than 300,000 acres of national forests and other public lands worth over $1 billion—a plan that privatizes treasured public lands to pay for tax cuts enjoyed by the wealthy. The Bush administration is currently advocating the sale of hundreds of thousands of acres of federal lands in order to raise $350 million to supplement the budget and help pay for the war in Iraq (which has already cost over half a trillion dollars).

The Bush administration is also awarding lucrative government contracts to some of the worst corporate polluters in the country (e.g., Halliburton around the cleanup of New Orleans and the Gulf coast in the wake of Hurricane Katrina). To undercut environmentalists and EJ activists, the White House announced two days after Christmas in 2002 the rejection of regulations that would have barred companies that repeatedly violate environmental and workplace standards from receiving government contracts. This is no trivial matter. A congressional report had found that in one recent year, the federal government had awarded $38 billion in contracts to at least 261 corporations operating unsafe or unhealthy work sites.[128] The rule was issued despite studies by the GAO revealing that a significant number of federal contractors violate federal laws, sometimes repeatedly. For example, the GAO found that eighty federal contractors receiving over $23 billion from 4,400 contracts had engaged in violations of the National Labor Relations Act.[129]

There are viable alternatives to corporate welfare. Many environmentalists are today calling for the use of pollution taxes as a more efficient way to reduce pollutants as well as greenhouse gases. Unlike subsidies or emissions credits, which tend to be given away, a tax actually raises revenue. A carbon tax makes more sense because the money can be used to cut taxes on positive developments (like clean, renewable energy) and to raise taxes on negative activities (like pollution and clearing forests). In short, ecological taxes offer more promise for addressing environmental injustices and greening American capitalism.[130] Unfortunately, they are not a central component of the neoliberal agenda.

Waiving EJ Enforcement in Favor of Voluntary Cleanups

In the rush to reduce costs and boost profits for corporate polluters, neoliberals are implementing regulatory waiver or variance programs. In these programs, the EPA allows polluters to avoid some command-and-control requirements in favor of more cost-effective approaches selected by the company. This includes agreements with specific corporations that allow environmental regulations to be avoided if alternative approaches yield "superior environmental results." Advocates of EJ have criticized these approaches, however, because it is often extremely difficult to ascertain whether such alternative projects actually decrease the pollution burden in a community. These projects may also result in reductions of certain kinds of less harmful pollutants and cause increases in other, potentially more dangerous types of pollutants in the same community. Pollutants might also be transferred from one medium to another or from one area to a marginalized community. And while such a project might seem, initially, to produce superior environmental results, it could aggravate health or environmental impacts to the surrounding community because of the synergistic or cumulative impacts of the new pollutant or new discharge coupled with existing pollution.

On June 11, 2003, the Office of Enforcement and Compliance Assurance issued a memorandum, "Expanding the Use of Supplemental Environmental Projects (SEPs)." The memo urged enforcement agents to make greater use of SEPs as a tool for addressing environmental injustice. An SEP is an environmentally beneficial project that a corporate violator of environmental law chooses to perform as part of the settlement of an EPA enforcement action. The EPA will agree to reduce the financial penalty imposed on a corporation if the company voluntarily agrees to implement an SEP. An SEP is supposed to compensate communities that are put at risk from the environmental violations. Although a violator is not legally required to perform an SEP, the cash penalty may be lowered significantly, in most cases reduced by half, if the company performs one.

On January 5, 2004, the Office of Enforcement and Compliance Assurance issued a second memorandum, "Recommended Ideas for Supplemental Environmental Projects," which included suggestions for types of potentially beneficial SEPs. Taken together, these memoranda lay the foundation for more aggressive use of environmentally significant SEPs in communities with EJ concerns. In fact, EPA's Supplemental Environmental Projects Policy states, in part,

> There is an acknowledged concern, expressed in Executive Order 12898 on environmental justice, that certain segments of the nation's population, i.e., low-income and/or minority populations, are disproportionately burdened by pollutant exposure. Emphasizing SEPs in communities where environmental justice concerns are present helps ensure that persons who spend significant portions of their times in areas, or depend on food and water sources located near, where the violations occur would be protected.[131]

In 2006, the National Refinery Reform Campaign and Public Citizen's Texas office issued a report examining the history of SEPs in Corpus Christi, Texas. Not surprisingly, the report revealed that the communities most impacted by the violations are not directly benefiting from the resulting SEPs. Corpus Christi's "Refinery Row" consists of several refinery and chemical plants that are in close proximity to low-income communities of color. The report found that companies responsible for the pollution often elect to undertake SEPs in lieu of a portion of the according fines for their actions. Ideally, these projects would create direct benefits in the most affected communities. However, a review of documents indicate that most SEPs do not directly benefit the communities affected by the violations. For example, an enforcement action against Citgo for the serious violations of operating a surface impoundment without a permit and emitting hydrogen fluoride, volatile organic compounds, and hydrogen sulfide without a permit resulted in the approval of an SEP contribution focused on improving a bird nesting site on Shamrock Island. This SEP was of no direct benefit to the affected community residents being harmed by the company's illegal actions. The report concludes that unless the power to choose SEPs are taken out of the hands of the polluter-industrial complex and instead placed in the hands of residents to decide what projects would be most beneficial to the community, environmental injustices are likely to worsen. These laws are granting special privileges to polluters, and these privileges are being abused.[132]

Similarly, the EPA advertises its "Performance Track" program as a haven for companies with exemplary environmental records. In return for a voluntary commitment to go "beyond compliance," corporations are promised additional regulatory incentives, an "exclusive" right to be shielded from "routine" inspections, free advertising, and insider access to senior decision makers in government." However, a 2006 investigation by the Environmental Integrity

Project found that some of the manufacturers reaping Performance Track rewards are releasing *more* toxic pollution to the environment than they were before signing up for the program. For instance, seven participating facilities reported increasing air emissions of toxic pollutants by *more than 2 million
pounds* between 2000 and 2004, including hundreds of thousands of pounds of
carcinogens and pollutants that cause birth defects.[133] The 3M chemical plant
in Guin, Alabama, led the pack by more than doubling its emissions of the carcinogen ethylbenzene over four years. Guin is a racially diverse, working-class
community of 2,257 people.

Five other plants in the program reported releasing at least 457,000 pounds
more toxic pollution into nearby rivers in 2004 than they did in 2000, including International Paper's Kraft mill in Mansfield, Louisiana, which nearly
tripled its reported toxic discharges. Mansfield is a poor, minority community
(74 percent black) with a household median income of $12,417. These ex-
amples and more suggest that there is a significant mismatch between the incentives the EPA offers—fewer inspections and less monitoring of toxic pollutants—and what the public gets out of this program in return. Furthermore,
the programs are left to be self-policed by the companies themselves, and the
results are confidential. And there are no consequences for not meeting com-
mitments—targets that are missed are simply adjusted downward to match
actual performance. In short, Performance Track offers corporate participants
the chance to pick their subjects, design their own tests, grade themselves,
and even change their own report cards after the fact in order to avoid a failing grade. In return, the EPA enthusiastically promises fewer regulations and
less enforcement.

Finally, under pressure from the White House, the EPA is making increased
use of *consent agreements*, which are abused regularly as a way of protecting
corporate interests. Not unlike a plea bargain, a consent agreement is a contract wherein a corporate defendant agrees to stop an illegal activity without
admitting guilt. However, consent agreements are drawn up in secret, with no
public review. As a result, politically connected corporations are able to secure consent agreements that grant them all sorts of privileges to which they
are not entitled, often in exchange for paltry fines. For example, when Chemical Waste Management was denied a permit to store carcinogenic PCBs at its
massive hazardous waste dump in Emelle, Alabama, a poor community of
color, they stored them anyway and later got caught. An eventual consent
agreement fined the company far less than the profits incurred by its illegal
action and threw in a PCB storage permit to boot. The agreement also exempted the firm from punishment for any other past violations, even those
that had not yet come to light. In short, for a $450,000 fine, Chemical Waste
Management received waivers worth more than $100 million. In effect, free-

market environmentalism is coddling the polluter-industrial complex. By creating the appearance of reform, these neoliberal programs are actually permitting capital to continue polluting in poor communities of color and working-class neighborhoods. As a result, environmental injustices in America are intensifying.

CONCLUSION

Neoliberal strategies to de-democratize the federal bureaucracy have accelerated in the new millennium. These strategies include the implementation of administrative mechanisms designed to bypass democratic processes and procedures built into the EPA, the Occupational Safety and Health Administration, the Interior Department, and other federal agencies. The Bush–Cheney administration has also appointed officials working directly for the polluter-industrial complex to key positions within the bureaucracy and implemented severe cuts in agency staffs and budgets, effectively crippling the research, monitoring, and enforcement activities of the EPA and other agencies. Neoliberals are also blocking or slowing the introduction of more progressive environmental legislation, preventing the enforcement of existing regulations, and delegating programs to financially strapped local and state governments lacking the capacity to assume the task. Finally, many older regulations requiring across-the-board compliance with environmental laws are being replaced with "cost-effective" reforms and "free-market" forms of environmental policy—pollution taxes and credits, effluent charges, subsidies for polluting industries, markets for pollution rights, and bubble schemes—all designed to increase capital's flexibility to meet weaker environmental regulations but continue polluting in a profitable manner. The cumulative impact of this assault is to exacerbate environmental health problems among the working class and especially poor people of color.

This attack has come at a critical juncture for the ecology and EJ movements. Since much of the key environmental legislation is already on the books, the Bush–Cheney administration is defining the issues in terms of how these laws will be implemented and enforced. The focus of activity has shifted from to Congress to the executive branch precisely at the moment when the latter has become captured by the polluter-industrial complex. Knowing that EJ policies and programs are invariably redistributive in that they impose substantial costs on capital and confer substantial benefits on the working class and people of color, the Bush administration is erecting profound institutional barriers to the enactment of such policies. Neoliberals realize that it is much easier to stop a law from being enacted than to secure new legislation. Nevertheless, the various forms of free-market environmentalism being implemented are deepening the ecological crisis. This crisis is being displaced onto marginalized communities inside and outside the United States. The political goal of the EJ movement should not be the defense of the old liberal regime of environmental regulation, for it is inadequate. Rather, a superior strategy would be to focus on preventing pollution in the first place—to build a clean economy and democratic society committed to principles of social justice for all Americans.

NOTES

1. Laura Pulido, *Environmentalism and Economic Justice: Two Chicano Struggles in the Southwest* (Tucson: University of Arizona Press, 1996), 210–11.

2. Robert J. Brulle, *Agency, Democracy, and Nature: The US Environmental Movement from a Critical Theory Perspective* (Cambridge, MA: MIT Press, 2000), 101–14.

3. Christopher J. Bosso, *Environment, Inc.: From Grassroots to Beltway* (Lawrence: University Press of Kansas, 2005), 6–7.

4. A Natural Resources Defense Council study (released on May 8, 1996) on 239 cities across the country found that some 64,000 Americans are dying each year from air pollution, even at levels that the federal government considers safe.

5. Robert J. Gilliom, Jack E. Barbash, Charles G. Crawford, Pixie A. Hamilton, Jeffrey D. Martin, Naomi Nakagaki, Lisa H. Howell, Jonathan C. Scott, Paul E. Stackelberg, Gail P. Thelin, and David M. Wolock, *Pesticides in the Nation's Streams and Ground Water, 1992–2001*, a report by the National Water-Quality Assessment Program of the United States Geological Survey (March 2006), 1–181.

6. Alex Knott, "EPA Document Lists Firms Tied to Superfund Sites: 100 Companies—and Federal Agencies—Are Connected to 40 Percent of the Worst Toxic Waste Dumps" (April 26, 2007), available at http://www.publicintegrity .org/superfund (accessed May 5, 2007).

7. Eric J. Krieg, "Toxic Wastes, Race, and Class: A Historical Interpretation of Greater Boston" (PhD diss., Northeastern University, 1995), 1–26.

8. For a review, see Environmental Research Foundation, *Rachel's Hazardous Waste News* 332 (April 8, 1993): 1–2.

9. Sandra Steingraber, *Living Downstream: An Ecologist Looks at Cancer and the Environment* (New York: Addison-Wesley, 1997).

10. American Cancer Society, *Cancer Facts and Figures, 2006*, available at http:// www.cancer.org/downloads/STT/CAFF2006PWSecured.pdf (accessed January 10, 2007).

11. Robert D. Bullard, Paul Mohai, Robin Saha, and Beverly Wright, *Toxic Wastes and Race at Twenty: 1987–2007—Grassroots Struggles to Dismantle Environmental Racism in the United States*, a report prepared for the United Church of Christ Justice and Witness Ministries (March 1987).

12. Devra Davis, *When Smoke Ran Like Water: Tales of Environmental Deception and the Battle against Pollution* (New York: Basic Books, 2002).

13. Joe Thornton, *Pandora's Poison: Chlorine, Health, and a New Environmental Strategy* (Cambridge, MA: MIT Press, 2000), vii–14.

14. David Roe, William Pease, Karen Florini, and Ellen Silbergeld, *Toxic Ignorance: the Continuing Absence of Basic Health Testing for Top-Selling Chemicals in the United States* (New York: Environmental Defense Fund, 1997).

15. Mary H. O'Brien, "When Harm Is Not Necessary: Risk Assessment as Diversion," in *Reclaiming the Environmental Debate: The Politics of Health in a Toxic Culture*, ed. Richard Hofrichter (Cambridge, MA: MIT Press, 2000), 113–34.

16. Institute of Medicine, *Toward Environmental Justice: Research, Education, and Health Policy Needs* (Washington, DC: National Academy of Sciences, 1999), chap. 1.

17. Stacy Malkan, *Not Just a Pretty Face: The Ugly Side of the Beauty Industry* (Gabriola Island, BC: New Society Publishers, 2007).

18. Jim Pirkle et al., *National Report on Human Exposure to Environmental Chemicals*, NCEH Publication No. 02-0716 (Atlanta: Centers for Disease Control and Prevention, January 31, 2003); see also "CDC Releases Most Extensive Assessment to Date of Americans' Exposure to Environmental Chemicals," available at http://www.cdc.gov (accessed June 25, 2007).

19. Fairbank, Maslin, Maullin & Associates, "PBT Opinion Research Report, 2005," cited in Pat Costner, Beverly Thorpe, and Alexandra McPherson, *Sick of Dust: Chemicals in Common Products—A Needless Health Risk in Our Homes* (Spring Brook, NY: Clean Production Action, March 2005).

20. Cited in Robert D. Bullard, "Environmental Justice in the Twenty-First Century," in *The Quest for Environmental Justice: Human Rights and the Politics of Pollution*, ed. Robert D. Bullard (San Francisco: Sierra Club Books, 2005), 29.

21. Richard Moore, "Confronting Environmental Racism," *Crossroads* 11, no. 2 (April 1992): 7–9.

22. Daniel Faber, "A More 'Productive' Environmental Justice Politics: Movement Alliances in Massachusetts for Clean Production and Regional Equity," in *Environmental Justice and Environmentalism: The Social Justice Challenge to the Environmental Movement*, ed. Ronald Sandler and Phaedra C. Pezzullo (Cambridge, MA: MIT Press, 2007), 135–64.

23. Terry L. Anderson and Donald R. Leal, *Free Market Environmentalism* (New York: Palgrave, 2001).

24. Jonathan H. Alder, ed., *Ecology, Liberty and Property: A Free Market Environmental Reader* (Washington, DC: Competitive Enterprise Institute, 2000); Peter Huber, *Hard Green: Saving the Environment from the Environmentalists—A Conservative Manifesto* (New York: Basic Books, 1999).

25. Richard A. Harris and Sidney M. Milkis, *The Politics of Regulatory Change: A Tale of Two Agencies* (New York: Oxford University Press, 1989).

26. Robert V. Bartless, "The Budgetary Process and Environmental Policy," in *Environmental Policy in the 1980s*, ed. Norman J. Vig and Michael E. Kraft (Washington, DC: Congressional Quarterly Press, 1984), 130.

27. J. Clarence Davies, "Environmental Institutions and the Reagan Administration," in Vig and Kraft, *Environmental Policy in the 1980s*, 146–48.

28. Richard N. L. Andrews, "Deregulation: The Failure at EPA," in Vig and Kraft, *Environmental Policy in the 1980s*, 164–65.

29. Bruce Barcott, "Changing All the Rules: How the Bush Administration Quietly—and Radically—Transformed the Nation's Clean-Air Policy," *New York Times Magazine* (April 4, 2004), 40–44.

30. Richard J. Lazarus, "A Different Kind of 'Republican Moment' in Environmental Law," *Minnesota Law Review* 87, no. 4 (April 2003): 999–1036, esp. 1031.

31. Brian Tokar, *Earth for Sale: Reclaiming Ecology in the Age of Corporate Greenwash* (Boston: South End Press, 1997).

32. In the words of DuPont Chairman Edgar Woolard, "We do not seek a wholesale dismantling of the regulatory framework . . . just smarter, more effective regulation where we need it." See Ronald Begley, "Deregulation: Two Much of a Good Thing?," *Chemical Week* (April 19, 1997), 68.

33. Joel Brinkley, "Out of Spotlight, Bush Overhauls US Regulations," *New York Times* (August 14, 2004).

34. *Reckless Abandon: How the Bush Administration Is Exposing America's Waters to Harm*, a report by Earthjustice, the National Wildlife Federation, the Natural Resources Defense Council, and the Sierra Club (August 2004).

35. Robert F. Kennedy Jr., "Foreword," in Robert S. Devine, *Bush versus the Environment* (New York: Anchor Books, 2004), xv.

36. Emily Cousins, Robert Perks, and Wesley Warren, *Rewriting the Rules: The Bush Administration's First-Term Environmental Record*, 3rd ed., a report by the Natural Resources Defense Council (January 2005), vii.

37. Reece Rushing, *Special Interest Takeover: The Bush Administration and the Dismantling of Public Safeguards*, a report by the Center for American Progress and OMB Watch on behalf of Citizens for Sensible Safeguards (May 2004).

38. Chris Mooney, *The Republican War on Science* (Cambridge, MA: Basic Books, 2005).

39. Rick Weiss, with Lucy Shackelford and Julie Tate, "Data Quality Law Is Nemesis of Regulation," *Washington Post* (August 16, 2004), A1.

40. Robert Perks, Wesley Warren, and Gregory Wetstone, *Rewriting the Rules: The Bush Administration's Assault on the Environment*, a report by the Natural Resources Defense Council (April 2002), v.

41. Kennedy, "Foreword," xv.

42. Environment2004, *Polluting Polluters First: The Bush Administration's Environmental Record*, a report by Environment2004 (June 2004), 5.

43. Barcott, "Changing All the Rules," 40–44.

44. Luke W. Cole and Sheila R. Foster, *From the Ground Up: Environmental Racism and the Rise of the Environmental Justice Movement* (New York: New York University Press, 2001), 161–63.

45. Judith M. Espinosa and Eileen Gauna, *Environmental Justice Background Report for the New Mexico Environment Department*, a report prepared by the Alliance for Transportation Research Institute (November 2004), 1–72.

46. Holly D. Gordon and Keith I. Harley, "Environmental Justice and the Legal System," in *Power, Justice, and the Environment: A Critical Appraisal of the Environmental Justice Movement*, ed. David Naguub Pellow and Robert J. Brulle (Cambridge, MA: MIT Press, 2005), 153–70.

47. National Advisory Council for Environmental Policy and Technology, *Report on the Title VI Implementation Advisory Committee: Next Steps for EPA, State, and Local Environmental Justice Programs* (1999); Eileen Gauna, Catherine A. O'Neill, and Clifford Rechtschaffen, "Environmental Justice," a Center for Progressive Regulation white paper, no. 505 (March 2005), 1–24.

48. Cole and Foster, *From the Ground Up*, 161–62.

49. Transnational Resource and Action Center, "The Big, the Bad and the Ugly: Major Polluters Blitz the EPA on Environmental Justice," May 29, 1998, available at http://www.corpwatch.org (accessed January 22, 2002).

50. Brian Hansen, "Tempers Flare at Environmental Justice Conference," *Environment News Service* (December 12, 2000), 1–3.

51. Monique Harden, *The Fight for Healthy and Safe Communities: Uncovering EPA's Anti-Civil Rights Agenda*, a report by the National Black Environmental Justice Network (October 2002).

52. Robert Benford, "The Half-Life of the Environmental Justice Frame: Innovation, Diffusion, and Stagnation," in Pellow and Brulle, *Power, Justice, and the Environment*, 37–53.

53. Denis Binder et al., "A Survey of Federal Agency Response to President Clinton's Executive Order No. 12898 on Environmental Justice 31," *Environmental Law Reporter* (2001): 11133–67.

54. Rebecca Porter, "EPA Rule-Making Gives Environmental Justice Short Shrift, GAO Says," *Trial* 41, no. 10 (October 2005): 81(3).

55. Gauna et al., "Environmental Justice," 3.

56. Holly D. Gordon and Keith I. Harley, "Environmental Justice and the Legal System," in Pellow and Brulle *Power, Justice, and the Environment*, 153–70.

57. Luke W. Cole, "Environmental Justice Litigation: Another Stone in David's Sling," *Fordham Urban Law Journal* 21 (1994): 523–40.

58. Alex Sugarman Broza, personal correspondence, February 1995.

59. Eugene B. Benson, "Commonwealth Makes Strides in Combating Environmental Injustice, but Journey Has Just Begun," *Massachusetts Bar Institute* 8, no. 2 (2006): 3–5.

60. David Pace, "AP: More Blacks Live with Pollution," *AberdeenNews.com* (December 13, 2005), 1–4.

61. Gordon and Harley, "Environmental Justice and the Legal System," 158–59.

62. U.S. Commission on Civil Rights, *Not in My Backyard: Executive Order 12898 and Title VI as Tools for Achieving Environmental Justice* (Washington, DC: U.S. Commission on Civil Rights, 2003).

63. U.S. Environmental Protection Agency, Office of the Inspector General, *EPA Needs to Consistently Implement the Intent of the Executive Order on Environmental Justice* (Washington, DC: U.S. Environmental Protection Agency and Government Accounting Office, September 18, 2006).

64. Government Accountability Office, *Environmental Justice: EPA Should Devote More Attention to Environmental Justice When Developing Clean Air Rules*, Report No. GAO-05-289 (July 2005).

65. Robert D. Bullard, testimony before the Senate Subcommittee on Superfund and Environmental Health of the Senate Environment and Public Works Committee regarding Environmental Justice (July 25, 2007), 6.

66. Eileen Gauna and Clifford Rechtschaffen, *Environmental Justice: Law, Policy, and Regulation* (Durham, NC: Carolina Academic Press, 2002).

67. "Hastings Calls for Major Changes in Administration's Environmental Justice 'Strategic Plan,'" available at http://alceehastings.house.gov (accessed July 21, 2005).

68. U.S. Environmental Protection Agency, Office of the Inspector General, *Evaluation Report: EPA Needs to Conduct Environmental Justice Reviews of Its Program, Policies, and Activities*, Report No. 2006-00034 (Washington, DC: U.S. Environmental Protection Agency, 2006), 7.

69. U.S. General Accountability Office, *Hurricane Katrina: EPA's Current and Future Environmental Protection Efforts Could Be Enhanced by Addressing Issues and Challenges Faced on the Gulf Coast*, a GAO report to congressional committees (June 2007).

70. Devine, *Bush versus the Environment*, 112–13.

71. Chris Bowman, "EPA Pumps Up Its Record: Bee Finds Drug and Terror Cases Mask Drop-Off in Pollution Probes," *Sacramento Bee* (July 6, 2003).

72. U.S. Environmental Protection Agency, *EPA Claims to Meet Drinking Water Goals despite Persistent Data Quality Shortcoming*, a report by the EPA's Office of the Inspector General (March 5, 2004).

73. Safe from Toxics, "2004 TRI Data Shows Increase in Water Pollution: EPA Proposal Would Keep Public in the Dark," a project of the State PIRGs and State Environment Groups, April 12, 2006, available at http://www.safefromtoxics.org/tx.asp?id2=23505 (accessed April 15, 2006).

74. Christy Leavitt, *Troubled Waters: An Analysis of Clean Water Act Compliance, July 2003–December 2004*, a report by the US PIRG Education Fund (March 2006), 1–38.

75. Safe from Toxics, "2004 TRI Data Shows Increase in Water Pollution."

76. The results were based on the responses by 233 corporate lawyers to the survey published in the *National Law Journal.* See Rick Henderson, "Crimes against Nature," available at http://www.reason.com/news/printer/29400.html (accessed April 30, 2007).

77. Associated Press, "Firms Dumped Chemicals during Pittsburgh Oil Spill," *San Francisco Chronicle* (February 22, 1998), A5.

78. Guy Gugliotta and Eric Planin, "Few Fined for Polluting Water," *Washington Post* (June 6, 2003).

79. Martha Mendoza and Christopher Sullivan, "Billions Uncollected in Penalties for Wrongdoing," Associated Press (March 18, 2006), 1–2.

80. William Greider, "The Man from Alcoa: Treasury Secretary Paul O'Neill Is Turning Out to Be a Dangerous Crank," *The Nation* 273, no. 3 (July 16, 2001): 11–14.

81. League of Conservation Voters, *Clean Air and Water Are among Top Concerns for American Voters* (March 9, 2000).

82. Joel A. Mintz, "Treading Water: A Preliminary Assessment of EPA Enforcement during the Bush II Administration," *Environmental Law Institute News and Analysis* 34 (October 2004): 10933–53.

83. "Group Asserts EPA Exaggerating Enforcement Claims," *BushGreenWatch* (November 19, 2004), 1–2.

84. Brad Heavner and Ellen R. Montgomery, *America's Environment at Risk*, a report by the Frontier Group, a policy center of the National Association of State Public Research Interest Groups (2003), 1–35.

85. The head of the agency's enforcement division, J. P. Suarez, resigned, while Bruce Buckheit, head of the air enforcement division, and his deputy Rich Biondi opted for early retirement. Sylvia K. Lowrance, the acting assistant administration for enforcement, also left in August 2002, followed later by EPA Director Christine Whitman.

86. Steve Schwarze, "The Silences and Possibilities of Asbestos Activism: Stories from Libby and Beyond," in Sandler and Pezzullo, *Environmental Justice and Environmentalism*, 165–88.

87. Jeff Krehely, Meaghan House, and Emily Kernan, *Axis of Ideology: Conservative Foundations and Public Policy* (Washington, DC: National Committee for Responsive Philanthropy, March 2004), 18–19.

88. Eric Schaeffer, "Polluters Breathe Easier: EPA Environmental Court Actions Decline," a report by the Environmental Integrity Project (October 12, 2004), 1–3.

89. Office of the Inspector General, U.S. Environmental Protection Agency, "New Source Review Rule Change Harms EPA's Ability to Enforce against Coal-Fired Electric Utilities," Report No. 2004-P-00034, September 30, 2004, available at http://www.epa.gov/oigearth/reports/air.htm (accessed May 12, 2007).

90. Martha H. Keating and Felicia Davis, *Air of Injustice: African Americans and Power Plant Pollution*, a report by the Black Leadership Forum, Clear the Air, the Georgia Coalition for the Peoples' Agenda, and the Southern Organizing Committee for Economic and Social Justice (October 2002), 4.

91. J. B. Andelman and D. W. Underhill, eds., *Health Effects from Hazardous Waste Sites* (Chelsea, MI: Lewis, 1987); National Research Council, *Environmental Epidemiology* (Washington, DC: National Research Council, 1991).

92. Joaquin Sapien, "Superfund Progress Drops Off under Bush: Focus on Tougher Sites Blamed for Decline in Cleanups, but Critics Point to Less Funding and Closer Ties to Industry" (April 26, 2007), available at http://www.publicintegrity.org/superfund (accessed May 10, 2007).

93. *The Truth about Toxic Waste Cleanups: How EPA Is Misleading the Public about the Superfund Program*, a report by the Sierra Club and the US PIRG Education Fund (February 2004); Alex Fidis, *Empty Pockets: Facing Katrina's Cleanup with a Bankrupt Superfund*, a report by the US PIRG Education Fund (December 2005), and "Taxpayers Pay to Clean Up after Polluters at Nation's Toxic Waste Sites" (April 13, 2006), available at http://www.safefromtoxics.org/tx.asp?id2=23502 (accessed May 10, 2007).

94. "Taxpayers Pay to Clean Up after Polluters at Nation's Toxic Waste Sites."

95. Joaquin Sapien, "Superfund Today: Massive Undertaking to Clean Up Hazardous Waste Sites Has Lost Both Momentum and Funding" (April 26, 2007), available at http://www.publicintegrity.org/superfund (accessed May 10, 2007).

96. Marianne Lavelle and Marcia Coyle, "Unequal Protection: The Racial Divide in Environmental Law," *National Law Journal* (September 21, 1992), 2–12.

97. Deeohn Ferris, "Communities of Color and Hazardous Waste Cleanup: Expanding Public Participation in the Federal Superfund Program," *Fordham Urban Law Journal* 21 (1994): 671–79.

98. Sandra George O'Neil, "Environmental Justice in the Superfund Clean-Up Process" (PhD diss., Boston College, April 2005).

99. Alex Knott, "EPA Document Lists Firms."

100. Anupama Narayanswamy, "Lobbying the EPA Takes Money—and Connections: 71 Companies Spent More Than $1 Billion and Hired Former Agency Officials" (April 26, 2007), available at http://www.publicintegrity.org/superfund (accessed May 10, 2007).

101. Joaquin Sapien, "Superfund's Shell Game: As Ownerships Change, Companies' Environmental Liabilities Sometime Get Lost in the Shuffle" (April 26, 2007), available at http://www.publicintegrity.org/superfund (accessed May 10, 2007).

102. Narayanswamy, "Lobbying the EPA Takes Money—and Connections."

103. See the "Money and Politics Databases" at http://www.politicalmoneyline.com/cgi-win/lp_sector.exe?DoFn=ye&Year=05. See also Jonathan D. Salant and Jeff St. Onge, "Lobbying Funds Spiral to $2.4b: General Electric Tops Corporate List of Spenders," *Boston Globe* (July 7, 2006), A6.

104. Richard Pollak, "Is GE Mightier Than the Hudson?," *The Nation* 272, no. 21 (May 28, 2001): 11–15.

105. Narayanswamy, "Lobbying the EPA Takes Money—and Connections."

106. Eric Goldscheider, "At GE, Former Enemies Are Now Employees: Switching Sides Angers Those in PCB Fight," *Boston Globe* (August 6, 2000), B1, B4.

107. Stephen M. Johnson, "Economics v. Equity: Do Market-Based Environmental Reforms Exacerbate Environmental Injustice?" *Washington and Lee Law Review* 56 (Winter 1999): 1–24, draft available at http://www.merlin.law.mercer.edu/elaw/economic.htm (accessed June 22, 2006). See also Stephen M. Johnson, *Economics, Equity, and the Environment* (Washington, DC: Environmental Law Institute, 2004).

108. PEER, *Trading Thin Air: EPA's Plan to Allow Open Market Trading of Air Pollution Credits*, a white paper report by the Public Employees for Environmental Responsibility (June 2000), 1–30, esp. 7.

109. Environmental Law Institute Research Report, *Opportunities for Advancing Environmental Justice: An Analysis of US EPA Statutory Authorities* (Washington, DC: Environmental Law Institute, November 2001).

110. Eric Mann with the Watchdog Organizing Committee, *L.A.'s Lethal Air: New Strategies for Policy, Organizing, and Action* (Los Angeles: Labor/Community Strategy Center, 1991).

111. Richard Toshiyuki Drury et al., "Pollution Trading and Environmental Injustice: Los Angeles' Failed Experiment in Air Quality Policy," *Duke Environmental Law and Policy Forum* 9 (1999): 231, cited in Gauna et al., "Environmental Justice," 6.

112. Gauna et al., "Environmental Justice," 6–25.

113. U.S. Environmental Protection Agency, Office of the Inspector General, *Evaluation Report: Air, Open Market Trading Program for Air Emissions Needs Strengthening* (September 30, 2002), available at http://www.epa.gov/oigearth (accessed June 20, 2006).

114. Daniel Faber and Eric Krieg, *Unequal Exposure to Ecological Hazards 2005: Environmental Injustices in the Commonwealth of Massachusetts*, produced by the Philanthropy and Environmental Justice Research Project, Northeastern University, Boston, MA (October 12), 2005, 1–59.

115. PEER, *Trading Thin Air*, 1–30.

116. Jason Corburn, "Emissions Trading and Environmental Justice: Distributive Fairness and the USA's Acid Rain Programme," *Environmental Conservation* 28, no. 4 (2001): 323–32.

117. Erik Reece, *Lost Mountain: A Year in the Vanishing Wilderness; Radical Strip Mining and the Devastation of Appalachia* (New York: Riverhead Books, 2006).

118. Winona LaDuke, *All Our Relations: Native Struggles for Land and Life* (Boston: South End Press, 1999); Jane Weaver and Russell Means, eds., *Defending Mother Earth: Native American Perspectives on Environmental Justice* (Maryknoll, NY: Orbis Books, 1996); Donald A. Grinde, Howard Zinn, and Bruce Elliott Johansen, *Ecocide of Native America: Environmental Destruction of Indian Lands and Peoples* (Santa Fe, NM: Clear Light Publishers, 1998).

119. Saleem H. Ali, *Mining, the Environment, and Indigenous Development Conflicts* (Tucson: University of Arizona Press, 2005).

120. Navin Nayak, Erich Pica, and Aideen Roder, *Green Scissors 2004: Cutting Wasteful and Environmentally Harmful Spending*, a report by Friends of the Earth, Taxpayers for Common Sense, and US PIRG (2004), 14–18.

121. David Cay Johnston, "More Americans Making Ends Meet with Less Money," *Boston Globe* (August 21, 2007), D3; Citizens for Tax Justice (http://www.ctj.org).

122. Charles M. Sennott, "The $150 Billion 'Welfare' Recipients: US Corporations," *Boston Globe* (July 7, 1996), A1, A8–A9.

123. Bill Mesler, "Al Gore: The Other Oil Candidate," a Corporate Watch report (August 29, 2000), available at http://www.corpwatch.org/feature/election/goreoil.html (accessed September 4, 2000); Alexander Cockburn and Jeffrey St. Clair, "Gore's Debts to Richardson and Coelho," *CounterPunch* 7, no. 6 (March 16–31, 2000): 2–3.

124. Thomas Shevory, *Toxic Burn: The Grassroots Struggle against the WTI Incinerator* (Minneapolis: University of Minnesota Press, 2007).

125. For a more comprehensive list of all environmental laws that the Bush administration has weakened, see http://www.nrdc.org/bushrecord.

126. Allison Cassady, *Big Money to Big Oil: How ExxonMobil and the Oil Industry Benefit from the 2005 Energy Bill*, a report by the US PIRG Education Fund (August 2005), 1–17.

127. See Shannon Collier, Navin Nayak, Erich Pica, and Aileen Roder, *Green Scissors 2003: Cutting Wasteful & Environmentally Harmful Spending*, a report by Friends of the Earth, Taxpayers for Common Sense, and US Public Interest Research Group (2003), 19–21.

128. David S. Broder, "The Game in Washington," *Boston Globe* (January 3, 2002), A11.

129. U.S. Government Accountability Office, "Worker Protection: Federal Contractors and Violations of Labor Law," a GAO report to the Honorable Paul Simon, U.S. Senate (October 1995).

130. Corburn, "Emissions Trading and Environmental Justice."

131. U.S. Environmental Protection Agency, Office of Regulatory Enforcement, Office of Enforcement and Compliance Assurance, "EPA Supplemental Environmental Project Policy" (2004).

132. Suzie Canales, *Supplemental Environmental Projects: The Most Affected Communities Are Not Receiving Satisfactory Benefits*, a report by the Refinery Reform Campaign and Public Citizen (June 2006), 2–23.

133. See Environmental Integrity Project, "Wrong Track? Some Performance Track Facilities Report Increased Levels of Toxic Pollution" (February 8, 2006), available at http://www.environmentalintegrity.org/pub360.cfm (accessed June 5, 2007).

Chapter Four

The Unfair Trade-Off: Globalization and the Export of Ecological Hazards

The benefits of international trade come from allowing countries to exploit their comparative advantage. . . . And much of the third world's comparative advantage lies, in one way or another, in the fact of its poverty; in particular, cheap labor and a greater tolerance of pollution.[1]

—Pam Woodall, economics editor, *The Economist*

THE GLOBAL ECOLOGICAL CRISIS

The age of globalization has witnessed the triumph of a distinctly hard-nosed brand of American capitalism in the world economy. Facilitated by the neoliberal agenda for global free trade (market liberalization), an end to most governmental regulatory "interference" with business practices (deregulation), the takeover of former public services and state agencies by domestic and/or international capital (privatization), and reductions in social welfare and environmental protection measures in both the North and the global South (fiscal conservatism), the growing pace of economic integration across the globe is unprecedented. Characterized by the increased mobility of capital and goods and services across national borders, globalization represents the emergence of a truly integrated international system of capitalist *production* and *distribution* under the hegemony of the United States. It is a process whereby all previous precapitalist residues of social life and domestic business formerly articulated within broader social formations are disintegrating into a transnational social structure that operates both "over" and "under" the nation-state system. As a result, world labor forces, natural resources and energy, technology and machinery, biosystems, and other "productive inputs"

171

are becoming more integrated into the circuits of global capital (economically) and the structures of transnational corporations and banks (organizationally), especially those institutions controlled by American interests. In this respect, the term "globalization" is often used as a cover word by U.S. policymakers to describe the imposition of neoliberal capitalist development models all around the world.

The capitalist world system, of course, is not new. Nor is the process of global economic integration, especially in terms of the internationalization of the commodity and money circuits of capital. However, there *is* something profoundly different about the current phase of globalization. Put simply, multinational corporations possess a newly developed capacity to locate capitalist production facilities in virtually every corner of the planet. The creation of modern global communications and transportation systems and the development of advanced infrastructure in the newly industrializing countries are granting industrial capital the geographic mobility to take advantage of more favorable business climates abroad. This is especially true in the countries of East Asia and the global South with large supplies of cheap and highly disciplined wage laborers, abundant natural resources and energy supplies, tax advantages, and weaker environmental regulations. The commodities and surplus profits produced by the factories are then exported back into the United States and other advanced capitalist countries. The pollution, however, remains behind. Even worse, the toxic waste, industrial pollution, discarded consumer goods, and other forms of "antiwealth" produced in the United States are becoming increasingly mobile and end up in the "pollution havens" of the Third World. Prior to the invention of environmental protection laws in the United States and elsewhere, it was not necessary (let alone cost effective) to export environmental problems to other countries. This is no longer the case. In short, it is the internationalization of the productive and waste circuits of capital that distinguishes the current period of corporate-led globalization from previous historical epochs.

Corporate-led globalization has also initiated a profound restructuring of the U.S. economy. Spurred by innovations in global communications, information, and transportation systems—as well as major improvements in infrastructure and the educational, skill, and productivity levels of labor power in the developing world—overseas industry and agriculture (particularly in the newly industrializing countries) have rapidly expanded in recent years to capture a growing share of the U.S. and world markets. While globalization has facilitated growth in some "new economy" sectors of the U.S. market, particularly industries exporting high technology and other capital goods and services of all kinds to both developed and newly industrializing countries overseas, many industries that have traditionally served as the backbone of the "old economy," as well as the trade union movement, have seen their competitive position for mass-produced consumer goods and finished raw materials (such as steel) steadily eroded.

In contrast, economic growth in the global South has been led by exports of energy, raw materials, and consumer goods to the North. This turn toward export-oriented industrialization is being driven by foreign direct investment (FDI) and foreign lending provided by the United States and other advanced capitalist countries and is intended to facilitate the appropriation and development of domestic business facilities, energy supplies, and natural resources by northern investors. Thus, global free trade is creating a new international division of labor in which the South favors exports of cheap raw materials, energy, technology components, and consumer goods to the United States on the one hand and the United States favors capital goods and services for export within the North and to the South on the other. In short, while the South produces wealth in the commodity form, the United States produces wealth in the "capital form."

Under processes of unequal ecological exchange, the massive quantities of physical wealth now entering the United States (in the form of energy, raw materials, foodstuffs, and durable consumer goods) are greatly undervalued in the world economy. With international trade largely under the control of northern-based transnational corporations, the concrete and potential natural wealth found in U.S. imports of energy and raw materials is in much greater proportion than the monetary (abstract) wealth that is exported back to the global South. Through exploitative world trade relations, the United States is appropriating the biocapacity of the global South. This process also includes the damage being done to the economies of the global South resulting from U.S. exports of pollution, hazardous waste, greenhouse gases, and other ecological hazards (externalities). It is estimated that the *ecological debt* owed by the United States and other advanced capitalist to the developing countries as a result of carbon emissions alone amounts to $13 trillion per year.[2] Moreover, America's *ecological debt* arising from excessive use of the South's environmental space is accelerating, even as the *economic* debt owed by many Third World countries to U.S. banks continues to grow.[3] The South's economic debt and the North's ecological debt are symptomatic of the "unfair" trade-off brought about by corporate-led globalization.

The plundering of the South's resources and the export of pollution and other environmental hazards by the United States are together creating an unparalleled ecological crisis of global dimensions. Almost 40 percent of the 58 million deaths occurring worldwide each year are now caused by pollution.[4] In addition, the landmark Millennium Report compiled by 1,300 researchers from ninety-five countries reveals that approximately 60 percent of the ecosystem services that support life on earth are being used unsustainably and/or already significantly degraded.[5] According to the report *Vital Signs 2006–2007* by the Worldwatch Institute, for instance, the world's forests have shrunk by 90 million acres since 2000. An estimated 20 percent of the earth's coral reefs are "effectively destroyed," and another 50 percent are threatened. Meanwhile, the global use of chemical poisons is skyrocketing. World exports of pesticides reached a record $15.9 billion in 2004 and have risen to almost two pounds for every acre of land on the planet (compared to less than half a pound per acre in 1961). Pesticides and industrial pollution in the global environment are contributing to a worldwide cancer epidemic that kills 7.6 million people annually. The World Health Organization estimated that cancer deaths will continue to rise and will eventually reach 9 million deaths in 2015. Over 70 percent of these deaths occur in the less developed countries.[6] Last but certainly not least, global warming is threatening to revamp the ecological face of the entire planet and displace tens of millions of people from their homes and means of livelihood, especially in the global South.[7]

In this chapter, I outline the manner in which trade policy is creating an unparalleled ecological crisis in the less developed countries through the export of environmental hazards (or externalities). The evidence will show that the United States has the largest *ecological footprint* (or impact) of any nation on earth. This impact occurs through U.S. FDI in environmental damaging industries and the relocation of U.S.-based dirty facilities to the global South as well as from the dumping of toxic waste and dangerous consumer goods in developing countries. In addition to the export of hazard, I examine the manner in which neoliberal economic policy is facilitating the confiscation of greater quantities of biomass from the South at prices highly advantageous to American industry. In short, this chapter will paint a disturbing picture of the role played by corporate-led globalization and unfair trade policies in provoking severe ecological problems and environmental injustices throughout the world.

GLOBALIZATION, UNFAIR TRADE, AND THE CORPORATE ASSAULT ON MOTHER EARTH

The Expansion of Foreign Trade

In the age of globalization, the expansion of foreign trade has become the engine of world capitalist growth and development. Since 1950, the rate of growth of world exports has exceeded the growth rate of world gross domestic product (GDP) and continues to accelerate.[8] The dramatic increases in the size, numbers, and sheer power of multinational corporations reflects this new global political-economic architecture. In 1992, there were 37,000 transnational corporations in the world, with over 200,000 foreign affiliates.[9] Today there are more than 64,000, with over 870,000 foreign affiliates. Transnationals now control more than 70 percent of world trade and have annual sales over $18 trillion. More than $6 trillion of world trade is intrafirm, occurring between units of the same corporation, many of them U.S.-based companies.[10] American multinational corporations also employ almost 10 million workers overseas.[11] In short, transnational corporations dominate the world economy.

Strong growth in the U.S. GDP and international trade during this time has transformed the American economy into the "world's cash register," from a net exporter into a net importer of commodities. As a result, the United States is serving as the supermarket for rest of the world—the primary source of global effective demand in the form of private consumption, investment, and government expenditures. Much of this spending, however, is being fueled via massive deficit spending. In 2006, the overall U.S. trade deficit in goods and services was $765.3 billion, a fifth consecutive record deficit.[12] An even more complete view on the state of the U.S. economy can be achieved when analyzing the current account deficit, which includes the difference between U.S. exports and imports of goods and services, income (salaries and investments), and net transfers (workers' remittances, donations, aids and grants, and so on). At $875 billion in 2006, the global current account deficit of the United States is the largest in history and now accounts for 7 percent of the country's GDP. Moreover, the deficit has been rising by an average of $100 billion a year since 2002. To finance the current account imbalance, the United States must attract capital inflows from the rest of the world of almost $4 billion a day (or about $1 trillion a year).[13] Despite the potential economic threats posed by the current account deficit, the capacity of U.S. capitalism to capture and employ so much of the world's material output and financial savings (much of which is reinvested abroad) reflects the strength of American empire, not its weakness.

Globalization and the Domestic Assault against Environmentalism

The advent of global free trade is subverting nationalist economic development models, compelling nations in both the North and the South to focus primarily on expanding foreign investments and export markets (over domestic markets) as a means of achieving growth. In a dialectical fashion, the decline of nation-state–oriented models of Keynesian economics (based on the progressive redistribution of wealth) has led the world political order to increasingly adopt neoliberal economic programs and policies as an alternative model of development (based on the regressive redistribution of wealth). In the United States, fearing that increased costs to business will undermine profitability in an increasingly competitive world market, the American business establishment has become unwilling to abide by the traditional accords brokered by the liberal wing of the Democratic Party on its behalf with the labor, environmental, civil rights, women's, environmental justice, and other progressive social movements. Instead, the rise of neoliberals committed to less governmental "control" of industry is now hegemonic. As a result, the defining characteristics of liberal capitalism historically enlisting the mass loyalty of ordinary working people—high wages, good benefits, job security and advancement, affirmative action, universal entitlements, and welfare protections—are being eroded by corporate-led globalization. This entails launching a *domestic political assault* on the environmental justice (EJ) movement, trade unions, environmentalists, and other progressive social movements.

The rise of neoliberalism in the United States and its subsequent near universalization entails the restructuring and opening of the world's nations, including ex-Communist ones, to economic competition, the free movement of capital, and the deepening of capitalist social relations. Both financial markets and international financial institutions play critical roles in facilitating this and in reinforcing American imperial power. In fact, the triumph of the "Third Way" neoliberalism model of globalization not only has undermined traditional New Deal liberalism and welfare state capitalism in the United States but has also dealt a death blow to bureaucratic state socialism in the East, import-substitution industrialization and other nationalist-based models of dependent development in the South, and Keynesian social democratic regimes in the West (as seen in the recent electoral defeats of the left in France and elsewhere in Europe as well as the hegemony of a more conservative Labor Party in Britain). Furthermore, former rivals in the form of Japanese and German corporatism have become sufficiently subordinated by American-style neoliberalism. Moreover, the growth of the integrated production processes spawned by U.S.-based multinational corporations, along with the increased dependency of most nations on American FDI and international "free trade," has largely restrained protectionist impulses. It has also reinforced Asian and European reliance on U.S. military power to maintain a favorable business climate for foreign capital throughout much of the world, including the Middle East. In this respect, the American imperial form of rule functions to reproduce the conditions for global capital accumulation and political-economic order (but ecological disorder) among nations as necessary for their own reproduction.

Ecological Armageddon and the Unfair Trade-Off

Operating in concert with multilateral institutions such as the World Bank and the International Monetary Fund, the World Trade Organization (WTO) has played a key role in organizing this new architecture of global economic governance. With the help of the General Agreement on Tariffs and Trade, the North American Free Trade Agreement (NAFTA), and other "free" trade agreements, multinational corporations and financial institutions are being granted the power to supersede democratic elements of the nation-state that guard the larger public interest, including the environment. As stated by political economist James O'Connor, "The function of neo-liberalism in general, and trade liberalization in particular, is to enlarge the WTO's powers to strengthen global capital vis-à-vis local and national capital world-wide. At the limit, this means to free global financial markets (organized by finance capital), global production (organized by transnational corporations), and the global market for goods and services from any and all local and national rules and regulations."[14]

Free-trade agreements are suppose to apply the same set of rules to all signatory nations, requiring conformity to a strict set of capital and commercial provisions and permit individual investors to directly sue nation-states for violations of the terms of the treaties. These lawsuits may be brought in special dispute settlement tribunals outside of national court systems. Ordinary citizens and popular social movements are denied any meaningful role in these deliberations. As a result, the structure of power in the WTO is fundamentally undemocratic. Instead, decision making around the structure of the world economy takes place in nontransparent backroom sessions rather than in formalized public plenaries. Majority-rule voting has been dispensed with in favor of a process called consensus, which is really a process in which the eight wealthiest capitalist countries in the world—Canada, Great Britain, France, Germany, Italy, Japan, Russia, and the United States—impose their will on the majority of the member countries. This arrangement allows U.S. investors and transnational corporations to consolidate their control over political life (the United States does not follow the same rules it promotes abroad in these free-trade agreements since the federal government heavily subsidizes American farmers and protects key sectors of the economy from foreign competition). Trade liberalization policies implemented under NAFTA and other free-trade agreements and enforced by the WTO profoundly impact the global environment. These agreements take specific aim at certain types of environmentally inspired trade restrictions as in fact being "illegal" restraints or barriers to trade. If transnational corporations or other countries perceive that another country's labor, consumer product safety, and environmental laws constitute a "nontariff barrier to trade," then these restrictions can be appealed to the WTO. As noted by environmental activists Kenny Bruno and Josh Karliner, "Since it was created in 1995, the WTO has ruled every environmental policy it has reviewed an illegal trade barrier that must be eliminated or changed."[15] Thus, in a "race to the bottom," free-trade agreements are resulting in a *downward harmonization* of environmental, labor, consumer, and worker health and safety regulations across the world, including the United States.

Nevertheless, some serious cracks are beginning to develop in this new global economic architecture. Growing frustration and anger at the United States for its refusal to budge from protectionist double standards is leading local ruling classes to resort to nationalist strategies of protection and state-backed competition for global markets and natural resources. Furthermore, the dissonance between the promises of globalization and free trade and the actual results of neoliberal policies—growing poverty, inequality, and ecological degradation—is creating a deep crisis of legitimacy for the International Monetary Fund, the World Bank, and the WTO, particularly in the global South. As stated by Walden Bello, "Global warming, peak oil, and other environmental events are making it clear to people that the rates and patterns of growth that come with globalization are a surefire prescription for ecological Armageddon."[16] Aware of these dangers, the global South is beginning to retreat from globalization. Bolivian President Evo Morales and Venezuelan President Hugo Chavez are forging new models of regional economic cooperation (over free trade) with little or no participation from U.S. multinational corporations. The Washington consensus is beginning to break down. Nevertheless, the U.S. government continues to impose a new form of neoconservative neoliberalism on other countries, where debt relief and grant aid (rather than loans provided by the World Bank and a nearly defunct International Monetary Fund) are now offered in exchange for the continued liberalization of markets and the privatization of domestic industries, land, and natural resources. The economic and ecological pillage of the less developed countries in the orbit of American capitalism continues to move forward.

DUMPING ON THE THIRD WORLD: THE EXPORT OF ECOLOGICAL HAZARDS AND ENVIRONMENTAL INJUSTICE

Similar to the "internal" strategy of reducing production costs by displacing ecological and public health hazards onto poor people of color and the working class *inside* the United States, corporations are also reducing costs by adopting the "external" strategy of exporting ecological hazards *outside* America's national boundaries. The worsening ecological crisis in the global South is directly related to an international system of economic and environmental stratification in which the United States and other advanced capitalist nations are able to shift or impose the environmental burden onto weaker states. In fact, one of the primary aims of U.S. economic planners is to cut costs by displacing environmental problems (externalities) onto poorer southern nations—countries with little power in global environmental policy decision-making institutions. Lawrence Summers, former undersecretary of the treasury of international affairs and key economic policymaker in the Clinton administration (and former president of Harvard University), is infamous for writing a 1991 memo as a chief economist at the World Bank that argued,

> Just between you and me, shouldn't the World Bank be encouraging *more* migration of the dirty industries to the LDCs [less developed countries]? . . . I think the economic logic behind dumping a load of toxic waste in the lowest wage country is impeccable and we should face up to that. . . . I've always thought that under-populated countries in Africa are vastly *under*-polluted.[17]

The Summers memo reflects the "thinking" of many U.S. policymakers aligned with the interests of U.S. multinational corporations: that human life in the Third World is worth much less than in the United States. If the poor and underemployed masses of Africa become sick or die from exposure to pollution exported from the United States, it will have a much smaller impact on the profits of international capital. Aside from the higher costs of pollution abatement in the United States, if highly skilled and well-compensated American workers fall prey to environmentally related health problems, then the expense to capital and the state can be significant. Although morally reprehensible, under the capitalist system it pays business to shift pollution onto the poor in the less developed countries.[18]

Given the willingness of undemocratic governments in the global South to trade off the environmental protection for economic growth, the growing mobility of capital (in all forms) is facilitating the export of ecological problems from the advanced capitalist countries to the Third World and subperipheral states.[19] This *export of ecological hazard* from the United States and other northern countries to the less developed countries takes place 1) *in the money circuit of global capital*, in the form of FDI in domestically owned hazardous industries as well as destructive investment schemes to gain access to new oil fields, forests, agricultural lands, mining deposits, and other natural resources; 2) *in the productive circuit of global capital*, with the relocation of polluting and environmentally hazardous production processes and polluting facilities owned by transnational capital to the South; 3) *in the commodity circuit of global capital*, as witnessed in the marketing of more profitable but also more dangerous foods, drugs, pesticides, technologies, and other consumer/capital goods; and 4) *in the waste circuit of global capital*, with the dumping of toxic wastes, pollution, discarded consumer products, trash, and other forms of "antiwealth" produced by northern industry.[20]

Hence, corporate-led globalization is facilitating the displacement of ecological hazards from richer to poorer countries. Although a few international agreements (such as the Basel Convention) have been put into place, they are for the most part ineffective at stemming the transfer of hazards. Since few peripheral countries have the ability to adequately evaluate and manage the risks associated with such hazards, the export practices of transnational corporations are increasing the health, safety, and environmental problems facing many peripheral countries. In effect, U.S. capital is appropriating carrying capacity for the core by transferring ("distancing") externalities to the global South.[21] As in the United States, it is the poorest and most politically repressed people in the South who are bearing the brunt of the global ecological crisis.

ANTIGREEN GREENBACKS: THE EXPORT OF ECOLOGICALLY HAZARDOUS INVESTMENT CAPITAL

U.S. FDI in "Dirty" Countries

Between 1999 and 2006, FDI from the United States totaled $1.094 trillion. In fact, from 2002 to 2005, U.S. FDI abroad was more than twice the amount foreigners invested in the U.S. economy.[22] Although labor costs and proximity to emerging markets (to service local clients or to acquire a strategic position themselves) are often the most important consideration of U.S. investors, the lack of environmental regulations and enforcement in much of the global South also promises profitable investment opportunities. Since the mid-1970s, the U.S. regime of environmental regulation has resulted in stricter laws, increased delays due to permitting, and higher costs related to pollution control technology, liability and insurance cases, and worker health and safety. These costs are especially significant for companies involved in the production of heavy metals, asbestos-containing products, copper and lead smelting, and leather tanning and has led these industries to relocate overseas.[23] The competition for foreign investment among the developing countries is fierce, and, combined with the imposition of structural adjustment policies by the International Monetary Fund and World Bank on indebted developing countries, more and more nations are opening themselves up to increased FDI by weakening environmental standards.

Historically, FDI was motivated principally by the availability of natural resources abroad and by a desire to internationalize companies' value chains in order to benefit from lower labor costs in other countries. Even today, FDI is concentrated heavily on a few dozen nations that possess abundant natural resources, including smaller nations such as Equatorial Guinea, Angola, Sudan, Venezuela, Azerbaijan, and Kazakhstan. However, some of the upsurge of FDI into the developing world since the mid-1990s is motivated by the privatization of public utilities, land, and resources in several countries. But with the expansion of international trade, brought about by the increased efficiencies of global transportation and communications networks, manufacturing operations can now be located in almost any corner of the world. To take advantage of these conditions, U.S. multinational corporations and financial institutions are increasing their investments in highly polluting and environmentally hazardous industries in the global South, including those involved in resource extraction, heavy manufacturing, chemicals, and electronics. As a consequence, the rate of growth in hazardous industries in the developing countries is now greater than the overall industrial growth in those same countries, indicating that the cost advantages stemming from weaker environmental protection are attracting investment. Again, this trend began the late 1970s, just as environmental regulations became more stringent in the United States and other advanced capitalist countries.[24]

China: The New Economic Superpower or Ecological Nightmare?

Investment havens for dirty industry are located in some of the world's most populous countries, including China, India, and Russia. FDI is an especially important driver of the Chinese economy. For the first time on record, China surpassed the United States as the world's foremost recipient of FDI in 2003. In fact, China now attracts almost one-third of the developing nations' FDI and is the fastest-growing economy in the world.[25] The development strategy rests on utilizing FDI provided by multinational corporations and northern banks to promote export-oriented industrialization, particularly in terms of supplying cheap exports directly to the U.S. market through Wal-Mart and other retailers. Foreign firms now dominate this export activity and control a 57 percent share of China's exports.[26] Drawn by a highly disciplined and abundant labor force willing to work for $4 a day or less, China has emerged as the world's low-cost manufacturing leader. As *BusinessWeek* marveled,

> "The China Price." They are the three scariest word in U.S. industry. In general, it means 30 percent to 50 percent less than what you can possibly make something for in the US. In the worst cases, it means below your cost of materials.[27]

Although China has excelled in providing low-quality consumer goods, the country is now ramping up to create more advanced industries, adding state-of-the-art capacity in cars, specialty steel, petrochemicals, and microchips.

Thus, while American petrochemical makers have invested in little new capacity inside the United States over the past decade, over 12,000 workers are constructing a $2.7 billion petrochemical complex in Nanjing, China. This facility will be among the world's largest, most modern complexes for making ethylene, the basic ingredient in plastics. Constructing such a plant in China offers sizable cost advantages over rival facilities in the United States, Europe, and Japan because of the lower environmental costs of doing business. The Chinese government allows industry to freely pollute the air, water, and ground, which (combined with the low cost of labor) easily allows industry to undercut the prices charged by companies abiding by strict standards elsewhere in the world. However, the economic incentives offered to foreign capital to invest in China, including few controls over pollution and worker health and safety violations, have created an ecological nightmare. As stated by journalists Joseph Kahn and Jim Yardley,

> Environmental woes that might be considered catastrophic in some countries can seem commonplace in China: industrial cities where people rarely see the sun; children killed or sickened by lead poisoning or other types of local pollution; a coastline so swamped by algal red tides that large sections of the ocean no longer sustain marine life. China is choking on its own success.[28]

The magnitude of this ecological crisis is apparent in a 2007 draft report by the World Bank and China's State Environment Protection Agency. The study finds that 750,000 people die prematurely in China each year, mainly from air pollution in the large cities. In fact, the numbers are so mind-boggling that the Chinese government "persuaded" the World Bank to remove nearly a third of the report's information on pollution prior to its official release because it would have provoked "social unrest" among the masses (the World Bank agreed to do so in a pared-down version of the final report). Missing from the final report are the original findings that high air pollution levels in Chinese cities is causing the deaths of 350,000 to 400,000 people each year. Another 300,000 people die prematurely each year from poor indoor air quality.[29] Incredibly, only 1 percent of the country's 560 million city dwellers breathe air considered safe by the European Union. And air quality is getting worse. The central government's most recent report put the cost of air pollution at $64 billion in 2004.[30]

Of the twenty most polluted cities in the world, according to the World Bank, sixteen are located in China. About one-third of China's lakes, rivers, and coastal waters are so polluted that they pose a threat to human health, according the Organization for Economic Cooperation and Development. As a result, 300 million Chinese do not have access to clean drinking water, resulting in about 60,000 premature deaths a year.[31] Acid rain falls on more than 30 percent of the country.[32] Industrial pollution is so extensive that the country's birth defect rate is triple that of the developed nations. At least a million Chinese babies born each year have birth defects.[33] As acknowledged in the World Bank report, China's poor are disproportionately affected by these environmental health burdens.[34] The World Bank puts the cost of China's pollution at 8 percent of GDP, although some economists say it is as high as 10 percent of GDP, which is equal to the country's rate of economic growth. Many Chinese people are fed up with the pollution; a number of environmental riots have erupted in China in recent years and are likely to become more numerous in the future.[35]

Africa's Black Gold: Investing in Repression and Environmental Injustice

Given the continuing U.S. war in Iraq and growing instability in the Middle East, the United States is funneling investment to other parts of the world in search of cheaper oil and natural resources. In 2001, Vice President Dick Cheney predicted that Africa would soon become the fastest-growing source of oil for the American market (as much as 25 percent of U.S. imports by 2015).[36] Investment capital has poured in to begin making this prediction a reality (West Africa currently supplies 15 percent of America's energy). For instance, energy companies have invested several billion dollars in Equatorial Guinea, including the construction of a major liquefied natural gas facility owned by Chevron. As a result, Equatorial Guinea has become the third-largest oil exporter in sub-Saharan Africa, after Nigeria and Angola. Oil production today stands at more than 300,000 barrels a day, or $5.5 billion a year. But despite its oil wealth, Equatorial Guinea remains one of the poorest countries in Africa.

Under the dictatorship of Teodoro Obiang, oil companies have bribed the government to gain access to Equatorial Guinea's rich natural resources at favorable prices and disregard safeguards required in the United States. The Securities and Exchange Commission is now investigating bribery under the Foreign Corrupt Practices Act. Investigations show that as much as $700 million in bribe payments were made to members of Obiang's regime and his family by ExxonMobil, Amerada Hass, Marathon Oil, and Chevron Texaco through Riggs Bank in Washington, D.C.[37] Although friendly to international investors, the dictatorship has treated its own people with brutality. Human rights abuses remain unchecked in the country. Opponents are often tortured. Nearly half of all children under the age of five are malnourished, and half a million people live in poverty. All the major cities lack clean water and basic sanitation, while the average Equatoguinean scrapes by on $2 a day.[38] The inflow of FDI and outflow of oil has done nothing to improve the quality of life for the majority of the people. Instead, it has come as a curse.

Nigeria is another country that has seen huge investments of U.S. capital to develop the oil fields and is the now the eighth-leading exporter of oil in the world (and the largest oil producer in Africa). More than $300 billion in oil has been exported since 1975. Petroleum companies such as Chevron and Royal Dutch Shell have invaded the oil-rich Niger delta, home to the Ogoni people and one of the most populated regions in all of Africa. At the invitation of a brutally repressive Nigerian government, the international oil companies ignore standard environmental protection measures in order to cut costs and maximize profits. Enjoying a complete lack of government oversight, the oil companies have created what the European Parliament calls "an environmental nightmare" for the Ogoni people. A constant barrage of oil spills—an average of 300 per year—have significantly contaminated waterways and groundwater, killed fish and other wildlife on which the local people are dependent, and decimated the resource base of numerous subsistence economies in the region. Petroleum pollution in Ogoni streams is 680 times greater than European Community permissible levels. Leaking pipes have also caught fire, exploded, and killed hundreds of people. Toxic wastes dumped in unlined pits litter the countryside, while continuous gas flares pollute nearby villages with 35 million tons of carbon dioxide a year (76 percent of natural gas in the oil-producing areas is flared, compared to 0.6 percent in the United States, along with 12 million tons of methane, which is more than any nation on earth). Local crops will not grow, and acid rain pervades the area.[39]

As the ecological crisis emerged full force in the early 1990s, the Ogoni people organized peaceful protests to raise international awareness of their plight. In response to the awareness that such actions were generating around the world, the then military government reacted with extreme repression. In November 1995, Ken Saro-Wiwa, the leader of the Movement for the Survival of Ogoni People (and a highly respected and renowned playwright in the international community) and eight other Ogoni leaders were arrested on trumped-up treason charges. They were immediately tried by a military tribunal, found guilty, and executed. Despite the military's unfounded allegations, the world knew that the "Ogoni 9" were killed for organizing peaceful protests against the country's large oil exporter, Royal/Dutch Shell. As stated in a recent report, "Shell failed to use its substantial influence with the Nigerian government to stop the execution. Indeed, Shell has publicly admitted that it had invited the Nigerian army to Ogoni land, provided them with ammunition and logistical and financial support for a military operation that left scores dead and destroyed many villages."[40] In defense of the company and the military regime following the execution, Naemeka Achebe, the general manager for Shell Nigeria, stated, "For a commercial company trying to make investments, you need a stable environment. . . . Dictatorships can give you that. Right now in Nigeria, there is acceptance, peace, and continuity."[41] According to Human Rights Watch, hundreds if not at least 2,000 people have been killed by the Nigerian military in a combination of ethnic strife and repression in the delta since the new millennium.[42]

In response to the repression, Nigerian villagers have brought suit in U.S. court against Chevron alleging that the company supported military attacks on protesters in the Niger delta. A Human Rights Watch investigation uncovered Chevron's use of a covert Nigerian security force known as the "kill-and-go" squad against the movement. In the trial, Chevron stated that the incident was "regrettable" but resulted from attempts by protesters to take control of weapons held by security personnel. Although the company was cleared of direct liability in 2004, the judge in the case noted that a reasonable juror could reason that the company had indirect responsibility and could be liable for reparations because of its "extraordinarily close relationship" with Chevron Nigeria. In August 2007, another judge allowed claims of wrongful death and other human rights suits to proceed.

Burma: Subordinating Human Rights and Environmental Protection to the Almighty Dollar

In partnership with the Burmese military regime, Western oil companies have also built natural gas pipelines in southern Burma, leading to countless human rights abuses against the local population and severe environmental destruction. In 2006, FDI in the oil and gas sector reached $2.635 billion, or roughly 35 percent of all FDI. The notorious Yadana and Yetagun pipelines are the largest of these foreign investment projects in Burma and have generated over $3 billion in hard currency for the regime (the largest single source of income for the military). This is an oppressive government that massacres nonviolent protesters (including religious leaders), ignores the result of democratic elections, and faces international sanctions for its human rights abuses. The military has provided key services to Unocal and other oil companies around the construction of the pipelines, including the forcible relocation of several villages. Burmese soldiers have conscripted thousands of civilians to perform forced labor (slavery) to build the pipelines and have murdered, raped, tortured, and forcibly relocated innocent villagers along the route of the pipeline. According to the World Wildlife Fund, the pipelines pass through the largest block of intact rain forests in Southeast Asia and are among the most destructive investment projects in the world. More recently, FDI has brought about an increase in large-scale resource extraction and an increase in human rights and environmental abuses connected to a plethora of other development schemes, including natural gas, dam, logging, and mining projects, mostly in ethnic minority areas.[43]

Despite international outrage over these incidents, the U.S. polluter-industrial complex has come to the defense of the Burmese government. While Dick Cheney was chief executive officer of Halliburton, the company did business on the Yadana project in Burma, including laying offshore portions of the pipeline. Halliburton is one of the driving forces behind USA-Engage, a corporate coalition that, along with the National Foreign Trade Council, has become a serious obstacle to the Burmese democracy movement. They oppose sanctions on Burma (renamed Myanmar by the junta) despite calls for the sanctions by popular opposition forces inside the country and supported the ruling by the U.S. Supreme Court in 1990 that struck down a Massachusetts law placing trade sanctions on Burma. The corporation's winning argument was that states should not be able to steer money away from the Burmese dictatorship because the federal government had already enacted very weak sanctions against Burma that preempt state laws (these same corporations also vigorously lobby Congress not to impose those same federal sanctions).[44]

The Bush administration has also acted to limit the ability of foreign nationals to obtain judgments against despots and U.S. corporations in American courts, arguing that such lawsuits have become a threat to American foreign policy and could undermine the War on Terror. For the past two decades, federal courts have allowed victims of torture and other abuse to file claims under an obscure 1789 statute for violations of human rights norms, commonly known as the Alien Torts Claims Act. Bush administration officials fear that the torts act will be used in claims against U.S. companies overseas. The Justice Department brief was filed in the San Francisco–based Court of Appeals for the Ninth Circuit in a case involving the Yadana pipeline in Burma and argued that because the "alleged injuries were incurred in a foreign country . . . with no connection whatsoever to the United States," the case should be dismissed. The filing prompted an outcry from human rights groups. Burmese citizens say their human rights were violated during the construction of the $1.2 billion gas pipeline, a joint venture of the Burmese military regime, Unocal (a multinational oil and gas company based in El Segundo, California), and two other private firms.[45] Only with the peaceful prodemocracy protests led by tens of thousands of Buddhist monks in Rangoon in late September 2007—to which the Burmese government responded by clubbing, shooting, and detaining demonstrators—was the Bush administration forced to announce sanctions against the Burmese government and some of its financial backers.

Since the 1980s, the military junta has detained and tortured thousands of political prisoners, including Aung San Suu Kyi, the prodemocracy leader who has been under house arrest for twelve of the past eighteen years. Again, the Burmese case is not unique in the age of corporate-led globalization. Similar human rights abuses, the weakening of ecological safeguards, and environmental injustices at the hands of multinational corporations can be found in Ecuador, India, Kenya, Mexico, Russia, Cambodia, Guatemala, and countless other countries seeking foreign investment. As stated in a recent report by Amnesty International and the Sierra Club,

> We live in a world where multinational corporations can make or break a nation's economy, where the chairman of Exxon tells the World Petroleum Congress in 1997 that developing nations should avoid strict environmental regulations or risk losing foreign investment. From emerging economies in the South to economic superpowers in the North, governments are lowering environmental standards to increase global trade and are allowing their foreign policies to be driven and directed by corporate, instead of democratic, values. In many parts of the world, corporations and governments are colluding to violate the rights of environmental activists in the name of profit and economic development.[46]

GLOBAL POLLUTION HAVENS: THE EXPORT OF ECOLOGICALLY HAZARDOUS INDUSTRY

In the age of corporate-led globalization, free-trade and neoliberal economic policies are encouraging countries to lower wages and environmental standards in order to cut costs and achieve a comparative advantage in the world economy. By pitting various nations against one another in this "race-to-the-bottom" phenomenon in which countries lower environmental regulations in order to gain a competitive edge, multinational corporations have acquired greater and greater power in relation to the nation-state. With the increased international mobility of industrial capital, various governments at all levels are pressured to reduce the financial burden of environmental regulations, taxation policy, labor rules, and consumer product safety requirements on industry. Otherwise, the manufacturer will simply pick up and move to another part of the world where the business climate is more favorable. The state is left with little choice but to grant such concessions if the jobs and other economic benefits are to be preserved.

Over the past three decades, those U.S.-based industries most heavily impacted by environmental regulations, including lead smelting, dye and chemical manufacturing, asbestos-related production, pesticides, textiles, copper smelting, vinyl chloride, and so on, have moved to other countries with weaker rules and enforcement.[47] American companies often make no secret of the fact that more stringent environmental regulations are a major factor in relocating facilities abroad. As stated by the U.S. agency Chemex, "As a result of tougher environmental regulations . . . many North American [mineral oil] refineries have ceased operations. Recognizing an opportunity, Chemex redirected its focus to the procurement of quality used refineries" for export to developing countries.[48] This process is now accelerating as double standards in worker and community health protection become more common in the world, especially in the less developed countries of the Caribbean, Africa, Latin America, and especially Asia. According to a UN study, over half the transnational firms surveyed in the Asia-Pacific region adopt lower standards in comparison to their country of origin in the North.[49] As a result, the increased mobility of U.S. capital is serving to relocate many of the worst public health risks and environmental injustices associated with "dirty industry" to the global South.

Union Carbide in India: A Disastrous Double Standard

Perhaps the case that best illustrates the disastrous impacts of the new double standard in the global economy can be found in India. On the night of December 2, 1984, a runaway chemical reaction and gas leak developed at a Union Carbide India Ltd pesticide factory in the city of Bhopal. By the time workers at the plant discovered the problem, it was too late. Poorly designed safety systems were either malfunctioning or turned off. The worst chemical disaster in history had begun. Over twenty-seven tons of methyl isocyanate (MIC) spewed from the plant and enveloped the city in a cloud of deadly poison. In the middle of the night, between 2:00 and 3:00 A.M., thousands of people woke up coughing and gasping for air, their eyes burning from the fumes. Coming outside their homes, there was no place to run, as the gases were everywhere. Many fell dead as they ran for safety. More than 2,500 people lost their lives that night, and more than 5,500 followed in the next three days. Over 520,000 people were exposed to the gases. Hardest hit were the poor living in substandard housing adjacent to the factory. Eventually, more than 15,000 to 20,000 people would die as a result of exposure-related illnesses in the following years, according to popular accounts. People are still dying today. An estimated 120,000 to 150,000 survivors remain chronically ill. The most common problems range from respiratory diseases and gynecological disorders to cancers, neurological problems, and immunological system disorders. It is perhaps the worst industrial disaster in history.[50]

   Given the lack of money spent on environmental safety by Union Carbide, it is clear that the Bhopal "accident" was a disaster waiting to happen. In comparison to Union Carbide's sister facility in Institute, West Virginia, there were significant health and safety shortcuts taken in the construction and operation of the Bhopal plant. Built in 1969 to provide pesticide products for India's agricultural, or "green," revolution, the plant proved profitable for many years (the year before the leak, the plant had sales of $202 million and prof-its of $8.8 million). Nevertheless, Union Carbide spent $5 million more in safety improvements for the Institute plant, including emergency scrubbers, flare towers, leak detection systems, and emergency dump tanks and backup systems. In order to save money, these safeguards were lacking at the Bhopal plant and probably would have prevented the accident. In addition, significant cost cutting in maintenance and safety procedures, including shutting down the refrigeration units that kept the MIC cool, allowed for a violent chemical reaction to occur. Incredibly, the company cut operating costs further by rou-tinely shutting down the plant's key safety systems (the flare tower and vent gas scrubber) even though MIC was being stored in very hot tanks with no re-frigeration. Finally, despite the greater dangers, Union Carbide's corporate engineering group overruled the Indian subsidiary's objections in deciding to store large amounts of MIC in large, substandard tanks. Although cheaper, this practice is regarded as far too dangerous in Germany, Japan, and the United States and is avoided. In short, weaker environmental standards and enforcement in India allowed Union Carbide to engage in a series of prac-tices—all designed to save the company money—that resulted in a horrific catastrophe. But this is not atypical of India. The *Hindustan Times* reports that "only 16 out of the 50 pesticide manufacturing units in the country have any worthwhile pollution control system working and the general system of su-pervision of pollution control is dangerously lax."[51]

In 1989, Union Carbide and the Indian government arrived at a negotiated settlement of $470 million for all gas disaster–related injuries. The average payout for the personal injury was between $370 and $533 per person (in con-trast, the penalty for the Exxon Valdez disaster, where no human lives were lost, was $5 billion). However, much of the money was not distributed for many years (in 2004, the Indian government released some $330 million in compensation to be split among all 578,000 victims of the disaster). In its 1989 annual report, Union Carbide told its shareholders that the Bhopal dis-aster had cost them forty-three cents per share. Despite the tragedy, Union Carbide became a wholly owned subsidiary of Dow Chemical Company in February 2001. Dow, which assumed Union Carbide assets, has refused to ac-cept its liabilities in India. The abandoned factory site remains littered with toxic waste, leaking poisons into the surrounding neighborhood. As a result, the survivors of this corporate disaster tour the United States demanding that Dow assume liability for the health impacts and lost livelihoods caused by the "accident" and engage in a full cleanup of the site. Over 20,000 people con-tinue to live in close proximity to the old factory site and exposed to toxic chemicals left behind. But despite the awful legacy of the Bhopal disaster, it's business as usual for corporate polluters in India.

Mexico: Environmental Troubles South of the Border

Since the passage of NAFTA in 1994, Mexico's environmental problems have worsened throughout the country. NAFTA is a free-trade agreement that reduces tariffs and other barriers to trade among Mexico, Canada, and the United States. Aided by the agreement, dirty industries are moving out of the United States to Mexico, where environmental standards are lax, unions are weak, and worker health and safety concerns are ignored.[52] Along the 2,100-mile U.S.–Mexico border running from the Pacific Ocean to the Gulf of Mexico, there are more than 2,000 factories, or maquiladoras, including U.S. companies, involved in textiles and clothing, chemicals, and electronics. A 1991 U.S. Government Accounting Office study even found that several Los Angeles furniture manufacturers relocated to Mexico after the establishment of stringent air pollution restrictions in California (80 percent of these businesses cited environmental costs in their decision to move).[53]

The explosive growth of the maquiladoras is creating an ecological disaster along both sides of the border. Factories big and small generate huge volumes of pollution (some 87 percent of maquiladoras use toxic materials in their production processes). Reports show that industrial waste is seldom treated before it is discharged into rivers, arroyos, the Rio Grande, or the ocean. Maquiladoras also generate a substantial amount of hazardous waste, including dangerous solvents such as trichloroethylene, acids, heavy metals like lead and nickel, paints, oils, resins, and plastics. Over 65 percent of such waste is unaccounted for in either the United States or Mexico.[54] The situation is growing worse because NAFTA no longer requires transnational corporations to return waste to the United States for proper disposal.[55]

Pollution problems along the border are not limited to manufacturing facilities. In July 2003, the U.S.-based Sempra Energy Company completed construction of a $350 million natural gas–fired power plant just three miles over the border in Mexico. The company built the plant in Mexico, near the own of Mexicali, in order to dodge California's stringent air quality regulations, even though the electricity is being sent back to consumers in southern California. A subsidiary of San Diego Gas & Electric, Sempra's plant annually emits approximately 378 tons per year of nitrogen oxides, 376 tons of carbon monoxide, and almost four megatons of carbon dioxide. The plant also uses up to 3 million gallons of water per day, depriving the arid and rain-starved city of Mexicali of valuable water from the New River. This is the first power plant in Mexico to be fully owned and operated by a foreign corporation and, in the words of CorpWatch, is turning the border region into a "dirty energy export zone."[56] Sempra is not alone. In an earlier survey of U.S. companies operating in Mexicali, 25 percent indicated that stiff environmental regulations in the United States and weaker ones in Mexico were either the main factor or a factor of importance in their decision to locate facilities in the town.[57]

Mexico is emblematic of the vast social and environmental problems that corporate-led globalization, NAFTA, and neoliberal economic policy have brought to the global South. The Mexican government, under pressure from various U.S. agencies and international financial institutions such as the World Bank, the International Monetary Fund, and the WTO, has adopted export-oriented industrialization policies aimed at attracting foreign capital into the country. This strategy requires that production costs be kept low if companies are to successfully compete with other export producers around the world. Production costs are relatively low in Mexico because of cheap labor, natural resources, and energy as well as low taxes and other subsidies but are also depressed by limited state control over industry with respect to the environment and public health.[58] Since the passage of NAFTA in 1994, real spending on environmental protection has declined by 45 percent in Mexico.[59] Contrary to prevailing assumptions, foreign companies are no more likely than domestic firms to comply with Mexican environmental law, according to a World Bank survey of over 200 firms across all of Mexico.[60] In other words, U.S. corporations are "equal opportunity" ecological offenders.

In comparison to the United States, the twelve largest industrial sectors in Mexico are alarmingly "dirtier." For instance, the textile industry is up to 1,225 times dirtier (depending on the pollutant) than its U.S.-based counterparts, while the paper industry is up to 592 times dirtier. On the whole, most Mexican-based industries are about six times dirtier than in the United States. However, Mexican-based companies involved in the production of certain chemical and pharmaceutical products, iron and steel, and nonferrous metals were much cleaner than their U.S.-based counterparts.[61] Nevertheless, despite the weak state of environmental enforcement, many of the dirtiest industries in Mexico are beginning to relocate to "pollution havens" in China, where labor is four times cheaper. As a result, the share of dirty industry is declining in *both* the United States and Mexico. Between 1988 and 2000, in terms of total production, pollution-intensive economic activity as a share of total production in the United States decreased by three percentage points and in Mexico by five.[62]

Despite the flight of dirty industry to China, the ecological crisis still continues to deepen in Mexico. More than $50 billion in damage is done each year to Mexican society from air and water pollution, soil erosion, and municipal solid waste. This is equivalent to 10 percent of the country's GDP. In other words, for every dollar the Mexican economy grows, ten cents is thrown away. As stated by environmental scholar Kevin Gallagher, to waste $50 billion per year is "a tragedy when half of Mexico's 100 million people live on less than $2 a day."[63]

Out with the Old and in with the New:
The Export of Polluting Factories and Equipment

The export of hazards in the productive circuit of capital is not limited to the siting of brand-new but "dirty" production facilities in the global South. Some of America's most highly polluting factories and equipment rendered obsolete by age and/or U.S. environmental regulations are being sold off in the international market and shipped to countries that cannot afford modern and/or cleaner technologies. This international trade in retired equipment (and vehicles) is estimated to be around $150 billion per year. A 2003 report by the German think tank Adelphi Research found that these relocated facilities in the steel, energy, cement, and mineral-oil industries create "additional pollution of a considerable dimension."[64] In fact, these polluting facilities and technology can have a second life in the global South that is longer than the first term in the United States, create enormous health problems, and serve to "hinder sustainable development." Estimates are that secondhand machinery exported to the developing countries consumes an average of 20 percent more energy than more modern equipment and therefore produces greater quantities of emissions that cause global warming. Three U.S. automobile manufacturers also recently sold emission control technology to China that did not meet U.S. air pollution standards.[65]

Old power plants are some of the worst offenders. The transfer of used fossil power stations alone, with an overall capacity of twenty-three gigawatts, cause additional annual emissions of approximately 2.2 billion tons of carbon dioxide in comparison with modern power stations.[66] In Turners Falls, Massachusetts, an old 2,600-ton coal-fired power plant is being dismantled and shipped to Guatemala. There it is being rebuilt in order to power a textile mill that will produce pants, shirts, and sportswear for export back to American consumers. The Turners Falls plant cost about $44 million when it was built in the late 1980s to power a paper mill and is being rebuilt in Guatemala at a cost of $22 million. Furthermore, the export of "dirty" production facilities and technologies also increases the demand for U.S.-produced cleanup technologies and services by the state and other corporations operating in the global South. The global cleanup industry is now valued at over $300 billion. It is the export of pollution abatement and cleanup technologies that enable waste-producing firms to meet the "minimal" regulatory requirements of most developing nations. As stated by CorpWatch founder Josh Karliner, "When the cleanup firms are subsidiaries of the same corporations that generate large amounts of hazardous waste in developing countries, the double benefits are obvious."[67]

BUYER BEWARE: THE EXPORT OF
ECOLOGICALLY HAZARDOUS COMMODITIES

Third World Testing Grounds for Dangerous Chemicals

In the era of corporate-led globalization, dangerous pesticides and other chemicals, biotechnology, drugs, and other consumer products that are highly restricted in the United States are still manufactured here and routinely exported to other nations. American corporations know that there is little government oversight or public pressure to inspect and regulate such products in overseas markets and that significant profits are to be made from shipping their hazardous products to unsuspecting consumers all around the world. This process has been under way for many decades but is accelerating with the expansion of world trade.

One of the most hazardous commodities exported by the United States to the rest of the world are pesticides. Roughly a billion pounds of pesticides are exported each year, or *forty-five tons per hour*. Tragically, American policymakers have done little to stop the export of pesticides forbidden in the United States. Under the Federal Insecticide, Fungicide and Rodenticide Act, the Environmental Protection Agency (EPA) does not review the health and environmental impacts of pesticides manufactured for export only, or what are termed "never-registered" pesticides. The most recent figures available indicate that nearly 22 million pounds of these exported pesticides are banned or severely restricted for use in the United States, an average of more than twenty-two tons per day. Furthermore, an average rate of more than thirty tons per day of "extremely hazardous" chemicals, as rated by the World Health Organization, are also exported. Nearly 1.1 billion pounds of known or suspected carcinogenic pesticides were exported by the United States between 1997 and 2000, an average rate of almost sixteen tons per hour.[68] As a result, many pesticides that the EPA has judged too dangerous for domestic use, as well as pesticides never evaluated by the EPA, are regularly shipped from U.S. ports.[69]

Under pressure from the polluter-industrial complex, the U.S. government has refused to adopt two key treaties that would address this problem: the Stockholm Convention, which eliminates chemicals the international community has agreed are extremely dangerous to human health and the environment, and the Rotterdam Convention, which controls the international trade of highly toxic chemicals. The Stockholm Convention focuses on persistent organic pollutants, which move up the food chain and accumulate in the body fat of humans and other animals. The chemicals can cause reproductive and development disorders, many different kinds of cancers, and damage to the immune and nervous systems. The Stockholm Convention identifies twelve pollutants for elimination, including nine pesticides (aldrin, endrin, dieldrin, chlordane, dichloro-diphenyl-trichloroethane [DDT], heptachlor, hexachlorobenzene, mirex, and toxaphene). Similarly, the Rotterdam Convention requires that any country importing pesticides and certain other hazardous chemicals be informed of bans or severe restrictions on those substances in other countries. The treaty gives a receiving country the power to refuse shipments of chemicals harmful to the environment and public health. As stated by Kristin Schafer of the Pesticide Action Network North America, "Washington's inability to adopt these treaties [Stockholm and Rotterdam]—now ratified by 127 and 110 countries, respectively—constitutes a failure not only of US leadership but of responsible participation in global efforts to protect human health."[70]

The U.S. failure to ratify these agreements permits the U.S. polluter-industrial complex to "legally" export deadly poisons to the rest of world. But as noted by Fatma Zora Ouhachi-Vesely, the special rapporteur to the UN Commission of Human Rights, "Just because something is not illegal, it may still be immoral. Allowing the export of products recognized to be harmful is immoral."[71] The most dangerous U.S. chemical exports are often destined for Third World countries where the prevailing working conditions—a lack of protective equipment, unsafe application and storage practices, and inadequate training of pesticide applicators—greatly magnify the health risks for agricultural workers and their families. In fact, about 57 percent of these products are shipped to the developing world, while most of the remaining chemicals are shipped to ports in Belgium and the Netherlands for reshipment to developing countries.[72] As a result, poisonings continue to mount. The World Health Organization estimates that 3 million severe pesticide poisonings occur each year, and, of these, a minimum of 300,000 people die, many of them children. Some 99 percent of these cases occur in developing countries.[73]

The Global Circle of Poison

The people of the global South are not the only ones being poisoned by pesticides exported from the United States. Third World agricultural exports contaminated with pesticides come back to the United States and other northern countries in a vicious "circle of poison." Although the U.S. environmental movement was successful in legally restricting or prohibiting the use of many hazardous chemicals such as DDT in the 1970s, multinational corporations continue to manufacture and export these same pesticides to the Third World. The circle of poison closes when U.S. citizens consume Third World exports contaminated with the pesticides. For instance, imports of Chilean grapes,

Canadian and Mexican carrots, Mexican broccoli and tomatoes, Argentine and Hungarian apple juice, and Brazilian orange juice are found to have worse levels of pesticide contamination than U.S.-grown crops.[74]

Food and Drug Administration (FDA) data show that food imports from developing countries are often contaminated with pesticides banned or restricted for health reasons in the United States, including a violation rate of 40.8 percent for all imports of Guatemalan green peas, 18.4 percent for Mexican strawberries, and 15.6 percent for Mexican lettuce.[75] FDA inspections of Chinese imports have also caught dried apples preserved with a cancer-causing chemicals, frozen catfish laden with banned antibiotics, scallops and sardines coated with bacteria, and mushrooms laced with illegal pesticides. These were among the 107 food imports from China that the FDA detained at U.S. ports in April 2007 along with more than 1,000 shipments of tainted Chinese dietary supplements and other products.[76]

Both U.S. and foreign corporations know that exporting tainted products into the United States poses little risk of being caught by an underfunded and understaffed FDA. FDA testing of food imports (and domestic products) is infrequent and restricted to only a few choice chemicals. Since 1997, FDA officials have examined just 1.5 percent of all food imports, while shipments skyrocketed from more than 4 million entries in 1997 to more than 15 million in 2006. Under assault from the Bush administration and the polluter-industrial complex, the FDA's regulatory affairs staff is getting leaner—it shrank from a high of 4,003 full-time employees in the 2003 fiscal year to 3,488 in 2007. As a result, noncriminal foreign and domestic inspections carried out by the FDA's Center for Food Safety and Applied Nutrition staffers amounted to 9,038 in 2005, down from 11,566 just two years earlier.[77]

In the few instances where testing is done, FDA health standards are inadequate. In some cases, consumption of a single food item contaminated with chemicals at levels allowed by the FDA, such as DDT in fish, would expose the consumer to more than fifty times the daily intake levels considered "safe" by the EPA. Persistent organic pollutants such as DDT and polychlorinated biphenyls (PCBs) are implicated in a breast cancer epidemic that impacts an estimated 2,044,000 women in the United States and claims about 40,000 lives each year.[78] In fact, a person eating the U.S. Department of Agriculture's recommended five servings of fruits and vegetables per day will eat illegal pesticides at least seventy-five times per year. In contrast, the average consumer has to eat about 100 pounds of fresh fruits and vegetables in order to eat from a shipment tested for pesticides by the FDA. This means that the average American is at least fifteen times more likely to eat an illegal pesticide than to eat from a shipment tested by the FDA.[79] A form of *toxic trespass*, these dangerous chemicals are invading the bodies of U.S. citizens and are linked to various types of cancers, learning disabilities and autism, immune system suppression, central nervous disorders, damage to reproductive systems, and numerous other disorders.[80] According to the U.S. Centers for Disease Control, the American people carry a "body burden" of the pesticides chlorpyrifos (Dursban) and methyl parathion that dramatically exceeds acceptable thresholds for chronic exposure.[81]

"Getting the Lead Out" of Chinese Imports

The "circle of poison" in the new global economy is not restricted to pesticides. To the contrary, the trade in dangerous consumer goods coming into the United States has become a regular feature on the front pages of American newspapers. China is one of the world's worst offenders. American imports of Chinese goods have nearly tripled since 2000, largely because of low prices stemming from the cheap costs of labor power, high labor productivity, and weak environmental and worker health and safety standards. These conditions also result in the manufacturing of dangerous consumer products and additives. In 2007, thousands of dogs and cats became ill or died across the United States after consuming pet food filled with the chemical melamine. The problem occurred when the Las Vegas firm ChemNutra imported about 1.7 million pounds of Chinese wheat gluten. Unknowing that it was tainted with the industrial chemical, ChemNutra added it to millions of containers of pet food. Melamine, which is used to make plastics, artificially inflates protein levels (and makes the food appear more nutritious) and raises the price of the product for Chinese exporters.[82] Similarly, in July 2007, toothpaste contaminated with diethylene glycol and imported into the United States from China and South Africa was discovered and confiscated by U.S. officials. Since 2006, American authorities have also recalled toxic seafood, juice made with unsafe color additives, and defective tires from China (Foreign Tire Sales Inc. of Union, New Jersey, was forced to recall as many as 450,000 imported tires because of tread separation).

In response to growing public outrage in the United States and political pressure on the Chinese government over these types of incidents, China executed Zheng Xiaoyu, who headed the State Food and Drug Administration from 1998 to 2005. Xiaoyu was accused and convicted of dereliction of duty and of taking about $850,000 in bribes from pharmaceutical companies.[83] Nevertheless, the importation of toxic products from China continues. In August and September 2007, Mattel Inc. ordered three high-profile recalls of more than 21 million toys. The toys were also made in China and decorated with dangerous levels of lead paint and/or designed by Mattel with small magnets and other hazards for small children (childhood ingestion of lead can result in reduced intelligence, hyperactivity, attention deficit disorders, and various other forms of brain damage or even death). Among the most popular children's toys in the nation, these products included Thomas the Tank engine toys, Barbie doll accessories, and toy cars (Mattel is the world's largest toy company and has about 65 percent of its products manufactured in China).[84] Much of the lead paint was used from a lower-cost third-party supplier (or subcontractor) in China instead of paint supplied directly from the contractor.[85]

Some Chinese-made vinyl baby bibs sold at Toys "R" Us stores also were contaminated with lead, as were vinyl lunch boxes and children's jewelry. In fact, Reebok International Ltd was earlier forced to recall about 300,000 charm bracelets made in China with excessive lead after a four-year-old Minnesota boy died. The Consumer Product Safety Commission was forced to recall 150 million pieces of Chinese-made children's jewelry sold in vending machines across the United States in 2004 because of excessive lead levels (since 2003, the commission has conducted about forty recalls of children's jewelry because of high levels of lead). Two recent studies suggest that the lead turning up in Chinese-made jewelry is being obtained from discarded computers and other electronic goods from the United States that are being dumped in China and disassembled for the materials inside at recycling centers.[86] The toxic trash exported abroad is coming back to haunt the American people.

DUMPING ON THE THIRD WORLD: THE EXPORT OF POLLUTION AND HAZARDOUS WASTE

The Global Trade in Hazardous Waste

The United States is the single largest producer of hazardous wastes in the world. Each year, the United States produces some 238 million tons.[87] Meanwhile, the cost of hazardous waste disposal in the United States has grown from $15 per ton in 1980 to over $250 per ton, while the costs of incineration has increased over threefold to between $1,500 and $3,000 per ton. Although capital has looked to reduce expenses by locating hazardous waste dumps and facilities in poor communities of color throughout the United States, there is also a growing incentive to export wastes to developing countries. The disposal cost per metric ton of hazardous waste in Africa, for instance, has historically hovered around $40 to $50 per ton (and, in the case of an agreement between the Gibraltar-based company and the Benin Republic government, for as low as $2.50 per ton).[88] These costs are so low because regulations governing toxic waste disposal are virtually nonexistent in developing countries.

The incentive to cut disposal costs by exporting toxics to the global South is also strong among other advanced capitalist countries. Hundreds of cases involving hundreds of millions of pounds of hazardous waste being exported from the advanced capitalist countries to the South have been documented over the past two decades. As if emboldened by the words of former World Bank chief economist Lawrence Summers—"I've always thought that under-populated countries in Africa are vastly *under*-polluted"—dump sites of toxic waste from Western nations can be found throughout Africa, from Senegal to Nigeria, Zimbabwe, Congo, and even South Africa. In some years, West Africa alone has imported up to 300 million tons of toxic waste from some twenty-four industrialized countries.[89]

A Toxic Terror in the Ivory Coast

The devastating impact of hazardous waste trade in Africa and the global South is illustrated by the case of the *Proba Koala* in the Ivory Coast. Exemplary of the growing integration of capital on a global scale, the *Proba Koala* was a Korean-built, Greek-managed, Panamanian-flagged tanker chartered by the London branch of a Swiss trading corporation the fiscal headquarters of which are in the Netherlands—the multi-billion-dollar Dutch global oil and metals trading company called Trafigura Beheer BV. The ship had been acting as a storage vessel for unrefined gasoline. In the summer of 2006, Trafigura had explored disposing of the ship's "washings" after a routine cleaning of the storage hull with caustic soda in Amsterdam. However, because of the cost estimate of $300,000 or more for disposing of the waste in that city, the company instead elected to take the ship to the Ivory Coast, even though there are no facilities capable of handling high-level toxic wastes. On arrival, the captain of the *Proba Koala* contacted a local company called Compaigne Tommy to dispose of the waste for a mere $15,000, representing a huge savings for Trafigura.

On August 19, 2006, the *Proba Koala* offloaded 528 tons of the washings onto more than a dozen tanker trucks. The washings were a toxic alkaline mix of water, gasoline, and caustic soda, which gave off many poisonous chemicals, including hydrogen sulfide. After loading up, Compaigne Tommy simply waited until after midnight. Under the cover of darkness, the tanker trucks fanned out to dump the waste in eighteen public open-air sites around the country's main city of Abidjan. These sites included the city's main garbage dump, a roadside field beside a prison, a sewage canal, and several neighborhoods. In a scene eerily reminiscent of the Bhopal disaster, citizens throughout the city awoke at night to an overpowering stench that burned the eyes and made it hard to breathe. By morning, nausea, vomiting, diarrhea, nosebleeds, stomachaches, chest pains, and breathing difficulties were affecting thousands of people. Tests later showed the sludge contained excessive levels of mercaptans and hydrogen sulfide, a potent poison that can quickly paralyze the nervous system and cause blackouts, respiratory failure, and death. More than 100,000 Abidjan residents sought medical treatment, and sixty-nine were hospitalized as a result of the dumping. Fifteen people died. The spreading illnesses sparked violent demonstrations from a population convinced that government corruption was to blame for the dumping. The political furor ultimately forced the prime minister and his government to resign in September 2006 (though many were later reinstated). Nevertheless, this mass resignation is unprecedented in the history of the Ivory Coast and symbolizes the anger among the African people that their home would be used as a dumping ground by the advanced capitalist nations.[90]

Limitations of the Basel Convention for Controlling Global Dumping of Toxic Waste

In 1989, some 118 countries signed onto the Basel Convention on the Transboundary Movement of Hazardous Wastes and Their Disposal. Enacted in 1992, the treaty was designed to better regulate the movement of hazardous waste between nations. Unfortunately, there were problems left unaddressed. For one, the convention did *not* prohibit waste exports to any location except Antarctica and instead merely required a notification and consent system known as "prior informed consent." As such, if a nation did consent to accept hazardous wastes for disposal but did not have the capacity to control and monitor such wastes in a safe and environmentally sound manner, then the prior informed consent rule was meaningless.[91] In addition, a number of key nations, including the Ivory Coast and the United States, undermined the agreement by failing to ratify the main amendment to the Basel Convention. The convention also did not adequately address the dumping of toxic products and materials through industrial recycling programs. Nevertheless, despite these problems, the Basel Convention established a new international norm that views the export of hazardous wastes from the North to the South as an unacceptable act of ecological imperialism.

Immediately after the adoption of the Basel Convention, the international environmental movement and less developed countries went to work on overcoming its limitations. Over the course of the 1990s, their actions proved successful. The convention has subsequently been strengthened through the adoption of hundreds of decisions, a protocol, an amendment, and the amendment of annexes. Of these agreements, the Basel Ban is the most important, as it puts into place a global ban on the export of hazardous wastes from members of the Organization for Economic Cooperation and Development (OECD) to non-OECD countries. It has, without question, in the words of the Basel Action Network, "transformed the Basel Convention from a control regime, to a no-exceptions, environmentally-justified trade barrier to hazardous waste."[92]

Unfortunately, even as a nonparty, the United States has vociferously opposed improvements to the Basel Convention. In fact, since the very beginning of the Basel negotiations, both Republican and Democratic administrations alike have joined with the polluter-industrial complex to strongly oppose the concept of a no-exceptions waste trade ban. Furthermore, the United States is attempting to redefine what constitutes hazardous wastes, including efforts to avoid the Basel Convention for the management of end-of-life American ships or to delist certain types of electronic wastes. However, as long as the United States remains a nonparty, efforts to dismantle the Basel Ban against the wishes of the global community will probably fail. Instead, the likely plan of a hostile U.S. government is to selectively ratify the original agreement and then punch loopholes in the Basel Ban on behalf of industry from inside the Basel Convention apparatus. This approach not only attempts to turn back the clock on the regulation of hazards but also violates the principles of environmental justice that the federal government itself adopted with Clinton's executive order.

The Export of Hazardous Wastes from the United States

Although the traditional means of exporting toxic wastes from the advanced capitalist countries for final disposal in developing countries has slowed down since the adoption of the Basel Convention, the United States still exports hazardous waste abroad.[93] And while U.S. law regulates hazardous waste exports, it imposes fewer controls than the Basel Convention. In a recent incident, a U.S. chemical firm, HoltraChem Manufacturing, attempted to export 260,000 pounds of spent mercury waste from its Maine plant to India, already the largest recipient of mercury exports from the United States. Despite the negative publicity surrounding the sale, the U.S. government exempted the shipment from regulations on waste exports because it considered the metal to have "trade value." Nevertheless, the Indian government ultimately denied the shipment entry into the country and forced its return to the United States.[94]

Thanks to the Basel Ban, many other countries are now unwilling to accept toxic waste from the United Sates. Instead, the United States has increasingly relied on Canada to receive toxic waste. Canada's hazardous waste laws are much less stringent and, in contrast to U.S. law, do not require treatment of waste to reduce toxicity prior to disposal in landfills. Canada is therefore a lower-cost alternative for U.S. waste exporters. As a result, about 30 percent of all imported wastes from the United States in the late 1990s ended up in a landfill in Sarnia, Ontario, that was owned by the U.S. company Safety-Kleen.[95]

NAFTA has figured into the export of hazards. Under Chapter 11, companies may sue governments for the expropriation of profits or actions that are tantamount to expropriation of profits, even in the case of environmental protection. For instance, S. D. Myers, a U.S. waste disposal company, won its challenge to a 1995 Canadian law banning the cross-border trade of PCBs. In this case, Canada claimed that the law on PCB waste was justified under the Basel Convention, but the NAFTA dispute panel did not accept this argument. Similarly, in a U.S.-threatened case before the WTO, Guatemala was forced to cancel a public health law that had forbidden infant formula companies, notably Gerber, from advertising their products as being healthier than breast milk. Infant death rates skyrocket for mothers using baby formula in the Third World because of the presence of bacteria and parasites in polluted water used to make the formula and because babies are denied the additional antibodies provided by breast milk to ward off illnesses stemming from polluted water. According to the World Health Organization, every year there are 1.6 million diarrheal deaths worldwide related to unsafe water—the vast majority among children under age five.

In another example of "cross deregulation," in August 2000 an international trade tribunal under the International Center for Investment Dispute Settlement (an arm of the World Bank) ruled that Mexico violated NAFTA's Chapter 11 investor provisions by not allowing California-based Metalclad Corporation to open a hazardous waste treatment and disposal site in San Luis Potosi, a state in central Mexico. Metalclad claimed that this action effectively expropriated its future expected profits. As a result, the Mexican government was ordered to pay the company $16.7 million as compensation. In the early 1990s, Metalclad received approval from the Mexican federal government to build the disposal plant, which would handle up to 360,000 tons of hazardous waste a year. Outraged by the secret agreement, public protests against the facility ultimately compelled local governmental authorities to investigate the potential environmental impacts, which were determined to be severe. The governor then refused to open the facility and eventually declared the site part of a 600,000-acre ecological zone.

This case demonstrates the manner in which provisions under Chapter 11 are being utilized to directly sue sovereign governments when any investment is infringed on by environmental or worker health and safety regulations. NAFTA also utilizes international standards and rules that in many cases are weaker than U.S., Canadian, and even Mexican law and regulation. For example, the international food safety standard in the NAFTA is *Codex Alimentarius*, which allows residues on food of substances banned in the United States or Canada, such as DDT. Weaker environmental standards and enforcement become a part of the competitive advantage in this race to the bottom.[96] Mexico's maquiladoras have also proven to be an important front for smuggling in hazardous wastes from the United States. Wastes are often sent hidden as cargo on trucks and trains that cross the border into Mexico.[97] It is estimated that 285,000 tons of hazardous waste flow from the United States to Mexico each year.[98] Once inside the country, the chemicals are released into waterways, sewers, municipal landfills, unregulated landfills, and numerous private property sites.

When waste is not labeled as hazardous waste, it is very difficult to track and regulate. For instance, four U.S. companies once mixed 1,000 tons of hazardous waste (including lead and cadmium) into a shipment of fertilizer bound for Bangladesh. The fertilizer was applied to fields before the contamination was discovered. In another case, some 15,000 tons of toxic incinerator ash of U.S. origin was shipped to Guinea in the late 1980s under the label of brick building materials. This toxic waste was dumped on the Guinean Island of Kassa, just off the coast of the country's capital city, Conakry, by a Norwegian waste management firm. In a surreal land reclamation project, several U.S. companies even attempted to convince the Marshall Islands that imported wastes could be used to build up landmass to ensure that the islands would survive possible sea-level rises caused by global warming (the United States and China are the world's largest producers of greenhouse gases).[99]

Recycling "Trash for Cash"

In the new millennium, a new wave of waste trade is developing in the form of various "trash for cash," or recycling schemes of postconsumer products. Loopholes in the rules allow waste transfers to legally continue under the auspices of recycling. These exported wastes take the form of used car (lead-acid) batteries, cell phones, plastics, heavy metals, old ships laden with asbestos, and lead scrap, shipped from the United States to southern China, India, Pakistan, the Philippines, Malaysia, and Taiwan for "recycling." In January 1993 alone, for instance, the United States sent over 1,985 tons of plastic waste to India.[100] These new types of waste products are becoming a far more serious form of toxic dumping in comparison to the export of toxic chemicals.

In the United States, the costs of emission control systems, liability insurance, and other environmental and occupational health regulatory safeguards associated with lead battery recycling facilities have skyrocketed. Meanwhile, the prices offered for secondary lead are so low that over half of North America's secondary lead smelters have gone out of business over the past two decades. In contrast, foreign smelters in the global South can afford to bid a higher price for scrap because their capital, labor, and environmental costs are much lower than those of U.S. producers. As a result, U.S. battery brokers are looking for higher profits by shipping lead-acid batteries to recycling facilities in Indonesia, the Philippines, Thailand, India, Brazil, South Korea, Mexico, and China. As early as the mid-1980s, for instance, the U.S. subsidiary of a Danish company, Bergsöe Metal Corporation went bankrupt and closed its lead battery recycling plant in St. Helens, Oregon. Today, Bergsöe operates a lead battery recycling plan in Suraburi, Thailand, where it receives thousands of pounds of battery scrap each year. The facility reportedly poisons the air, groundwater, and soil beyond the plant's property with lead and arsenic.[101]

Similarly, the city of Tianying in China is now ranked by the Blacksmith Institute as one of ten most polluted places in the world. Tianying is among the largest lead production bases in China. Studies have found average lead concentrations in the city's air and soil that are 8.5 times and ten times higher than allowed by national health standards. Over 140,000 people live in close proximity to the recycling plants, and elevated rates of health problems related to lead poisoning, such as brain damage, encephalopathy, learning disabilities, and impaired physical growth, are reported.[102] The abundance of low-cost lead produced by the city's vast number of recycling facilities is then sold to corporations producing consumer goods for export back to the United States. Chinese factory owners and some multinational corporations look to maximize profits in intensely competitive markets by cutting safety corners and incorporating lead into their manufacturing processes. Paint with higher levels of lead, for instance, often sells for a third of the cost of paint with low levels. As we have seen, these lead compounds and paints are used to make toys, jewelry, and countless other products and eventually end up in the hands of American consumers.

Electronic waste (or e-waste) is perhaps the most rapidly growing waste problem in the world. According to the United Nations, about 20 million to 50 million tons of e-waste are generated worldwide annually. Such waste contains toxins like lead, mercury, and other chemicals that can poison waterways, the land, or air (if burned). The United States, which uses most of the world's electronic products and generates most of the e-waste, is able to significantly reduce disposal costs by shipping e-wastes to the developing countries. In addition to U.S. efforts to undermine the Basel Convention, the U.S. government has also intentionally exempted e-wastes from the Resource Conservation and Recovery Act.[103] In short, the export of e-waste to developing countries serves as an economic escape valve for American industry. Rather than designing products that are less toxic and that can be more easily rebuilt and reused, American business maximizes profits by building products with very hazardous components with a short life span. Some 20 million computers become obsolete each year in the United States, generating some 5 million to 7 million tons of e-waste.[104]

In the era of corporate-led globalization, toxic waste disposal is running "downhill" on the path of least resistance. About 80 percent of the e-waste handled by traders is exported to Asia, and 90 percent of that is destined for China, where environmental regulations are weak and poorly enforced. E-waste today contains a witches' brew of toxic substances such as lead and cadmium in circuit boards, lead oxide and cadmium in monitor cathode ray tubes, mercury in switches and flat-screen monitors, cadmium in computer batteries, PCBs in older capacitors and transformers, and brominated flame retardants on printed circuit boards, plastic casings, cables, and polyvinyl chloride cable insulation.[105]

The open burning, acid baths, and toxic dumping that take place around recycling centers release vast quantities of pollution. In the Guiyu region of China, lead levels in drinking water are 2,400 times higher than what the World Health Organization considers to be safe. Similar environmental problems can be found in Indian and Pakistani recycling operations.[106] As in the United States, poor communities surrounding the plants bear the greatest health impacts from these operations.

GLOBALIZATION, UNEQUAL ECOLOGICAL EXCHANGE, AND ENVIRONMENTAL INJUSTICE

The Colonization of Nature in the South

The economic prosperity of American capitalism is dependent on the appropriation of surplus environmental space from the global South. A primary function of corporate-led globalization is to facilitate the importation of cheaper (with high quality/price ratios) consumer goods into the United States, which in turn cheapens the reproduction costs of labor power. As a result, living standards for American workers can systematically increase without a corresponding increase in actual money wages, thus preventing inflation and protecting the value of Wall Street assets. Aside from oil, where the Organization of Petroleum Exporting Countries (OPEC) has successfully restricted supplies and inflated prices in recent years, globalization is making available to the U.S. economy cheaper raw materials and energy supplies from other nations. Because natural resources and energy serve as inputs for both the consumer and the capital goods industries, these lower costs become generalized throughout the economy as a whole. Corporate profits go up because the costs of labor power and manufacturing go down. In this respect, the expansion of American capitalism is becoming increasingly predicated on the consumption of ever-greater quantities of undervalued natural resources from the global South as well as the export of hazards to the developing world.

Over the past two decades and more, the United States has provided international aid packages and loans in order to promote the modernization and expansion of capitalist export agriculture, the extraction of renewable and nonrenewable resources, and industrial development in the global South. In addition, tens of billions of dollars have also been provided every year by the United States and the World Bank (and its regional counterparts) to finance the construction of roads, bridges, coal-fired and nuclear power plants, large dam and irrigation projects, and other infrastructure essential to the conversion of nature into capitalist private property.[107]

Laboring in the service of this new global order but receiving few of its benefits are the popular majorities of the developing world—the poor peasants, workers, ethnic minorities, and indigenous peoples who make up the subsistence sector. Unfortunately, international capital and the U.S. government favor the acquisition of land and natural resources by American corporations as well as large landowners, corrupt government officials and security forces, and various domestic economic elites allied with multinational corporations and U.S. banks. As a result, access to natural resources such as rivers, forests, and fisheries is being restricted by the transformation of these resources and subsistence-based ecosystems into capitalist private property. Utilizing financial assistance provided by multilateral lending agencies, large-scale development projects typically transfer access and control over natural sources from popular classes at the local level to the state, elite land speculators, or private companies (including many multinational corporations).[108] Those peoples in the South who draw their livelihood directly from communal access to land, water, forests, coastal mangroves, and other ecosystems are being the hardest hit by the construction of large dams, mining and oil industry operations, and the capitalization of agriculture and fisheries.[109]

Displaced from their homelands by government policies, economic acquisition, or military force, the displaced masses of the global South migrate to ecologically fragile areas, including rugged hillsides prone to erosion, barren deserts regions lacking water, and pristine tropical rain forests. Once resettled, they try to eke out an existence by overexploiting the limited resource base to which they have access. After a few years of abuse, the resource base eventually collapses, as in much of Central America. In the fragile highlands of El Salvador, for instance, hundreds of thousands of desperately poor family farmers displaced by the expansion of export coffee estates are attempting to survive in a landscape already irreversibly destroyed by erosion, gully formation, and deforestation. More than 77 percent of the country now suffers serious soil erosion.[110] As a result, poverty is increasing dramatically throughout the country. This pattern of impoverishment is repeated in country after country throughout the global South. Of the world's population of about 6.5 billion, 58 percent are malnourished (compared with 20 percent of the world population in 1950).[111]

Unable to support themselves off the land, many migrate to the cities to live in the vast ghettos surrounding the major cities, hoping to find work as cheap wage laborers in the burgeoning factories producing cheap consumer goods for export to the United States and other core countries. Lacking access to potable water, sewage and water treatment facilities, good jobs, adequate housing, and garbage disposal services, the living conditions in these urban areas are often horrendous. With 1.2 billion people lacking access to clean water and adequate sanitation worldwide, waterborne infections are spreading, killing millions of people each year. As these globalization-inspired development models become increasingly unviable, popular movements for social and ecological justice—an *environmentalism of the poor*—are developing all over the world.[112]

EJ movements in the global South encounter great resistance (and often repression) from the ruling power structure and the U.S. government. After all, social and ecological impoverishment of Third World people is advantageous for both domestic and foreign capital (including U.S. multinational corporations), as it functions to create a vast supply of cheap labor for the agricultural plantations, mining and logging operations, and manufacturing facilities producing shoes, electronics, toys, clothing, and countless other commodities for the world export market. Social struggles that disrupt the steady stream of cheap natural resource, energy, and consumer goods coming into America are treated as a threat to "national security" and likely to draw a harsh response from the U.S. government.[113]

Unequal Ecological Exchange and the Ecological Footprint of American Capitalism

Corporate-led globalization is exacerbating unequal trade relations between the United States and developing nations in both economic and ecological terms. Under ecological unequal exchange, the concrete and potential natural wealth found in energy and raw materials flow into the United States in much greater proportion to the monetary (abstract) wealth that is returned (via international trade) to the global South. This occurs because physical wealth imported into the United States is "undervalued" in the world economy. With the dramatic expansion of U.S. FDI in export-oriented industries in the global South, most raw material producers (with the exception of oil-producing nations that are OPEC members) are engaged in fierce price competition with one another in the world market. Moreover, since giant transnational corporations (particularly U.S. multinational corporations engaged in intrafirm transfers) control the purchase and distribution of most agricultural products, raw materials, and consumer goods in the world market, Third World producers and domestic corporations typically exercise little control over global pricing mechanisms.

In order to compete, foreign producers must maximize exports by minimizing production costs, especially wages and "nonproductive" expenditures relating to environmental protection. The profits derived from foreign capital penetration are repatriated to the United States, where the FDI originated. The repatriation of profits serves to retard domestic economic development and increase inequality and poverty. As a result, corporate-led globalization reinforces a system of international trade that facilitates a net transfer of cheap energy and raw materials into the advanced capitalist countries at the ecological expense of the less developed countries. These imported resources are transformed into quantities of products vastly greater than the fraction that is returned to their peripheries. In this respect, "a reasonable market price conceals the fact that what is being exchanged are intact resources for products representing resources already spent."[114] Increases in the U.S. gross national product are therefore directly linked to the expansion of deforestation, mining, energy development, and export agriculture in the poorer nations. That is a primary function of world trade policy.

Evidence of unequal ecological exchange in the world economy can be seen in the *ecological footprint* of the United States and other nations. The ecological footprint is a widely used tool for measuring and analyzing human natural resource consumption and waste output within the context of nature's renewable and regenerative capacity (biocapacity). It represents a quantitative assessment of the biologically productive area (the amount of nature in the form of croplands, pasture, fisheries, forests, and so on) required on a continuous basis to produce resources (food, energy, and materials) consumed by the population and to absorb the wastes that the population produces, wherever on earth that may be located. It therefore estimates human demand (or "load") on the earth in terms of the ecosystem area required to provide basic material support for any population.[115] If a country's ecological footprint is within the annual regenerative capabilities of nature, it is a sustainable economy. However, if a country exceeds ecological limits by using resources more quickly than they can be renewed—a process called *overshoot*—then the economy runs *ecological deficits* and is unsustainable. In this situation, the country's natural capital is drawn down and nature's absorptive sinks are swamped. This leaves less nature for future generations.

When the ecological footprint of a nation's economy is greater than the biophysical capacity of its territory, the country must either import that extra ecological capacity from other territories, reduce the consumption of resources, and/or continue to erode its own ecological capacity. There are currently 28.2 billion global acres of biologically productive land on the planet, covering roughly one-quarter of the earth's surface. The amount of global biocapacity available on a sustainable basis is estimated at about 38 acres per person. However, with the dramatic expansion of capitalist accumulation and world trade over the past three decades or more, the degradation and destruction of ecosystems around the world is accelerating. The actual average global ecofootprint now stands at a whopping fifty-four acres per person. As a result, the world capitalist system is exceeding the ecological limits of the planet by 39 percent, an ecological overshoot of about sixteen acres per person.[116] The manifestation of ecological overshoot is overwhelming, as witnessed in the daily headlines surrounding pollution, land degradation, fisheries collapse, mass extinctions and lost biodiversity, deforestation, acute water shortages, expanding deserts, and spreading diseases.

Globalization is greatly enhancing processes of ecological unequal exchange, allowing the United States to dramatically expand the size of its ecological footprint on the rest of the world. Put another way, economic neoliberalism is enabling a net import of the global South's biocapacity as embodied in energy and natural resource flows. This is being accomplished through the drawdown (or consumption) of a stock of natural capital that resides outside the United States.[117] In fact, the United States exceeds its biological capacities more than any other nation on earth, save for the United Arab Emirates and Kuwait.[118] The differences between the United States and the global South are staggering. Africa, for one, has a population that is nearly 480 million people larger than the United States yet possesses a continental ecofootprint that is 3.95 billion acres smaller.[119] The United States has a much larger global footprint (on a per capita basis) because Africa's consumption of natural resources and commodities produced by dirty industry is much lower. In fact, ecofootprints per capita in Africa are only 18.5 acres, compared to an incredible *270 acres* in the United States. Even burgeoning China has an ecofootprint of only 30.8 acres.[120]

Under corporate-led globalization, the United States is exporting excess ecological impacts to other countries through international trade. This process also includes the displacement of pollution onto the global commons, such as the release of greenhouse gases that cause global warming. The carbon dioxide portion, for instance, accounts for approximately 50 percent of the U.S. total per capita footprint.[121] Failing to curb greenhouse gases from the United States (and other countries) will eventually impact the global economy "on a scale of the Great Depression," according to a 2006 report by the British government. Authored by Sir Nicholas Stern, who heads Britain's Government Economic Services, the high-profile report estimates that the environmental devastation caused by global warming could cost between 5 and 20 percent of the world's gross domestic production.[122]

The Stern report echoes what most climate scientists are predicting: that the melting or collapse of the ice sheets will eventually threaten land that is home to one in every twenty people, and that there will be hundreds of millions more people without sufficient water or food to survive. And while all countries will be affected, it is the poorest countries that will suffer earliest and most intensely, even though they have contributed least to the causes of climate change. The impacts of climate change will be especially devastating for the poorest people already living on the edge of survival in the global South. Given that climate change brings more severe storms and hurricanes of greater intensity, desertification and increased droughts, sea-level rise, more flooding and landslides, and other "natural" disasters, the International Red Cross/Red Crescent estimates that hundreds of million of ecological refugees will be created in the next fifty years. People affected by natural disasters in low-income countries are already four times more likely to die than those in high-income countries. Indeed, there are today more than 25 million ecological refugees in the world—people displaced by ecological degradation and natural disaster. And their numbers are growing by at least 5,000 per day. For the first time in history, more people are being displaced by environmental degradation than war.[123] Ecological disasters are becoming normative occurrences in the age of globalization.

The United States is somewhat insulated from some of the most severe forms of ecological degradation and disaster (Hurricane Katrina notwithstanding). This is so because American capitalism "imports" sustainability from the global South and thereby preserves a greater share of its own ecological capital in the process. In other words, the United States is better able to maintain stronger environmental protection measures inside the country because it consumes so much biomass and sink capacity that is produced outside the country.[124] Known as the "Netherlands fallacy," whereby a supposedly "green" society imports bioresources in order to preserve its own, the higher rates of ecological degradation in the global South are subsidizing the profits of U.S. corporations and the existing consumption patterns of American citizens.[125]

Natural capital is not being significantly eroded because the ecological deficit of the United States is smaller than the sum of its net imports of biomass and of sink capacity (both measured in land area).[126] The importation of commodities produced via the superexploitation of nature and labor is the sine qua non of corporate-led globalization and the world capitalist system under the hegemony of the United States. Free trade and neoliberal economic policy is giving international capital or any other agent who is rich enough the power to decide how global biocapacity is to be used. And so far, the decision is clear. The world's ruling classes are depleting the earth's resources at the expense of the poorest segments of society as well as future generations.

As biomass throughout the world becomes scarcer—because of depletion or appropriation by other nations—*resource wars* (both large and small) are likely to increase, as seen in the U.S. war in Iraq over control of the country's vast oil reserves.[127] Countries with one or two primary export resources already have more than a one-in-five chance of civil war in any given year.[128] Pressures to increase exploitation of domestic biomass is also likely to become more intense as China begins to compete with the United States for foreign oil reserves and other resources. This is already occurring in the United States, as seen in the assault by both major political parties and the polluter-industrial complex on environmental regulations. This burden weighs particularly heavily on poor people of color as the impacts of resource exploitation and industrial pollution are shifted onto populations with less political-economic power. Hence, the growing ecological sacrifice and segregation ("ecoapartheid") of the world's people along economic and racial lines have led to charges of environmental racism and calls for environmental justice in countries as economically and socially disparate as South Africa and the United States.

A BETTER WORLD IS POSSIBLE?

In the era of neoliberalism and corporate-led globalization, EJ movements in the both the United States and the global South have a mutual interest in developing coordinated strategies. The growing ability of multinational corporations and transnational financial institutions to evade environmental safeguards and worker/community health and safety regulations and to dismantle unions and the social safety net in the United States is being achieved by crossing national boundaries into politically repressive and economically oppressive countries. And in this context, abetted by "free-trade" agreements and economic liberalization enforced by the WTO, various nationalities and governments are increasingly being pitted against one another to attract capital investment by dismantling labor and environmental laws seen as damaging to profits. In this respect, corporate-led globalization is weakening the power of the EJ movement to win concessions from the state and American industry.

At the same time, any potential victory by a community of color in the United States against the disposal of toxic incinerator ash in their own locality is quite limited if the result is the transport and disposal of the same waste in a poor West African community. If multinational corporations flee to the Third World to avoid environmental regulations and liability in the North, then the actions of U.S. environmentalists may be indirectly exacerbating environmental injustices elsewhere in the world.[129] Stringent environmental standards must be applied to all nations in order to foster global environmental justice. A reworking of established "free-trade" agreements in favor of more positive "fair-trade" agreements are an important first step in the struggle to defeat neoliberal economic policy. Such a "fair-trade" agreement would establish minimum standards, or "floors," for regulations rather than "ceilings." In other words, rather than a "race to the bottom" whereby the nation with the weakest environmental regulations sets the standard "ceiling" that all trading partners must accept, a transnational EJ movement must work for a series of mandatory strong standards that apply to all nations. Such a regulatory harmonization process would privilege nations with the strictest environmental laws as establishing a standard "floor" to which all other countries must comply if trade is to be conducted between them.[130]

A word of caution, however, to the adoption of narrow liberal policy prescriptions. The implementation of new international agreements and treaties to address the environmental injustices fostered by corporate-led globalization cannot be piecemeal in approach. Strong baseline standards around particular issues is not enough. Agreements must be comprehensive in nature, taking into account *all* the interconnected processes by which ecological hazards are displaced and transferred between countries and especially between the North and South. For instance, in response to the Basel Convention (and Basel Ban), there is evidence that as dirty industries are deterred from exporting hazardous wastes abroad, many factories are relocating from their home bases in the United States to more permissive investment locations in the poorer countries. Once relocated, industry is able to take advantage of the less stringent environmental regulations to more cheaply dispose of hazardous waste directly inside the new country. As a result, the intent of the Basel Ban will be defeated.

Unless comprehensive international rules are also put into place to govern FDI in "toxic" industries, hazardous wastes may still wind up in other countries via this alternative route. The migration of dirty industries to maquiladora zones in Mexico is a strong example of the migration process.[131] Regulating the export of hazards must be comprehensive in scope. As we shall see in chapter 5, there are signals that a new transnational EJ movement devoted to tackling the export of ecological hazards to poor communities of color inside and outside the United States is beginning to take shape. The Southwest Network for Economic and Environmental Justice and the Environmental Health Coalition, for instance, are placing pressure on multinational corporations and government agencies to clean up pollution along the U.S.–Mexico border. In addition, a coalition of Canadian, U.S., and Mexican organizations has successfully expanded right-to-know legislation in Mexico, including the establishment of a Pollutant Release and Transfer Register that is similar to those in Canada and the United States.[132] Although still in its infancy, the rise of an environmentalism of the poor in the global South and new transnational networks of EJ organizations in the North are among the most promising vehicles for curbing the ecological horror stories brought about by corporate-led globalization.

In the short run, only by achieving greater social governance over trade and lending institutions and regulatory bodies can the process that leads different countries to sacrifice human and environmental health in order to compete in the world economy be overcome. This includes efforts to reestablish popular control over the United Nations as a counterweight to the WTO.[133] There is no doubt that we are witnessing a profound antidemocratic counterrevolution in which globalization and its neoliberal imperatives are being used by capital to weaken popular and elected authority. Therefore, the fight for environmental justice and sustainable development must involve strategies to democratize the national and international institutions that shape world policy. These institutions, including transnational corporations and large banks, the International Monetary Fund and the World Bank, the United Nations, and the General Agreement on Tariffs and Trade, must be opened up to greater public participation in decision making.[134] The antiglobalization movement, in the form of the International Forum on Globalization, has prepared alternative proposals for building a more just and sustainable international system that ends corporate dominance over the world economy. These proposals include a system of unified global economic governance under a restructured United Nations.[135] In the long run, however, even larger transformations are necessary. Successfully challenging the instruments of neoliberal globalization will require opposing U.S. imperialism and the system of global capitalism itself.[136] Absent a postcapitalist future devoted to substantive social equality and sustainable development, the global ecological crisis is destined to deepen.[137]

NOTES

1. Pam Woodall, "The Global Economy: War of the Worlds," *The Economist* (October 1, 1994), 36.

2. John Bellamy Foster and Brett Clark, "Ecological Imperialism: The Curse of Capitalism," in *Socialist Register 2004: The New Imperial Challenge*, ed. Leo Panitch and Colin Leys (London: Merlin Press, 2003), 186–201; Aurora Donoso, "No More Looting! Third World Owed an Ecological Debt" (2000), available at http://www.cosmovisions.com/DeudaEcologica/a_looting.html (accessed March 6, 2003).

3. Joan Martinez-Alier, "Marxism, Social Metabolism, and International Trade," in *Rethinking Environmental History: World-System History and Global Environmental Change*, ed. Alf Hornborg, J. R. McNeill, and Joan Martinez-Alier (Lanham, MD: AltaMira Press, 2007), 221–38, esp. 233.

4. Air pollution alone kills 3 million people a year. These figures come from an upcoming report by Cornell University Professor David Pimentel and a research team that examined more than 120 published papers on malnutrition and environmental degradation. Their findings will be presented in the December 2008 issue of *Human Ecology*.

5. Millennium Ecosystem Assessment, *Ecosystems and Human Well-Being: Synthesis Report* (Washington, DC: Island Press, 2005).

6. World Health Organization, *The World Health Organization's Fight against Cancer: Strategies That Prevent, Cure, and Care* (Geneva: WHO Press, 2007).

7. J. Timmons Roberts and Bradley C. Parks, *A Climate of Injustice: Global Inequality, North-South Politics, and Climate Policy* (Cambridge, MA: MIT Press, 2007).

8. James O'Connor, "House Organ," *Capitalism, Nature, Socialism* 11, no. 3 (2000): 162–73.

9. Kenny Bruno and Joshua Karliner, *Earthsummit.biz: The Corporate Takeover of Sustainable Development* (Oakland, CA: Food First Books, 2002), 8.

10. Joshua Karliner, *The Corporate Planet: Ecology and Politics in the Age of Globalization* (San Francisco: Sierra Club Books, 1997), 5; Bruno and Karliner, *Earthsummit.biz*, 8; United Nations, *World Investment Directory: Latin America and the Caribbean* 9, pts. 1 and 2 (New York: United Nations Conference on Trade and Development, 2004), iii.

11. Leo Panitch and Sam Gindin, "Superintending Global Capital," *New Left Review* 35 (September/October 2005): 101–23, esp. 113–15.

12. Associated Press, "Oil Imports Push Up US Trade Gap: Retailers Post Weak Sales Figures in April," *Boston Globe* (May 11, 2007), C2.

13. C. Fred Bergsten, "The Current Account Deficit and the US Economy," testimony before the Budget Committee of the United States Senate (February 1, 2007), 1–5, available at http://www.iie.com/publications/prinit.cfm?doc=pub&ResearchID=705 (accessed May 16, 2007).

14. O'Connor, "House Organ."

15. Bruno and Karliner, *Earthsummit.biz*, 9.

16. Walden Bello, "The Capitalist Conjuncture: Overaccumulation, Financial Crises, and the Retreat from Globalization," *Third World Quarterly* 27, no. 8 (2006): 7; Walden Bello, "The Post-Washington Dissensus" (Washington, DC: Foreign Policy in Focus, September 24, 2007), 1–3.

17. Excerpts from a December 12, 1991, internal memo by Lawrence Summer that was leaked to the press in 1992. Summers was at the time the chief economist at the World Bank. Summers would later become U.S. treasury secretary under the Clinton administration and a major figure in organizing international trade arrangements.

18. John Bellamy Foster, "Let Them Eat Pollution: Capitalism in the World Environment," in *Ecology Against Capitalism* (New York: Monthly Review Press, 2002), 60–68.

19. Francis O. Adeola, "Cross-National Environmental Injustice and Human Rights Issues: A Review of Evidence in the Developing World," *American Behavioral Scientist* 43, no. 4 (2000): 686–706, esp. 691.

20. Kate O'Neill, *Waste Trading among Rich Nations: Building a New Theory of Environmental Regulation* (Cambridge, MA: MIT Press, 2000); Barry Castleman and Vicente Navarro, "International Mobility of Hazardous Products, Industries, and Wastes," *Annual Review of Public Health* 8 (May 1987): 1–19.

21. R. Scott Frey, "The Transfer of Core-Based Hazardous Production Processes to the Export Processing Zones of the Periphery: The *Maquiladora* Centers of Northern Mexico," *Journal of World-Systems Research* 9, no. 2 (Summer 2003): 317–54.

22. James K. Jackson, "Foreign Direct Investment: Effects of a 'Cheap' Dollar," *CRS Report for Congress*, no. RS43000 (May 11, 2007), 1–14.

23. Jennifer Clapp, *Toxic Exports: The Transfer of Hazardous Wastes from Rich to Poor Countries* (Ithaca, NY: Cornell University Press, 2001), 109–10.

24. Robert Lucas, David Wheeler, and Hemamala Hettige, "Economic Development, Environmental Regulation, and the International Migration of Toxic Industrial Pollution, 1960–88," *Policy Research Working Papers*, WPS 1602 (Washington, DC: World Bank, 1992), 14.

25. Hans Christiansen and Ayse Bertrand, "Trends and Recent Developments in Foreign Direct Investment," a report by the OECD Directorate for Financial and Enterprise Affairs (June 2004), 1–24.

26. Martin Hart-Landsberg and Paul Burkett, "China, Capitalist Accumulation, and Labor," *Monthly Review* 59, no. 1 (May 2007): 17–39.

27. Pete Engardioi and Dexter Roberts, "The Three Scariest Words in U.S. Industry: The China Price," *BusinessWeek* (December 6, 2004): 104–12.

28. Joseph Kahn and Jim Yardley, "Amid China's Boom, Pollution Reaches Deadly Extremes," *Boston Globe* (August 26, 2007), A9.

29. World Bank, *The Cost of Pollution in China: Economic Estimates of Physical Damages*, a report prepared by the World Bank and State Environmental Protection Administration, People's Republic of China (2007), 1–111.

30. Jim Jubak, "How Long Can China Pollute for Free?," *Jubak's Journal* (February 9, 2007), 1–8; Elizabeth C. Economy, *The River Runs Black: The Environmental Challenge to China's Future* (Ithaca, NY: Cornell University Press, 2004).

31. World Bank, *The Cost of Pollution in China*, 1–111.

32. Jubak, "How Long Can China Pollute for Free?," 1–8.

33. Blacksmith Institute, *The World's Most Polluted Places: The Top Ten of the Dirty Thirty*, a report prepared by the Blacksmith Institute (September 2007).

34. World Bank, *The Cost of Pollution in China*.

35. Tim Johnson, "Environment: A Social Issue—Bad Air and Toxic Water Spark Protests and Reflect Political Conflicts," *Philadelphia Inquirer* (November 25, 2005), A1, A18.

36. Michael Watts, "Violent Environments: Petroleum Conflict and the Political Ecology of Rule in the Niger Delta, Nigeria," in *Liberation Ecologies: Environment, Development, Social Movements*, 2nd ed., ed. Richard Peet and Michael Watts (New York: Routledge, 2004), 273–98.

37. Report by Lucinda Low on FCPA prosecutions, May 5, 2006. *United States v. ABB Vetco Gray, Inc. and ABB Vetco Gray UK, Ltd.* (case no. 04-CV-279-01) (S.D. Tex. July 2004); SEC Accounting and Auditing Enforcement Release No. 2049 (July 6, 2004); Davi Leigh and David Pallister, "Revealed: The New Scramble for Africa," *Guardian Unlimited* (June 1, 2005), available at http://www.guardian.co.uk/hear-africa05/story/0,15756,1496561,00.html (accessed October 10, 2007).

38. Peter Maass, "A Touch of Crude," *Mother Jones* (January–February 2005), 49–53, 86–89.

39. Watts, "Violent Environments," 273–98.

40. Amnesty International USA, *Environmentalists under Fire: 10 Urgent Cases of Human Rights Abuses* (Washington, DC: Amnesty International USA and the Sierra Club, 2000), 22–23.

41. Joshua Hammer, "Nigeria Crude: A Hanged Man and an Oil-Fouled Landscape," *Harper's* (June 1996), 68, cited in Karliner, *The Corporate Planet*, 86.

42. Derrick Z. Jackson, "The Iraq War and America's Oil Addiction," *Boston Globe* (April 11, 2003), A23.

43. Ken MacLean, *Capitalizing on Conflict: How Logging and Mining Contribute to Environmental Destruction in Burma*, a report by EarthRights International with Karen Environmental and Social Action Network (October 2003), 1–72.

44. Kenny Bruno, "Halliburton's Destructive Engagement: How Dick Cheney and USA-Engage Subvert Democracy at Home and Abroad," *Corporate Watch Report* (October 11, 2000), available at http://corpwatch.org/feature/elections/halliburton.html (accessed October 12, 2000), 1–3.

45. Dan Eggen and Charles Lane, "Bush Seeks to Restrict Foreign Nationals' Suits," *Boston Globe* (June 2, 2003), A5.

46. Amnesty International USA, *Environmentalists under Fire*, 3.

47. Jeffrey Leonard, *Are Environmental Regulations Driving US Industry Overseas?* (Washington, DC: Conservation Foundation, 1985), 155.

48. Jorg Janischewski, Mikael P. Henzier, and Walter Kahlenborn, *The Export of Second-Hand Goods and the Transfer of Technology: An Obstacle to Sustainable Development in Developing Countries and Emerging Markets?* (Berlin: German Council for Sustainable Development and Adelphi Research, May 2003), 29.

49. ESCAP/UNCTC, *Environmental Aspects of Transnational Corporation Activities in Pollution-Intensive Industries in Selected Asian and Pacific Developing Countries* (Bangkok: UN/ESCAP, 1990), 61.

50. William Bogard, *The Bhopal Tragedy: Language, Logic, and Politics in the Production of Hazard* (San Francisco: Westview Press, 1989); David Weir, *The Bhopal Syndrome: Pesticide Manufacturing and the Third World* (Penang, Malaysia: International Organization of Consumers Unions, 1986).

51. Cited in Larry Everest, *Behind the Poison Cloud: Union Carbide's Bhopal Massacre* (Chicago: Banner Press, 1985), 313.

52. Frey, "The Transfer of Core-Based Hazardous Production Processes to the Export Processing Zones of the Periphery," 317–54.

53. U.S. General Accounting Office, *U.S.-Mexico Trade: Some U.S. Wood Furniture Firms Relocated from the Los Angeles Area to Mexico* (Washington, DC: U.S. General Accounting Office, 1991).

54. D. M. Perry, Roberto Sanchez, and William H. Glaze, "Binational Management of Hazardous Waste: The *Maquiladora* Industry in the US-Mexico Border," *Environmental Management* 14 (1998): 441.

55. Clapp, *Toxic Exports*, 116.

56. J. P. Ross, "Sempra: Exporting Pollution," *Corpwatch Report* (May 27, 2002), 1–5.

57. Robert A. Sanchez, "Health and Environmental Risks of the Maquiladora in Mexicali," *Natural Resources Journal* 30 (Winter 1990): 163–70.

58. R. Scott Frey, "The Hazardous Waste Stream in the World-System," in *The Environment and Society Reader*, ed. R. Scott Frey (Boston: Allyn and Bacon, 2001), 106–20.

59. Kevin P. Gallagher, "Is NAFTA Working for Mexico?," *Environmental Forum* (May/June 2006), 21–27.

60. Gallagher, "Is NAFTA Working for Mexico?," 26.

61. Kevin Gallagher, *Trade Liberalization and Industrial Pollution in Mexico: Lessons for FTAA*, Global Development and Environment Institute working paper no. 00-07 (October 2000).

62. Gallagher, "Is NAFTA Working for Mexico?," 21–27.

63. Kevin Gallagher, *Free Trade and the Environment: Mexico, NAFTA, and Beyond* (Palo Alto, CA: Stanford University Press, 2004).

64. Janischewski et al., *The Export of Second-Hand Goods and the Transfer of Technology*.

65. Maria Cramer, "US Castoffs Resuming Dirty Career: Old Plants, Buses Are Sold to Poorer Nations," *Boston Globe* (August 19, 2007), A1, A22.

66. Janischewski et al., *The Export of Second-Hand Goods and the Transfer of Technology*, iv.

67. Joshua Karliner, "The Environmental Industry," *Ecologist* 24, no. 2 (1994): 60–61.

68. These findings come from a special issue of the *International Journal of Occupational and Environmental Health* 7, no. 4 (2002), and summarized in the Pesticide Action Network Updates Service, "US Pesticide Exports Remain High" (January

11, 2002), available at http://www.panna.org/resources/panups/panup_20020111.dv .html (accessed September 15, 2007), 1–2.

69. Foundation for Advancements in Science and Education, *Exporting Risk: Pesticide Exports from US Ports, 1995–1996* (Los Angeles: Foundation for Advancements in Science and Education, 1998), 1–18; Carl Smith, "US Pesticide Traffic—Exporting Banned and Hazardous Pesticides," *Global Pesticide Campaigner* 3, no. 3 (1993): 1.

70. Kristin S. Schafer, "One More Failed U.S. Environmental Policy," *Foreign Policy in Focus* (September 6, 2006), 1–6.

71. "U.N. Human Rights Investigator Deems U.S. Export of Banned Pesticides 'Immoral,'" *Common Dreams Progressive Newswire* (December 17, 2001), available at http://www.commondreams.org/news2001/1217-03.htm (accessed September 15, 2007), 1–2.

72. Foundation for Advancements in Science and Education, *Exporting Risk*, 1.

73. Flemming Konradsen, "Acute Pesticide Poisoning—A Global Public Health Problem," *Danish Medical Bulletin* 54, no. 1 (February 2007): 58–59.

74. Edward Groth III, Charles M. Benbrook, and Karen Lutz, *Do You Know What You're Eating? An Analysis of US Government Data on Pesticide Residues in Foods*, a report by the Consumers Union (February 1999).

75. Environmental Working Group, *Forbidden Fruit: Illegal Pesticides in the US Food Supply* (Washington, DC: Environmental Working Group, February 1, 1995), 2.

76. Rick Weiss, "Chinese Exports Drawing Scrutiny: Push On to Address Food Safety Issues," *Boston Globe* (May 21, 2007), A2.

77. Diedtra Henderson, "Food Imports Seldom Checked: Odds Favor Rogue Producers over Underfunded, Understaffed FDA, Critics Say," *Boston Globe* (May 1, 2007), C1, C5.

78. Kristin S. Schafer, Susan E. Kegley, and Sharyle Patton, *Nowhere to Hide: Persistent Toxic Chemicals in the U.S. Food Supply* (San Francisco: Pesticide Action Network North America, March 2001), 8, 21–23.

79. Environmental Working Group, *Forbidden Fruit*, 3.

80. Schafer et al., *Nowhere to Hide*, 24.

81. For a discussion of the 2004 CDC report, see Kristin S. Schafer, Margaret Reeves, Skip Spitzer, and Susan E. Kegley, *Chemical Trespass: Pesticides in Our Bodies and Corporate Accountability*, a report by the Pesticide Action Network North America (May 2004).

82. Henderson, "Food Imports Seldom Checked."

83. Mark Magnier, "Food Safety Head's Execution in China Stirs Internet Cheers," *Boston Globe* (July 12, 2007), A15.

84. Robert Gavin, "In Low-Priced Imports, Worrisome Costs," *Boston Globe* (August 3, 2007), A1, A10.

85. Jenn Abelson, "Safety Recalls Linked to China Could Hurt Holiday-Season Sales," *Boston Globe* (August 25, 2007), C1, C4.

86. Gordon Fairclough, "China: Lead Toxins Take a Global Round Trip," *Wall Street Journal* (July 12, 2007), A1.

87. R. Scott Frey, "The Transfer of Core-Based Hazardous Production Processes to the Export Processing Zones of the Periphery," and "The Hazardous Waste Stream in the World System," 109.

88. Segun Gbadegesin, "Multinational Corporations, Developed Nations, and Environmental Racism: Toxic Waste, Oil Exploration, and Eco-Catastrophe," in *Faces of Environmental Racism: Confronting Issues of Global Justice*, 2nd ed., ed. Laura Westra and Bill E. Lawson (Lanham, MD: Rowman & Littlefield, 2001), 187–202, esp. 190.

89. Gbadegesin, "Multinational Corporations, Developed Nations, and Environmental Racism," 190.

90. Lydia Polgreen and Marlise Simons, "Global Sludge Ends in Tragedy for Ivory Coast," *New York Times* (October 2, 2006), available at http://www.nytimes.com/2006/10/10/02/world/africa/02ivory.html (accessed September 12, 2007).

91. Frey, "The Hazardous Waste Stream in the World System," 115.

92. Basel Action Network, "The US Must Ratify the Entire Basel Convention (or Not at All)," Briefing Paper no. 2 (September 2007), 1–2.

93. Mary Tiemann, "Waste Trade and the Basel Convention: Background and Update," Committee for the National Institute for the Environment (December 30, 1998), 1–4.

94. Jennifer Clapp, "Seeping through the Regulatory Cracks," *SAIS Review* 22, no. 1 (Winter–Spring 2002): 146.

95. Clapp, "Seeping through the Regulatory Cracks," 146–49.

96. Jim Puckett, *When Trade Is Toxic: The WTO Threat to Public and Planetary Health*, a report by the Asia Pacific Environmental Exchange and the Basel Action Network (1999), 1–33.

97. "Enforcement Actions Taken against Polluters on U.S.-Mexico Border," *EPA Environmental News* (June 3, 1992).

98. Cyrus Reed, Marisa Jacott, and Alejandro Villamar, *Hazardous Waste Management in the United States–Mexico Border States: More Questions Than Answers*, a report by the Red Mexicana de Accion Frente al Lebre Comercio and the Texas Center for Policy Studies (March 2000), 34.

99. Greenpeace USA, *Pacific Waste Invasion* (Washington, D.C.: Greenpeace, 1992).

100. Anne Leonard, "South Asia: The New Target of International Waste Traders," *Multinational Monitor* 14 (December 1993): 21–24, esp. 22.

101. Madeleine Cobbing and Simon Divecha, "The Myth of Automobile Recycling," *Greenpeace Report* (1993), available at http://www.things.org/~jym/greenpeace/myth-of-battery-recycling.html (accessed September 12, 2007).

102. Blacksmith Institute, *The World's Most Polluted Places*, 13–14.

103. Jim Puckett, Leslie Byster, Sarah Westervel, Richard Gutierrez, Sheila Davis, Asthma Hussain, and Madhumitta Dutta, *Exporting Harm: The High-Tech Trashing of Asia*, a report by the Basel Action Network and the Silicon Valley Toxics Coalition (February 25, 2002).

104. National Safety Council, *Electronic Product Recovery and Recycling Baseline Report* (Washington, DC: National Safety Council, 1999).

105. Puckett et al., *Exporting Harm*, 6–9.

106. Puckett et al., *Exporting Harm*, 9, 22.

107. Bruce Rich, *Mortgaging the Earth: The World Bank, Environmental Impoverishment, and the Crisis of Development* (Boston: Beacon Press, 1994).

108. Vandana Shiva, *Staying Alive: Women, Ecology, and Development* (London: Atlantic Highlands, NJ: Zed Books, 1998).

109. Ramachandra Guha, *Environmentalism: A Global History* (New York: Longman, 2000).

110. Faber, *Environment under Fire*, 45–82.

111. Cornell University Professor David Pimentel and a research team examined more than 120 published papers on malnutrition and environmental degradation. Their findings will be presented in the December 2008 issue of *Human Ecology*.

112. Joan Martinez-Alier, *The Environmentalism of the Poor: The Study of Ecological Conflicts and Valuation* (Northampton, MA: Edward Elgar, 2002).

113. John Bellamy Foster and Robert W. McChesney, eds., *Pox Americana: Exposing the American Empire* (New York: Monthly Review Press, 2004).

114. Alf Hornborg, "Towards an Ecological Theory of Unequal Exchange: Articulating World System Theory and Ecological Economics," *Ecological Economics* 25 (1998): 127–36.

115. Nicky Chambers, Craig Simmons, and Mathis Wackernagel, *Sharing Nature's Interests: Ecological Footprints as an Indicator of Sustainability* (London: Earthscan, 2000), 31.

116. Jason Venetoulis and John Talberth, *Ecological Footprint of Nations: 2005 Update* (Oakland, CA: Redefining Progress, 2005), 7–8.

117. Paul H. Templet, "Externalities, Subsidies and the Ecological Footprint: An Empirical Analysis," *Ecological Economics* 32 (2000): 381–83.

118. Venetoulis and Talberth, *Ecological Footprint of Nations*, 8.

119. Jason Venetoulis, Dahlia Chazan, and Christoper Gaudet, *Ecological Footprint of Nations 2004* (Oakland, CA: Redefining Progress, March 2004), p.7.

120. Craig R. Humphrey, Tammy L. Lewis, and Frederick H. Buttel, *Environment, Energy, and Society: A New Synthesis* (Belmont, CA: Wadsworth, 2002), 100.

121. Andrew K. Jorgenson, "Consumption and Environmental Degradation: A Cross-National Analysis of the Ecological Footprint," *Social Problems* 50, no. 3 (2003): 387.

122. Nicholas Stern, *Stern Review: The Economics of Climate Change* (Cambridge: Cambridge University Press, 2006).

123. Red Cross and Red Crescent Societies, *World Disasters Report: Focus on Recovery* (Geneva: International Federation of Red Cross and Red Crescent Societies, 2001).

124. Andersson and Lindroth, "Ecologically Unsustainable Trade," 113–22.

125. Jorgenson, "Consumption and Environmental Degradation," 377.

126. Andersson and Lindroth, "Ecologically Unsustainable Trade," 116.

127. Michael Klare, "The New Geopolitics," in Foster and McChesney, *Pox Americana*, 51–56.

128. Paul Collier and Anke Hoeffler, "Greed and Grievance in Civil War," *Oxford Economic Papers* (October 2004), cited in William K. Tabb, "Resource Wars," *Monthly Review* 58, no. 8 (January 2007): 32–42.

129. Adeola, "Cross-National Environmental Justice and Human Rights Issues," 703.

130. Mark Ritchie, "Trading Away the Environment: Free-Trade Agreements and Environmental Degradation," in *Toxic Struggles: The Theory and Practice of Environmental Justice*, ed. Richard Hofrichter (Philadelphia: New Society Publishers, 1993), 209–18.

131. Clapp, "Seeping through the Regulatory Cracks," 141–55.

132. Talli Nauman, "Mexico's Right-to-Know Movement," *Citizen Action in the Americas* (February 2003), cited in Frey, "The Transfer of Core-Based Hazardous Production Processes," 338–41.

133. Karliner and Bruno, *Earthsummit.biz*, 2002.

134. Martin Khor Kok Peng, "Economics and Environmental Justice: Rethinking North-South Relations," in Hofrichter, *Toxic Struggles*, 219–25.

135. International Forum on Globalization, *Alternatives to Economic Globalization: A Better World Is Possible* (San Francisco: Berrett-Koehler Publishers, 2002).

136. John Bellamy Foster, "Monopoly Capital and the New Globalization," *Monthly Review* 53, no. 8 (January 2002): 1–16.

137. James O'Connor, *Natural Causes: Essays in Ecological Marxism* (New York: Guilford Press, 1998); Istvan Meszaros, "Sustainable Development and Equality," *Monthly Review* 53, no. 7 (December 2001): 10–19.

Chapter Five

Transforming Green Politics: Challenges Confronting the Environmental Justice Movement

This struggle emerging from the environmental experience of oppressed people brings forth a new consciousness . . . to make a true connection between humanity and nature. This struggle to resolve environmental problems may force the nation to alter its priorities; it may force the nation to address issues of environmental justice and, by doing so, it may ultimately result in a cleaner and healthier environment for all of us.

—Bunyan Bryant[1]

A DEEPER SHADE OF GREEN POLITICS

In the United States, communities of color and lower-income neighborhoods are historically the hardest hit by pollution from industrial factories and incinerators, the illegal dumping of chemical wastes on vacant lots, lead contamination in building materials, a lack of parklands and other environmental amenities, and decrepit housing, schools, and public transportation. Yet these neighborhoods and the organizations that represent them typically possess few resources to confront these threats. These injustices are not so much the failing of technology or the law as they are the product of the political marginalization of people of color and working-class families. Moreover, with the corporate assault on the liberal regime of environmental regulation and environmental justice (EJ) policy, racial and class-based disparities in the exposure to ecological hazards are intensifying. Unfortunately, despite some initiatives of the Sierra Club, Friends of the Earth/Environmental Policy Institute, the Natural Resources Defense Council, and the Wilderness Society, the mainstream environmental movement largely ignores the interconnections among poverty, racism, social injustice, and environmental policy.

221

In reaction to the economic and ecological injustices accentuated by the rise of neoliberalism and corporate-led globalization as well as the neglect of the mainstream environmental movement, a deeper shade of green politics is evolving in the United States. In Latino and Asian-Pacific neighborhoods in the inner cities, small African American townships, depressed Native American reservations, Chicano farming communities, and white working-class districts all across the country, peoples traditionally relegated to the periphery of the ecology movement are challenging the wholesale degradation of their land, water, air, and community health by corporate polluters and indifferent governmental agencies and nongovernmental organizations. At the forefront of this new wave of grassroots activism are hundreds of community-based EJ organizations working to reverse the disproportionate social and ecological hardships borne by people of color and poor working-class families.

The growth of community-based organizations, strategic regional networks, and constituency-based national networks committed to the principles of economic and environmental justice are essential to the efforts of people of color and lower-income communities to organize and mobilize the resources needed to eradicate these environmental and public health threats. The continued growth and prosperity of these EJ organizations and networks is essential to constructing a more inclusive, democratic, and proactive environmental politics in the United States. This chapter explores the major challenges confronting EJ activists as they try to forge a global movement. These challenges include the formation of a master "frame" that allows citizens to identify with the goals of the movement, the adoption of suitable organizational structures that will allow the movement to grow and prosper, and the utilization of appropriate political strategies and tactics necessary to bring about real social change.

THE EVOLUTION OF THE ENVIRONMENTAL
JUSTICE MOVEMENT IN THE UNITED STATES

There have been three stages in the evolution of the U.S. EJ movement. The first stage began in the fall of 1982, when the state of North Carolina attempted to dump over 6,000 truckloads of polychlorinated biphenyls (PCBs) in the mostly African American and rural Warren County. More than 500 people were jailed for protesting the siting of the landfill, marking the first time African Americans had mobilized from around the country to defend a local group opposing what they defined as environmental racism. Inspired by this struggle, numerous locally based EJ organizations were created all over the country during the 1980s, although most remained isolated or loosely connected to one another.

The second stage in the movement's evolution began with the 1991 First National People of Color Environmental Leadership Summit, the single most important event in the movement's history. In addition to adopting the Principles of Environmental Justice, the summit led to a recognition of the need to build stronger institutional linkages between these local and sometimes isolated community-based groups.[2] As a result, a number of regionally based networks, as well as national constituency-based and issue-based networks for environmental justice, were created and/or consolidated during the 1990s. Regional networks included the Southern Organizing Committee for Economic and Social Justice (SOC), the Southwest Network for Economic and Environmental Justice (SNEEJ), and the Northeast Environmental Justice Network. The Asian Pacific Environmental Network (APEN), the Indigenous Environmental Network (IEN), and the Farmworker Network for Economic and Environmental Justice (FWNEEJ) constituted the principal national constituency-based networks, as did the African American Environmental Justice Action Network, the People of Color Disenfranchised Communities Environmental Health Network, and the National Black Environmental Justice Network.

In the new millennium, the movement is now entering a third stage of development. As witnessed by the evolution of a number of new organizational entities, such as the Environmental Justice Fund, the National Environmental Justice Advisory Council (NEJAC), and the National People of Color Environmental Leadership Summit in 2002, and the consolidation of the regional and national constituency-based networks, attempts are now being made to create a transnational EJ movement that is greater than the sum of its parts. However, as we shall see, these efforts are proving difficult. The movement remains very young and is experiencing severe growing pains. Nevertheless, some progress has been made in creating new infrastructures for building intergroup collaboration and coordinated programmatic initiatives that can have a broader policy impact at the state, national, and international levels. The EJ movement led by people of color might have only been born with the local Warren County fight in 1982, but it is beginning to come of age.[3]

The diversity of people participating in these local, regional, and national organizations is matched by the diversity of political paths and approaches taken to achieving environmental justice. For the most part, activists in the EJ movement represent a convergence of seven formerly independent social movements, including (1) the *civil rights movement*, focused on issues of *environmental racism* and the disproportionate impacts of pollution in communities of color, the racial biases in government regulatory practices, and the glaring absence of affirmative action and sensitivity to racial issues in the established environmental advocacy organizations; (2) the *occupational health and safety movement*, working for the labor rights of nonunion immigrants and undocumented workers; (3) the *indigenous lands movement*, emerging out of the struggles by Native Americans, Chicanos, African Americans, and other marginalized indigenous communities to retain and protect their traditional lands; (4) the *environmental health movement*, which developed largely out of the mainstream environmental movement in general and the antitoxics movement in particular; (5) *community-based movements for social and economic justice* that have expanded their political horizons to incorporate issues such as lead poisoning, abandoned toxic waste dumps, the lack of parks and green spaces, poor air quality, and other issues of environmental justice into their agenda for community empowerment; (6) the *human rights, peace, and solidarity movements*, particularly those campaigns that first emerged in the 1980s around apartheid in South Africa and U.S. intervention in Nicaragua and Central America; and (7) *the immigrant rights movements* that expand the basic struggle for citizenship to include basic rights of citizenship—including the right to clean air, and water.

Fighting Environmental Racism: The Civil Rights Movement and EJ

The U.S. EJ movement is heavily grounded in the civil rights movement (as well as African American churches that are so central to the struggle for civil rights) and heavily focused on racial biases and discrimination with respect to environmental policy. Targeting issues of environmental racism, this component of the EJ movement is committed to battling the disproportionate impacts of pollution in communities of color, the racial biases in government regulatory practices, and the glaring absence of affirmative action and sensitivity to racial issues in the established environmental advocacy organizations.[4] According to a landmark 1987 report by the United Church of Christ's Commission on Racial Justice, three out of five African Americans and Latinos nationwide live in communities that have illegal or abandoned toxic dumps.[5] Unequal exposure to environmental hazards is thus experienced by people of color in terms of where they "work, live, and play."[6]

In 1988, a Southern Environmental Assembly was held in coordination with the Super Tuesday primary elections. Dr. Benjamin Chavis Jr. of the National Association for the Advancement of Colored People was joined by Joseph Lowery of the Southern Christian Leadership Conference, among other civil rights leaders, in a series of eighty workshops over two days that joined community-based and national environmental groups to link environmental concerns with social justice ones. In 1992, the National Urban League's *State of Black America* included—for the first time in the seventeen years the report has been published—a chapter on environmental threats to African Americans.

The growing linkages among civil rights, racial justice, and environmental protection have also inspired investigations into the class, gender, and ethnic dimensions of disproportionate exposure to environmental hazards.[7]

The civil rights orientation has led to major institutional innovations in environmental decision making. On February 11, 1994, then President Clinton issued Executive Order 12898, titled "Federal Action to Address Environmental Justice in Minority Populations and Low-Income Populations," which directs all federal agencies with a public health or environmental mission to make environmental justice an integral part of their policies and activities. The order reinforces the Civil Rights Act of 1964, prohibiting discriminatory practices in programs receiving federal support. Section 5.5 of the order specifically outlines processes for public participation and access to information. In his *Memorandum on Environmental Justice* that accompanied the order, President Clinton declared that the order was intended to, among other things, "*provide minority communities and low-income communities access to public information on, and an opportunity for public participation in, matters relating to human health or the environment.*"

To ensure that the Environmental Protection Agency (EPA) would receive significant input from affected stakeholders, NEJAC was established prior to the executive order in 1993. NEJAC is a federal advisory committee that provides independent advice to the EPA and was chartered to meet until September 2001. Members are appointed by the EPA and represent community-based groups, academic and educational institutions, state and local governments, tribal governments, nongovernmental organizations, business and industry, and environmental organizations. These representatives help NEJAC serve as a forum for integrating environmental justice with other EPA priorities and initiatives. A number of NEJAC subcommittees related to waste and facility siting, enforcement, health and research, public participation and accountability, indigenous peoples, and international issues have contributed to significant changes in EPA practices. These accomplishments include the creation of research projects and health programs that identify high-risk communities, reviews of the agency's enforcement and compliance work plan, conducting public dialogue meetings in five major cities concerning possible solutions to urban problems resulting from the loss of economic opportunities caused by pollution and the relocation of businesses, and the development of a public forum protocol for interagency meetings.

The EPA's Office of Environmental Justice and regional offices throughout the country have established relations with local EJ organizations and begun projects. As a result, in a few short years, the movement has overcome exclusionary practices to have meaningful impacts on policy development and enforcement. For instance, one victory of the EPA Accountability Campaign helped force Chevron to abate emissions in the primarily African American/Laotian community of Richmond, California, resulting in a settlement for the community and $5 million for community programs and worker trainings. NEJAC also worked closely with the EPA, the Environmental Counsel of the States, and other groups to very recently produce the EPA document "Public Involvement in Environmental Permits: A Reference Guide," which can be used by all stakeholders to improve the quality of citizen participation in the agency's permitting decisions.

People Organized in Defense of Earth and her Resources (PODER), for instance, formed in East Austin, Texas, in 1991 to address hazards facing a largely Latino and African American community. Dedicated to facilitating broader community participation in corporate and governmental decision making on issues of environmental quality and economic development, PODER has worked to successfully revise the city's enterprise zone/tax abatement ordinance, relocate a gasoline storage tank facility, close a garbage truck facility, relocate the Robert Mueller Municipal Airport and a BFI recycling plant, close the Holy Street Power Plant, and develop comprehensive alternatives to discriminatory land use and economic development policies. Most recently, PODER was successful in having the East Austin Overlay amended to ensure greater public participation by the community in commercial, industrial, and city land use planning, allowing residents to further eliminate hazardous sites in their neighborhoods. Similarly, SOC was formed in the mid-1970s from roots in the civil rights and peace movements. SOC played a critical role in building new multiracial/cultural and multistate organizing efforts and alliances for environmental justice in the South. For instance, SOC stimulated a new level of networking activity by convening the Southern Community/Labor Conference for Environmental Justice in New Orleans in December 1992, which was attended by over 2,000 people (including 500 youth). SOC has continued to work on the conference mandate for a campaign to develop state networks that will feed into a regional structure based on collective and democratic decision making.

Dying for a Living: The Occupational Health Movement and EJ

The EJ movement also emerges out of the longtime struggles for labor rights and better occupational health and safety conditions for vulnerable workers. Some 16,000 workers are injured on the job *every day*, of which about seventeen will die. Another 135 workers die *every day* from diseases caused by longer-term exposure to toxins in the workplace.[8] These types of occupational hazards are even more profound for workers lacking the minimal protections afforded by unions or formal rights of citizenship, such as immigrant farmworkers. Over 313,000 of the 2 million farmworkers in the United States—

90 percent of whom are people of color and undocumented immigrants—suffer from pesticide poisoning each year.[9]

The plight of such vulnerable workers is spurring new coalitions between farmworker associations such as the United Farm Workers, immigrant rights groups, consumer and environmental organizations, labor, and the EJ movement. Recent examples include legislative right-to-know campaigns, farmworkers' struggles against pesticide abuses impacting workers in the field and nearby communities, and campaigns against the reproductive dangers of high-tech industry. At the national level, the constituency-based FWNEEJ has taken the lead in linking labor rights issues with workplace and community hazards. Created in 1993 by farmworker membership organizations from the United States and the Caribbean, FWNEEJ's primary goals are to enlarge resources for directing organizing around pesticide hazards to farmworker families and their communities, promote exchange and mutual support among farmworker organizations on health and environmental issues, support the sustainability of agriculture, ensure higher standards of safety and quality in agricultural products for consumers, and forge a common voice for farmworkers in the EJ movement and related policy debates over regulation, sustainable agriculture, and occupational health and safety.

There have been a number of significant accomplishments. For instance, one FNEEJ membership organization—the Farmworker Association of Florida—has gained significant improvements in wages and working conditions for workers in over forty central Florida companies. It has also secured passage of Florida's right-to-know law to protect farmworkers; filed successful complaints for violations and advocated for better government enforcement of pesticides, field sanitation, and other health and safety issues; conducted a study on the effects of pesticides on farmworkers; and continues to address injustices suffered by farmworkers in the workplace and community. Likewise, the Farm Labor Organizing Committee has successfully worked to raise wages in the pickle industry by 100 percent between 1986 and 1996, established protections for members from pesticide exposure beyond EPA minimum standards, eliminated the "independent contractor system," and created the first workable mechanism midwestern farmworkers have ever had to enforce pay, safety, working and housing regulations—a union contract—which is now overseen by the Dunlop Commission (an independent, private lab board chaired by former Labor Secretary John Dunlop).

Protecting Cultural and Biological Diversity: The Native Lands Rights Movement

The EJ movement also emerges out of struggles by Native Americans, Chicanos, African Americans, and other marginalized indigenous communities to retain and protect their traditional lands. A key component of the polluter-industrial complex offensive against environmentalism involves efforts to contain and roll back policies establishing national parks as well as protections for wilderness, forests, wild rivers, wetlands, and endangered species. These include efforts to exploit the majestic old-growth forests in Alaska's Tongass National Forest and the ancient redwoods in the Pacific Northwest, habitat of the endangered spotted owl; the rich deposits of low-sulfur coal that lie underneath the Black Mesa homelands of the Hopi and Navajo Indians in the Four Corners region of the American Southwest; and the vast oil and natural gas reserves that lay in the Arctic National Wildlife Refuge in Alaska and to open up more wetlands and fragile ecosystems to agricultural, commercial, and residential developers.

Much of the land richest in natural resource wealth targeted for acquisition by business interests is home to indigenous communities established long ago by Spanish and Mexican land grants in the eighteenth to nineteenth centuries or during Reconstruction following the Civil War or by treaty with the U.S. government. The Native American land base alone amounts to 100 million acres and is equivalent in size to all "wilderness lands" in the national wilderness preservation system. The Navajo Reservation alone is five times the size of Connecticut and twice the size of Maryland. Two-thirds of the uranium and one-third of all low-sulfur coal reserves lie on Native lands. Some 50 billion board feet of timber standing on reservation forests is currently threatened by logging interests and hydroelectric dam projects. In an attempt to gain control over and exploit the low-cost resources on these lands, a nationwide corporate attack on Native Americans has been initiated, including calls for the termination of treaty rights.[10] In addition, there have been more than a hundred separate proposals to dump toxic waste in Native communities over the past decade. Many communities are still demanding cleanup of old dump and Superfund sites. For more than a decade, Native Americans have worked with other EJ groups to protest plans by the nuclear power industry to bury highly radioactive waste in Ward Valley in California's East Mojave Desert, approximately twenty miles from the Colorado River, on sacred Indian lands.[11] Decades of uranium mining has resulted in catastrophic death and disablement from environmentally related disease in dozens of Native communities. Since the 1950s, uranium tailings and mining wastes have so contaminated the environment, for instance, that elevated rates of cancer, birth defects, and other health problems are common among the Navajo.[12]

To tackle the social and ecological crises confronting indigenous communities, the EJ movement is linking concerns for natural resource protection and sustainability with issues of land and sovereignty rights, cultural survival, racial and social justice, alternative economic development, and religious freedom. At the forefront of these struggles is the national constituency-based IEN. Formed in 1992, IEN is a resource network committed to building mutual support strategies by providing technical and organizational assistance to over 600 Native American organizations and activists across North America. Working primarily on reservation-based environmental issues, including forestry, nuclear weapons and waste, mining, toxic dumping, water quality, and water rights, IEN is now moving to create regional intertribal networks that build the capacity of local organizations as well as the national structure. Its National Council and annual conference are in themselves important centers for collaboration, advocacy, and consensus building among activists representing indigenous peoples from all over the world.

Challenging Poisonous Profit Making: The Environmental Health Movement

The environmental health movement in general and community-based antitoxics organizations in particular constitute another critical foundation from which the EJ movement has emerged.[13] In thousands of communities across the United States, billions of gallons of highly toxic chemicals including mercury, dioxin, PCBs, arsenic, lead, and heavy metals such as chromium have been dumped in the midst of unsuspecting neighborhoods. These sites poison the land, contaminate drinking water, and potentially cause cancer, birth defects, nerve and liver damage, and other health effects. Coupled with the assault on the regulatory capacities of the state, American business is now externalizing more costs and spending less on prevention of health and safety problems inside and outside the factory as well as on reducing pollution and the depletion of natural resources.

Ever since the environmental decade of the 1970s, thousands of local citizen organizations have been created to fight for the cleanup of toxic waste dumps, the regulation of pollutants from industrial facilities, the enforcement and improvement of federal and state environmental standards, and many other issues. A number of prominent activists of color emerged from these white-led antitoxics and environmental health organizations (such as the now-defunct National Toxics Campaign) to take up leadership roles in the EJ community. Today, there are a great variety of multiracial local and national organizations organizing people of color and/or lower-income communities to protect their health and environment. Now emerging from a more diverse array of settings, including poor working-class communities, with notably high numbers of women in key activist and leadership positions, these local organizations are increasingly making the links between issues of corporate power, governmental neglect, and citizen disenfranchisement. As a result, many of these organizations are working in close collaboration with or evolving into EJ organizations.

At the national level, organizations such as the Center for Health, Environment and Justice (CHEJ; formerly the Citizen's Clearinghouse on Hazardous Waste) have taken a lead role in galvanizing the antitoxics movement to address the issue of political-economic power, with most of their efforts concentrated in white working- and middle-class communities. Founded by Lois Gibbs following the 1978–1980 struggle at Love Canal, New York, where 900 lower-income families fought for and won relocation after they discovered that their neighborhood was built next to a massive toxic waste dump, CHEJ has since worked with a network of over 8,000 local grassroots environmental groups on issues ranging from hazardous waste dumps, incinerators, pollution from chemical plants, radioactive waste, and recycling. CHEJ trains and assists local people to fight for justice, become empowered to protect their communities from environmental threats, and build strong, locally controlled organizations. CHEJ connects these strong groups with each other to build a movement from the bottom up so that grassroots groups can collectively change the balance of power. This is accomplished by providing scientific and technical assistance, organizing and leadership training, and information services. CHEJ has also produced over 100 guidebooks and information packages as well as the quarterly magazine *Everyone's Backyard*, which includes a state-by-state chronicle of victories won by grassroots EJ organizations.

Communities for a Better Environment (CBE) was formerly a white-led organization named Citizens for a Better Environment working on issues of toxics and environmental health in Los Angeles. Since the name change in 1996, CBE has become a statewide voice for environmental justice and health. Today, people of color comprise 60 percent of the staff, 80 percent of management, and 70 percent of the board of directors (including members directly from organized communities). Through projects such as LA CAUSA (Los Angeles Comunidades Asambleadas Unidas para un Sostenible Ambiente), CBE is developing leadership and membership among grassroots activists throughout California, researching cumulative exposures to environmental hazards, educating health care providers on health risks, developing critiques of market incentive programs that may adversely affect communities of color, and developing pollution prevention projects. Successes include the closing and cleanup of the La Montana recycling plant, the relocation of two others (including the installation of dust containment processes), the EPA-enforced closing of the Maywood incinerator, and an investigation by the California Department of Toxic Substance Control that resulted in the closing of a hexavalent chrome–plating operation adjacent to the Suva Elementary School in Bell Gardens (the school was also decontaminated).

The Export of Ecological Hazards to the South: Human Rights and the Solidarity Movement

The human rights and solidarity movements, including the South African antiapartheid and anti-intervention in Central America struggles in the 1980s, among others, provide an important foundation for the emergence of the contemporary EJ movement. Solidarity movements in support of popular-based environmental organizations in the Third World are assuming an ever-greater importance in the era of corporate-led globalization. The growing ability of multinational corporations and transnational financial institutions to dismantle unions, evade environmental safeguards, and weaken worker/community health and safety regulations in the United States is being achieved by crossing national boundaries into politically repressive and economically oppressive countries, such as in Mexico, Indonesia, Burma, Nigeria, and Central America generally.[14] As a result, various nationalities and governments are increasingly pitted against one another as never before in a bid to attract capital investment, leading to one successful assault after another on labor and environmental regulations seen as damaging to profits. Aided by recent "free-trade" initiatives such as the North American Free Trade Agreement (NAFTA) and enforced by bodies such as the World Trade Organization (WTO), corporate-led globalization is leading to the export of more profitable yet more dangerous production processes and consumer goods as well as waste disposal methods to developing countries where environmental standards are lax, unions weak, and worker health and safety issues ignored.[15]

The efforts of entities such as SNEEJ have increased attention on the U.S.-Mexico border, where there are more than 2,000 factories, or maquiladoras, many of them relocated U.S.-based multinational corporations. One study of the border town of Mexicali indicated that stiff environmental regulations in the United States and weaker ones in Mexico were either the main factor or a factor of importance in their decision to leave the United States.[16] To address the export of environmental injustices, SNEEJ was established in 1990 as a regional, binational network by representatives of eighty grassroots organizations based throughout the U.S. Southwest, California, and northern Mexico. One of the network's primary points of focus is the Border Justice Campaign, which is developing a movement to hold industrial and government agencies accountable for environmental and social problems along the U.S.–Mexico border. Others include the Worker Justice Campaign as well as efforts on EPA accountability, high-tech industry, sustainable communities and youth leadership, support for farmworker communities against pesticide abuses, and environmental support work on Native land issues. Each of these initiatives assists community-based organizations

on both sides of the border to build collective understandings of and responses to the problems resulting from globalization. For instance, through
the EPA Accountability Campaign in 1994, SNEEJ forced the EPA to sub-
poena the records of over ninety-five U.S. corporations operating in Mexico
for their contamination of the New River.

Forging links with Third World popular movements combating such abuses
is yet another profound challenge confronting the U.S. EJ movement. Given
the repression faced by environmental activists in much of Mexico and the
developing world, however, perhaps the most fundamental prerequisite in the
quest for sustainable development is the struggle for human rights. Initially
led by organizations such as the Environmental Project on Central America
and Third World Network in the 1980s, a host of EJ organizations in the
United States and abroad are now focusing on the interconnections between
corporate-led globalization and growing problems of poverty, human rights
violations, environmental degradation, and the lack of democracy for poor
Third World peoples. For instance, the Sierra Club and Amnesty International
have combined to support the work of EarthRights International and other organizations around human rights issues. Unless popular movements in the
United States and the developing world can unify into a larger international
movement for social and environmental justice, living standards and environmental quality throughout the world will continue to deteriorate. The EJ
movement is proving crucial to these organizing efforts for "fair trade" and
sustainable development, promoting strategies that emphasize grassroots mobilization, international solidarity with popular movements in the developing
countries, and cross-movement alliance building.

Organizing for Social Change and Economic Reform:
The Community Empowerment Movement

A significant element of EJ activism has also evolved out of movements for social and economic justice, particularly in poorer communities of color. Emphasizing issues of affordable and safe housing, crime and police conduct (including racial profiling and police brutality), unemployment and underemployment,
a living wage, accessible public transportation, city services, redlining and discriminatory lending practices by banks, affordable day care, deteriorating
schools and inferior educational systems, job training and welfare reform, and
a host of other issues, many of these organizations have expanded their political horizons to incorporate problems related to lead poisoning, abandoned toxic
waste dumps, the lack of parks and green spaces, poor air quality, and other
manifestations of environmental injustice into their agenda for community empowerment. Although many organizations are not strictly self-defined as "envi-

ronmental," they may devote considerable attention to environmental issues in their own communities. In fact, in recent years some of the most impressive environmental victories at the local level have been achieved by economic justice organizations oriented around multiple issues.

The Southwest Organizing Project (SWOP) is an example of a multiracial, multi-issue, statewide grassroots membership organization in New Mexico that addresses environmental contamination as part of a broad agenda for social, racial, and economic justice. A key anchor group in SNEEJ, SWOP focuses on increased citizen participation and building leadership skills so that residents can participate in decision making on issues affecting their lives, including racial and gender equality, environmental justice, and community and worker protection. As seen in the Community Environmental Program and other organizing efforts, SWOP's priority is to ensure greater corporate accountability on environmental and labor issues, particularly as they relate to regional economic development. SWOP is also a leader in the EJ movement among grassroots groups that engage in cross-border organizing and exchanges.

Another example of this type of community-based organization is Direct Action for Rights and Equality (DARE). DARE was established in 1986 to bring together low-income families in communities of color within Rhode Island to work for social, economic, and environmental justice. A multi-issue, multiracial, dues-paying membership-based organization made up of 900 low-income families, members are organized into block clubs (similar to chapters), identify issues of common concern at regular organizational meetings, and develop a strategy to address the problem. Since its establishment, DARE has successfully campaigned for the cleanup of over 100 polluted vacant lots and improved neighborhood playgrounds and parks throughout Providence. One of DARE's most significant victories was recently achieved when Rhode Island became the first state in the nation to guarantee health care coverage for day care providers. Through this agreement with DARE, Rhode Island has set a new standard for other states to follow and implement. DARE is beginning work on campaigns to win jobs and career training from local companies for young people and implementing further strategies to reduce pollution in low-income neighborhoods.

Also included in this corner of EJ activism are the contributions of social justice–oriented religious groups and alliances, particularly those located in disenfranchised communities of color. For instance, the Los Angeles Metropolitan Churches is a network of forty African American congregations in Los Angeles County. The Environmental Justice Project organizes these churches to facilitate environmental cleanup and other positive changes in South Central Los Angeles. In Minnesota, the St. Paul Ecumenical Alliance of Congregations (SPEAC) began faith-based organizing in 1990 through a wide variety of civic and religious-based institutions within St. Paul, Minnesota's lowest-income census tracts. Today, SPEAC's nineteen congregations of color and low income have strategically expanded their alliances at the neighborhood, metropolitan, and regional levels to impact St. Paul's core city issues of reclaiming metro-polluted land for living wage job creation as well as related issues of regional tax base sharing and reinvestment, public finance reform, affordable home ownership, and fair welfare reform. Working in close collaboration with aging inner-ring suburban municipalities, SPEAC and the Interfaith Action of Minneapolis recently won a total of $68 million in state funds that is being utilized to turn polluted dirt into pay dirt by redirecting funds from outer-ring suburban development on agricultural land ("greenfields") into the reclamation of abandoned, polluted industrial land in the inner cities ("brownfields"). This funding, when fully spent and matched by private investment over the next six years, will yield about 2,000 permanent, good-wage industrial jobs that will be easily accessible to people who need them most rather than promoting urban sprawl. This campaign has become a model for metropolitan stability throughout the country.

Live Free or Die: The Immigration Rights Movement and EJ

Finally, the EJ movement has substantial roots in immigration rights activism. Over the past decade, anti-immigration sentiments have grown in conservative policy circles. Some mainstream environmental organizations also support anti-immigration policies. Immigration has also proved to be one of the most divisive issues of the Sierra Club's history when advocates of tighter restrictions on immigration attempted a "hostile takeover" of the board of directors in 2004. This effort followed a vote six years earlier by members on whether to officially favor immigration limits. Approval of the measure would have translated into Sierra Club policy in support of a reduction in immigration from 900,000 a year to around 200,000. However, EJ and other progressive activists mobilized an educational campaign that helped defeat the initiative in April 1998.[17]

Today, many groups in the EJ movement, such as SWOP, the Environmental Health Coalition (EHC), the Political Ecology Group, and APEN, among others, work on the interconnections between environmental justice and immigrant rights. APEN was formed in 1993 to encourage grassroots organizing and leadership development in Asian American and Pacific Islander communities around such problems as lead poisoning, industrial pollution, workplace safety, and community development. Working primarily in the Bay Area of California, APEN has played a leading role in interjecting Asian Pacific perspectives on debates within the environmental movement relating to immigration rights and community empowerment, completed community-driven surveys on the consumption of contaminated seafood, organized healthy community garden projects, and organized the first ever West Contra County Environmental Health Festival, in which over 500 community members and forty organizations participated. APEN also serves as a clearing-house and resource for a variety of diverse Asian Pacific groups working on multi-issue projects in their own communities. Most recently, the Laotian Organizing Project mobilized hundreds of high school students in Richmond, California, to win approval for a pilot teacher-advisory program to strengthen counseling services and improve the school-based environment, while in Contra Costa County, APEN coorganized a campaign to secure resources for the implementation of a multilingual emergency warning system in case of a chemical accident at nearby industrial plants.

In summary, although the community-based organizations and regional/national networks for environmental justice often bear the distinctive political imprints of the original movements from which they emerged, *all are united in the larger struggle* to link grassroots activism and participatory democracy to problem solving around the issues of environmental abuse, racial oppression, poverty and social inequality, and political disempowerment.[18] In this respect, there is occurring a steady and undeniable sublation of these various political heritages into a larger EJ body politic whereby these differing elements are achieving a deeper appreciation and understanding of the other and merging it with their own political consciousness and movement-building strategies. The movement is becoming greater than the sum of its parts. Nevertheless, as was evident at the Second National People of Color Environmental Leadership Summit, significant divisions and political differences exist between these different wings, leading some to refer to these as different *movements* for environmental justice.[19]

FRAMING "ENVIRONMENTAL JUSTICE" AND BUILDING AN IDENTITY FOR THE MOVEMENT

The Postmaterialist Perspective

Many theoretical critiques of environmental activism in the United States, Europe, and throughout the rest of the world utilize a "postmaterialist" perspective. This view holds that the transformation from "Fordist" to "post-Fordist" modes of accumulation in the advanced capitalist states under the weight of globalization is resulting in a decline in traditional trade-union occupations devoted to mass production in favor of more knowledge-based, service-oriented economies oriented to the salariat. This growing "new middle class" of professionals and white- and pink-collar workers have grown up politically in the long postwar period of peace and economic prosperity. Their experiences of increased material well-being have created a libertarian shift in society from material to postmaterial values, with an emphasis on value participation, self-actualization, and aesthetic needs more than material wealth and its distribution.[20] As a result, postmaterialism is linked to a decline in economic issues and class-based politics and solidarity associated with the labor movement and to the increased salience of individual lifestyles and "subjective" political issues of the professional classes, central among which is political ecology and environmental quality.[21] Indeed, many ecological economists argue that the demand for environmental amenities and other "quality of life" improvements only increases with income and that, implicitly, the poor are "too poor to be green."[22]

There are significant problems with this formulation. First, environmentalism in the advanced capitalist countries is diverse, ranging from middle-class advocates concerned with the "effluents of affluence" to more "materialist" varieties focused on severe health threats to working-class and subaltern populations.[23] Moreover, in the United States, there is significant evidence that class-based and subaltern forms of environmental politics are becoming *more* relevant, not less so. To bolster profits and competitiveness, capital typically exploits nature in ways that are not only most cost efficient but also the most politically expedient. The path of least resistance compels American capital (as in most countries) to displace ecological externalities onto the least politically powerful segments of the popular classes—oppressed peoples of color, poor working-class communities, industrial blue-collar workers, farmers and farmworkers, and undocumented immigrants.[24] With its focus on the interrelationships between racism, poverty and economic inequality, and ecological hardships confronting marginalized peoples, the U.S. EJ movement clearly defies characterization as a postmaterialist form of environmentalism.

Likewise, when analyzing the character of environmental activism in the global South, the flaws of the postmaterialist perspective are further pronounced. In developing countries, where the ecological space of the popular classes is being confiscated for the benefit of domestic elites and international capital, a "materialist" *environmentalism of and for the poor* is becoming dominant.[25] As a result, there is a strong belief in environmental protection among the popular classes in poor countries of the global South.[26] These *liberation ecology movements* of the poor are organized primarily as a defense of livelihood.[27] As such, they are firmly grounded in "spiritual" *and* "material" conflicts, with the claims of economic and environmental justice—that is, the rights of poor communities to natural resources—being the central component of the movement discourse.[28] In contrast to the reformist character of the mainstream-oriented *environmentalism of affluence* and *enhanced quality of life* of the northern middle classes, the *environmentalism of survival* and *livelihood* of the southern poor is much more radical in orientation, confronting structures of political-economic power that lie at the root of the ecological crisis. Examples include the struggles by poor peasants on behalf of *revolutionary ecology* in Nicaragua,[29] villages contesting the massive hydroelectric projects in Turkey, the Chipko movement and the fights led by rural women against the Narmada dam in India,[30] efforts by the late Chico Mendes and the *seringueiros* in the rainforests of Brazil, the Green Belt movement in Kenya, confrontations led by indigenous peoples with logging and mining companies in Latin America and Asia, and other popular-led movements for environmental justice in South Africa and throughout the world.[31]

Identity Politics and EJ

In these movements, how "environmental injustice" comes to be defined and framed in the United States versus the global South depends on a complex set of interactions and interpretations between various "claims makers" who construct their own interpretations of the problem using the frames made available to them. As stated by the scholars Mark Shibley and Annette Prosterman, "Whether an environmental issue becomes a social problem"—the perception that lead poisoning or illegal toxic dumping is pervasive and harmful rather than a minimal threat, for example—"is related to how social events are framed."[32] Frames, according to Erving Goffman, are schemata of interpretation that allow people to locate, perceive, identify, and label events taking place around them.[33] Collective behavior occurs only after existing environmental "strains" are identified and defined as unjust. Environmental injustices may exist in an objective reality, but until they are recognized as such, collective action and social movement formation to address the causes and/or symptoms of the problem are not possible.[34] But how the environmental "injustice" is framed also determines the course of collective actions that are to be undertaken.[35]

Community members and the EJ organizations that represent them are likewise constantly framing social issues and related events "in ways that are intended to mobilize potential adherents and constituents, to garner bystander support, and to demobilize antagonists."[36] *Frame transformation*, or the systematic recasting of a dominant interpretive frame, may be necessary when it is found that the values, causes, or programs being promoted by the EJ movement do not resonate with the government officials, community residents, general public, or other constituencies that activists wish to mobilize.[37] Transnational coalition building requires that activists frame EJ issues in ways that resonate with those in both the global South and the global North, and experience shows that this is often difficult to do.

Broadly speaking, there are presently three competing frames or discourses that dominate EJ politics. *Identity politics* in the EJ movement emphasizes a constituency solidarity based on the shared ascriptive, quasi-ascriptive, and related (constructed) *cultural characteristics* of people, based primarily on race, ethnicity, and heritage. This discourse identifies *cultural oppression*, or the deliberate targeting of communities of color via the dominant culture (institutionalized environmental racism), as the primary source of environmental injustice. This orientation is dominant within the U.S. EJ movement.

Radical/liberal democratic politics in the EJ movement emphasizes a constituency solidarity based on the shared *legal-political rights* of people, based primarily on citizenship, community membership, or fellowship with humanity. This discourse identifies *political domination*, or the subordination of citizen, civil, and human rights (for a healthy and clean environment) to the private property rights of large corporations and antidemocratic structures of state power (including northern imperial power), as the primary source of environmental injustice. This orientation is dominant within the international EJ movement.

Finally, *socialist politics* in the EJ movement emphasizes a constituency solidarity based on the shared *material (or political-economic) interests* of working people, based primarily on social class. This discourse identifies *economic exploitation*, or the manner in which the integrity of nature and all working people are continuously violated by the systemic profit imperatives of the capitalist system, as the primary source of environmental injustice. Class antagonisms and differing class interests related to the appropriation of nature are seen as central. This orientation is gaining momentum among southern (and some northern) EJ activists in the era of neoliberalism and globalization, as international capital and the law of value (or Adam Smith's invisible hand) increasingly colonize formerly independent cultures, nation-states, and economies alike.[38]

These EJ frames or discourses are not always mutually exclusive. There is a great deal of overlap in the identity politics and liberal democratic discourses around "civil rights" and "environmental racism," for instance, that focus on the denial of specific political-legal rights to culturally oppressed racial and ethnic minorities in both the North and the South. In fact, what many EJ-oriented movements share is a *subaltern* consciousness and location, that is, a recognition of the multiple forms of political domination, cultural oppression, economic exploitation, environmental degradation, and social resistance experienced by the most marginalized members of society at the hands of the ruling political and economic elites. The subaltern consciousness is more "deep" than narrower applications of traditional conceptions of working-class consciousness in that racism, colonialism, caste and ethnic structures, patriarchy, and/or other forms of oppression are seen as having some important "relative autonomy" from labor movement politics and systems of class exploitation under the larger capitalist system.[39]

In the United States, the EJ movement has evolved into a people-of-color movement dominated by an *identity politics* orientation that privileges environmental racism over other possible frames as the primary axis of domination. It is this priority placed on race, ethnicity, and culture as explanations of environmental damage that distinguish this movement from the more traditional political-economic critiques of capitalism.[40] As stated by Laura Pulido, "People of color in the environmental justice movement have articulated a broad but problematic conceptualization of racism that has allowed racism to subsume and become a metaphor for all forms of inequality impacting nonwhite groups."[41] More often than not, the racial identity politics orientation has led to the adoption of nationalist or civil rights strategies in relation to the state. These strategies mobilize *people-of-color constituencies* to become more integrated into established and/or alternative (autonomous) decision-making processes to ensure the equal application of environmental law and policy. EJ frames emphasizing the potential for solidarity with the white working-class or white middle-class citizens are typically deemphasized, if not completely discounted, by broad sectors of the EJ movement in the United States, particularly among the networks.

Given the vicious legacy of racism in American culture, particularly in terms of the genocidal acts committed against indigenous peoples and the brutal legacy of slavery and Jim Crow, the dominance of a racial identity–oriented EJ frame is understandable. But the implications of this identity orientation are enormous. In the United States, EJ politics are largely a *politics of the minority*, in comparison to the developing world, where EJ politics are largely a *politics of the majority*. This is not to say that subaltern forms of environmentalism in the global South built around racial and ethnic identity are not common. The struggles on behalf of indigenous peoples around the world to protect cultural and ecological diversity from intrusion are obvious.[42] State policy in the South has especially targeted the "assimilation" of communal groups for repression and appropriation of their resources. Indigenous populations, ethnoclasses, and other minorities and their rights to land, natural resources, clean air, good health, and environmental protection are viewed by the dominant culture as expendable for the sake of national security, national unity, and economic development.[43]

In Nigeria, for instance, the Ogoni people and environment of the Niger delta region are devastated by oil exploration and toxic pollution by multinational oil corporations like the Royal Dutch/Shell Oil Company. The Ogoni people represent one of many diverse minority ethnic groups in Nigeria marginalized by the Hausa, Igbo, Yoruba, and other majority ethnic groups. The Nigerian government actively promotes the control and exploitation of natural resources in oil-rich minority communities for the benefit of these core ethnic-centered groups as well as transnational corporations and domestic political-economic elites. In 1990, under the leadership of the playwright Kenule Saro-Wiwa, the Movement for the Survival of the Ogoni People drafted the Ogoni Bill of Rights, which seeks to secure a reasonable share of the oil revenues from Ogoniland, reductions in environmental degradation by oil-producing multinational corporations, and greater political autonomy to participate in the affairs of the republic as a distinct and separate entity.[44] In response, the military government of Nigeria hanged nine of the movement's leaders, including Saro-Wiwa, in 1991, on trumped-up charges (with the complicity of Dutch Shell).[45]

Nevertheless, despite the examples provided by Nigeria and elsewhere, *environmentalism of the poor* in the South largely operates from a progressive nationalist (or anti-imperialist), populist, and/or communitarian perspective.[46] These popularly based EJ movements typically move beyond a strictly racial identity politics framework to incorporate recognition of national and international structures of political-economic power. In this respect, the civil rights orientation for protecting the rights of minorities of the United States as adopted by much of the U.S. EJ movement has limited applicability in the global South, where majoritarian movements are engaged in struggles for their basic human rights, particularly in terms of threats to the environmental basis of livelihood. Likewise, a liberal-pluralist orientation emphasizing advocacy and policy-oriented approaches typically embraced by the mainstream U.S. environmental movement is also poorly equipped to support an environmentalism of the poor in the global South.

Can Class and Racial Politics Be Reconciled?

The primacy of the racial identity politics frame in the U.S. EJ movement has created another obstacle to the development of a transnational movement. In the eyes of EJ activists, mainstream environmental organizations have long neglected to incorporate oppressed people of color into a more democratic, mass-based environmental movement. Far too many mainstream environmental organizations ignore the central interconnected social and environmental issues of poor people of color and are often insufficiently accountable to their own membership as well.[47] As a result, the creation of EJ community groups, regional strategic networks, and nationally based constituency networks has finally given voice to people of color and constructed autonomous organizational avenues for identifying and addressing environmental problems. Evolving out of the *Principles of Environmental Justice* and understanding developed at the 1991 and 2002 People of Color Environmental Leadership Summits and embodied in the slogan *we speak for ourselves*, the dominant view is that the U.S. EJ movement should be led exclusively by people of color.[48]

This principle raises some important questions regarding the EJ frame and strategy.[49] Why is racial identity, rather than class or gender, the category that binds constituents to leaders? Do not poor, working-class whites suffer gross environmental abuses as well? Would EJ activists want to see the evolution of self-described "white-only" environmental organizations? Does the exclusiveness of racial identity politics create a type of disjuncture between the multiracial membership base and exclusively people of color leadership structure of the EJ movement?

As noted previously, there are primarily six different wings of the EJ movement. Aside from the constituency-based national networks, such as the IEN, many of the community-based organizations inside and outside the regional networks are multiracial in terms of membership, staff, and/or leadership. For instance, one of the more effective EJ organizations in the country—the EHC of San Diego—has a white executive director, even though the staff and membership are multiracial. But since the EJ networks only allow people of color to serve as representatives in network decision-making settings, the result is a segregated leadership structure (even though the base is often multiracial and inclusive of whites). Thus, the Center for Health, Environment and Justice (headed by Lois Gibbs of Love Canal fame) and other grassroots environmental organizations and other movements representing white working-class communities are isolated from many of the decision-making processes of the EJ movement. As argued by social movements scholar Barbara Epstein, "In a movement that includes people of all races, distinguishing between people of color and whites in terms of access to leadership positions is not only undemocratic in principle but also distorts the relation between membership and leadership by assuming sharper racial distinctions among local groups than actually exist in many cases."[50] Although instituted to preempt the very real threat of organizational colonization by whites and white-led groups with different political agendas—agendas that are often indifferent to oppressed people of color and poor working-class whites—this principle can also effectively prevent local memberships from nominating leaders who more effectively represent their interests. This strong tension between racial exclusion at the top and racial inclusion at the bottom poses a challenge to EJ activists and could ultimately hamper the continued fusion of the movement.

ISSUES OF ORGANIZATION FOR BUILDING A
TRANSNATIONAL ENVIRONMENTAL JUSTICE MOVEMENT

Sublating EJ Discourses around Identity, Citizenship, and Class

Beyond the organizing efforts of indigenous peoples in the United States and around the world, the exclusivity aspects of racial identity politics limits the ability of the U.S. EJ movement to form transnational coalitions. Currently, there is no openly formalized process or national organizational structure by which the EJ movement as a whole (representing all people of color) can negotiate differences and develop unified strategies with either grassroots or mainstream environmental organizations "representing" primarily working-class and middle-class whites. An earlier attempt to maintain a central, Washington, D.C.–based office on environmental justice in the early 1990s that included a coordinated focus on federal policy failed. In fact, other than the Environmental Justice Fund, which was originally created to focus on alternative fund-raising techniques for the movement, there has been no regular institutional framework for local groups and the networks as a whole to engage in coordinated debate, strategizing, and decision making with each other and other popular social movements inside and outside the United States. The place- and constituency-specific character of the movement, as expressed in the slogan "we speak for ourselves,"[51] potentially inhibits the formation of deep national and international organizational structures and coalitions of activists who don't share a similar cultural identity.

In the age of globalization, unless the EJ movement can "act and think both locally and globally" to confront the power of the polluter-industrial complex and develop transnational forms of organization to supplement the current focus on the local and regional, the potential of the movement will remain quite limited. For this reason, many movements representing an *environmentalism of the poor* in the global South engage in outreach to traditional environmental organizations in the United States, organizations that movements in the global South perceive as being more receptive and having greater capacity than the EJ movement. To address this deficiency, the Environmental and Economic Justice Project (EEJP) in Los Angeles assumed the mission of facilitating international collaboration of grassroots environmental and economic justice organizations in the United States and six Third World countries. Founded in 1993, EEJP provides organizational training and support to local and regional environmental and economic justice groups around the country. Programs are designed to build organizational capacity at the local, regional, and national levels, to assist in the strategic development of EJ networks, and to encourage the creation of a strong international grassroots EJ movement. Four convenings have been organized since 1996 to build relationships and foster discussions among the international participants on strategies and campaigns countering the negative impacts of globalization. EEJP has also organized two international activist exchanges (to Brazil and the Philippines) to build understanding and strengthen opportunities for organizations to develop collaborative work.

In the meantime, there is currently no consensus in the U.S. EJ movement as to whether the segregation of whites from positions of leadership within the movement, as well as "white-oriented" groups from outside the movement, is a temporary or permanent practice necessary to prevent colonization of the movement.[52] Broader definitions of environmental injustice beyond "environmental racism" will one day certainly necessitate the creation of linkages between people of color and whites, between the working poor and middle classes, and between peoples of the global South and North. This will require the sublation of identity politics, radical democratic, anti-imperialist, and socialist discourses into a new master EJ frame. Few other movements in the United States hold the potential for developing such a liberating vision and program for all peoples.

Philanthropic Marginalization of the EJ Movement

In the United States, the capabilities of the EJ movement are inhibited by the fact that, unlike many traditional environmental organizations, nonprofits led by people of color remain sorely undersupported by the philanthropic community at large. In addition, traditional foundation grant-making practices are often inappropriate for the types of nonprofit organizations working on EJ issues.[53] Both of these factors threaten to constrain the continued development and effectiveness of the movement, particularly in terms of developing transnational coalitions—a very expensive endeavor.

The U.S. environmental movement is now one of the most powerful social movements in the United States. Over 10,000 environmental organizations now operate in the country, with a combined membership of between 19 million and 41 million members. These organizations employ approximately 28,000 staff, receive a total annual income of $2.6 billion, and possess assets of $5.8 billion.[54] Foundation support plays a fundamental role in sustaining the environmental movement. It is estimated that 5.4 percent, or $1.23 billion, of total foundation giving ($22.8 billion) went to the environment in 1999.[55] The bulk of foundation funding, however, goes to a small handful of the more politically moderate national environmental organizations. As documented by social scientists Robert Brulle and J. Craig Jenkins in their comprehensive analysis of environmental movement funding between 1970 and 2000, over 80 percent of foundation funding goes to staff-dominated professional movement organizations that lack a grassroots base and over 90 percent to organizations that rely exclusively on institutional tactics rather than base building and community organizing.[56] In short, the foundation community is throwing its financial weight behind a sector of the movement governed largely by white, middle- to upper-class advocacy organizations without active memberships.[57]

In contrast, aside from a few progressive grant makers, the foundation community as a whole neglects the EJ movement. Given the high number of organizations and the large size of the constituencies being served, *the EJ movement is one of the most underfunded major social movements in the country.* Based on the most recent estimates available, only $27.498 million in grants came to the EJ movement in 1996 and rose to just over $49 million in 1999.[58] The lack of resources for organizations serving people of color and lower-income communities is particularly noticeable given the funding of the traditional environmental organizations. In comparison, just eight mainstream environmental organizations—including the Leadership for Environment and Development, The Nature Conservancy, the World Wildlife Fund/Conservation Foundation, the Golden Gate National Parks Association, the Environmental Defense Fund, the National Audubon Society, the Population Council, and the Natural Resources Defense Council—received 212 foundation grants totaling over $48 million in 2000, *an amount equivalent to all 200 or more grassroots EJ organizations in the country.* To provide another, more extreme example, the Nature Conservancy alone received approximately $97 million in foundation grants in 1994, a figure significantly higher than any other environmental organization in the country.

The long-term success of the ecology movement in general and the EJ movement in particular depends on the reorientation of foundation priorities to support grassroots organizing and base-building strategies that democratically incorporate people into problem solving around the social and environmental ills plaguing communities. Building an international EJ movement will demand a dramatic expansion of capacity building, allowing the movement to strengthen organizational structures, increase staffing, conduct trainings, hold and attend conferences, and enhance communication and technical capabilities. There is evidence that some EJ organizations and/or networks have a thin membership base, even in their own backyards.[59] Other organizations lack a multilayered leadership structure, resulting in an overwhelming workload and burnout among the founders and key leaders in the EJ movement. The ability to engage in international travel to attend such meetings between base EJ organizations and colleagues is particularly burdensome financially but crucial for engaging in cross-border work. The EJ movement cannot evolve into a transnational movement without the creation of a strong organizational infrastructure, yet securing the funds and support from foundations needed to make this a reality is proving extremely difficult. In this respect, the lack of funding is the number one impediment to developing strong coordinated international campaigns for environmental justice. The recent creation of the progressive-oriented Funders Network on Trade and Globalization and other foundation entities are beginning to address the disparities and assist the EJ movement in developing these capacities.[60]

ISSUES OF STRATEGY FOR BUILDING A TRANSNATIONAL ENVIRONMENTAL JUSTICE MOVEMENT

Taking on the Export of Hazard

In the United States, the EJ movement has achieved some impressive results over the past twenty-plus years. Poor neighborhoods and communities of color across the country have successfully cleaned up hazardous waste sites, redeveloped brownfields, stopped and shut down incinerators, established accessible parks and conservation areas, eliminated local pollution threats, demanded the provision of cleaner and more convenient means of public transportation, and protected unique habitats and wildlands. Most recently, residents of the African American community in Norco, Louisiana (part of an area known as "Cancer Alley"), and the Environmental Health Fund won a historic battle to relocate from the fence line of Shell Chemical LP, which bought the homes of families wanting to leave. Perhaps more important, in the process of winning these victories, the EJ movement enlarged its power building capacities by engaging in *movement fusion* strategies, expanding its base of support by coming together with other movements for social justice and developing a common agenda.[61]

In the global South, environmental degradation; growing unemployment and falling wages; diminished local control over land, agriculture, and seeds by peasants and small indigenous farmers; government deregulation of markets; dwindling power of national governments to create their own beneficial trade policies; economic destabilization; and increasing poverty are features of corporate-led globalization. In response, the voices of environmentalists, indigenous peoples, women, and other marginalized peoples traditionally subordinated by parties on both the right and the left are now asserting themselves politically. Recognizing the diminished power of the nation-state to counteract the dictates of the International Monetary Fund (IMF), the World

Bank, the WTO, and the G-8 and thereby to effectively address environmental and social problems, efforts in cross-border organizing among these popular "new social movements" have greatly expanded in recent years.[62] An exclusive focus on domestic power structures is now inadequate.[63]

In the era of neoliberalism and corporate-led globalization, EJ movements in the both the global South and North have a mutual interest in developing coordinated strategies. The growing ability of multinational corporations and transnational financial institutions to evade environmental safeguards and worker/community health and safety regulations and to dismantle unions and the social safety net in both the advanced capitalist states and the periphery is being achieved by crossing national boundaries into politically repressive and economically oppressive countries. This *export of ecological hazard* from the United States and other core countries to the global South includes the following: 1) *the money circuit of global capital*, in the form of foreign direct investment in domestically owned hazardous industries as well as destructive investment schemes to gain access to new oil fields, forests, agricultural lands, mining deposits, and other natural resources; 2) *the productive circuit of global capital*, or the movement of polluting and environmentally hazardous production processes and polluting facilities owned by transnational capital to newly industrialized countries; (3) *the commodity circuit of global capital*, or the marketing of more profitable but also more dangerous foods, drugs, pesticides, technologies, and other consumer/capital goods in the periphery; and 4) *the waste circuit of global capital*, or the dumping of toxic wastes and other pollutants produced by northern industry in the global South. And in this context, abetted by "free-trade" agreements and economic liberalization enforced by the WTO, various nationalities and governments are increasingly being pitted against one another to attract capital investment by weakening labor and environmental laws seen as damaging to profits. In this respect, globalization weakens the bargaining power of the U.S. EJ movement and mainstream environmental movement.

Likewise, victories by communities of color in the United States against the disposal of toxic incinerator ash in their own localities are quite limited if the result is the transport and disposal of the same waste in a community of color in West Africa. If multinational corporations flee to the Third World to avoid environmental regulations and liability in the North, then the actions of the U.S. EJ movement may be indirectly exacerbating environmental injustices elsewhere. Clearly, stringent environmental standards must be applied to all nations in order to foster environmental justice. Only by achieving greater social governance over trade and lending institutions and regulatory bodies can the process that leads different countries to sacrifice human and environmental health in order to compete in the world economy be overcome. This includes efforts to reestablish popular control over the United Nations as a counterweight to the WTO.[64]

Rather than a "race to the bottom," whereby the nation with the weakest environmental regulations sets the standard "ceiling" that all trading partners must accept, a transnational EJ movement must work for strong standards that apply to all nations. Such a regulatory harmonization process would privilege nations with the strictest environmental laws as establishing a standard "floor" to which all other countries must comply if trade is to be conducted between them. The U.S. EJ movement, in coordination with southern EJ movements, has initiated the first steps of such a strategy by concentrating on the actions of U.S.-based subsidiaries operating overseas. For instance, EarthRights International (ERI) recently launched a new "International Right to Know" campaign, with the goal of extending the existing reporting requirements of domestic environmental, occupational health and safety, and labor rights legislation to U.S. corporate activities in other countries. The campaign is being built in coalition with the AFL-CIO, the Sierra Club, the Center for International Environmental Law, Friends of the Earth, and Amnesty International but has the potential for incorporating broad segments of the EJ movement.

In addition to a "general reporting requirement" strategy aimed at all U.S. corporations operating overseas, the movement has also adopted regional and country-specific campaigns aimed at improving public accountability of both foreign and domestic capital as well as government agencies around issues of environmental justice. Cross-border organizing around NAFTA and Mexico is particularly important for SNEEJ, which provides networking, training, technical assistance, and capacity building to local affiliates. One of the network's primary efforts includes the Border Justice Campaign, which works with the EHC in San Diego and SWOP in Albuquerque and other affiliates to hold industrial and government agencies accountable for environmental and social problems along the U.S.–Mexico border. Through the EPA Accountability Campaign in 1994, the EHC and SNEEJ forced the EPA to disclose the records of U.S. corporations polluting the New River from inside Mexico. This was the first enforcement action that used NAFTA environmental "sidebars" and the executive order for environmental justice and became one of the largest single enforcement actions ever taken by the EPA.

Creating Model Approaches to Specific EJ Issues

Another strategy increasingly employed by the EJ movement is the identification of a *specific EJ issue* that links the "local" and the "global." By developing an organizing strategy and "model regulatory solution" to a specific EJ issue that has a wider application beyond the local community, international bridges can be crossed. For instance, the EHC is a community-based organization in San Diego that combines grassroots organizing, advocacy, technical assistance, research, education, and policy development. EHC's programs concentrate on problems of toxic contamination of local neighborhoods, the workplace, San Diego Bay, Tijuana, and the border region. EHC won a five-year battle with the San Diego Port District in July 1997, ending the use of the toxic pesticide methyl bromide as a fumigant on imported produce unloaded at the port. Methyl bromide is a toxic pesticide that causes birth defects and other health problems and is an ozone destroyer. The practice posed significant health risks to dockworkers, consumers, and nearby communities, including Barrio Logan, one of San Diego's poorest neighborhoods. Surrounded by more than 100 toxic polluting facilities, residents in Barrio Logan had experienced high rates of asthma, headaches, sore throats, rashes, damaged vision, and other health problems.

EHC's unprecedented local victory resulted in the first policy in the world to prohibit the common practice of using methyl bromide as a port fumigant. In fact, EHC was the only local environmental group to participate with national and international nongovernmental organizations in 1997 during discussions on the Montreal Protocol, an international treaty regarding the phasing out of ozone-depleting chemicals. The EHC campaign has become a model that many other EJ, labor, and environmental health organizations are now using to pressure ports to reduce the use of dangerous pesticides. Because the strategy was implemented in coordination with dockworkers organizing around job health and safety issues, the strategy also accomplished the *movement fusion* principle, whereby labor and the EJ movement expand their domestic and international base by developing a common agenda around a specific issue.[65]

Promoting Greater Corporate and Governmental Accountability

Another major strategy of the EJ movement is aimed at promoting greater *corporate and governmental accountability*, or increased democratic control over capital and the state, via selective targeting of victimizers. This strategy often implies the EJ movement identifying and then targeting a particularly egregious "leader" corporation within a particular industry or country for special campaign work. By organizing highly public campaigns that economically "punish" and alter the destructive behavior of such an industry leader, the potential is that other corporations (or countries) will follow suit in order to avoid the same stigmatic fate. This type of strategy can draw increased international attention to the plights being suffered in the affected communities and also win (with enough pressure) important economic and political concessions for the various stakeholders impacted by the corporation's behavior.

An example of such is the *Justice in Bhopal: Holding Dow Chemical Accountable* speaking tour with survivors of the Bhopal disaster that took place in the spring of 2002. The purpose of the U.S. tour was to demand that Dow Chemical assume the liabilities of Union Carbide. In one of the most powerful cases of globalization gone wrong, in December 1984, deadly gases leaked from the U.S. multinational Union Carbide's plant in Bhopal, India, killing over 8,000 people immediately. Over 20,000 have died since, making it the worst corporate-created environmental disaster of all time. More than thirty people continue to die every month as a result of the gas exposure. Toxic waste left behind at the site has contaminated the drinking water of the community. Dow Chemical merged with Union Carbide in 2001. While Dow has assumed all the assets of Union Carbide, Dow refuses to assume the liabilities of Union Carbide. Dow Chemical, now in India, is also manufacturing and promoting products in India that are being banned in the United States—practicing double standards just like Union Carbide. As part of the trip, Bhopal Survivors Tour representatives went to Michigan to demand justice at Dow's shareholder meeting. The tour was hosted by a number of EJ organizations, including the Alliance of South Asians Taking Action, APEN, CorpWatch, Laotian Organizing Project, PODER, and the Second National People of Color Environmental Leadership Summit.

In another case, the indigenous U'wa people of Colombia were able to establish international support groups to bring about pressure on the Colombian government and California-based Occidental Petroleum and its partner, Royal Dutch Shell, to halt oil drilling in the U'wa's migratory territory. This organizing strategy for the U'wa and other EJ-oriented movements abroad is made possible through the increased availability of communication technologies and networks. One of the more important of these information networks is CorpWatch. Founded in 1996, CorpWatch conducts broad public education activities including publications, workshops, media outreach, and an Internet website utilized by EJ advocates throughout the world. The site not only highlights CorpWatch's overall work but also has links to corporations and industries, research tools, publications, related websites, and government resources as well as a section on how to research corporations. CorpWatch also coordinates a fax- and cyber-based action alert on global environmental and social justice issues. Two campaigns are being conducted at present that focus on climate justice and on reforming the United Nations.[66]

Fighting for Human Rights and EJ

Given the severe repression faced by EJ activists and other popular movements in the world, perhaps the most fundamental prerequisite in the quest for environmental justice is the struggle for human rights.[67] The use of various instruments of state repression, including torture, imprisonment without justification, harassment, assassination, and even the forced removal or military extermination of entire villages (including acts of genocide against indigenous peoples and other communal groups), has long been prevalent in the global South, especially in places such as Indonesia, Nigeria, Burma, and Central America. Furthermore, despite the rhetoric of neoliberals regarding the "democratizing effect" of globalization, human rights abuses in many parts of the world are intensifying. At the insistence of the World Bank and IMF, newly written treaties and laws promoting economic liberalization consistently promote the interests of foreign investors over international standards of human rights and environmental regulation. The Universal Declaration of Human Rights, which makes it obligatory for every nation to protect human rights, is considered a barrier to "free trade." Even in the United States, rules initiated in Massachusetts to restrict trade with Burma in order to punish that country for its gross human rights violations (including the use of slave labor captured from villages being displaced by a massive oil pipeline being built for U.S. multinational oil corporations) was recently overturned by the courts, which ruled that only the federal government has the authority to regulate international commerce.

In the era of corporate-led globalization, environmental injustices and human rights violations are inextricably interwoven.[68] But because most popular movements in the global South lack the political space, resources, or regulatory instruments to adequately protect themselves from predatory corporations and state repression, international support is badly needed. For this reason, EJ movements in the global South are increasingly coming to recognize the critical role that American activists can play in forcing the U.S. government to take the lead in defending human rights and protecting the environment. This includes the application of political pressure on U.S. multinational corporations, the IMF, and other international bodies such as the United Nations. In yet another example of movement fusion, the human rights and EJ movements are now beginning to come together and form coalitions and campaigns in order to apply such pressure. This process of *environmentalization*, defined as when a formerly nonenvironmental issue such as trade and human rights comes to be seen substantially as an EJ issue, is now coming to fruition.[69] The overall strategy being employed is to uphold the Universal Declaration of Human Rights by developing explicit campaigns on human rights and the environment with strong international standards and to develop mechanisms for monitoring and reporting on compliance with these standards (much like the tactics currently employed by the international antisweatshop networks).

The importance of human rights for building transnational coalitions is gaining momentum. In collaboration with Amnesty International USA, the

Sierra Club, the oldest and largest grassroots environmental organization in the world, with over 550,000 members and 400 local groups, has taken up environmental justice and international human rights. The focus of the Human Rights and the Environment Campaign titled "Defending Those Who Give the Earth a Voice" is to bring public attention and pressure on governments and corporations to halt human rights abuses committed against environmental activists. By raising awareness, educating, and motivating the public to take action, the project demands accountability. The effort includes the Goldman Environmental Prize (with support from the Richard and Rhoda Goldman Fund), which recognizes activists from around the world who have braved human rights abuses to defend their communities and environment from abuses.[70]

Earth Rights International (ERI) was cofounded in 1995 by the Southeast Asian activist Ka Hsaw Wa, a recent recipient of the Goldman Prize. ERI is leading a worldwide effort to create a new understanding that the abuse of human rights and the environment go hand in hand. Programs are designed to investigate, monitor, and expose human rights and environmental abuses occurring in the name of development; increase the accountability of governments, transnational corporations, and international financial institutions; protect individuals and communities at work defending the earth; and ensure biodiversity, conservation, and ecological integrity. ERI achieves these goals through grassroots organizing, education, and training; litigation; documentation and publications; advocacy at local, national, regional, and international venues; and media work. The EarthRights Resource Center, located in Washington, D.C. (and working in cooperation with the Sierra Club's Human Rights and the Environment Campaign), also provides information, legal assistance, and strategic advice to groups involved in joint human rights and environmental work. Most recently, ERI teamed with the Center for Constitutional Rights to bring suit against Unocal for human rights abuses associated with the company's pipeline project in Burma. Burmese peasants suffered egregious violations at the hands of army units hired by Unocal to secure the pipeline, including forced labor, murder, rape, and torture. In June 2002, the Superior Court of California issued a decision which will make Unocal the first company in U.S. history to stand trial for human rights abuses committed abroad.[71]

BUILDING A BETTER MOVEMENT

The U.S. EJ movement is still developing, having gained some national organizational coherence in only the past ten years. For a movement so young and underresourced, it would be unreasonable, as often stated by Richard Moore of SNEEJ, to expect "too much, too soon." There is still much to be learned, particularly in terms of international EJ issues and building a transnational movement. In this respect, the fundamental work of popular education and information sharing are still very important tools for developing such an understanding. This is also true for EJ activists in the global South. In May and June 2002, South African activists visited communities of color around the United States as part of Project X-Change, an EJ youth exchange. The South African youth met with their U.S. counterparts in order to obtain a greater appreciation of political realities in the United States and to share their organizing experiences in South Africa. Cities visited included Boston; Jackson, Mississippi; "Cancer Alley" near New Orleans; San Antonio; El Paso; Los Angeles; and the San Francisco Bay Area. The tour was organized by the South African Exchange Program on Environmental Justice and the South African Development Fund. In many ways, these types of exchanges seem trivial but are actually critical to grassroots base building for a transnational EJ movement. As stated by James Scott, "Under the appropriate conditions, the accumulation of petty acts [of resistance] can, rather like snowflakes on a steep mountainside, set off an avalanche."[72]

Still, among seasoned EJ activists working on cross-border and transnational movement building, the ultimate goals are becoming increasingly clear. These aims go well beyond lessening poverty, redistributing income and wealth, and decreasing environmental health problems. Rather, the alternatives being advocated challenge the hegemonic structures of political-economic power in favor of more participatory, rights-based, and autonomously controlled local and national economies.[73] These strategies move beyond approaches aimed at ending the unequal distribution of environmental problems (*distributional justice*) to address the political-economic structures that produce the environmental problems in the first place (*productive justice*)—to move beyond a "not-in-my-backyard" to a "not-in-anyone's backyard" politics.[74] The more radical and far-reaching of these alternative visions sublate radical democracy, socialist, and identity politics into a new synthesis.

Under the banner of *revolutionary ecology* following the overthrow of the Somoza dictatorship in 1979, for instance, the new Nicaraguan government initiated what would become the single most important national experiment in radical environmentalism that the world has ever seen. Incorporating four mutually reinforcing principles—social and environmental justice, national sovereignty and self-determination, sustainable development, and ecological democracy—Nicaragua provided an alternative development model to the destructive tendencies of dependent capitalist development on the one hand and bureaucratic state socialism on the other.[75] The efforts of the U.S. environmental movement to rescue the Nicaraguan revolution from the aggression of the Reagan and Bush administrations during the 1980s was an important watershed in U.S. environmental politics. Not only did major environmental organizations such as Earth Island Institute, Friends of the Earth and the Environmental Policy Institute (now merged), Greenpeace, Earth First!, National Toxics Campaign (now defunct), and the Rainforest Action Network team with the Environmental Project on Central America make the unprecedented move of opposing U.S. policy and military intervention in Central America on both *human rights* and environmental grounds but also many of the activists involved in these organizational efforts in the 1980s were later instrumental in catalyzing transnational EJ organizing efforts in the 1990s and beyond. As a result, the potential offered by the Nicaraguan model remains an important source of inspiration to the movement.

Today, many of the world's EJ-oriented coalitions, networks, and movements articulate detailed policy positions regarding new forms of international economic and political organization. The message is clear: corporate-led globalization, as embodied by the WTO, NAFTA, World Bank, and IMF policies and corporate investment practices undermines democracy, local economies, ecological sustainability, labor unions, and human rights. This understanding is reflected in many of the transnational strategies aimed at increasing corporate and governmental accountability with regard to EJ issues. The eventual political necessity is to expand these EJ coalitions—still in their infancy—to work in harmony with other transnational movements to invent a more transformative political ecology.

As indicated by the "Battle in Seattle," in which labor, environmentalists, indigenous peoples, women's movements, farmers, consumer product safety advocates, and antiglobalization activists combined to partially shut down the WTO meetings, there are signs that such a transformative political ecology movement is beginning to develop in the United States. The revitalization of grassroots environmental organizations committed to genuine base building and political-economic reform is a reaction to the new challenges posed by neoliberalism and globalization and includes the use of direct action against timber companies, polluters, the WTO, the World Bank, and the IMF as well as criticism toward the "corporatist" and exclusionary approaches of mainstream environmental organizations. Pressing for greater economic equality, "fair trade" and stricter systems of international environmental regulation and labor rights, greater corporate and government accountability (such as the "right to know" about hazards facing the community), and more comprehensive approaches to environmental problem solving (such as the adoption of the precautionary principle over risk assessment, source reduction and pollution *prevention* over pollution *control* strategies, "just transition" for workers out of polluting industries over job blackmail, and so on), the struggle for ecological democracy represents the birth of a *transformative* environmental politics.[76]

NOTES

1. Bunyan Bryant, "Summary," in *Environmental Justice: Issues, Policies, and Solutions*, Bunyan Bryant, ed. (Washington, DC: Island Press, 1995), 212.

2. Held in Washington, D.C., the four-day summit was attended by more than 560 grassroots and national leaders from around the world. On September 27, 1991, delegates adopted seventeen "Principles of Environmental Justice," which now serve as a common guide for the movement. See Charles Lee, *Proceedings: The First National People of Color Environmental Leadership Summit* (New York: United Church of Christ Commission for Racial Justice, 1992), and Dana Alston, "Transforming a Movement: People of Color Unite at Summit against Environmental Racism," *Sojourner* 21 (1992): 30–31.

3. Daniel R. Faber and Deborah McCarthy, "The Evolution of the Environmental Justice Movement in the United States: New Models for Democratic Decision-Making," *Social Justice Research* 14, no. 4 (2001): 405–21.

4. Robert Bullard, ed., *Unequal Protection: Environmental Justice and Communities of Color* (San Francisco: Sierra Club Books, 1994); Bunyan Bryant and Paul Mohai, eds., *Race and the Incidence of Environmental Hazards: A Time for Discourse* (Boulder, CO: Westview Press, 1992).

5. Benjamin Chavis and Charles Lee, *Toxic Wastes and Race in the United States: A National Report on the Racial and Socioeconomic Characteristics of Communities Surrounding Hazardous Waste Sites* (New York: United Church of Christ Commission for Racial Justice, 1987).

6. Dana Alston, *We Speak for Ourselves: Social Justice, Race, and Environment* (Washington, DC: The Panos Institute, 1991).

7. Daniel R. Faber and Eric Krieg, "Unequal Exposure to Ecological Hazards: Environmental Injustices in the Commonwealth of Massachusetts," in "Advancing Environmental Justice through Community-Based Participatory Research," a special issue of *Environmental Health Perspectives* 110 (Supplement 2) (April): 277–88; Robert Bullard, *Dumping in Dixie: Race, Class, and Environmental Quality* (Boulder, CO: Westview Press, 1990).

8. Charles Levenstein and John Wooding, "Dying for a Living: Workers, Production, and the Environment," in Bryant and Mohai, *The Struggle for Ecological Democracy*, 60–80.

9. Ivette Perfecto, "Farm Workers, Pesticides and the International Connection," in Bryant and Mohai, *Race and the Incidence of Environmental Hazards*, 172–86.

10. Winona LaDuke, *All Our Relations: Native Struggles for Land and Life* (Boston: South End Press, 1999); Jane Weaver and Russell Means, eds., *Defending Mother Earth: Native American Perspectives on Environmental Justice* (Maryknoll, NY: Orbis Books, 1996); Donald A. Grinde, Howard Zinn, and Bruce Elliott Johansen, *Ecocide of Native America: Environmental Destruction of Indian Lands and Peoples* (Santa Fe, NM: Clear Light Publishers, 1998).

11. Robert D. Bullard, ed., *The Quest for Environmental Justice: Human Rights and the Politics of Pollution* (San Francisco: Sierra Club Books, 2005).

12. Barbara Rose Johnston, *Who Pays the Price? The Sociocultural Context of Environmental Crisis* (Washington, DC: Island Press, 1994).

13. Andrew Szasz, *Ecopopulism: Toxic Waste and the Movement for Environmental Justice* (Minneapolis: University of Minnesota Press, 1994).

14. Daniel R. Faber, *Environment under Fire: Imperialism and the Ecological Crisis in Central America* (New York: Monthly Review Press, 1993).

15. Joshua Karliner, *The Corporate Planet: Ecology and Politics in the Age of Globalization* (San Francisco: Sierra Club Books, 1997).

16. R. A. Sanchez, "Health and Environmental Risks of the Maquiladora in Mexicali," *Natural Resources Journal* 30 (1990): 163–70.

17. Leslie King, "Charting a Discursive Field: Environmentalists for U.S. Population Stabilization," *Sociological Inquiry* 77, no. 3 (August 2007): 301–25; Leslie King, "Ideology, Strategy and Conflict in a Social Movement Organization: The Sierra Club Immigration Wars," unpublished manuscript (July 2007), 1–39.

18. Ann Bastian and Dana Alston, "An Open Letter to Funding Colleagues: New Developments in the Environmental Justice Movement," New World Foundation and the Public Welfare Foundation (September 1993), 1–4.

19. Daniel R. Faber, ed., *The Struggle for Ecological Democracy: Environmental Justice Movements in the United States* (New York: Guilford Press, 1998).

20. Ronald Inglehart, *Culture Shift in Advanced Industrial Society* (Princeton, NJ: Princeton University Press, 1990).

21. Paolo Donati, "Environmentalism, Postmaterialism and Anxiety: The New Politics of Individualism," *Arena Journal*, no. 8 (1997): 147–72.

22. Steven R. Brechin, "Objective Problems, Subjective Values, and Global Environmentalism: Evaluating the Postmaterialist Argument and Challenging a New Explanation," *Social Science Quarterly* 80, no. 4 (1999): 793–809.

23. Brechlin, "Objective Problems, Subjective Values, and Global Environmentalism," 793–809.

24. Jim Schwab, *Deeper Shades of Green: The Rise of Blue-Collar and Minority Environmentalism in America* (San Francisco: Sierra Club Books, 1994).

25. Joan Martínez-Alier, "Retrospective Environmentalism and Environmental Justice Movements Today," *Capitalism, Nature, Socialism* 11, no. 4 (June 2000): 45–50.

26. Brechin, "Objective Problems, Subjective Values, and Global Environmentalism," 793–809.

27. Richard Peet and Michael Watts, eds., *Liberation Ecologies: Environment, Development, Social Movements* (London: Routledge, 1996).

28. Ramachandra Guha, *Environmentalism: A Global History* (New York: Longman, 2000).

29. Daniel R. Faber, "A Revolution in Environmental Justice and Sustainable Development: The Political Ecology of Nicaragua," in *Environmental Justice: Discourses in International Political Economy, Energy, and Environmental Policy*, ed. John Byrne, Leigh Glover, and Cecilia Martinez (New Brunswick, NJ: Transaction Books, 2002), 39–70.

30. Shobita Jaine, "Standing Up for the Trees: Women's Role in the Chipko Movement," in *Women and the Environment: Crisis and Development in the Third World*, ed. Sall Sontheimer (New York: Monthly Review Press, 1991), 163–78; Vandana Shiva, *Staying Alive: Women, Ecology, and Development* (London: Zed Books, 1998).

31. John Byrne, Leigh Glover, and Cecilia Martinez, eds., "A Brief on Environmental Justice," in *Environmental Justice*, 3–17; Julian Agyeman, Robert Bullard, and Bob Evans, eds., *Just Sustainabilities: Development in an Unequal World* (London: Transaction Books, 2002).

32. Mark A. Shibley and Annette Prosterman, "Silent Epidemic, Environmental Injustice, or Exaggerated Concern? Competing Frames in the Media Definition of Childhood Lead Poisoning as a Public Health Problem," *Organization and Environment* 11, no. 1 (1998): 33.

33. Erving Goffman, *Frame Analysis: An Essay on the Organization of Experience* (Cambridge, MA: Harvard University Press, 1974), 21.

34. Stella M. Capek, "The 'Environmental Justice' Frame: A Conceptual Discussion and an Application," *Social Problems* 40 (1993): 5–24.

35. Sherry Cable and Thomas Shriver, "The Production and Extrapolation of Meaning in the Environmental Justice Movement," *Sociological Spectrum* 15 (1995): 419–42.

36. David A. Snow and Robert D. Benford, "Ideology, Frame Resonance, and Participant Mobilization," in *From Structure to Action: Social Movement Participation across Cultures*, ed. B. Klandermans, H. Kriesi, and Sydney Tarrow (Greenwich, CO: JAI Press, 1988), 198.

37. David A. Snow, R. Burke Rochord Jr., Steven Worden, and Robert D. Benford, "Frame Alignment Process, Micromobilization, and Movement Participation," *American Sociological Review* 51 (1986): 464–481.

38. James O'Connor, "A Political Strategy for Ecology Movements," *Capitalism, Nature, Socialism* 3, no. 1 (1992): 1–5.

39. Laura Pulido, *Environmentalism and Economic Justice: Two Chicano Struggles in the Southwest* (New York: Simon & Schuster, 1996), 3–56.

40. Byrne et al., "A Brief on Environmental Justice," 3–17.

41. Pulido, *Environmentalism and Economic Justice*, 17.

42. Barbara Rose Johnston, *Who Pays the Price? The Sociocultural Context of Environmental Crisis* (Washington, DC: Island Press, 1994).

43. Francis O. Adeola, "Cross-National Environmental Injustice and Human Rights Issues: A Review of Evidence in the Developing World," *American Behavioral Scientist* 43, no. 4 (2000): 686–706.

44. Adeola, "Cross-National Environmental Injustice and Human Rights Issues," 699–700.

45. Kenny Bruno and Joshua Karliner, *Earthsummit.biz: The Corporate Takeover of Sustainable Development* (Oakland, CA: Food First Books, 2002), 15–16.

46. Leigh Glover, "globalization.com vs. ecologicaljustice.org: Contesting the End of History," in Byrne et al., *Environmental Justice*, 233.

47. Paul Almeida, "The Network for Environmental and Economic Justice in the Southwest: An Interview with Richard Moore," in Faber, *The Struggle for Ecological Democracy*, 159–87; William Shutkin, *The Land That Could Be: Environmentalism and Democracy in the Twenty-First Century* (Cambridge, MA: MIT Press, 2000).

48. Alston, *We Speak for Ourselves*, 5–13.

49. Barbara Epstein, "The Environmental Justice/Toxics Movement: Politics of Race and Gender," *Capitalism, Nature, Socialism* 8, no. 3 (1997): 63–87.

50. Epstein, "The Environmental Justice/Toxics Movement," 85.

51. Alston, *We Speak for Ourselves*, 1–25.

52. Epstein, "The Environmental Justice/Toxics Movement," 63–87.

53. Daniel R. Faber and Deborah McCarthy, *Green of Another Color: Building Effective Partnerships between Foundations and the Environmental Justice Movement* (Boston: Philanthropy and Environmental Justice Research Project, Northeastern University, 2001).

54. Robert J. Brulle, *Agency, Democracy, and Nature: The US Environmental Movement from a Critical Theory Perspective* (Cambridge, MA: MIT Press, 2000), 114.

55. The methodology and techniques utilized for obtaining these estimates is provided in Faber and McCarthy, *Green of Another Color.*

56. Robert J. Brulle and Craig Jenkins, "Foundations and the Environmental Movement: Priorities, Strategies, and Impact," in *Foundations for Social Change: Critical Perspectives on Philanthropy and Popular Movements*, ed. Daniel R. Faber and Deborah McCarthy (Lanham, MD: Rowman & Littlefield, 2005), 151–74.

57. Faber and McCarthy, *Foundations for Social Change.*

58. Faber and McCarthy, *Green of Another Color*, 29–40.

59. David Naguub Pellow and Robert J. Brulle, *Power, Justice, and the Environment: A Critical Appraisal of the Environmental Justice Movement* (Cambridge, MA: MIT Press, 2005), 14.

60. Daniel R. Faber and Deborah McCarthy, "Breaking the Funding Barriers: Philanthropic Activism in Support of the Environmental Justice Movement," in Faber and McCarthy, *Foundations for Social Change*, 175–210.

61. Luke W. Cole and Sheila R. Foster, *From the Ground Up: Environmental Racism and the Rise of the Environmental Justice Movement* (New York: New York University Press, 2001), 164.

62. Peter Waterman, *Globalisation, Social Movements and the New Internationalism* (London: Continuum, 2001).

63. Beverly Bell, *Social Movements and Regional Integration in the Americas* (Albuquerque, NM: Center for Economic Justice, 2002), 5.

64. Kenny Bruno and Joshua Karliner, *Tangled Up in Blue: Corporate Partnerships at the United Nations*, a report by CorpWatch (September 1, 2000).

65. Cole and Foster, *From the Ground Up*, 164.

66. Karliner and Bruno, *Earthsummit.biz*, 15–80.

67. Andrew Rowell, *Green Backlash: Global Subversion of the Environmental Movement* (New York: Routledge, 1996).

68. Adeola, "Cross-National Environmental Injustice," 687–703.

69. Frederick H. Buttel, "Environmentalization: Origins, Processes, and Implications for Rural Social Change," *Rural Sociology* 57 (1992): 1–27; Frederick H. Buttel and Peter J. Taylor, "Environmental Sociology and Global Environmental Change: A Critical Assessment," *Society and Natural Resources* 5 (1992): 211–30.

70. "Defending Those Who Give the Earth a Voice," *Environmentalists under Fire: 10 Urgent Cases of Human Rights Abuses* (Washington, DC: Amnesty International USA and the Sierra Club, 2001).

71. Specifically, the Court found evidence that would allow a jury to find that Unocal's joint venture hired the military and that Unocal is therefore vicariously liable for the military's human rights abuses and to conclude that Unocal breached California

constitutional and statutory law in its operations. For transcripts of the decision, see http://www.earthrights.org/unocal.

72. James Scott, *Domination and the Art of Resistance* (New Haven, CT: Yale University Press, 1990), 192.

73. Bell, *Social Movements and Regional Integration in the Americas*, 6.

74. Robert Lake, "Volunteers, NIMBYs, and Environmental Justice: Dilemmas of Democratic Practice," *Antipode* 28 (1996): 160–74.

75. Faber, "A Revolution in Environmental Justice and Sustainable Development," 39–70.

76. Daniel R. Faber, "The Struggle for Ecological Democracy and Environmental Justice," in *The Struggle for Ecological Democracy*, 1–26.

Conclusion

What Does the Future Hold?
The Struggle for "Productive"
Environmental Justice

Injustice anywhere is a threat to justice everywhere.

—Dr. Martin Luther King Jr.

NEOLIBERALISM, DEMOCRACY,
AND THE CRISIS OF ENVIRONMENTALISM

In the new millennium, democracy is under assault. In its efforts to hijack the American government, the polluter-industrial complex is pouring money into the campaigns of neoliberal candidates in both major political parties. The aim of these corporate polluters is to colonize the state and to implement neoliberal economic policies aimed at freeing capital of costly regulations intended to protect the environment and worker/consumer health and safety. These efforts are complemented by neoconservative social policy, which places a greater emphasis on the moral authority and responsibility of individuals and private organizations to assume the roles previously performed by the government for those in need. By subordinating the regulatory state to the economic imperatives of corporate capital and by dismantling the welfare state in favor of the moral impulses of voluntary charitable institutions, the business class and its political allies are reasserting their power in relation to environmental, labor, civil rights, women's, and environmental justice (EJ) movements. The American people are now being told by the ruling political establishment to fend for themselves and ask for charity rather than to demand sound government services and safeguards.

Although a liberal political agenda has often displaced more profound calls by the "left" for social and economic reforms, the gains won by these popular

259

movements over the past four decades or more—higher wages, good benefits, job security and advancement, environmental preservation, affirmative action, progressive taxation, occupational health and safety regulations, universal entitlements such as Social Security, good public educational opportunities, and various welfare programs—are significant. But as a result of the recent political offensive by the business establishment, the defining characteristics of liberal democratic capitalism that have brought such great benefits to much of America's working and middle classes are eroding. Consequently, a plethora of severe economic stresses and social strains are emerging, ranging from stagnant wages and increased indebtedness, the lack of affordable health care insurance, the disintegration of public education, the rollback of environmental protection and EJ policies, regressive taxation policies and declining services, and the sacrifice of civil liberties and human rights in the war on terrorism.

America's social and ecological problems can be partly traced to what the influential sociologist Robert Putnam has termed the decline in *social capital*, or those social networks and assets that facilitate the education, coordination, and cooperation of citizens for mutual benefit.[1] Under the pressures generated by global economic restructuring, the increased demands for labor mobility and longer hours spent at work, and the increased privatization of formerly independent civic institutions and public spaces, the social networks that integrate citizens into their local communities are deteriorating. The resulting decline in social capital inhibits genuine citizen participation in the affairs of civil society and real engagement in the realm of politics, including the ability to tackle social and environmental problems in an equitable and effective fashion. With interactions that build mutual trust eroded, large sectors of the American people are increasingly cynical about their ability to collectively effect meaningful social and ecological changes. Instead, a growing number of people retreat into what Jürgen Habermas terms *civil privatism*, with an emphasis on improving personal lifestyles through career advancement, social mobility, and conspicuous consumption.[2] When social and environmental problems are confronted, increasingly privatized "marketplace-driven" approaches, collective "voluntarism," escapist, or "individual-choice" solutions as promoted by the New Right become the favored response.

The scapegoating of the disadvantaged by conservative media pundits and mean-spirited talk show hosts such as Rush Limbaugh and Bill O'Reilly further decry notions of economic equality and progressive political action for the common good. Blaming the victims deflects potential criticism away from the failings of neoliberal capitalism. Portrayed by right-wing journalists, politicians, and government officials as "looters" or as "too lazy or dumb to leave," the demonization of poor African American residents of New Orleans is one such example. Instead of pondering why there was no adequate government relief mission or emergency evacuation plan for those without means to flee the storm, former House Leader Newt Gingrich blamed the 22,000 victims in New Orleans's Ninth Ward for a "failure of citizenship" by being "so uneducated and so unprepared, they literally couldn't get out of the way of a hurricane." Senator Rick Santorum of Pennsylvania even suggested punishing people who had ignored prestorm evacuation orders.[3] In this conservative blame game, the various racial, ethnic, class, and religious divides in American society become accentuated, as the "haves" increasingly disregard the needs of the "have nots," as seen in the attack on affirmative action, the social safety net, labor rights, consumer safeguards, public education, environmental justice, ecological protection, and federal emergency management.

The U.S. environmental movement has contributed to this problem by neglecting to reach out to poor people of color and working-class families. The movement has also largely failed to form more substantive organizational ties with labor and other progressive social movements in order to create a larger political agenda around such issues as affordable housing and health care, a living wage and economic justice, civil liberties and human rights, and the conversion of the U.S. economy to a more just and sustainable model. Instead, environmentalists and other social movements remain locked into narrow and increasingly ineffectual policy silos in Washington, D.C.[4] As stated by Pablo Eisenberg of Georgetown University's Public Policy Institute, "Although we know that our socioeconomic, ecological, and political problems are interrelated, a growing portion of our nonprofit world nevertheless continues to operate in a way that fails to reflect this complexity and connectedness."[5] As a result, the linkages between environmental abuses, poverty and economic inequality, racism, human health problems, crime, the lack of democracy, and the consolidation of corporate power are typically ignored.

Unfortunately, too many mainstream environmental organizations adopt corporate-like organizational models that further inhibit broad-based citizen involvement in environmental problem solving. For some groups, citizen engagement means simply sending in membership dues, signing a petition, and writing the occasional letter to a government official. As stated by William Shutkin, there is a "tendency for many non-profit environmental organizations to treat members as clients and consumers of services, or volunteers who help the needy, rather than as participants in the evolution of ideas and projects that forge our common life."[6] In the effort to conduct studies, draft legislation, and support lawsuits against polluters, much of the mainstream movement has gravitated toward a greater reliance on law and science conducted by professional experts rather than grassroots organizing. Lacking a highly mobilized political base, environmental organizations are compelled to engage in acts of political compromise in order to protect policy gains.

The aim of this move toward increased professionalization is to regain legitimacy in increasingly hostile neoliberal policy circles. The effect, however, is to reduce internal democratic practices within some environmental organizations and state regulatory agencies. The focus on technical-rational questions, solutions, and compromises rather than larger issues of political power and democratic decision making is causing a decline of public participation in national environmental politics. In addition, some nationally based, memberless environmental organizations assume the responsibility of deciding what are the primary environmental problems and issues of local communities, invent the special projects or campaigns designed to "remedy" the problem, and then select the strategies that will result in the "needed" projects or policies. Under this model, environmental organizations often speak and act on behalf of a community but are not necessarily *grounded* in the community. This does not promote participatory democracy or community self-determination.

FORGING A NEW ENVIRONMENTAL CITIZENSHIP

The retreat into civil privatism and the crisis of environmentalism have many sources but are fundamentally linked to the forces of civic disempowerment sweeping the nation. The disengagement of ordinary citizens from civic institutions is linked to a withering away of the democratic state. It is also linked to the increased encroachment of capitalist economy into the American lifeworld—the social networks and institutions that shape our shared and personal lives. The colonization of civil society by a host of undemocratic institutions under the control of the capitalist class and political elites—large corporations, quasi-private government agencies, private foundations, business-funded think tanks and policy institutes, and "top-down, memberless" nonprofit organizations—is rendering representative forms of political decision making devoid of any meaningful public deliberation and input. The dominance of corporate money in the Democratic and Republican parties further distorts democratic discourse. As a result, poor people of color and working-class whites, along with a growing proportion of the middle class, are increasingly hindered from engaging in civil society as equal citizens. Rendered politically passive by institutional elites, citizens retreat into civil privatism and/or increasingly embrace the New Right agenda.

To overcome this crisis of democracy and the corporate assault on nature requires the reinvigoration of an *active environmental citizenship* dedicated to the *principles of ecological democracy*, including (1) *grassroots democracy and inclusiveness*—a commitment to the vigorous participation of working people from all walks of life in the decision-making processes of business, government, and other social institutions that regulate their lives as well as civic organizations and social movements that represent their interests; (2) *social and economic justice*—meeting all basic human needs and ensuring fundamental human and civil rights for all members of society; and (3) *sustainability and environmental protection*—ensuring that the integrity of nature is preserved for both present and future generations of all citizens. These three pillars on which the concept of ecological democracy rests provide a meaningful vision for building a more just and ecologically sound American society.

Fortunately, there are signs that a powerfully new active environmental citizenship committed to the principles of ecological democracy is emerging in America and throughout the world. The revitalization of grassroots environmental organizations committed to rebuilding democratic institutions from the bottom up (i.e., base building*)* and implementing comprehensive reforms of the capitalist system is a reaction to the new challenges posed by neoliberalism and corporate-led globalization and includes the use of direct action against indifferent government agencies, corporate polluters, and the World Trade Organization. Pressing for greater economic equality, greater business and government accountability (such as the "right to know" about hazards facing the community), and more comprehensive approaches to environmental problem solving, the struggle for ecological democracy potentially represents the birth of a *transformative* environmental politics.

Base-building strategies aim to create accountable, democratic organizational structures and institutional procedures that facilitate the inclusion of ordinary citizens and especially dispossessed people of color and working-class families in the public and private decision-making practices affecting their lives. Traditional forms of "top down" advocacy, service, and litigation strategies are subordinated in favor of grassroots organizing efforts that facilitate *community empowerment*. In short, a transformative environmental politics aims to create a infrastructure that mobilizes a broad base of citizens to be directly involved in the identification of social and environmental problems and the implementation of potential solutions. This approach utilizes environmental advocacy, service, and litigation strategies that are informed by direct citizen participation in community decision making.

THE PROMISE OF THE ENVIRONMENTAL JUSTICE MOVEMENT FOR TRANSFORMING GREEN POLITICS

At the forefront of the struggle for ecological democracy and a new active environmental citizenship is the EJ movement. Along with the clean production movement, no other force within the broader context of grassroots environmentalism currently offers the same potential as the EJ movement for 1) bringing new constituencies into environmental activism, particularly in terms of oppressed peoples of color, the working poor, and other populations who bear the greatest ecological burden; 2) broadening and deepening our understanding of ecological impacts, particularly in terms of linking issues to larger structures of corporate power; 3) constructing and implementing new grassroots organizing and base-building strategies over traditional forms of advocacy as well as developing new organizational models that rebuild social capital and maximize democratic participation by community residents in decision-making processes; 4) connecting grassroots and national layers of environmental activism; 5) creating new pressure points for policy change; 6) building coalitions and coordinated strategies with other progressive social movements, including much of the labor movement; and 7) bringing more innovative and comprehensive approaches to environmental problem solving, particularly in terms of linking sustainability with issues of social justice.[7]

EJ activists clearly recognize the importance of community building, promoting active forms of citizen participation in decision-making processes, and forging stronger partnerships with other community organizations in order to build a more vibrant and democratic civil society.[8] As stated by Mark Gerzon, "Strengthening the capacity of communities for self-governance — that is, making the crucial choices and decisions that affect their lives" — is the most critical task confronting the EJ movement in rebuilding social capital and a vibrant ecological democracy.[9] By organizing base-building campaigns that address the common links between various social and environmental problems (in contrast to isolated single-issue-oriented groups that treat problems as distinct), EJ activists function as community capacity builders. In this respect, the movement has done an outstanding job of enlarging the constituency of the environmental movement as a whole by incorporating poorer communities and oppressed peoples of color into strong, independent organizational structures. The movement has done important work in helping to span community boundaries by crossing difficult racial, class, gender-based, and ideological divides that weaken and fragment communities.[10] It remains to be seen whether the dominance of an identity politics that privileges environmental racism as the primary manifestation of environmental injustice will deter or assist the formation of larger alliances between people of differing races, ethnic histories, and cultural backgrounds within the movement as well as between people of color in the movement and working- and middle-class whites currently outside the EJ movement.[11]

Finally, the movement is facilitating community empowerment by emphasizing grassroots organizing and base building over traditional forms of environmental advocacy. Under the traditional advocacy model, professional activists create organizations that speak and act on behalf of a community. In contrast, the grassroots organizing approach by the EJ movement emphasizes the mobilization of community residents to push through the systemic barriers that bar poor people of color from directly participating in the identification of problems and solutions—so that they may, in the words of the late EJ advocate Dana Alston, "*speak and act for themselves.*"[12] If the EJ movement continues to build on the already impressive successes it has established in these areas and can find ways to collaborate with the broad array of grassroots citizens' groups representative of the white working class and salariat, we may witness the creation of a truly broad-based ecology movement that is capable of implementing a national and international strategy to end the abuses of nature wrought by corporate America.

FINDING GREENER PASTURES: A MORE "PRODUCTIVE" ENVIRONMENTAL JUSTICE POLITICS

The most immediate mission of the EJ movement is to dismantle the mechanisms by which capital and the state disproportionately displace the social and ecological costs of production onto oppressed communities of color. Despite the movement's infancy, there have been a number of successes in recent years. Engaging in public protests, lobbying, media relations, electoral work, and other direct-action tactics, including mass-based civil disobedience, the EJ movement and other grassroots activists has won a number of important victories in recent years. EJ organizing efforts have helped to kill 80 percent of all planned municipal incinerators, protected the natural resources and unique wilderness areas of many communities, stopped ocean dumping of radioactive wastes and sewage sludge, facilitated the cleanup of toxic waste sites in poor communities of color, and created government policies and programs for addressing environmental injustices at the local, state, and federal levels.[13]

Although the tactics for attacking environmental inequities are quite varied, one common political demand of these movements is for greater democratic participation in the governmental decision-making processes affecting their communities. By gaining greater access to policy makers and agencies, EJ activists hope to initiate better governmental regulation of the discriminatory manner in which the market distributes environmental risks. At the national level, this has led important segments of the EJ movement to draw on liberal-democratic strategies aimed at reforming the Environmental Protection Agency's institutional focus, particularly the manner by which the agency drafts and enforces environmental policy. Movement pressure led President Clinton to sign Executive Order 12898 for environmental justice, ordering all federal agencies to begin initiatives aimed at reducing environmental inequities, although (as we have seen in chapter 3) the order is now under assault by the Bush administration and the polluter-industrial complex.

Despite these achievements, there are limitations to this reformist approach to environmental injustice. Aside from failing to transform the manner in which corporate money and power now dominate the electoral and policy-making processes, including the mechanisms by which the Environmental Protection Agency, the Department of Interior, and other related state agencies become captured and subsumed by the polluter-industrial complex, liberalist-oriented environmentalism fails to address the "essential cause" of ecological problems in America—the workings of a capitalist economy and market-place.[14] This is evident in a movement discourse that defines environmental justice in terms of eliminating the *discriminatory* or *unequal distribution* of ecological hazards rather than eliminating the *root causes* of the hazards for all Americans. President Clinton's executive order for environmental justice, for instance, specifically associates environmental justice with federal agencies "identifying and addressing, as appropriate, disproportionately high and adverse human health or environmental effects of their programs, policies and activities on minority populations and low income populations in the United States." Similarly, the Department of Energy, in announcing its "Environmental Justice" policy in 1994, defined its approach as promoting "non-discrimination among minority, American Indian, and low-income communities."[15]

But the struggle for environmental justice is not just about distributing environmental risks equally but also about preventing them from being produced in the first place so that no one is harmed at all. A movement for environmental justice is of limited efficacy if the end result is to have all Americans poisoned to the same perilous degree, regardless of race, color, or class. The struggle for environmental justice must be about the politics of capitalist production per se and the elimination of the ecological threat, not just the "fair" distribution of ecological hazards via better government regulation of racial/class-based inequities in the marketplace.

The benefits of greater participatory democracy are extremely limited if communities are presented with only false choices. Poorer communities often face the option of rejecting construction of a toxic waste facility that poses significant health hazards or of accepting such a site because of the greater job opportunities and tax revenues it affords. Unless movements for environmental justice can address the political-economic dynamics of capitalism that force communities to make such trade-offs, their conception of environmental justice as "greater participatory democracy" and an "end to racial discrimination" will remain extremely limited. The enemy is profit. Disease, hunger, racism, inadequate health care, and the ecological reconstruction of America will not be solved by corporations. While increased participatory democracy by popular forces in governmental decision making and community planning is desirable (if not essential) and should be supported, it is in and of itself insufficient for achieving true environmental justice. What is needed is a richer conception of environmental justice grounded in the traditions of the New Left.

From an ecosocialist perspective, organizing efforts against the procedures that result in the unequal *distribution* of environmental problems (distributional inequity) cannot ultimately succeed unless EJ activists address the procedures by which the problems are *produced* in the first place (procedural inequity). In the words of Robert Lake,

> Probing the nature of procedural environmental equity as self-determination suggest that solving the distributional problem may be necessary but will not be sufficient for producing environmental justice. Stated differently, environmental justice will not have been achieved in the event that marginalized communities are no longer subjected to a disproportionate share of environmental problems. We will not have eliminated environmental inequity when a benevolent Environmental Protection Agency succeeds in redistributing environmental problems such that no community is disproportionately burdened. Removing the environmental burden on a community, say through facility licensing and monitoring, site remediation, and environmental cleanups, may well be a significant accomplishment but it will not have empowered that community to control its environment. Redistributing outcomes will not achieve environmental justice unless it is accompanied and, indeed, preceded by a procedural redistribution of power in decision-making.[16]

In Lake's view, any attempt to rectify distributional inequities without attacking the fundamental processes that produce the problems being distributed focuses on symptoms rather than causes and is therefore only a partial, temporary, and necessarily incomplete and insufficient solution. What is needed is an ecosocialist politics for procedural equity that emphasizes democratic participation in the capital investment decisions through which environmental burdens are *produced* and then distributed. This view holds a much broader concept of ecological democracy and environmental justice. As stated by Michael Heiman, "If we settle for liberal procedural and distributional equity, relying upon negotiation, mitigation, and fair-share allocation to address some sort of 'disproportional' impact, we merely perpetuate the current production system that by its very structure is discriminatory and nonsustainable."[17] It is precisely this distinction between *distributional justice* and *productive justice* that many in the EJ movement are now confronting.

Rather than existing as a collection of organizations and networks fighting defensive "not-in-my-backyard" battles (as important as they may be), the EJ movement must continue to evolve into a political force capable of challenging the systemic causes of social and ecological injustices as they exist "in everyone's backyard."[18] Only by bringing about what Barry Commoner calls "the social governance of the means of production"[19]—a radical democratization of the major political, social, and economic institutions in society—can humanity begin to gain control over the course of social and environmental history. Such a program for social governance would require sublating the institutions of workplace and local direct democracy, liberal democratic procedures and constitutional guarantees, state planning, and the initiatives of popular-based social and environmental movements into a genuine ecological democracy.[20]

Ecological democracy offers the potential for overcoming the anarchy of the free market and the primacy of economic growth. Oriented first and foremost to the short-term interests of the corporate capital at the expense of nature, American capitalism must be subsumed to long-term democratic planning aimed at meeting the human and environmental needs of all present and future generations. Only then can the environmental movement succeed in moving beyond single-issue or band-aid policy approaches to embrace more comprehensive solutions to the ecological crisis. This would include adopting *pollution prevention* measures that eliminate the use of dangerous chemicals, production processes, and consumer goods altogether (source reduction) rather than relying on costly and ineffective *pollution control* measures aimed at "containing" and "fairly" distributing environmental hazards once they are produced. In this respect, ecological democracy not only is a form of praxis (practice) but also must become the telos (purpose) of movements for environmental justice.

The transition to *clean production* and the utilization of the *precautionary principle* are key components of a more "productive" EJ politics. The precautionary principle posits that if there is a strong possibility of harm (instead of scientifically proven certainty of harm) to human health or the environment from a substance or activity, precautionary measures should be taken. Standard environmental policy approaches in the United States utilize risk assessments to determine "acceptable" levels of public exposure to industrial pollutants applied as a general standard on industry. However, from an EJ perspective, there are a number of significant flaws with this approach. For instance, policymakers often assume that "dilution is the solution," that the wide dispersion of environmental pollution from various sources leads to what are considered safe levels of public exposure. However, if pollution is highly concentrated in certain communities, as demonstrated in chapter 1, then this approach can be grossly inadequate. All communities (and especially overburdened EJ communities) must be granted additional protections as offered by the precautionary principle, including promoting additional study of activities of concern, shifting the burden of proof onto capital to prove that a chemical/activity is safe (rather than the public to prove it is harmful), providing incentives for preventive behavior, and/or enacting clean production measures such as bans or phaseouts of substances suspected of causing harm.[21]

Around the country, new organizing efforts around clean production and environmental justice are gaining momentum. In Massachusetts, for instance, a statewide coalition of more than 160 environmental, labor, consumer product safety, health-affected groups (breast cancer, asthma, learning and behavioral disabilities, and others), scientific and public health associations, religious and faith-based organizations, student groups, and community-based EJ organizations has recently joined hands under the umbrella of the Alliance for a Healthy Tomorrow. This group is working for the adoption of proactive, prevention-oriented policies that make use of a precautionary approach (the precautionary principle) to hazardous chemicals, call for the adoption of safer alternatives in place of dangerous chemicals (the substitution principle), and provide a transition blueprint to a toxic-free economy that provides good jobs and other benefits for workers, people of color, and middle-class families (clean production). More specifically, all member organizations throughout the coalition are educating and mobilizing their constituencies to assist in the design and adoption of model legislation that is mutually beneficial to all the groups.

The most comprehensive approach has recently been integrated in the proposed legislation "An Act for a Healthy Massachusetts: Safer Alternatives to Toxic Chemicals." This bill aims to create a model for the gradual replacement of toxic chemicals with safer alternatives. It targets substances that are currently replaceable with feasible safer alternatives. It accomplishes this goal by laying out a careful process to examine all available evidence to identify safer alternatives and manufacturing processes that will benefit the health of workers, customers, children, the environment, and the economy. The proposed program would stimulate research and development on new technologies and solutions when a safer alternative is not currently feasible. It would also create programs to assist workers and businesses in the transition to the safest available alternatives, with funding provided through a fee on toxic chemicals. The goal of this legislation is to ensure that the targeted chemical be phased out from use only when the state determines that there is a feasible safer alternative available within a reasonable period of time. At the same time, the state would try to avoid seeing companies simply moving to another equally toxic alternative.[22]

WHAT DOES THE FUTURE HOLD?

If the traditional environmental movement continues to conceive of the ecological crisis as a collection of unrelated problems and if the reigning paradigm is defined in either liberal or neoliberalist terms, then it is possible that some combination of regulations, incentives, and technical innovations can keep pollution and resource destruction at "tolerable" levels for many people of higher socioeconomic status. However, poorer working-class communities and people of color who lack the political-economic resources to defend themselves will continue to suffer the worst abuses. If, however, the interdependency of issues is emphasized, as in the EJ movement, so that environmental devastation, ecological racism, poverty, crime, and social despair are all seen as aspects of a multidimensional web rooted in a larger structural crisis, then a transformative ecology movement can be invented.[23] The American people can play an instrumental role in facilitating this transformation of green politics in America by joining forces with those organizations championing the sorts of fundamental social and institutional changes needed to address the ecological crisis.

In order to build itself into a political force capable of addressing the fundamental roots of America's social and ecological crises, a series of challenges confront grassroots movements for environmental justice. First, in that the environmental movement as a whole (as well as the labor movement) has weakened itself by its failure to revive the struggle to democratize the state and the workplace, the EJ movement must build greater unity with trade unions and the labor movement around issues of productive justice. Similarly, in that the environmental movement has failed to fight against ecological racism, the EJ movement must incorporate and build unity between oppressed people of color and broader segments of the white working class and salariat, especially around issues of environmental health. Otherwise, struggles against ecological hazards in poor communities of color could evoke a political backlash if such hazards are relocated to white working- and middle-class communities. Only by gaining greater democratic governance over community planning and national economic development can a potentially divisive "not-in-my-backyard" politics oriented to distributive justice be replaced with a truly transformative "not-in-anyone's-backyard" politics oriented to productive justice.[24]

Finally, in that the environmental movement has been slow to combat the globalization of capital and export of ecological hazard, the EJ movement must develop solidarity with those movements and governments in the Third World that know that capitalist economic development, ecological degradation, and human poverty are different sides of the same general problem. The growing ability of multinational corporations and transnational financial institutions to evade and dismantle unions, environmental safeguards, and worker/community health and safety regulations in the United States is being achieved by crossing national boundaries into politically repressive and economically oppressive countries, such as in Mexico and China. As a result, peoples and governments of the world are increasingly being pitted against one another in a bid to attract capital investment, leading to one successful assault after another on labor and environmental regulations seen as damaging to profits. And in this context, utilizing the rhetoric of "free trade" and "jobs versus the environment," capital has further weakened and divided America's social movements against one another and worsened economic inequities and ecological injustices of all kinds. Only by achieving greater social governance over trade and lending institutions can the process that leads different countries to sacrifice human and environmental health in order to compete in the world economy be overcome.

And as the ecological crisis of U.S. capitalism deepens and global ecological conditions worsen, the need for a mass-based international ecology movement that unites the struggle for both social and ecological justice will become more pressing. Just as in the 1930s, when the labor movement was forced to change from craft to industrial unionism, so today does it appear to many that labor needs to transform itself from industrial unionism into an international, conglomerate union (inclusive of women and all racial/ethnic minorities)—merely to keep pace with the restructuring of international capital. And just as in the 1960s, when the environmental movement changed from a narrowly based conservation/preservation movement to include the middle class and sections of the white working class, so today does it seem to many that it needs to change from single-issue local and national struggles to a broad-based, multiracial international movement. This will ultimately require a merger and new synthesis with the EJ movement. Environmentalists, EJ activists, and other social movements in the United States must be made to realize that they need strong environmentalism and worker health and safety throughout the rest of the world in order to protect local initiatives and gains.

In summary, the challenge confronting the EJ movement is to help forge a truly broad-based political movement for ecological democracy. While the traditional environmental movement has played a critical and progressive role in stemming many of the worst threats posed to the health of the planet and its inhabitants, the movement is now rapidly losing power in the age of neoliberalism and corporate-led globalization. Traditional liberal environmental strategies are now, at best, limited or ineffective and, at worst, increasingly self-defeating. Environmentalists and social justice activists must embrace a multi-issue/multimovement approach that emphasizes productive justice for all Americans if this power is to ever be restored. To do so requires developing a more comprehensive understanding of the political-economic terrain on which it now struggles. Socialist ecology is essential to this endeavor. This historic task now confronts the EJ movement as well as all people of the United States and the world.

NOTES

1. Robert Putnam, *Bowling Alone: The Collapse and Revival of American Community* (New York: Simon and Schuster, 2000), 19–20.

2. Jürgen Habermas, *The Structural Transformation of the Public Sphere* (Cambridge, MA: MIT Press, 1989), and *Legitimation Crisis* (Boston: Beacon Press, 1975).

3. "Hurricane Katrina: Blaming the Victims" (September 29, 2007), available at http://www.sourcewatch.org/index.php?title=Hurricane_Katrina:_Blaming_the_Victims (accessed September 27, 2005).

4. Robert O. Bothwell, "Up against Conservative Public Policy: Alternatives to Mainstream Philanthropy," in *Foundations for Social Change: Critical Perspectives on Philanthropy and Popular Movements*, ed. Daniel Faber and Deborah McCarthy (Lanham, MD: Rowman & Littlefield, 2005), 115–50.

5. Pablo Eisenberg, "A Crisis in the Nonprofit Sector," *National Civic Review* 86, no. 4 (Winter 1997): 331–41.

6. William Shutkin, *The Land That Could Be: Environmentalism and Democracy in the Twenty-First Century* (Cambridge, MA: MIT Press, 2001), 1–20.

7. Ann Bastian and Dana Alston, "An Open Letter to Funding Colleagues: New Developments in the Environmental Justice Movement," New World Foundation (September 1993), 1–7, and "An Update on Developments in the Environmental Justice Movement: An Open Letter to Funding Colleagues," New World Foundation (January 1996), 1–12.

8. Daniel Faber and Deborah McCarthy, *Green of Another Color: Building Effective Partnerships between Foundations and the Environmental Justice Movement*, a report by the Philanthropy and Environmental Justice Research Project, Northeastern University (Boston, 2001).

9. Mark Gerzon, "Reinventing Philanthropy: Foundations and the Renewal of Civil Society," *National Civic Review* 84, no. 2–3 (Summer–Fall 1995): 188–95.

10. David Mathews, "Changing Times in the Foundation World," *National Civic Review* 86, no. 4 (Winter 1997): 275–80.

11. Daniel Faber, "Building a Transnational Environmental Justice Movement: Obstacles and Opportunities in the Age of Globalization," in *Coalitions across Borders: Transnational Protest and the Neoliberal Order*, ed. Joe Bandy and Jackie Smith (Lanham, MD: Rowman & Littlefield, 2005), 43–70.

12. Dana Alston, ed., *We Speak for Ourselves: Social Justice, Race, and Environment* (Washington, DC: The Panos Institute, 1991).

13. For a short summary, see Peter Montague, "Where We Are Now," *Rachel's Environment and Health Weekly*, no. 500 (June 27, 1996), 1–2.

14. James O'Connor, *Natural Causes: Essays in Ecological Marxism* (New York: Guilford Press, 1998).

15. Cited in Robert Gottlieb and Andrew Fisher, "'First Feed the Face': Environmental Justice and Community Food Security," *Antipode* 28, no. 2 (1996): 193–203.

16. Robert W. Lake, "Volunteers, NIMBYs, and Environmental Justice: Dilemmas of Democratic Practice," *Antipode* 28, no. 2 (1996): 169.

17. Michael K. Heiman, "Race, Waste, and Class: New Perspectives on Environmental Justice," *Antipode* 28, no. 2 (1996): 120.

18. See *Everyone's Backyard: The Journal of Grassroots Movements for Environmental Justice* (Citizen's Clearinghouse for Hazardous Waste, P.O. Box 6806, Falls Church, VA 22040).

19. Barry Commoner, *Making Peace with the Planet* (New York: Pantheon, 1990).

20. James O'Connor, "A Red Green Politics in the U.S.?," *Capitalism, Nature, Socialism* 5, no. 1 (March 1994): 1–20.

21. Mary O'Brien, *Making Better Environmental Decisions: An Alternative to Risk Assessment* (Cambridge, MA: MIT Press, 2000).

22. Daniel Faber, "A More 'Productive' Environmental Justice Politics: Movement Alliances in Massachusetts for Clean Production and Regional Equity," in *Environmental Justice and Environmentalism: The Social Justice Challenge to the Environmental Movement*, ed. Ronald Sandler and Phaedra C. Pezzullo (Cambridge, MA: MIT Press, 2007), 135–64.

23. John Rodman, "Paradigm Change in Political Science: An Ecological Perspective," *American Behavioral Scientist* 24, no. 1 (September–October 1980): 49–78.

24. Eric Krieg and Daniel Faber, "Not So Black and White: Environmental Justice and Cumulative Environmental Impacts," *Environmental Impact Assessment Review* 24, no. 7–8 (October–November 2004): 667–94.

Selected Bibliography

Adeola, Francis O. "Cross-National Environmental Injustice and Human Rights Issues: A Review of Evidence in the Developing World." *American Behavioral Scientist* 43, no. 4 (2000): 686–706.

Agyeman, Julian, Robert Bullard, and Bob Evans, eds. *Just Sustainabilities: Development In An Unequal World*. London, England: Transaction Books, 2003.

Ali, Saleem H. *Mining, the Environment, and Indigenous Development Conflicts*. Tuscon: University of Arizona Press, 2005.

Almeida, Paul. "The Network for Environmental and Economic Justice in the Southwest: An Interview with Richard Moore." In *The Struggle for Ecological Democracy: Environmental Justice Movements in the United States*, ed. Daniel Faber, 159–97. New York: Guilford Press, 1998.

Alston, Dana. "Transforming a Movement: People of Color United at Summit Against Environmental Racism." *Sojourner* 21 (1992): 30–31.

———. *We Speak for Ourselves: Social Justice, Race, and Environment*. Washington, DC: Panos Institute, 1991.

Amnesty International USA. *Environmentalists Under Fire: 10 Urgent Cases of Human Rights Abuses*. Washington, DC: Amnesty International USA and the Sierra Club, 2000.

Anderson, Judith T. L., Katherine Hunting, and Laura S. Welch. "Injury and Employment Patterns Among Hispanic Construction Workers." *Journal of Occupational and Environmental Medicine* 42, no. 2 (February 2000): 176–86.

Anderson, Terry L., and Donald R. Leal. *Free Market Environmentalism*. New York: Palgrave, 2001.

Athanasiou, Tom. *Divided Planet: The Ecology of Rich and Poor*. Boston: Little, Brown, 1996.

Baldwin, Robert E. *The Decline of US Labor Unions and the Role of Trade*. Washington, DC: Institute for International Economics, 2003.

Barrow, Clyde W. *Critical Theories of the State: Marxist, Neo-Marxist, Post-Marxist*. Madison: University of Wisconsin Press, 1993.

Bastian, Anne, and Dana Alston. "An Open Letter To Funding Colleagues: New Developments in the Environmental Justice Movement." *New World Foundation & Public Welfare Foundation* (1993): 1–4.

Beder, Sharon. *Global Spin: The Corporate Assault on Environmentalism*. White River Junction, VT: Chelsea Green Books, 1997.

Bell, Beverly. *Social Movements and Regional Integration in the Americas*. Albuquerque, NM: Center for Economic Justice, 2002.

Bello, Walden. "The Capitalist Conjuncture: Overaccumulation, Financial Crises, and the Retreat from Globalization," *Third World Quarterly* 27, no. 8 (2006): 1175–91.

——. "The Iron Cage: The World Trade Organization, The Bretton Woods Institutions, and the South." *Capitalism, Nature, Socialism* 11, no. 1 (2000): 3–32.

Belsky, Martin H. "Environmental Policy Law in the 1980s: Shifting Back the Burden of Proof," *Ecology Law Quarterly* 12, no. 1 (1984): 1–24.

Berman, Daniel. *Death on the Job: Occupational Health and Safety Struggles in the United States*. New York: Monthly Review Press, 1978.

Bezdek, Roger H. "The Net Impact of Environmental Protection on Jobs and the Economy." In *Environmental Justice: Issues, Policies, and Solutions*, ed. Bunyan Bryant, 86–106. Washington, DC: Island Press, 1995.

Bogard, William. *The Bhopal Tragedy: Language, Logic, and Politics in the Production of Hazard*. San Francisco: Westview Press, 1989.

Bohme, Susanna Rankin, John Zorabedian, and David S. Egilman. "Maximizing Profit and Endangering Health: Corporate Strategies to Avoid Litigation and Regulation." *International Journal of Occupational and Environmental Health* 11, no. 4 (October/December 2005): 338–48.

Bond, Patrick. *Unsustainable South Africa: Environment, Development, and Social Protest*. South Africa: University of Natal Press, 2002.

Bothwell, Robert O. "Up Against Conservative Public Policy: Alternatives to Mainstream Philanthropy." In *Foundations for Social Change: Critical Perspectives on Philanthropy and Popular Movements,* ed. Daniel Faber and Deborah McCarthy, 115–47. Lanham, MD: Rowman & Littlefied, 2005.

Bourne, Jr., Joel K. "Gone with the Water," *Natural Geographic* (October 2004): 88–105, 96.

Bouwes, Nicolaas W., Steven M. Hassur, and Marc D. Shapiro. *Empowerment Through Risk-Related Information: The EPA's Risk-Screening Environmental Indicators Project*. A report prepared by the Political Economy Research Institute, University of Massachusetts at Amherst (February 2001), 16.

Brechin, Steven R. "Objective Problems, Subjective Values, and Global Environmentalism: Evaluating the Postmaterialist Argument and Challenging a New Explanation." *Social Science Quarterly* 80, no. 4 (1999): 793–809.

Brown, Phil. *Toxic Exposures: Contested Illnesses and the Environmental Health Movement*. New York: Columbia University Press, 2007.

Brulle, Robert J. *Agency, Democracy, and Nature: The U.S. Environmental Movement from a Critical Theory Perspective*. Cambridge, MA: MIT Press, 2000.

Brulle, Robert J., and J. Craig Jenkins. "Foundations and the Environmental Movement: Priorities, Strategies, and Impact," in *Foundations for Social*

Change: Critical Perspectives on Philanthropy and Popular Movements, ed. Daniel Faber and Deborah McCarthy. Philadelphia: Temple University Press, 2003.

Bruno, Kenny, and Joshua Karliner. *Earthsummit.biz: The Corporate Takeover of Sustainable Development.* Oakland, CA: Food First Books, 2002.

Bryant, Bunyan. *Environmental Justice: Issues, Policies, and Solutions.* Washington, DC: Island Press, 1995.

Bryant, Bunyan, and Paul Mohai. *Race and the Incidence of Environmental Hazards: A Time for Discourse.* Boulder, CO: Westview Press, 1992.

Bullard, Robert D. "Environmental Justice in the Twenty-first Century." In *The Quest for Environmental Justice: Human Rights and the Politics of Pollution,* ed. Robert D. Bullard, 28–42. San Francisco: Sierra Club Books, 2005.

———. *Unequal Protection: Environmental Justice and Communities of Color.* San Francisco: Sierra Club Books, 1994.

———. *Dumping in Dixie: Race, Class, and Environmental Quality.* Boulder, CO: Westview Press, 1990.

———. ed., *Confronting Environmental Racism: Voices from the Grassroots.* Boston: South End Press, 1993.

Bullard, Robert D., Paul Mohai, Robin Saha, and Beverly Wright. *Toxic Wastes and Race at Twenty: 1987–2007 Grassroots Struggles to Dismantle Environmental Racism in the United States.* A report prepared for the United Church of Christ Justice and Witness Ministries (March 2007), 58–60.

Burns, Thomas, Jeffrey Kentor, and Andrew K. Jorgenson. "Trade Dependence, Pollution, and Infant Mortality in Less Developed Countries." In *Crises and Resistance in the 21st Century World-System,* ed. Wilma A. Dunaway, 14–28. Westport, CT: Praeger, 2003.

Buttel, Frederick H. "Environmentalization: Origins, Processes, and Implications for Rural Social Change." *Rural Sociology* 57 (1992): 1–27.

Buttel, Frederick H., and Peter J. Taylor. "Environmental Sociology and Global Environmental Change: A Critical Assessment." *Society and Natural Resources* 5 (1992): 211–30.

Byrne, John, Leigh Glover, and Cecilia Martinez eds., *Environmental Justice: Discourses in International Political Economy, Energy and Environmental Policy.* New Brunswick, NJ: Transaction, 2002.

Byrne, John, Cecilia Martinez, and Leigh Glover, "A Brief on Environmental Justice." In *Environmental Justice: Discourses in International Political Economy, Energy, and Environmental Policy,* ed. J. Byrne, L. Glover, and C. Martinez, 3–17. New Brunswick, NJ: Transaction, 2002.

Cable, Sherry, and Charles Cable. *Environmental Problems, Grassroots Solutions: The Politics of Grassroots Environmental Conflict.* New York: St. Martin's Press, 1995.

Cable, Sherry, and Thomas Shriver. "The Production and Extrapolation of Meaning in The Environmental Justice Movement." *Sociological Spectrum* 15 (1995): 419–42.

Capek, Stella M. "The 'Environmental Justice' Frame: A Conceptual Discussion and an Application." *Social Problems* 40 (1993): 5–24.

Cassady, Alison, and Alex Fidis. *Toxic Pollution and Health: An Analysis of Toxic Chemicals Released in the Communities across the United States.* Washington, DC: US PIRG Education Fund, March 2006.

Castleman, Barry, and Vicente Navarro. "International Mobility of Hazardous Products, Industries, and Wastes." *Annual Review of Public Health* 8 (1987): 1–19.

Chambers, Nicky, Craig Simmons, and Mathis Wackernagel. *Sharing Nature's Interests: Ecological Footprints as an Indicator of Sustainability.* London: Earthscan, 2000.

Chavis, Benjamin, and Charles Lee. *Toxic Wastes and Race in the United States: A National Report on the Racial and Socioeconomic Characteristics of Communities Surrounding Hazardous Waste Sites.* New York: United Church of Christ Commission for Racial Justice, 1987.

Christiansen, Hans, and Ayse Bertrand. "Trends and Recent Developments in Foreign Direct Investment," a Report by the OECD Directorate for Financial and Enterprise Affairs. June 2004.

Clapp, Jennifer. *Toxic Exports: The Transfer of Hazardous Wastes from Rich to Poor Countries.* Ithaca, NY: Cornell University Press, 2001.

Claybrook, Joan, and the Staff of Public Citizen. *Retreat from Safety: Reagan's Attack on America's Health.* New York: Pantheon Books, 1984.

Clifford, Mary, ed. *Environmental Crime: Enforcement, Policy, and Social Responsibility.* Gaithersburg, MD: Aspen Publishers, 1998.

Colburn, Theo, Dianne Dumanoski, and John Peterson Myers. *Our Stolen Future.* New York: Dutton, 1996.

Cole, Luke W., and Sheila R. Foster. *From the Ground Up: Environmental Racism and the Rise of the Environmental Justice Movement.* New York: New York University Press, 2001.

Commoner, Barry. *Making Peace with the Planet.* New York: Pantheon Books, 1990.

Cornes, Richard, and Todd Sandler. *The Theory of Externalities, Public Goods, and Club Goods.* New York: Cambridge University Press, 1986.

Costner, Pat, and Joe Thornton. *Playing with Fire.* Washington, DC: Greenpeace, 1990.

Curlee, C. K., S. J. Broulliard, M. L. Marshall, T. L. Knode, and S. L. Smith. *Upstream Oil and Gas Fatalities: A Review of OSHA's Database and Strategic Direction for Reducing Fatal Accidents*, a report presented at the Society of Petroleum Engineers, Environmental Protection Agency, and Department of Energy Exploration and Production Environmental Conference, Galveston, TX (March 7–9 2005). http://www.spe.org/jpt.

Davis, Devra. *When Smoke Ran Like Water: Tales of Environmental Deception and the Battle Against Pollution.* New York: Basic Books, 2002.

Davis, Mike. "Who Is Killing New Orleans?," *The Nation* 282, no. 14 (April 10, 2006), 11–20.

Dicken, Peter. *Global Shift: The Internationalization of Economic Activity*, 2nd ed. New York: Guilford Press, 1992.

Domhoff, G. William. *The Power Elite and the State: How Policy Is Made in America.* NewYork: Aldine de Gruyter, 1990.

———. *The Powers That Be: Processes of Ruling Class Domination in America.* New York: Vintage Books, 1979.

———. *Who Rules America?* Englewood Cliffs, NJ: Prentice-Hall, 1967.

Donati, Paolo. "Environmentalism, Postmaterialism and Anxiety: The New Politics of Individualism." *Arena Journal* 8 (1997): 147–72.

Dowie, Mark. *Losing Ground: American Environmentalism at the Close of the Twentieth Century.* Cambridge, MA: MIT Press, 1995.

Dyson, Michael Eric. *Come Hell or High Water: Hurricane Katrina and the Color of Disaster.* New York: Basic Civitas, 2006.

Economy, Elizabeth C. *The River Runs Black: The Environmental Challenge to China's Future.* Ithaca, NY: Cornell University Press, 2004.

Egen, Rachel. *Buying a Movement: Right-Wing Foundations and American Politics.* A Report by the American Way (1996): 1–43.

Egilman, David S., and Susanna Rankin Bohme. "Over a Barrel: Corporate Corruption of Science and its Effects on Workers and the Environment." *International Journal of Occupational and Environmental Health* 11, no. 4 (October/December 2005): 331–37.

Ehrenreich, Barbara. *Fear of Falling: the Inner Life of the Middle Class.* New York: Perennial, 1990.

Engardio, Peter, and Dexter Roberts. "The Three Scariest Words in U.S. Industry: The China Price." *BusinessWeek* (December 6, 2004), 102–12.

Environmental Working Group. *Forbidden Fruit: Illegal Pesticides in the US Food Supply.* Washington, DC: Environmental Working Group, 1995.

Epstein, Barbara. "The Environmental Justice/Toxics Movement: Politics of Race and Gender." *Capitalism, Nature, Socialism* 8, no. 3 (1997): 63–88.

Estabrook, Thomas. *Labor-Environmental Coalitions: Lessons from a Louisiana Petrochemical Region.* Amityville, NY: Baywood Publishing, 2007.

Evers, David C. *Mercury Connections: The Extent and Effects of Mercury Pollution in Northeastern North America, A Report by the BioDiversity Research Institute.* Gorham, ME: 2005.

Faber, Daniel. "A Revolution in Environmental Justice and Sustainable Development: The Political Ecology of Nicaragua." In *Environmental Justice: Discourses in International Political Economy, Energy, and Environmental Policy,* ed. John Byrne, Leigh Glover, and Cecilia Martinez, 39–70. New Brunswick, NJ: Transaction, 2002.

———. "Central America: A Disaster that Was Waiting To Happen." *Z Magazine* 12, no. 1 (1999): 5–6.

———. "The Political Ecology of American Capitalism: New Challenges for the Environmental Justice Movement." In *The Struggle for Ecological Democracy: Environmental Justice Movements in the United States,* ed. Daniel Faber, 27–59. New York: Guilford Press, 1998.

———. *Environment Under Fire: Imperialism and the Ecological Crisis in Central America.* New York: Monthly Review Press, 1993.

———. "The Ecological Crisis of Latin America: A Theoretical Introduction," *Latin American Perspectives* 19, no. 1 (1992): 3–16.

———. "Building a Transnational Environmental Justice Movement: Obstacles and Opportunities in the Age of Globalization." In *Coalitions Across Borders: Transna-*

tional Protest and the Neoliberal Order, ed. Joe Bandy and Jackie Smith, 43–70. Lanham, MD: Rowman & Littlefield, 2005.

———. "A More 'Productive' Environmental Justice Politics: Movement Alliances in Massachusetts for Clean Production and Regional Equity." In *Environmental Justice and Environmentalism: The Social Challenge to the Environmental Movement*. ed. Ronald Sandler and Phaedra C. Pezzullo, 135–64. Cambridge, MA: MIT Press, 2007.

Faber, Daniel, ed. *The Struggle for Ecological Democracy: Environmental Justice Movements in the United States*. New York: Guilford, 1998.

Faber, Daniel, and Deborah McCarthy. *Green of Another Color: Building Effective Partnerships Between Foundations and the Environmental Justice Movement*. Boston: Philanthropy and Environmental Justice Research Project, Northeastern University, 2001.

Faber, Daniel, and Deborah McCarthy. "The Evolution of the Environmental Justice Movement in the United States: New Models for Democratic Decision-Making." *Social Justice Research* 14, no. 4 (2001): 405–21.

Faber, Daniel, and James O'Connor. "Capitalism and the Crisis of Environmentalism." In *Toxic Struggles: The Theory and Practice of Environmental Justice*, ed. Richard Hofrichter. Philadelphia: New Society, 1993.

Faber, Daniel R., and Eric J. Krieg. *Unequal Exposure to Ecological Hazards 2005: Environmental Injustices in the Commonwealth of Massachusetts,* A Report by the Philanthropy and Environmental Justice Research Project, Northeastern University. Boston, MA: October 12, 2005.

Figueroa, Robert Melchior. "Other Faces: Latinos and Environmental Justice." In *Faces of Environmental Racism: Confronting Issues of Global Justice*, 2nd ed., ed. Laura Westra and Bill E. Lawson, 167–84. New York: Rowman & Littlefield, 2001.

Fireside, Daniel, Toussaint Losier, Adria Scharf, Thad Williamson, and the Dollars and Sense Collective, eds. *The Environment in Crisis*. 3rd ed. Boston: Dollars and Sense, 2006.

Foreman, Jr., Christopher H. T*he Promise and Peril of Environmental Justice*. Washington, DC: Brookings Institute, 1998.

Foster, John Bellamy. "Let Them Eat Pollution: Capitalism in the World Environment." In *Ecology Against Capitalism*, ed. John Bellamy Foster, 60–28. New York: Monthly Review Press, 2002.

Foster, John Bellamy, and Brett Clark. "Ecological Imperialism: The Curse of Capitalism." In *Socialist Register 2004: The New Imperial Challenge*, ed. Leo Panitch and Colin Leys, 186–201. London: The Merlin Press, 2003.

Foster, John Bellamy, and Robert W. McChesney, eds. *Pox Americana: Exposing the American Empire*. New York: Monthly Review Press, 2004.

Fox, Stephen. *The American Conservation Movement: John Muir and His Legacy* (Madison: University of Wisconsin Press, 1985).

Frank, Thomas. W*hat's the Matter with Kansas?: How Conservatives Won the Heart of America.* New York: Metropolitan Books, 2004.

Freudenburg, William R., and Robert Gramling. *Oil in Troubled Waters; Perceptions, Politics, and the Battle Over Offshore Drilling.* Albany, NY: State University of New York Press, 1993.

Frey, R. Scott. "The Transfer of Core-Based Hazardous Production Processes to the Export Processing Zones of the Periphery: The *Maquiladora* Centers of Northern Mexico." *Journal of World-Systems Research* 9, no. 2 (Summer 2003): 317–54.

———. "The Hazardous Waste Stream in the World-System." In *The Environment and Society Reader*, ed. R. Scott Frey, 106–20. Boston: Allyn and Bacon, 2001.

Friedman, David. "The 'Environmental Racism' Hoax." *The American Enterprise* 9, no. 6 (November–December 1989): 75–78.

Friedman-Jimenez, George. "Achieving Environmental Justice: The Role of Occupational Health." *Fordham Urban Law Journal* 21 (1993–94): 605–31.

Gallagher, Kevin P. "Is NAFTA Working for Mexico?" *Environmental Forum* (May/June 2006): 21–27.

———. *Free Trade and the Environment: Mexico, NAFTA, and Beyond.* Palo Alto, CA: Stanford University Press, 2004

———. *Trade Liberalization and Industrial Pollution in Mexico: Lessons for FTAA.* Working Paper no. 00-07, Global Development and Environment Institute (October 2000).

Gbadegesin, Segun. "Multinational Corporations, Developed Nations, and Environmental Racism: Toxic Waste, Exploration, and Eco-Catastrophe." In *Faces of Environmental Racism: Confronting Issues of Global Justice.* 2nd ed., ed. Laura Westra and Bill E. Lawson, 187–202. Lanham, MD: Rowman & Littlefield, 2001.

Gedicks, Al. "Resource Wars against Native Peoples." *The Quest for Environmental Justice: Human Rights and the Politics of Pollution*, ed. Robert D. Bullard, 168–87. San Francisco: Sierra Club Books, 2005.

———. "Racism and Resource Colonization." In *The Struggle for Ecological Democracy: Environmental Justice Movements in the United States*, ed. Daniel Faber, 272–92. New York: Guilford Press, 1998.

Geiser, Ken. *Materials Matter: Toward a Sustainable Materials Policy.* Cambridge, MA: MIT Press, 2001.

Gerzon, Mark. "Reinventing Philanthropy: Foundations and the Renewal of Civil Society." *National Civic Review* 84, no. 2/3 (Summer–Fall 1995): 188–95.

Gierzynski, Anthony. *Money Rules: Financing Elections in America.* Boulder, CO: Westview Press, 1999.

Glover, Leigh. "Globalization.com vs. ecologicaljustice.org: Contesting the End of History." In *Environmental Justice: Discourses in International Political Economy, Energy and Environmental Policy*, ed. John Byrne, Leigh Glover, and Cecilia Martinez, 231–60. New Brunswick, NJ: Transaction Publishers, 2002.

Goffman, Erving. *Frame Analysis: An Essay on the Organization of Experience.* Cambridge, MA: Harvard University Press, 1974.

Goldman, Benjamin, and Laura Fitton. *Toxic Waste and Race Revisited: An Update of the 1987 Report on the Racial and Socioeconomic Characteristics of Communities with Hazardous Waste Sites*. New York: United Church of Christ Commission for Racial Justice, 1994.

Goldman, Michael. "House Organ." *Capitalism, Nature, Socialism* 11, no. 4 (2000): 1–2, 157–58.

Gonzalez, George A. *Corporate Power and the Environment: The Political Economy of US Environmental Policy*. Lanham, MD: Rowman & Littlefield, 2001.

Gordon, David. *The Fat and the Mean: The Corporate Squeeze of Working Americans and the Myth of Managerial "Downsizing."* New York: Free Press, 1996.

Gordon, David, Thomas E. Weisskopf, and Samuel Bowles. "Power, Accumulation, and Crisis: The Rise and Demise of the Postwar Social Structure of Accumulation." In *The Imperiled Economy: Macroeconomics from a Left Perspective*, ed. Robert Cherry, Christine D'Onofrio, Cigdem Kurdas, Thomas R. Michl, Fred Moseley, and Michele I. Naples. New York: The Union for Radical Political Economics, 1987.

Gottlieb, Robert. *Forcing the Spring: The Transformation of the American Environmental Movement* (Washington, DC: Island Press, 1993).

Gould, Kenneth. "Response to Eric J. Krieg's 'The Two Faces of Toxic Waste: Trends in the Spread of Environmental Hazards.'" *Sociological Forum* 13, no. 1 (1998): 21–23.

———. "The Sweet Smell of Money: Economic Dependency and Local Environmental Political Motivation." *Society and Natural Resources* 4, no. 2 (April/June 1991): 133.

Green, Mark. *Selling Out: How Big Corporate Money Buys Elections, Rams Through Legislation, and Betrays Our Democracy*. New York: HarperCollins, 2004.

Greider, William. "The Man from Alcoa: Treasury Secretary Paul O'Neill Is Turning Out to be a Dangerous Crank." *The Nation* 273, no. 3 (July 16, 2001), 11–14.

Grinde, Donald A., Howard Zinn, and Bruce Elliott Johansen. *Ecocide of Native America: Environmental Destruction of Indian Lands and Peoples*. Santa Fe, NM: Clear Light Publishers, 1998.

Grossman, Richard. *Fear at Work: Job Blackmail, Labor and the Environment*. New York: Pilgrim Press, 1982.

Guha, Ramachandra. *Environmentalism: A Global History*. New York: Longman, 2000.

Gullason, Edward T. "The Dynamics of the U.S. Occupational Structure during the 1990s." *Journal of Labor Research* 21, no. 2 (April 2000): 363–75.

Habermas, Jürgen. *The Structural Transformation of the Public Sphere*. Cambridge, MA: MIT Press, 1989.

Hall, Kathy. "Changing Woman, Tukunavi and Coal: Impacts of the Energy Industry on the Navajo and Hopi Reservations." *Capitalism, Nature, Socialism* 3, no. 1 (March 1992): 49–78.

Hart-Landsberg, Martin, and Paul Burkett. "China, Capitalist Accumulation, and Labor." *Monthly Review* 59, no. 1 (May 2007): 17–39.

Hartman, Chester, and Gregory D. Squires. *There Is No Such Thing as a Natural Disaster: Race, Class, and Hurricane Katrina*. New York: Routledge, 2006.

Hays, Samuel P. *Conservation and the Gospel of Efficiency: The Progressive Conservation Movement, 1880–1920*. Cambridge, MA: Harvard University Press, 1959.

Hearne, Shelley A. *Harvest of Unknowns: Pesticide Contamination in Imported Foods*. New York: Natural Resources Defense Council, 1984.

Held, David, and Anthony McGrew, eds. *The Global Transformations Reader: An Introduction to the Globalization Debate*. Malden, MA: Blackwell Publishing, 2004.

Helvarg, David. *The War Against the Greens: The 'Wise Use" Movement, the New Right, and Anti-Environmental Violence*. San Francisco: Sierra Club Books, 1994.

Humphrey, Craig R., Tammy L. Lewis, and Frederick H. Buttel. *Environment, Energy, and Society: A New Synthesis*. Belmont, CA: Wadsworth, 2002.

Inglehart, Ronald. *Culture Shift in Advanced Industrial Society*. Princeton, NJ: Princeton University Press, 1990.

International Forum on Globalization. *Alternatives to Economic Globalization: A Better World is Possible*. San Francisco: Berrett-Koehler Publishers, 2002.

Ireland, Doug. "Whitman: A Toxic Choice." *The Nation* 272, no. 4 (January 29, 2001), 18.

Jain, Shobita. "Standing Up for the Trees: Women's Role in the Chipko Movement." In *Women and the Environment: Crisis and Development in the Third World,* ed. Sally Sontheimer, 163–78. New York: Monthly Review Press, 1991.

Jenkins, J. Craig, and Craig M. Eckert. "The Right Turn in Economic Policy: Business Elites and the New Conservative Economics." *Sociological Forum* 15 (2000): 307–38.

Jenkins, Rhys. *Transnational Corporations and Uneven Development: The Internationalization of Capital and the Third World*. New York: Routledge, 1991.

Johnston, Barbara Rose. *Who Pays the Price?: The Sociocultural Context of Environmental Crisis*. Washington, DC: Island Press, 1994.

Jorgenson, Andrew K. "Consumption and Environmental Degradation: A Cross-National Analysis of the Ecological Footprint." *Social Problems* 50, no. 3 (2003): 379–80.

Karliner, Joshua. *The Corporate Planet: Ecology and Politics in the Age of Globalization*. San Francisco: Sierra Club Books, 1997.

——. "The Environmental Industry." *Ecologist* 24, no. 2 (1994): 60–61.

Keating, Martha. *Cradle to Grave: The Environmental Impacts from Coal*, A Report by the Clean Air Task Force (Boston: June, 2001), 1–9.

Khor, Martin. *Globalization and the Crisis of Sustainable Development*. Penang: Third World Network, 2001.

——. "Economics and Environmental Justice: Rethinking North-South Relations." In *Toxic Struggles: The Theory and Practice of Environmental Justice*, ed. Richard Hofrichter, 219–25. Philadelphia: New Society Publishers, 1993.

King, Leslie. "Charting a Discursive Field: Environmentalists for U.S. Population Stabilization." *Sociological Inquiry* 77, no. 3 (August 2007): 301–25.

Klare, Michael. "The New Geopolitics." In *Pox Americana: Exposing the American Empire*, ed. John Bellamy Foster and Robert W. McChesney, 51–56. New York: Monthly Review Press, 2004.

Kline, Benjamin. *First Along the River: A Brief History of the U.S. Environmental Movement*. San Francisco: Acadia Books, 2000.

Koenig, Thomas, and Michael Rustad. "Toxic Torts, Politics and Environmental Justice: The Case for Crimtorts." *Law & Policy* 26, no. 2 (April 2004): 189–207.

Kovel, Joel. *The Enemy of Nature: The End of Capitalism or the End of the World?* New York: Zed Books, 2002.

Krieg, Eric, and Daniel Faber, "Not So Black and White: Environmental Justice and Cumulative Environmental Impacts," *Environmental Impact Assessment Review* 24, Issues 7–8 (October–November 2004): 667–94.

Krimsky, Sheldon. *Science in the Private Interest*. Lanham, MD: Rowman & Littlefield, 2003.

LaDuke, Winona. *All Our Relations: Native Struggles for Land and Life*. Boston: South End Books, 1999.

Lake, Robert. "Volunteers, NIMBYs, and Environmental Justice: Dilemmas of Democratic Practice." *Antipode* 28 (1996): 160–74.

Landy, Marc, Marc Roberts, and Stephen Thomas. *The Environmental Protection Agency: Asking the Wrong Questions*. Oxford: Oxford University Press, 1990.

Lash, Jonathan, Katherine Gillman, and David Sheridan. *A Season of Spoils: The Story of the Reagan Administration's Attack on the Environment*. New York: Pantheon Books, 1984.

Lavelle, Marianne, and Marcia Coyle. "Unequal Protection: The Racial Divide in Environmental Law." *National Law Journal* 21 (1992): 2–12.

Lazarus, Richard J. "A Different Kind of 'Republican Movement' in Environmental Law," *Minnesota Law Review* 87, no. 4 (April 2003): 999–1036.

Lee, Charles. *Proceedings: The National People of Color Environmental Leadership Summit.* New York: United Church of Christ Commission for Racial Justice, 1992.

Levenstein, Charles, and John Wooding. "Dying for a Living: Workers, Production, and the Environment." In *The Struggle for Ecological Democracy: Environmental Justice Movements in the United States*, ed. Daniel Faber, 68–80. New York: Guilford Press, 1998.

Lofdahl, Corey L. *Environmental Impacts of Globalization and Trade: A Systems Study*. Cambridge, MA: MIT Press, 2002.

Logan, John, and Harvey Molotch. *Urban Fortunes*. Berkeley: University of California Press, 1987.

Loh, Katherine, and Scott Richardson. "Foreign-born Workers: Trends in Fatal Occupational Injuries, 1996–2001." *Monthly Labor Review* (June 2004): 42–54.

Malkan, Stacy. *Not Just a Pretty Face: The Ugly Side of the Beauty Industry*. Gabriola Island, BC: New Society Publishers, 2007.

Martinez-Alier, Joan. "Marxism, Social Metabolism, and International Trade." In *Rethinking Environmental History: World-System History and Global Environmental Change*, ed. Alf Hornborg, J. R. McNeill, and Joan Martinez-Alier, 221–38. Lanham, MD: AltaMira Press, 2007.

———. *The Environmentalism of the Poor: The Study of Ecological Conflicts and Valuation*. Northampton, MA: Edward Elgar, 2002.

———. "Retrospective Environmentalism and Environmental Justice Movements Today." *Capitalism, Nature, Socialism* 11, no. 4 (June 2000): 45–50.

Martínez-Alier, Juan. "Retrospective Environmentalism and Environmental Justice Movements Today." *Capitalism, Nature, Socialism* 11, no. 4 (2000): 45–50.

———. "Environmental Justice: Local and Global." *Capitalism, Nature, Socialism* 8, no. 1 (1997): 91–107.

Massey, Douglas, and Nancy Denton. *American Apartheid: Segregation and the Making of the Underclass.* Cambridge, MA: Harvard University Press, 1993.

McCarthy, John D., and Mayer N. Zald. "Resource Mobilization and Social Movements: A Partial Theory." *American Journal of Sociology* 82 (1977): 1212–41.

Millennium Ecosystem Assessment. *Ecosystems and Human Well-Being: Synthesis Report.* Washington, DC: Island Press, 2005.

Mishel, Lawrence, Jared Bernstein, and Sylvia Allegretto. *The State of Working America, 2006–2007.* Ithaca, NY: Cornell University Press, 2007.

Mogensen, Vernon. *Worker Safety Under Siege: Labor, Capital, and the Politics of Workplace Safety in a Deregulated World.* Armonk, NY: M. E. Sharpe, 2005.

Montrie, Chad. *To Save the Land and People: A History of Opposition to Surface Coal Mining in Appalachia.* Chapel Hill: University of North Carolina Press, 2003.

Moore, Gwen, Sarah Sobieraj, J. Allen Whit, Olga Mayorova, and Daniel Beaulieu, "Elite Interlocks in Three US Sectors: Nonprofit, Corporate, and Government." *Social Science Quarterly* 83 (2002): 726–44.

Morello-Frosch, Rachel. "Discrimination and the Political Economy of Environmental Inequality." *Environment and Planning C: Government and Policy* 20 (2002): 477–96.

Morello-Frosch, Rachel, Manuel Pastor, and James Sadd. "Environmental Justice and Southern California's Riskscape: The Distribution of Air Toxics Exposures and Health Risks Among Diverse Communities." *Urban Affairs Review* 36 (2001): 551.

Muradian, Roldan, and Joan Martinez-Alier. "Trade and the Environment: From a 'Southern' Perspective." *Ecological Economics* 36 (2001): 281–97.

Murray, Douglas. *Cultivating Crisis: The Human Costs of Pesticides in Latin America.* Austin: University of Texas Press, 1994.

Nash, Roderick. *Wilderness and the American Mind.* New Haven, CT: Yale University Press, 1967.

National Research Council. *Waste Incineration and Public Health.* Washington, DC: National Academy Press, 2004.

Natural Resources Defense Council. *Breathtaking: Premature Mortality Due to Particulate Air Pollution in 239 American Cities.* Washington, DC: May 1996.

Noble, Charles. *Liberalism at Work: The Rise and Fall of OSHA.* Philadelphia: Temple University Press, 1986.

Norris, Ruth. *Pills, Pesticides, and Profits.* New York: North River Press, 1982.

Nwoke, Chibuzo. *Third World Minerals and Global Pricing: A New Theory.* Atlantic Highlands, NJ: Zed Press, 1987.

Nyhard, Nick. "The Myth of Small-Donor Clout: Large Contributors' Importance Grew in 2004, Contrary to Popular Perception." *The Nation* 280, no. 25 (June 27, 2005), 25–27.

O'Brien, Jim. "Environmentalism as a Mass Movement: Historical Notes," *Radical America* 17, no. 2/3 (1983): 75–85.

O'Brien, Mary H. "When Harm Is Not Necessary: Risk Assessment as Diversion." In *Reclaiming the Environmental Debate: The Politics of Health in a Toxic Culture*, ed. Richard Hofrichter, 113–34. Cambridge, MA: MIT Press, 2000.

O'Connor, James. "House Organ." *Capitalism, Nature, Socialism* 11, no. 1 (2000): 1–2.

———. "House Organ," *Capitalism, Nature, Socialism* 11, no. 2 (2000): 1–2, 156–73.

———. "House Organ," *Capitalism, Nature, Socialism*, 11, no. 3 (2000): 1–2, 155–72.

———. *Natural Causes: Essays in Ecological Marxism*. New York: Guilford Press, 1998.

———. "A Political Strategy for Ecology Movements." *Capitalism, Nature, Socialism* 3, no. 1 (1992): 1–5.

Oliver, Melvin L., and Thomas A. Shapiro. *Black Wealth/White Wealth: A New Perspective on Racial Inequality*. New York: Routledge, 1995.

O'Neil, Sandra George. "Environmental Justice in the Superfund Clean-Up Process." Ph.D. Dissertation. Boston College, Department of Sociology, April 2005.

O'Neill, Kate. *Waste Trading Among Rich Nations: Building a New Theory of Environmental Regulation*. Cambridge, MA: MIT Press, 2000.

Paehlke, Robert C. *Environmentalism and the Future of Progressive Politics*. New Haven, CT: Yale University Press, 1989.

Palast, Greg. *The Best Democracy Money Can Buy*. New York: Plume, 2003.

Peet, Richard, and Michael Watts, eds. *Liberation Ecologies: Environment, Development, Social Movement*. London: Routledge, 1996.

Pellow, David Naguib, and Robert J. Brulle. "Poisoning the Planet: The Struggle for Environmental Justice." *Contexts* 6, no. 1 (Winter 2007): 37–41.

Pellow, David Naguib, and Robert J. Brulle, eds., *Power, Justice, and the Environment: A Critical Appraisal of the Environmental Justice Movement*. Cambridge, MA: MIT Press, 2005.

Perfecto, Ivette. "Farm Workers, Pesticides and the International Connection." In *Race and the Incidence of Environmental Hazards,* ed. Bunyan Bryant and Paul Mohai. Boulder, CO: Westview, 1992.

Perry, D. M., Roberto Sanchez, and William H. Glaze. "Binational Management of Hazardous Waste: The *Maquiladora* Industry in the US-Mexico Border." *Environmental Management* 14 (1998): 441.

Plotkin, Sidney. *Keep Out: The Struggle for Land Use Control*. Berkeley: University of California Press, 1987.

Political Ecology Group. *Toxic Empire: The WMX Corportion, Hazardous Waste and Global Strategies for Environmental Justice*. San Francisco: PEG, 1995.

Puckett, Jim. *When Trade Is Toxic: The WTO Threat to Public and Planetary Health*, a Report by the Asia Pacific Environmental Exchange and the Basel Action Network, 1999.

Pulido, Laura. "Rethinking Environmental Racism: White Privilege and Urban Development in Southern California." *Annals of the Association of American Geographers* 90, no. 1 (2000): 12–40.

———. *Environmentalism and Economic Justice: Two Chicano Struggles in the Southwest*. New York: Simon & Schuster, 1996.

Putnam, Robert D. *Bowling Alone: The Collapse and Revival of American Community*. New York: Simon & Schuster, 2000.

Putnam, Robert D., and Lewis M. Feldstein, with Don Cohen. *Better Together: Restoring the American Community*. New York: Simon & Schuster, 2003.

Rechtschaffen, Clifford. "Competing Visions: EPA and the States Battle for the Future of Environmental Protection." *Environmental Law Reporter* 30 (2000): 10,803–17.

Redclift, Michael. *Sustainable Development: Exploring the Contradictions*. London: Metheun, 1987.

Red Cross and Red Crescent Societies. *World Disasters Report: Focus on Recovery*. Geneva: International Federation of Red Cross and Red Crescent Societies, 2001.

Regenstein, Lewis. *How to Survive in America the Poisoned*. Washington, DC: Acropolis Books, 1986.

Rich, Bruce. *Mortgaging the Earth: The World Bank, Environmental Impoverishment, and the Crisis of Development*. Boston: Beacon Press, 1994.

Richter, Elihu D., C. Soskolne, J. LaDou, and T. Berman. "Whistleblowers in Environmental Science, Prevention of Suppression Bias and the Need for a Code of Action." *International Journal of Occupational and Environmental Health* 7 (2001): 68–71.

Ringquist, Evan J. "Equity and the Distribution of Environmental Risk: The Case of TRI Facilities." *Social Science Quarterly* 78 (1997): 811–18.

Ritchie, Mark. "Trading Away the Environment: Free-Trade Agreements and Environmental Degradation." In *Toxic Struggles: The Theory and Practice of Environmental Justice*, ed. Richard Hofrichter, 209–18. Philadelphia: New Society Publishers, 1993.

Roberts, J. Timmons, and Bradley C. Parks. *A Climate of Injustice: Global Inequality, North-South Politics, and Climate Policy*. Cambridge, MA: MIT Press, 2007.

Robinson, William I. "Beyond Nation-State Paradigms: Globalization, Sociology, and the Challenge of Transnational Studies." *Sociological Forum* 13, no.4 (1998): 561–94.

Rodman, John. "Paradigm Change in Political Science: An Ecological Perspective," *American Behavioral Scientist* 24, no. 1 (September–October 1980): 49–78.

Roe, David, William Pease, Karen Florini, and Ellen Silbergeld. *Toxic Ignorance: The Continuing Absence of Basic Health Testing for Top-Selling Chemicals in the United States*. New York: Environmental Defense Fund, 1997.

Roque, Julie. "Review of EPA Report: 'Environmental Equity: Reducing Risk for All Communities.'" *Environment* 35 (1993): 25–28.

Rosenthal, Erika. "Who's Afraid of National Laws?: Pesticide Corporations Use Trade Negotiations to Avoid Bans and Undercut Public Health Protections in Central America." *International Journal of Occupational and Environmental Health* 11, no. 4 (October/December 2005): 437–43.

Ross, Robert, and K. Trachte. *Global Capitalism: The New Leviathan*. Albany: State University of New York Press, 1990.

Rowell, Andrew. *Green Backlash: Global Subversion of the Environment Movement*. New York: Routledge, 1996.

Sachs, Wolfgang. "Ecology, Justice, and the End of Development." In *Environmental Justice: Discourses in International Political Economy, Energy and Environmental Policy*, ed. John Byrne, Leigh Glover, and Cecilia Martinez, 19–35. New Brunswick, NJ: Transaction, 2002.

Sanchez, Robert A. "Health and Environmental Risks of the *Maquiladora* in Mexicali." *Natural Resources Journal* 30 (1990):163–70.

Sandbach, Francis. *Environment, Ideology, and Policy*. Montclair, NJ: Allanheld, Osmun, 1980.

Schafer, Kristin S., Susan E. Kegley, and Sharyle Patton. *Nowhere to Hide: Persistent Toxic Chemicals in the U.S. Food Supply*. San Francisco: Pesticide Action Network North America, March 2001.

Schwab, Jim. *Deeper Shades of Green: The Rise of Blue-Collar and Minority Environmentalism in America*. San Francisco: Sierra Club Books, 1994.

Scott, James. *Domination and the Arts of Resistance*. New Haven, CT: Yale University Press, 1990.

Shabecoff, Philip. *A Fierce Green Fire: The American Environmental Movement*. Washington, DC: Island Press, 2003.

Shanks, Bernard. *This Land Is Your Land: The Struggle to Save America's Public Lands*. San Francisco: Sierra Club Books, 1984.

Shibley, Mark A., and Annette Prosterman. "Silent Epidemic, Environmental Injustice, or Exaggerated Concern?: Competing Frames in the Media Definition of Childhood Lead Poisoning as a Public Health Problem." *Organization & Environment* 11, no. 1 (1998): 33–58.

Shiva, Vandana. *Staying Alive: Women, Ecology, and Development*. Atlantic Highlands, NJ: Zed Books, 1991.

———. *Biopiracy: The Plunder of Nature and Knowledge*. Boston: South End Press, 1997.

———. "Conflicts of Global Ecology: Environmental Activism in a Period of Global Reach." *Alternatives* 19, no. 2 (1994): 195–207.

———. *The Violence of the Green Revolution: Third World Agriculture, Ecology and Politics*. Atlantic Highlands, NJ: Zed Books, 1991.

Shulman, Seth, with Kate Abend and Alden Meyer. *Smoke, Mirrors, & Hot Air: How ExxonMobil Uses Big Tobacco's Tactics to Manufacture Uncertainty on Climate Science*. Cambridge, MA: Union of Concerned Scientists, 2007.

Shutkin, William. *The Land That Could Be: Environmentalism and Democracy in the Twenty-First Century*. Cambridge, MA: MIT Press, 2000.

Snow, David A., and Robert Benford. "Ideology, Frame Resonance, and Participant Mobilization." In *From Structure to Action: Social Movement Participation Across Cultures,* ed. B. Klandermans, H. Kriesi, and Sydney Tarrow, 197–217. Greenwich, CT: JAI, 1988.

Snow, David A., E. Rochford, Jr., S. Worden, and Robert Benford. "Frame Alignment Process, Micromobilization, and Movement Participation." *American Sociological Review* 51 (1986): 464–81.

South, Scott J., and Kyle D. Crowder. "Escaping Distressed Neighborhoods: Individual, Community, and Metropolitan Influences." *The American Journal of Sociology* 102, no. 4 (January 1997): 1040–84.

Stauber, John, and Sheldon Rampton. *Toxic Sludge Is Good for You: Lies, Damn Lies, and the Public Relations Industry*. Monroe, ME: Common Courage Press, 1995.

Stern, Nicholas. *Stern Review: The Economics of Climate Change.* Cambridge: Cambridge University Press, 2006.

Szasz, Andrew. *Ecopopulism: Toxic Waste and the Movement for Environmental Justice.* Minneapolis: University of Minnesota Press, 1994.

Templet, Paul H. "Externalities, Subsidies and the Ecological Footprint: An Empirical Analysis." *Ecological Economics* 32 (2000): 381–83.

Thomas, Pat. "The Lethal Consequences of Breathing Fire." *The Ecologist* 36, no. 7 (September 2006): 44–48.

Thornton, Joe. *Pandora's Poison: Chlorine, Health and a New Environmental Strategy.* Cambridge, MA: MIT Press, 2000.

Thrupp, Lori Ann. "Pesticides and Policies: Approaches to Pest-Control Dilemmas in Nicaragua and Costa Rica." *Latin American Perspectives* 15, no. 4 (Fall 1988).

Tokar, Brian. *Earth For Sale: Reclaiming Ecology in the Age of Corporate Greenwash.* Boston: South End Press, 1997.

Twombly, Renee. "Urban Uprising." *Environmental Health Perspectives* 105, no. 7 (July 1997): 696–701.

US General Accounting Office. *Siting of Hazardous Waste Landfills and Their Correlation with Racial and Economic Status of Surrounding Communities.* Washington, DC: US Government Printing Office, 1983.

Vaclav, Smil. *China's Environmental Crisis: An Inquiry into the Limits of National Development.* New York: M. E. Sharpe, 1997.

Venetoulis, Jason, Dahlia Chazan, and Christoper Gaudet. *Ecological Footprint of Nations 2004.* Oakland, CA: Redefining Progress, March 2004.

Washburn, Jennifer. *University Inc: The Corporate Corruption of Higher Education.* New York: Basic Books, 2005.

Waterman, Peter. *Globalisation, Social Movements and the New Internationalism.* London: Continuum, 2001.

Watts, Michael. "Violent Environments: Petroleum Conflict and the Political Ecology of Rule in the Niger Delta, Nigeria." In *Liberation Ecologies: Environment, Development, Social Movements.* 2nd ed., ed. Richard Peet and Michael Watts, 273–98. New York: Routledge, 2004.

Weaver, Jane, and Russell Means, eds. *Defending Mother Earth: Native American Perspectives on Environmental Justice.* Maryknoll, NY: Orbis Books, 1996.

Weir, David. *The Bhopal Syndrome: Pesticide Manufacturing and the Third World.* Penang, Malaysia: International Organization of Consumers Unions, 1986.

Wernette, D. R., and L. A. Nieves. "Breathing Polluted Air: Minorities Are Disproportionately Exposed." *EPA Journal* (March/April 1992), 16.

Westra, Laura. "The Faces of Environmental Racism: Titusville, Alabama, and BFI." In *Faces of Environmental Racism: Confronting Issues of Global Justice.* 2nd ed. ed. Laura Westra and Bill E. Lawson, 113–40. Lanham, MD: Rowman & Littlefield, 2001.

Whitman, Christine Todd. *It's My Party Too: The Battle for the Heart of the GOP and the Future of America.* New York: Penguin, 2005.

Williams, Bob. *US Petroleum Strategies in the Decade of the Environment.* Tulsa, OK: PennWell Books, 1991.

Wisner, Ben, Piers Blaikie, Terry Cannon, and Ian Davis. *At Risk: Natural Hazards, People's Vulnerability and Disasters*. 2nd ed. New York: Routledge, 2005.

Witness for Peace. *A Hemisphere for Sale: The Epidemic of Unfair Trade in the Americas*. Washington, DC: Witness for Peace, 2001.

Woodall, Pam. "The Global Economy: War of the Worlds." *The Economist* (October 1, 1994), 36.

World Bank. *The Cost of Pollution in China: Economic Estimates of Physical Damages*, a Report prepared by the World Bank and State Environmental Protection Administration, P.R. China, 2007.

World Coal Institute. *The Coal Resource: A Comprehensive Overview of Coal*. London: WCI, May 2005.

World Health Organization. *The World Health Organization's Fight Against Cancer: Strategies That Prevent, Cure, and Care*. Geneva: WHO Press, 2007.

Wu, Brandon. "Paying to Pollute: Campaign Contributions and Lobbying Expenditures by Polluters Working to Weaken Environmental Laws," a Report by the US PIRG Education Fund (April 2004), 1–45.

Wyant, William K. *Westward in Eden: The Public Lands and the Conservation Movement*. Berkeley: University of California Press, 1982.

Index

About the Author

Daniel Faber is Director of the Northeastern Environmental Justice Research Collaborative, and professor of sociology at Northeastern University. A longtime environmental justice advocate, researcher, and scholar, he cofounded the Environmental Project On Central America (EPOCA), Earth Island Institute in 1984. Dr. Faber is also a cofounding editor of the international journal *Capitalism, Nature, Socialism*, and a founding Board Member of the *Alliance for a Healthy Tomorrow (AHT)*, a broad-based coalition of citizens, scientists, health professionals, labor unions, business leaders, and environmentalists working to implement a more precautionary and preventive approach to environmental policy in Massachusetts. He is the author of numerous publications on environmental injustice, including *Environment Under Fire: Imperialism and the Ecological Crisis in Central America*, and the edited collections, *The Struggle for Ecological Democracy* and *Foundations for Social Change*.